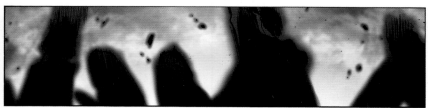

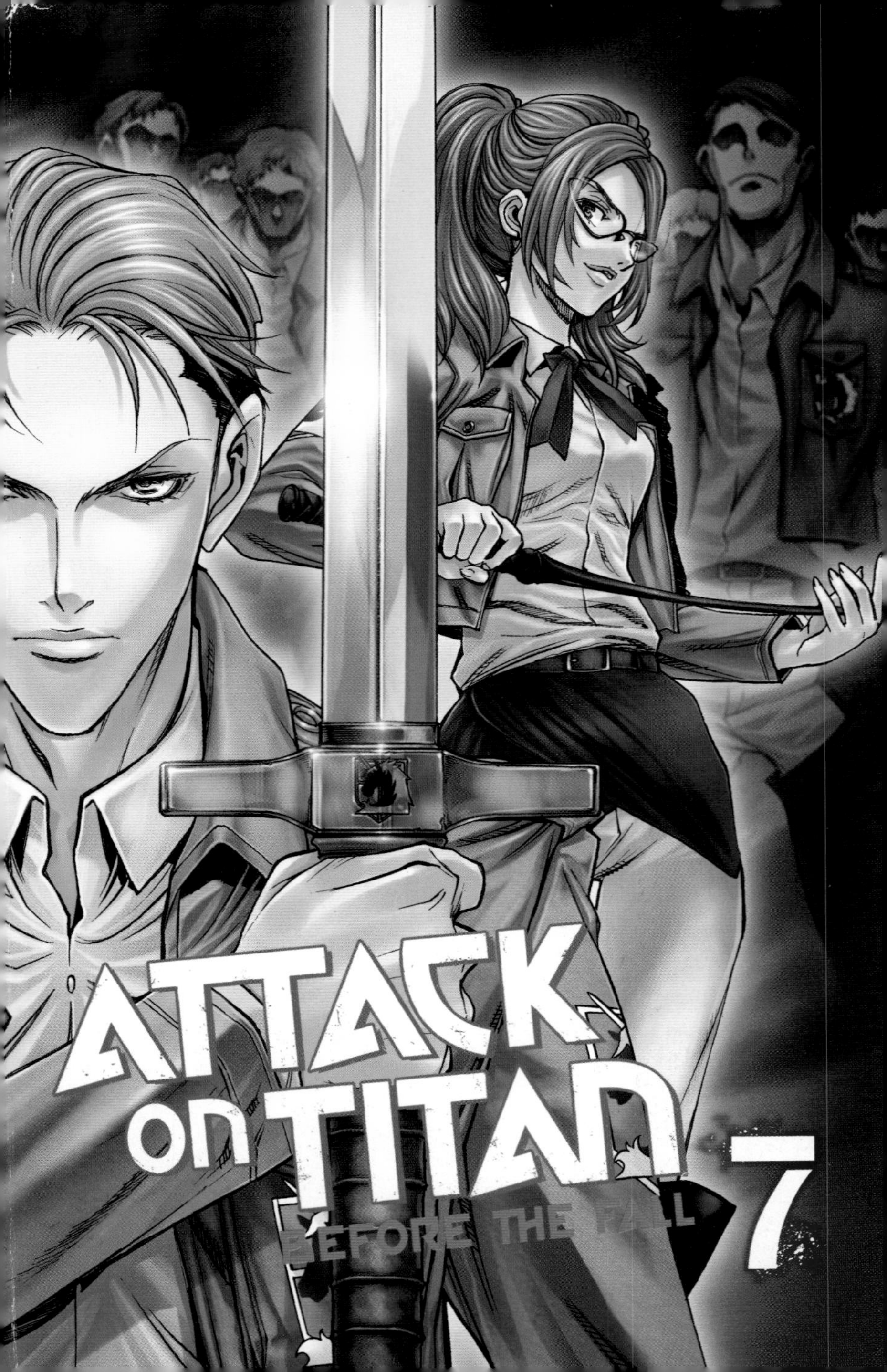
ATTACK on TITAN
BEFORE THE
7

Based on "Attack on Titan"
created by Hajime Isayama
Story by: Ryo Suzukaze
Art by Satoshi Shiki
Character Designs by: Thores Shinamoto

Contents:

Chapter 21: Den of Treachery... 1
Chapter 22: Abyss Below the Wall... 61
Chapter 23: Rondo of Darkness... 113
Chapter 24: Wall from the Shadows... 165
Swear Upon Wall Maria... 217

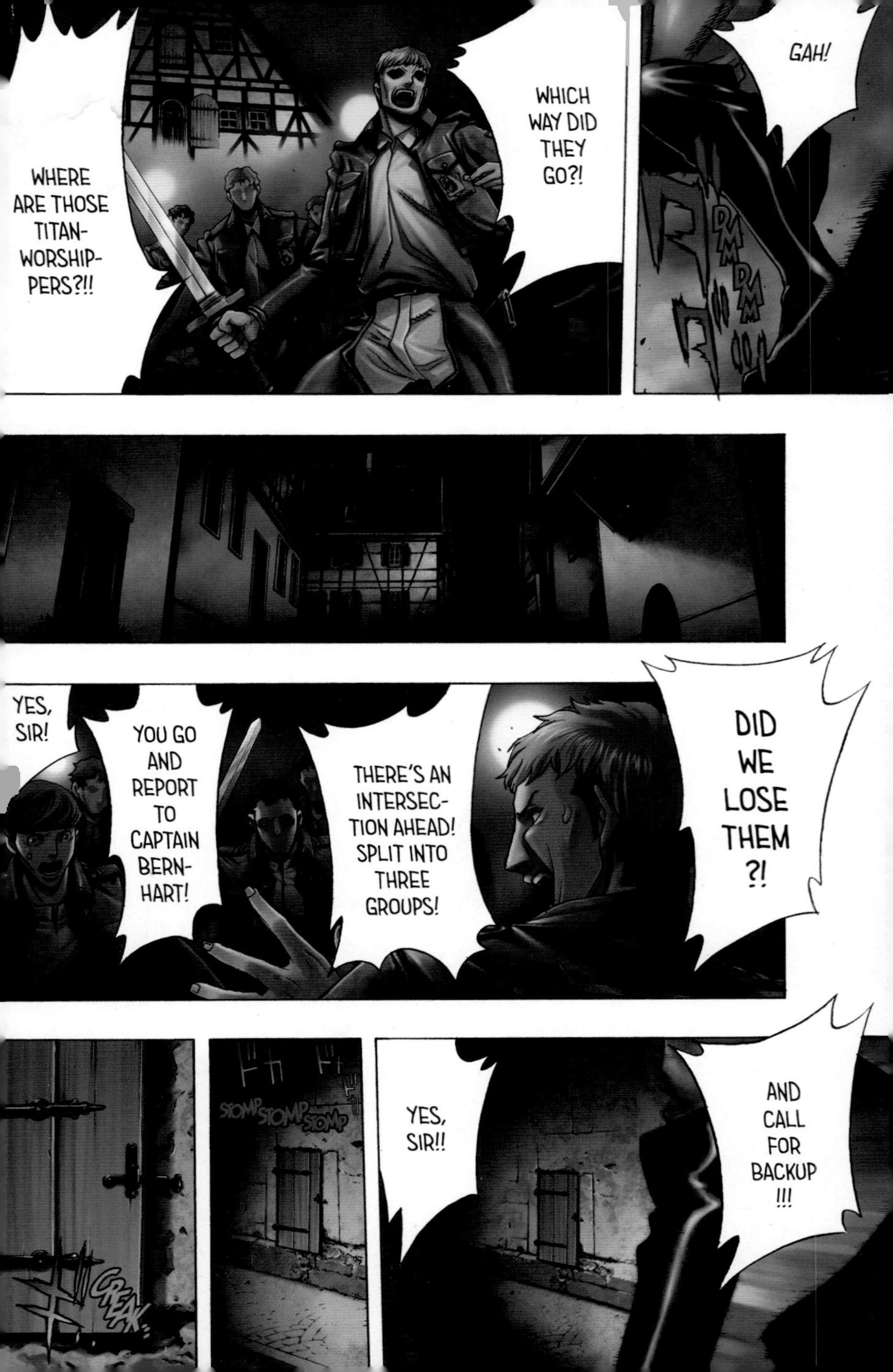
GAH!
DMDMDM
WHICH WAY DID THEY GO?!
WHERE ARE THOSE TITAN-WORSHIPPERS?!!
DID WE LOSE THEM?!
THERE'S AN INTERSECTION AHEAD! SPLIT INTO THREE GROUPS!
YOU GO AND REPORT TO CAPTAIN BERNHART!
YES, SIR!
AND CALL FOR BACKUP!!!
YES, SIR!!
STOMP STOMP STOMP
CREAK

Before the fall Character Profile

Kuklo

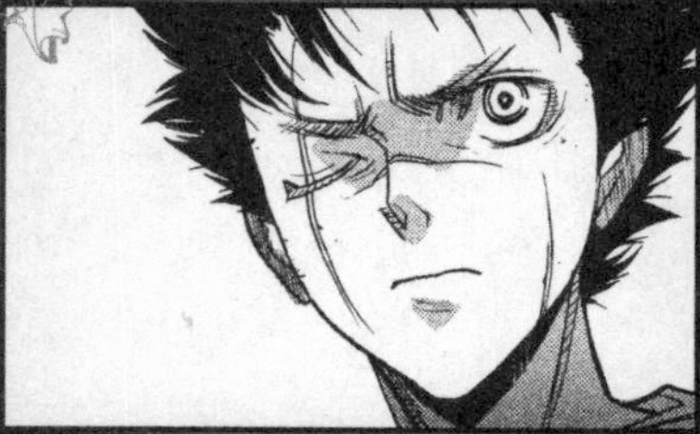

A fifteen-year-old boy born from a dead body packed into the vomit of a Titan, which earned him the moniker, "Son of a Titan." He is fascinated with the Device as a means to defeat the Titans. The protagonist of this story.

Sharle Inocencio

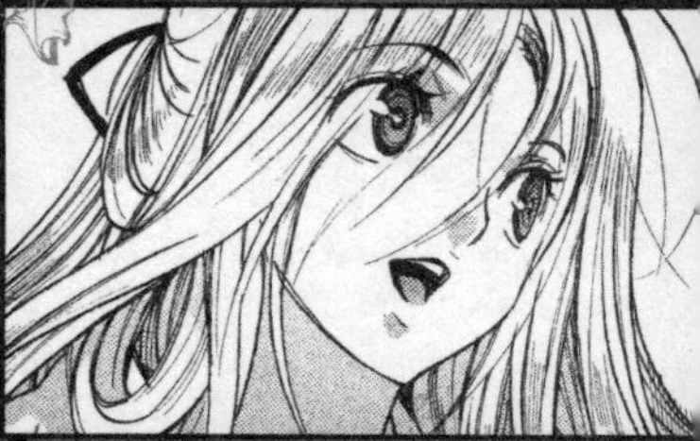

First daughter of the Inocencios, a rich merchant family within Wa Sheena. When she realized that Kuklo was a human, she taught hir to speak and learn. Currently an apprentice craftsman unde Xenophon in the industrial city.

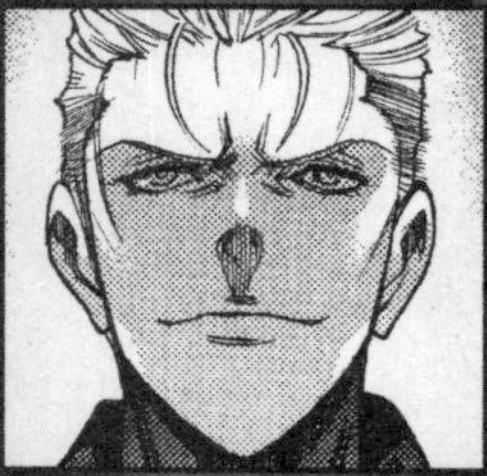

Xavi Inocencio

Head of the Inocencio family and Sharle's brother. Member of the Military Police in Shiganshina District.

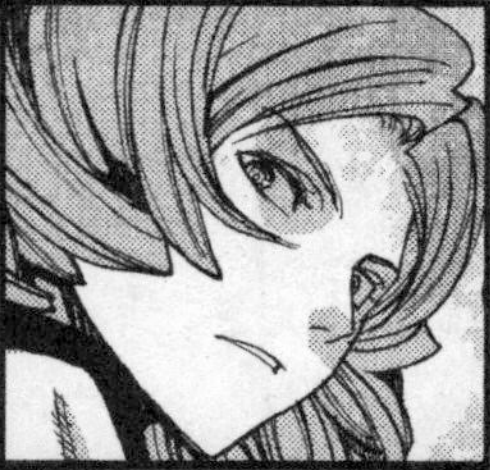

Cardina Baumeister

Kuklo's first friend in the outside world, and his companion in developing the Device.

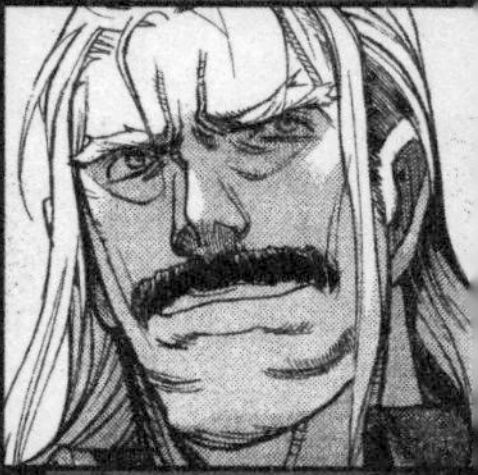

Jorge Pikale

Training Corps instructor. A former Survey Corps captain who was hailed as a hero for defeating a Titan.

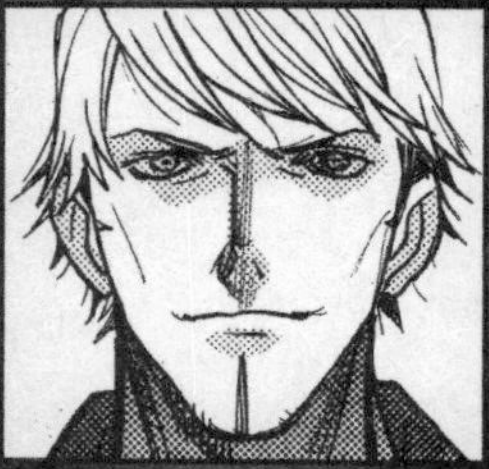

Carlo Pikale

Jorge's son and current captain of the Survey Corps. After they battled Titans together, he has great respect for Kuklo.

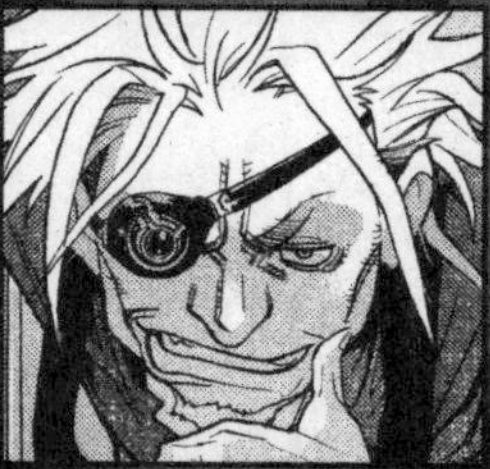

Xenophon Harkimo

Foreman at the industrial city. He took over development of the Device from its inventor, Angel.

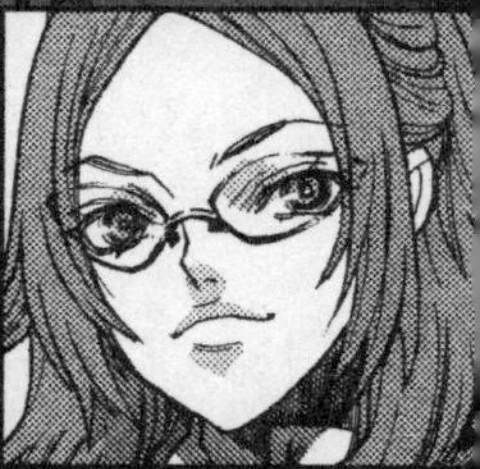

Gloria Bernhart

Captain of the Military Police in Shiganshina District. A powerful MP officer with a cold, tactical mind.

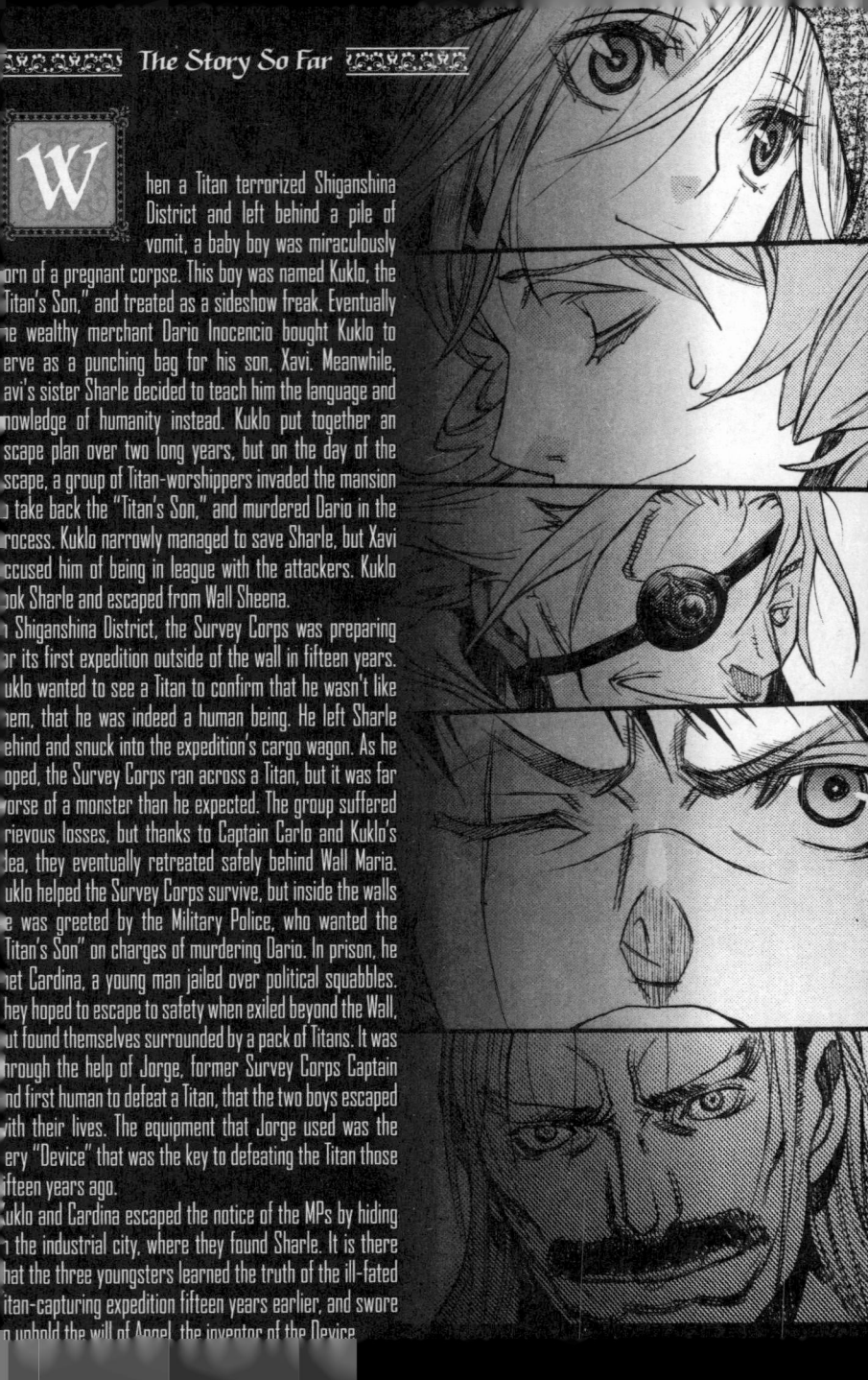

When a Titan terrorized Shiganshina District and left behind a pile of vomit, a baby boy was miraculously born of a pregnant corpse. This boy was named Kuklo, the "Titan's Son," and treated as a sideshow freak. Eventually the wealthy merchant Dario Inocencio bought Kuklo to serve as a punching bag for his son, Xavi. Meanwhile, Xavi's sister Sharle decided to teach him the language and knowledge of humanity instead. Kuklo put together an escape plan over two long years, but on the day of the escape, a group of Titan-worshippers invaded the mansion to take back the "Titan's Son," and murdered Dario in the process. Kuklo narrowly managed to save Sharle, but Xavi accused him of being in league with the attackers. Kuklo took Sharle and escaped from Wall Sheena.

In Shiganshina District, the Survey Corps was preparing for its first expedition outside of the wall in fifteen years. Kuklo wanted to see a Titan to confirm that he wasn't like them, that he was indeed a human being. He left Sharle behind and snuck into the expedition's cargo wagon. As he hoped, the Survey Corps ran across a Titan, but it was far worse of a monster than he expected. The group suffered grievous losses, but thanks to Captain Carlo and Kuklo's idea, they eventually retreated safely behind Wall Maria. Kuklo helped the Survey Corps survive, but inside the walls he was greeted by the Military Police, who wanted the "Titan's Son" on charges of murdering Dario. In prison, he met Cardina, a young man jailed over political squabbles. They hoped to escape to safety when exiled beyond the Wall, but found themselves surrounded by a pack of Titans. It was through the help of Jorge, former Survey Corps Captain and first human to defeat a Titan, that the two boys escaped with their lives. The equipment that Jorge used was the very "Device" that was the key to defeating the Titan those fifteen years ago.

Kuklo and Cardina escaped the notice of the MPs by hiding in the industrial city, where they found Sharle. It is there that the three youngsters learned the truth of the ill-fated Titan-capturing expedition fifteen years earlier, and swore to uphold the will of Angel, the inventor of the Device.

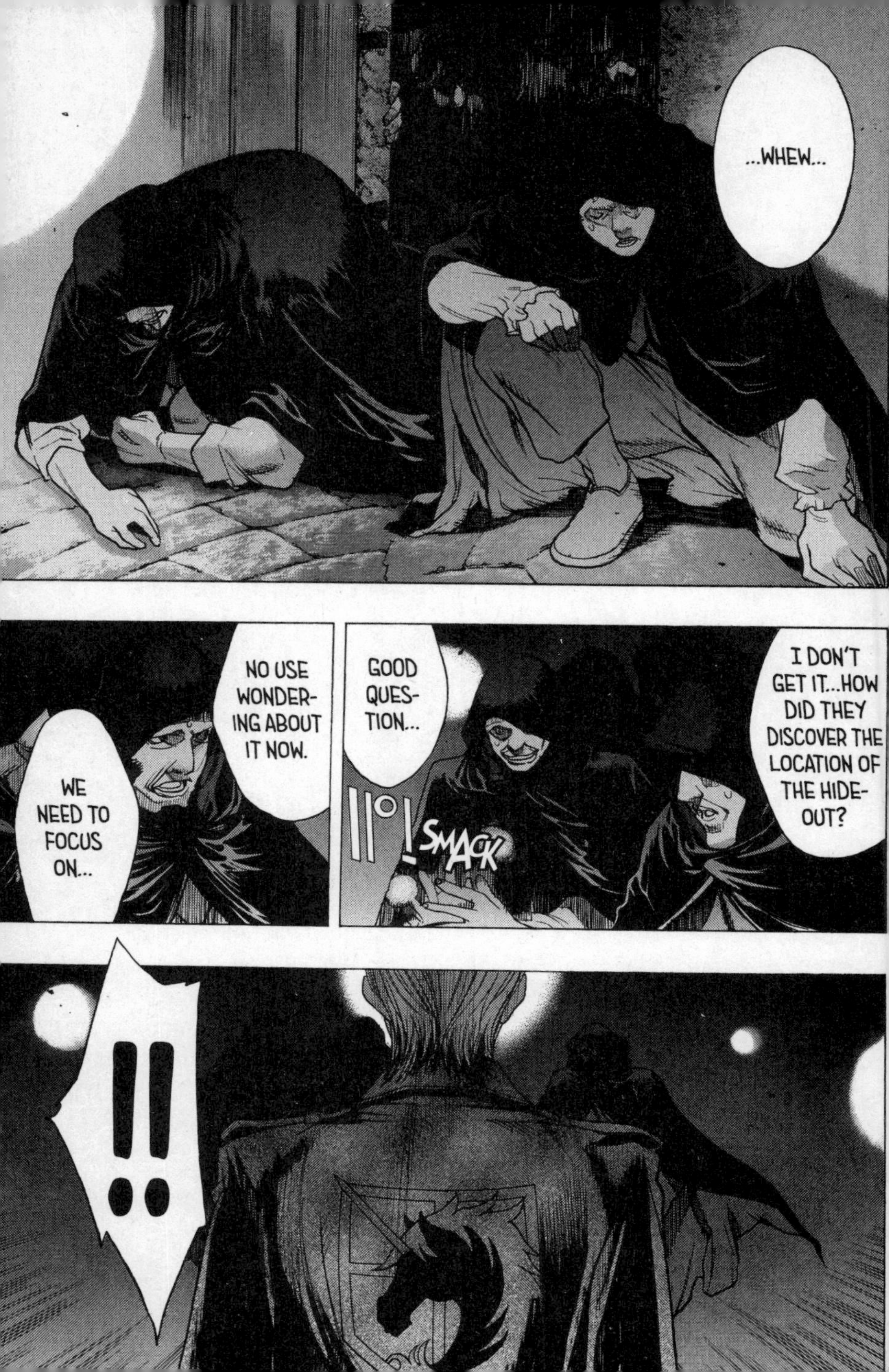
...WHEW...
I DON'T GET IT...HOW DID THEY DISCOVER THE LOCATION OF THE HIDE-OUT?
SMACK
GOOD QUES-TION...
NO USE WONDER-ING ABOUT IT NOW.
WE NEED TO FOCUS ON...
!!

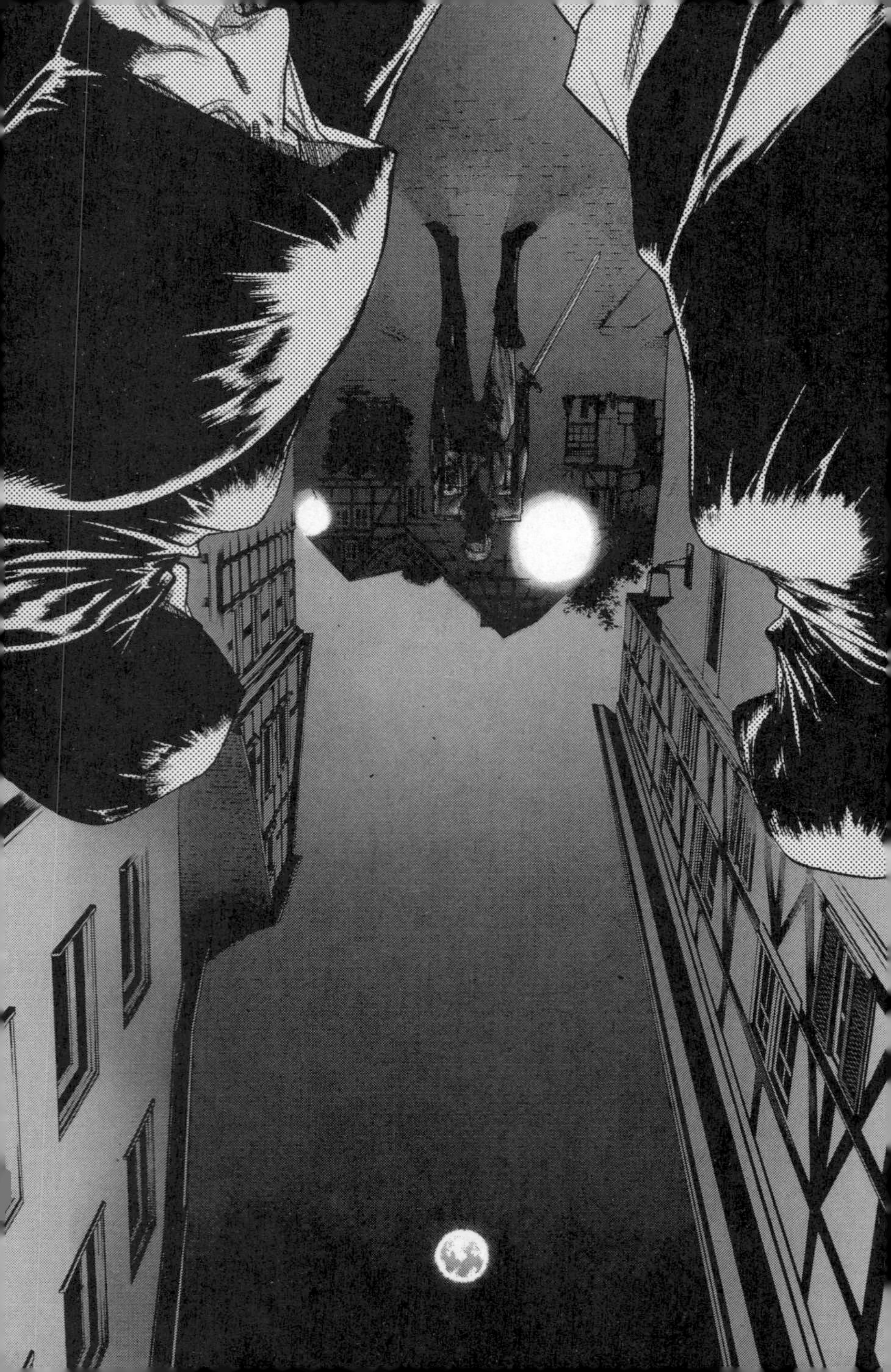

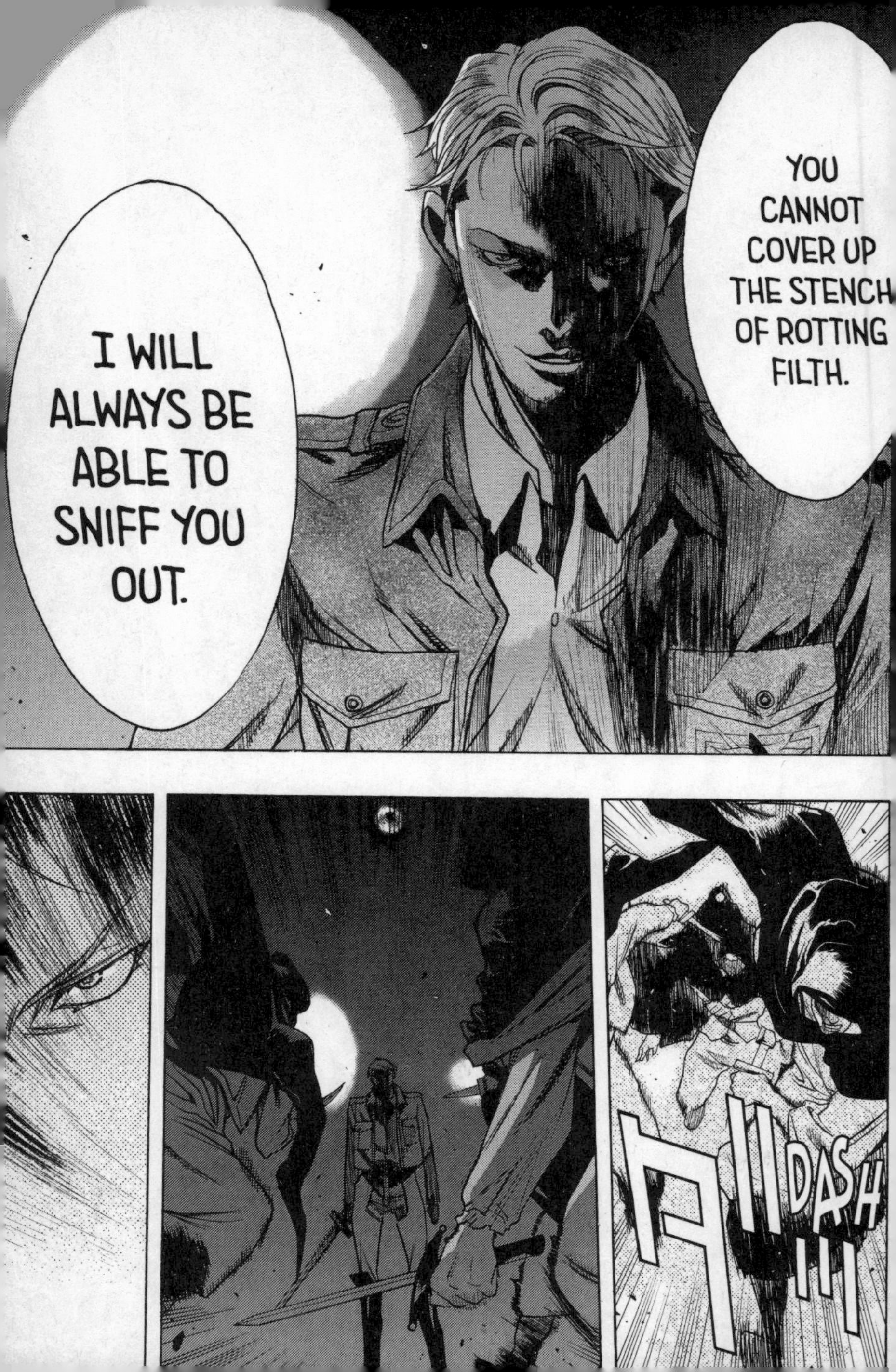
YOU CANNOT COVER UP THE STENCH OF ROTTING FILTH.
I WILL ALWAYS BE ABLE TO SNIFF YOU OUT.
DASH

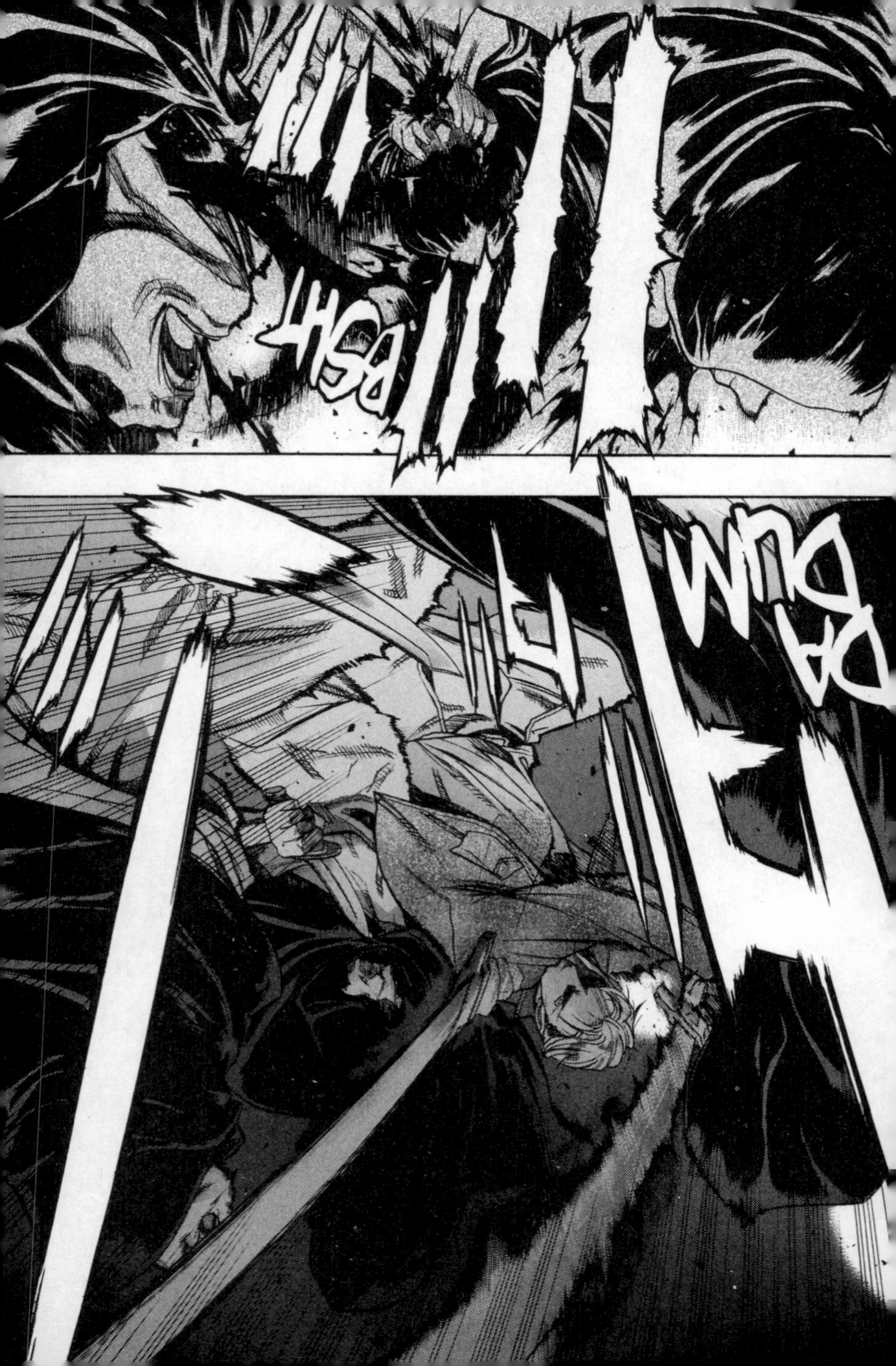
BASH
BUM

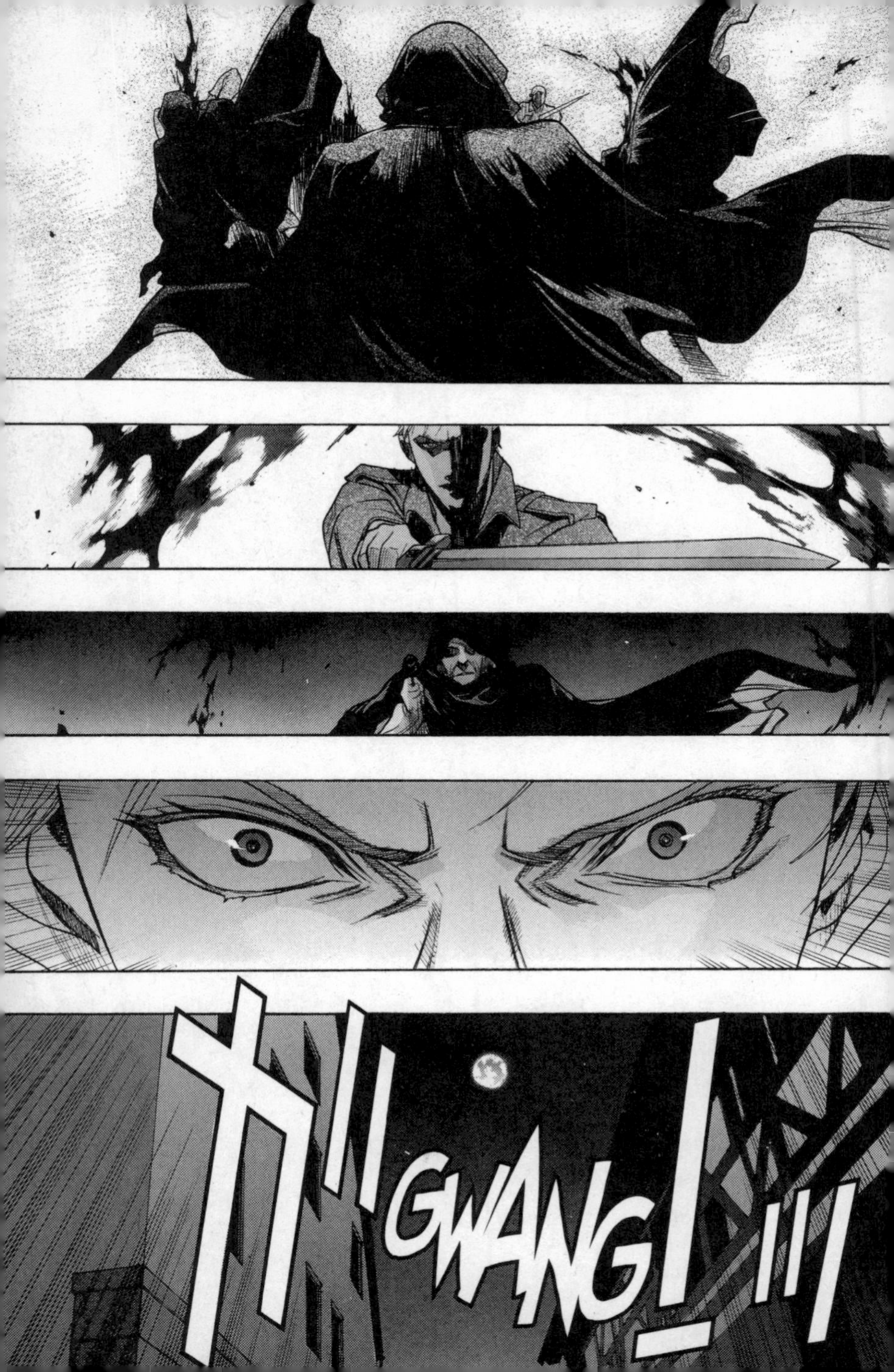
ガ GWANG!!!

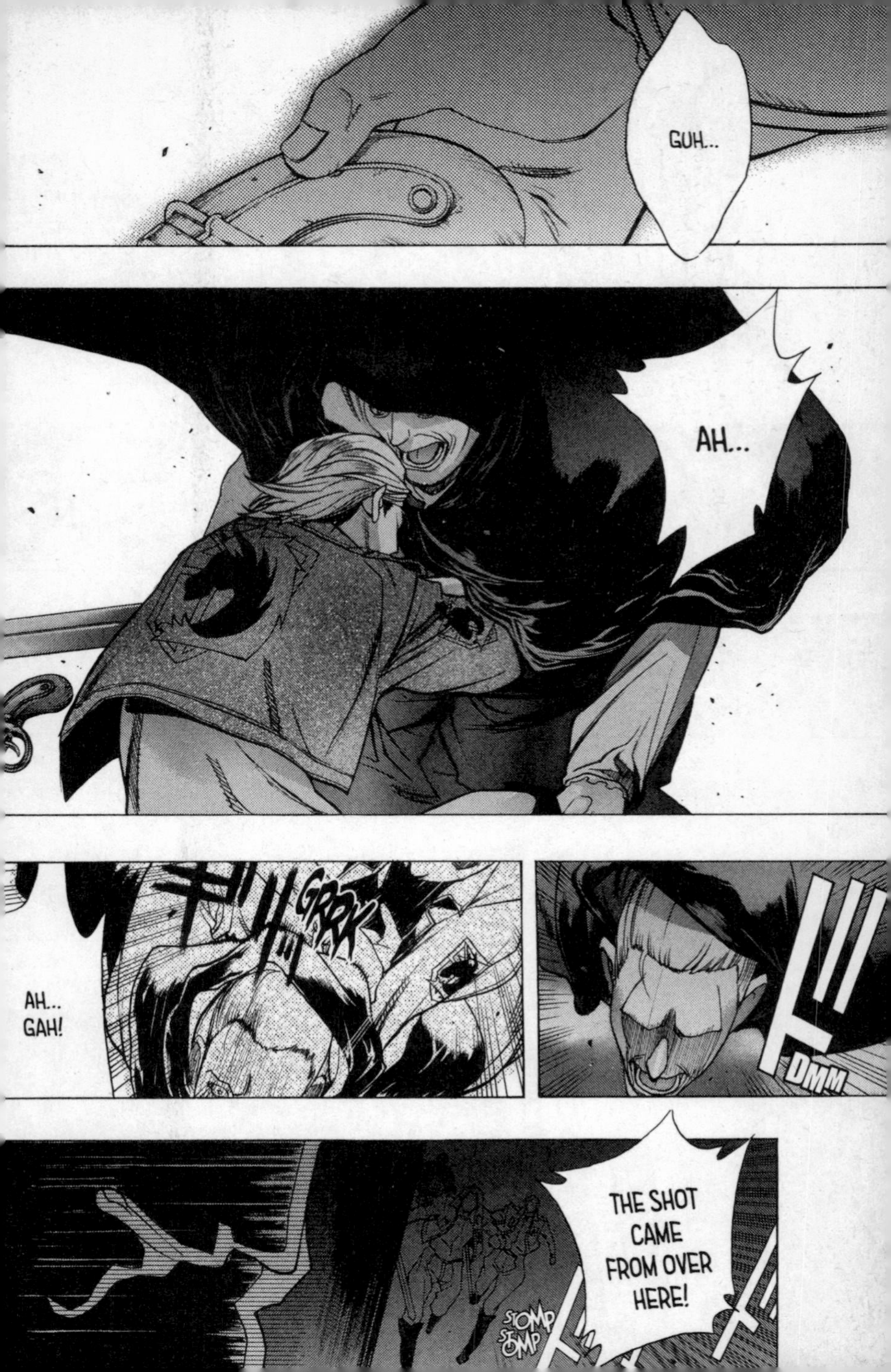
GUH...
AH...
DMM
AH... GAH!
GRRK
THE SHOT CAME FROM OVER HERE!
STOMP STOMP

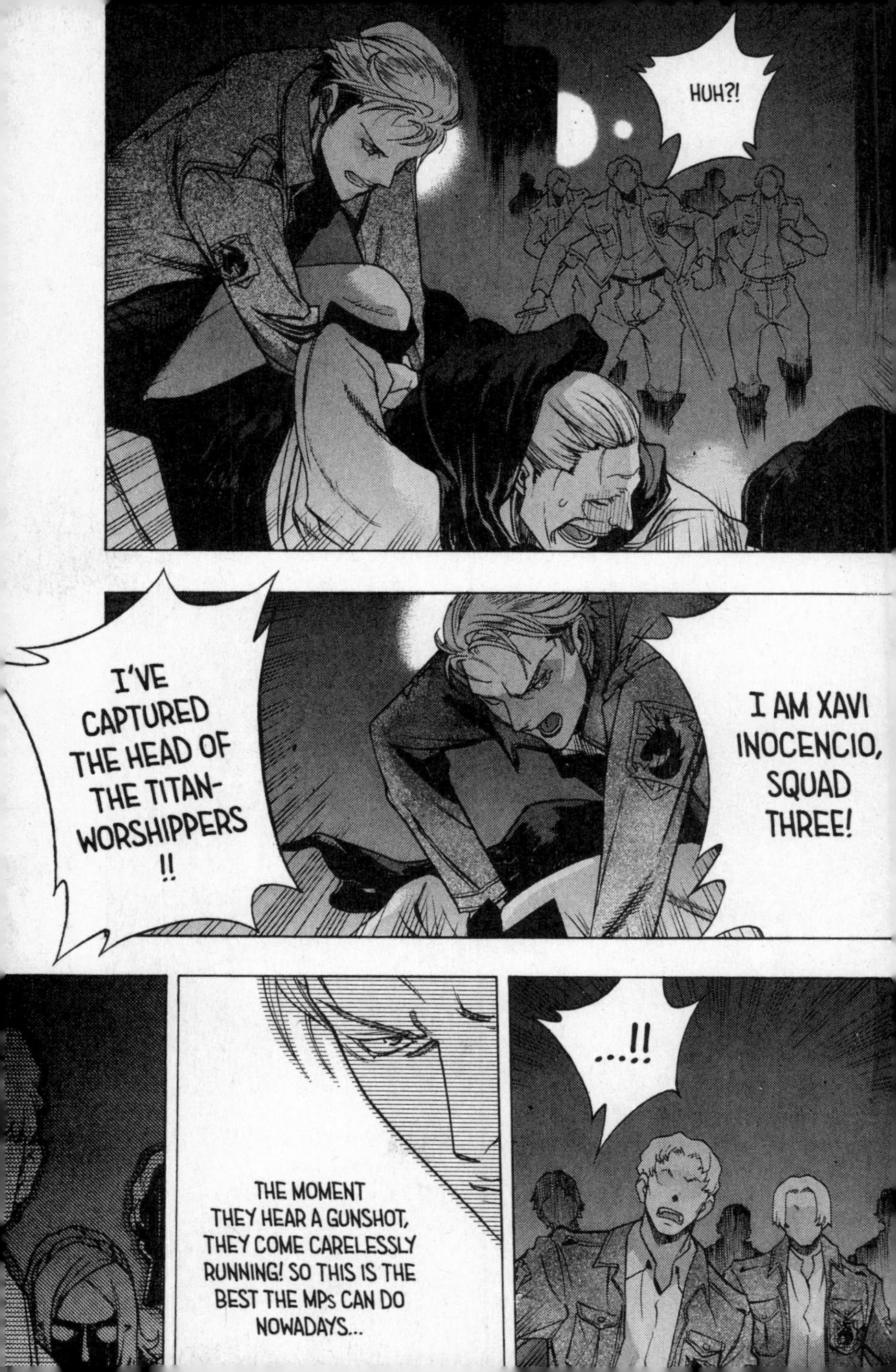
HUH?!
I AM XAVI INOCENCIO, SQUAD THREE!
I'VE CAPTURED THE HEAD OF THE TITAN-WORSHIPPERS !!
...!!
THE MOMENT THEY HEAR A GUNSHOT, THEY COME CARELESSLY RUNNING! SO THIS IS THE BEST THE MPs CAN DO NOWADAYS...

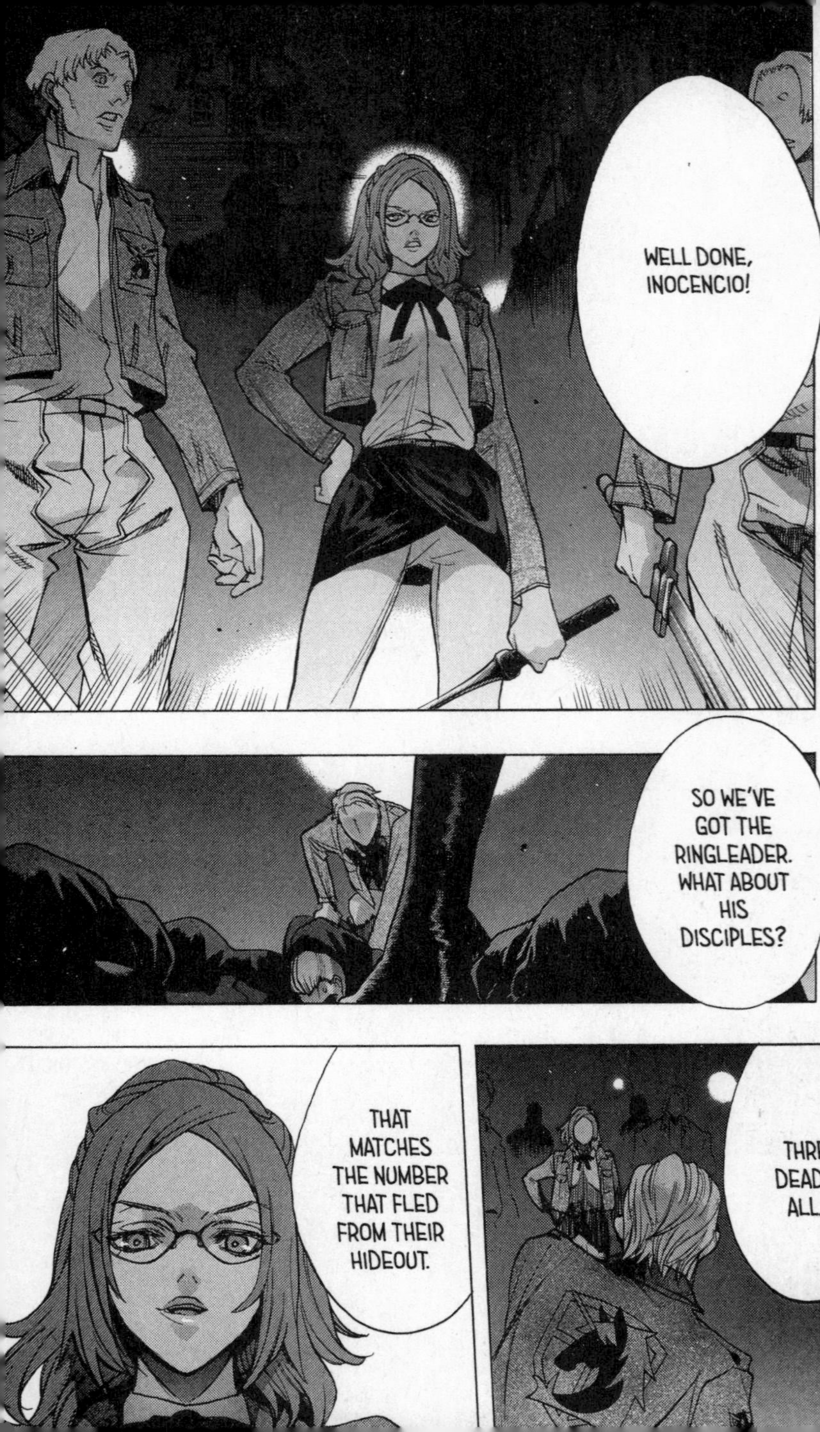
WELL DONE, INOCENCIO!
SO WE'VE GOT THE RINGLEADER. WHAT ABOUT HIS DISCIPLES?
THREE DEAD IN ALL...
THAT MATCHES THE NUMBER THAT FLED FROM THEIR HIDEOUT.

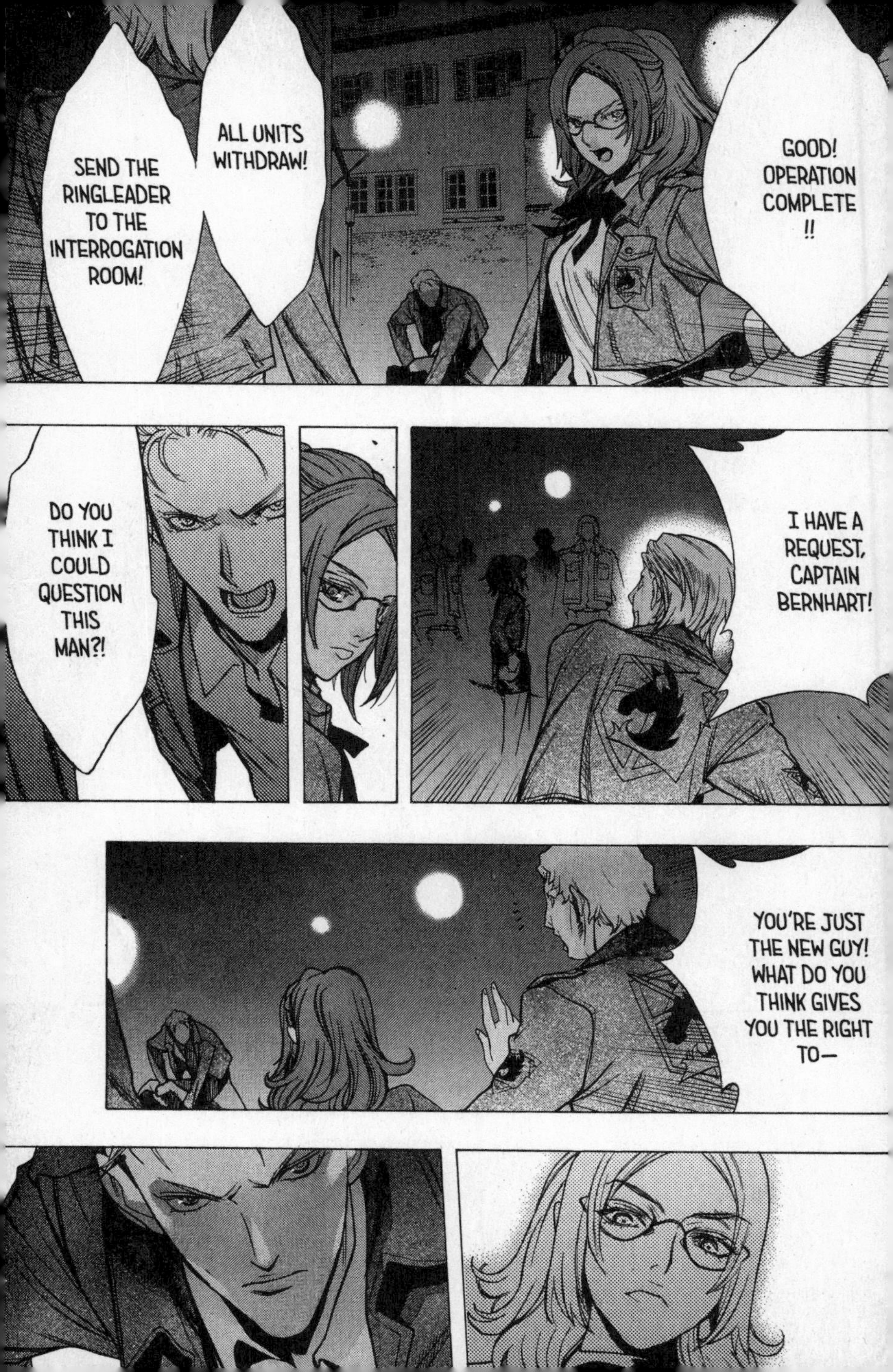
GOOD! OPERATION COMPLETE !!
ALL UNITS WITHDRAW!
SEND THE RINGLEADER TO THE INTERROGATION ROOM!
I HAVE A REQUEST, CAPTAIN BERNHART!
DO YOU THINK I COULD QUESTION THIS MAN?!
YOU'RE JUST THE NEW GUY! WHAT DO YOU THINK GIVES YOU THE RIGHT TO—

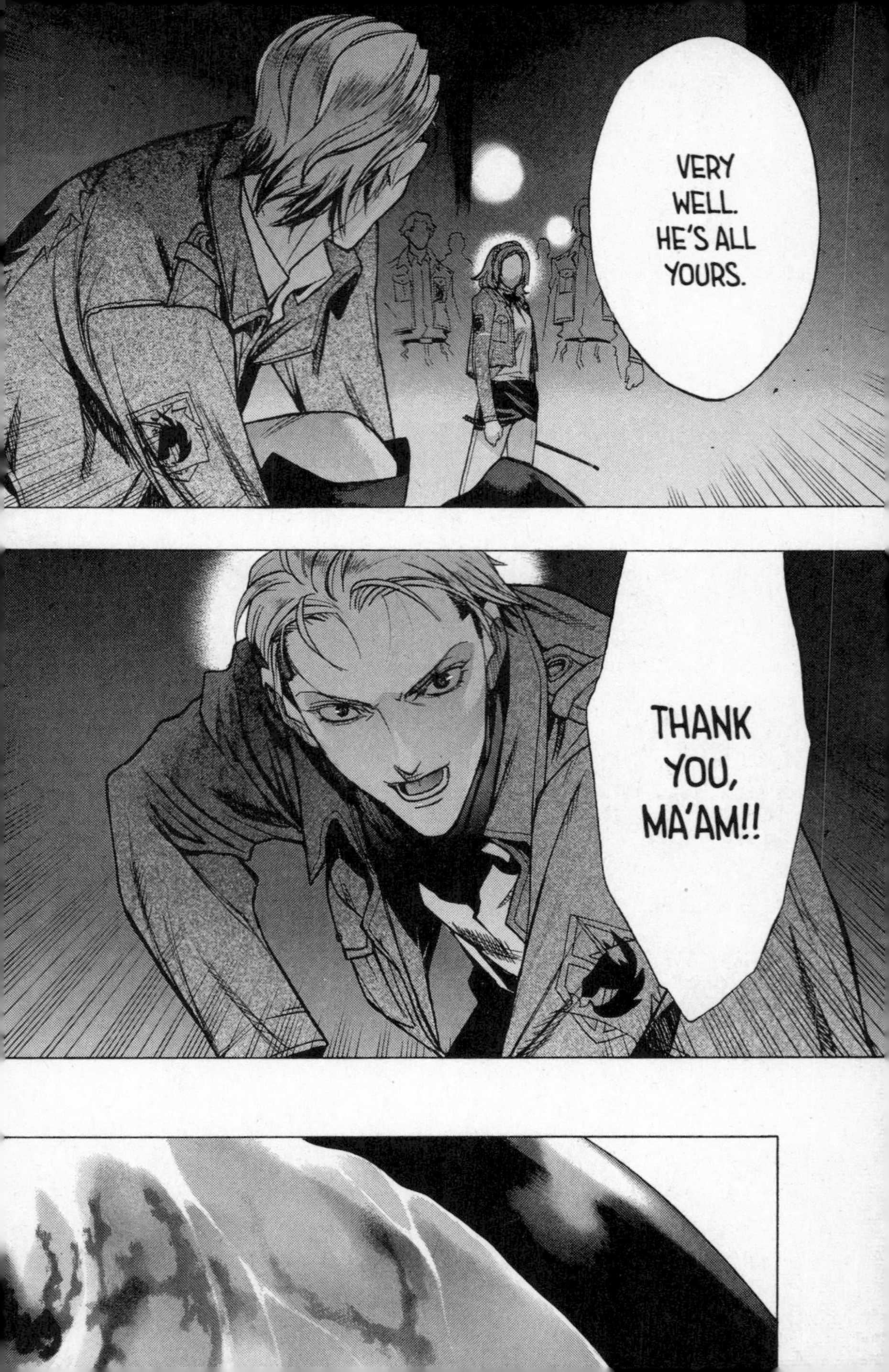
VERY WELL. HE'S ALL YOURS.
THANK YOU, MA'AM!!

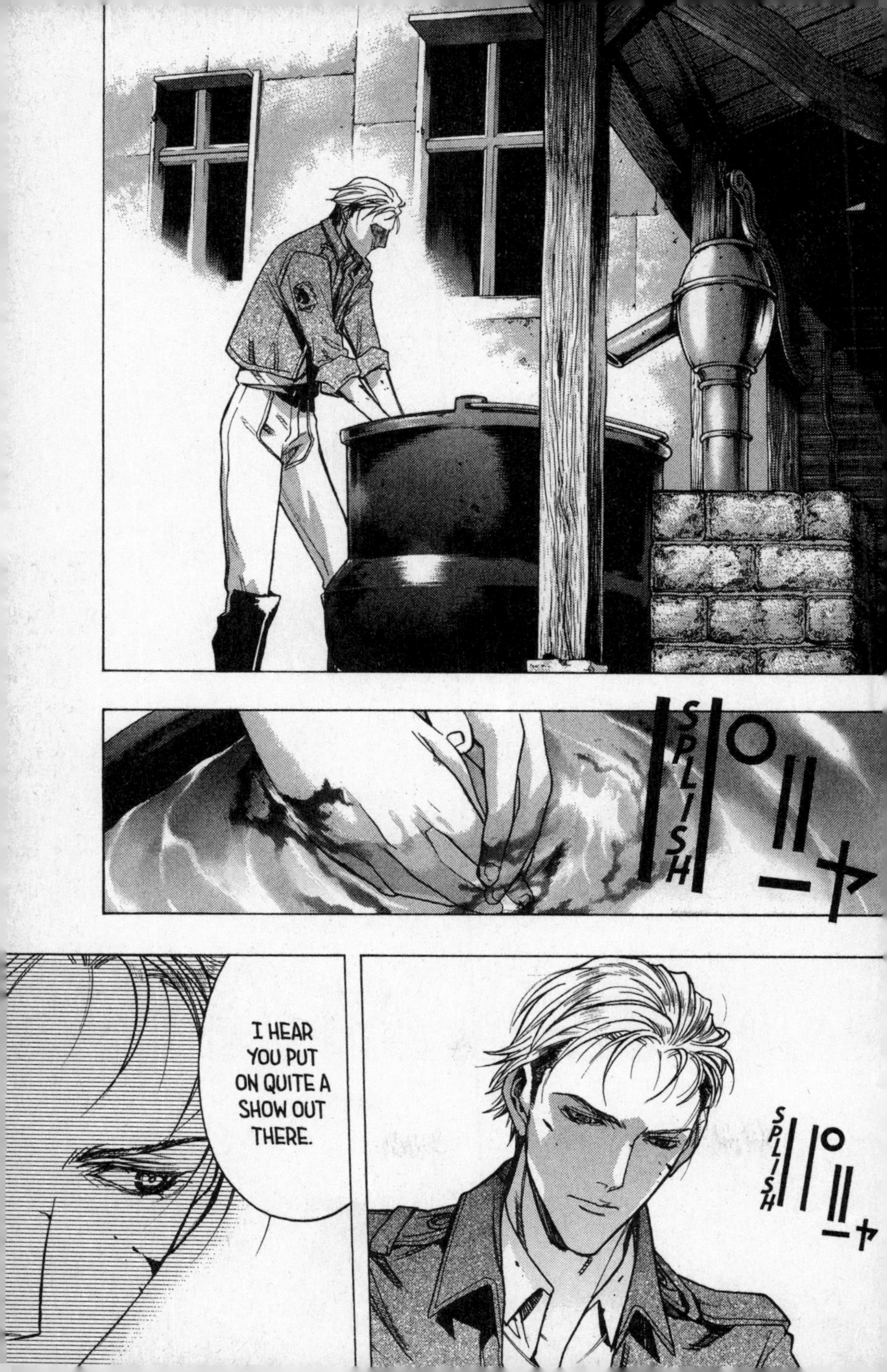
パシャ
SPLISH
パシャ
SPLISH
I HEAR YOU PUT ON QUITE A SHOW OUT THERE.

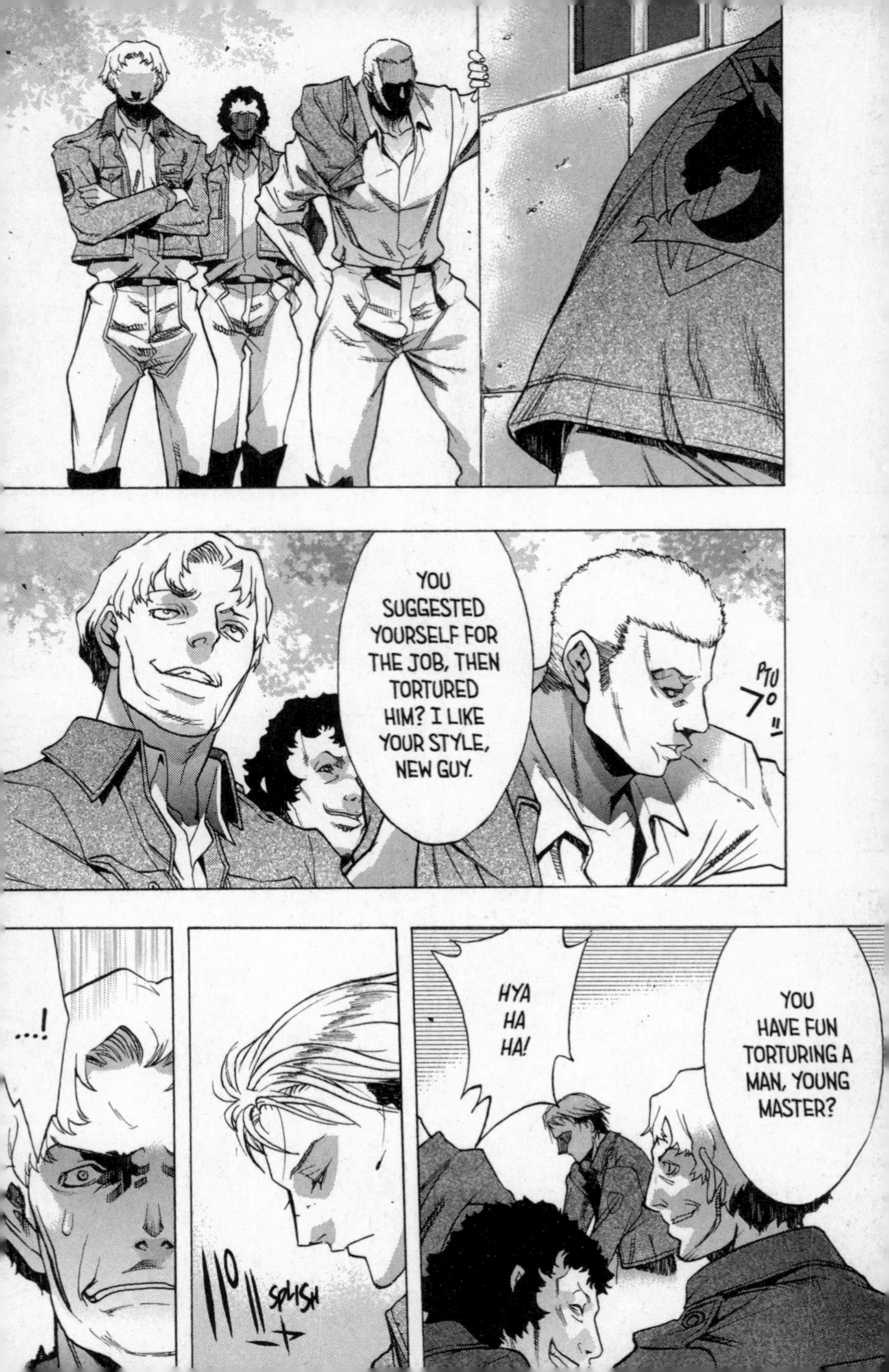
PTU
YOU SUGGESTED YOURSELF FOR THE JOB, THEN TORTURED HIM? I LIKE YOUR STYLE, NEW GUY.
YOU HAVE FUN TORTURING A MAN, YOUNG MASTER?
HYA HA HA!
SPLISH
...!

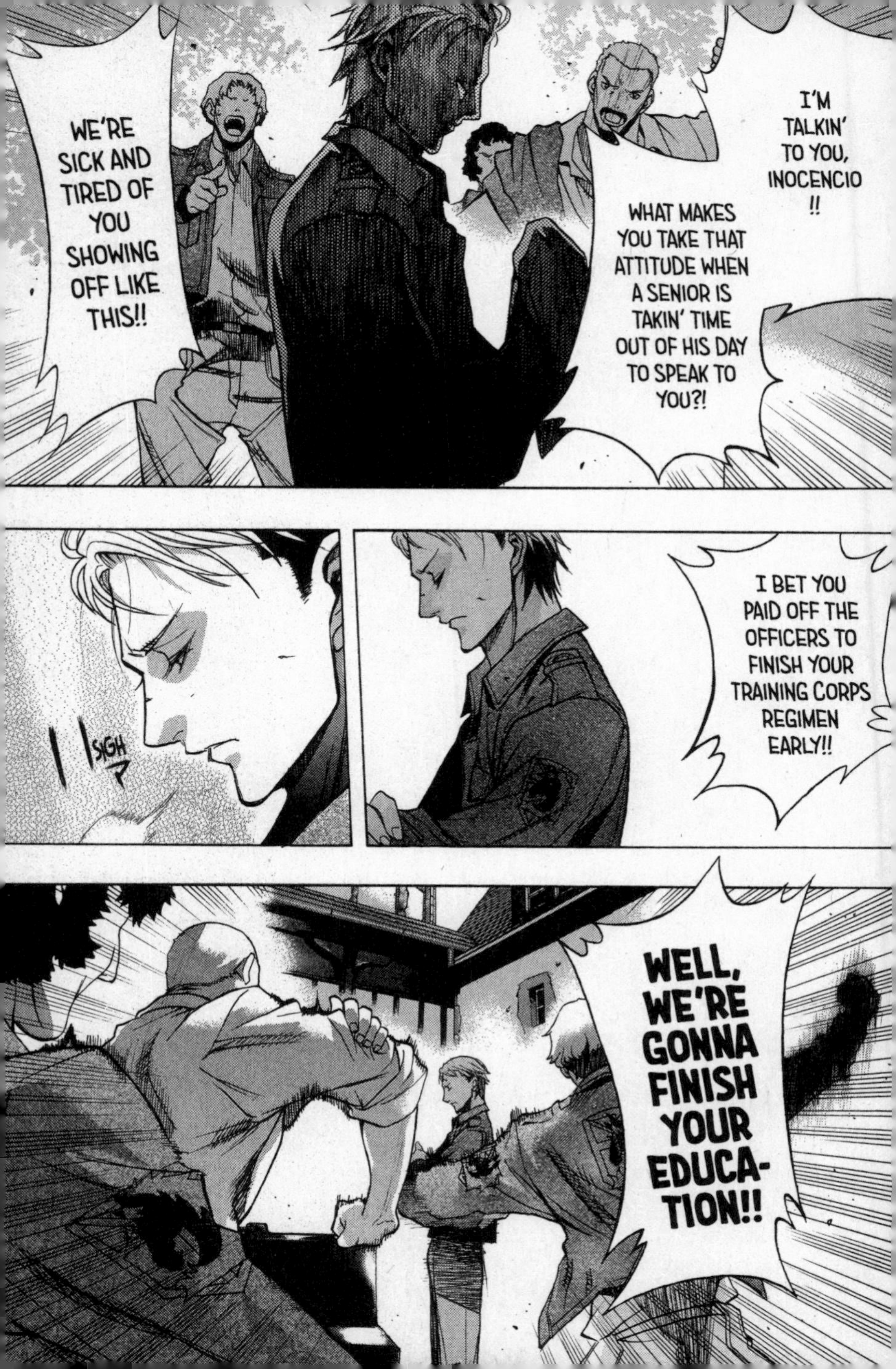
I'M TALKIN' TO YOU, INOCENCIO !!
WHAT MAKES YOU TAKE THAT ATTITUDE WHEN A SENIOR IS TAKIN' TIME OUT OF HIS DAY TO SPEAK TO YOU?!
WE'RE SICK AND TIRED OF YOU SHOWING OFF LIKE THIS!!
I BET YOU PAID OFF THE OFFICERS TO FINISH YOUR TRAINING CORPS REGIMEN EARLY!!
SIGH
WELL, WE'RE GONNA FINISH YOUR EDUCA-TION!!

THANK YOU FOR YOUR INSTRUCTION.

SHFF

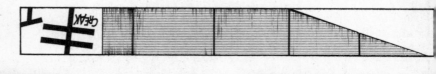

CREAK

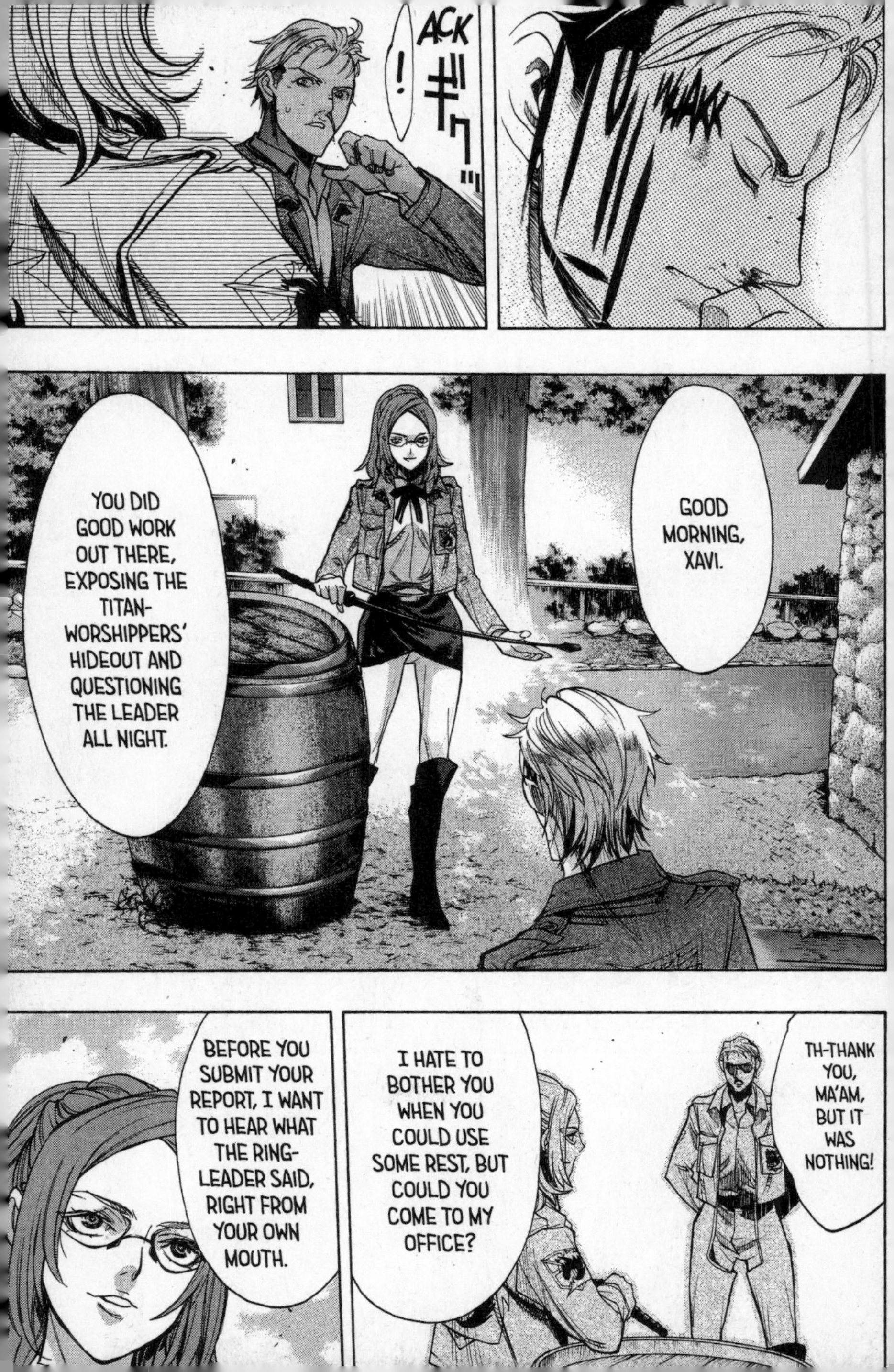
WHAKK
ACK
ギク
!
GOOD MORNING, XAVI.
YOU DID GOOD WORK OUT THERE, EXPOSING THE TITAN-WORSHIPPERS' HIDEOUT AND QUESTIONING THE LEADER ALL NIGHT.
TH-THANK YOU, MA'AM, BUT IT WAS NOTHING!
I HATE TO BOTHER YOU WHEN YOU COULD USE SOME REST, BUT COULD YOU COME TO MY OFFICE?
BEFORE YOU SUBMIT YOUR REPORT, I WANT TO HEAR WHAT THE RING-LEADER SAID, RIGHT FROM YOUR OWN MOUTH.

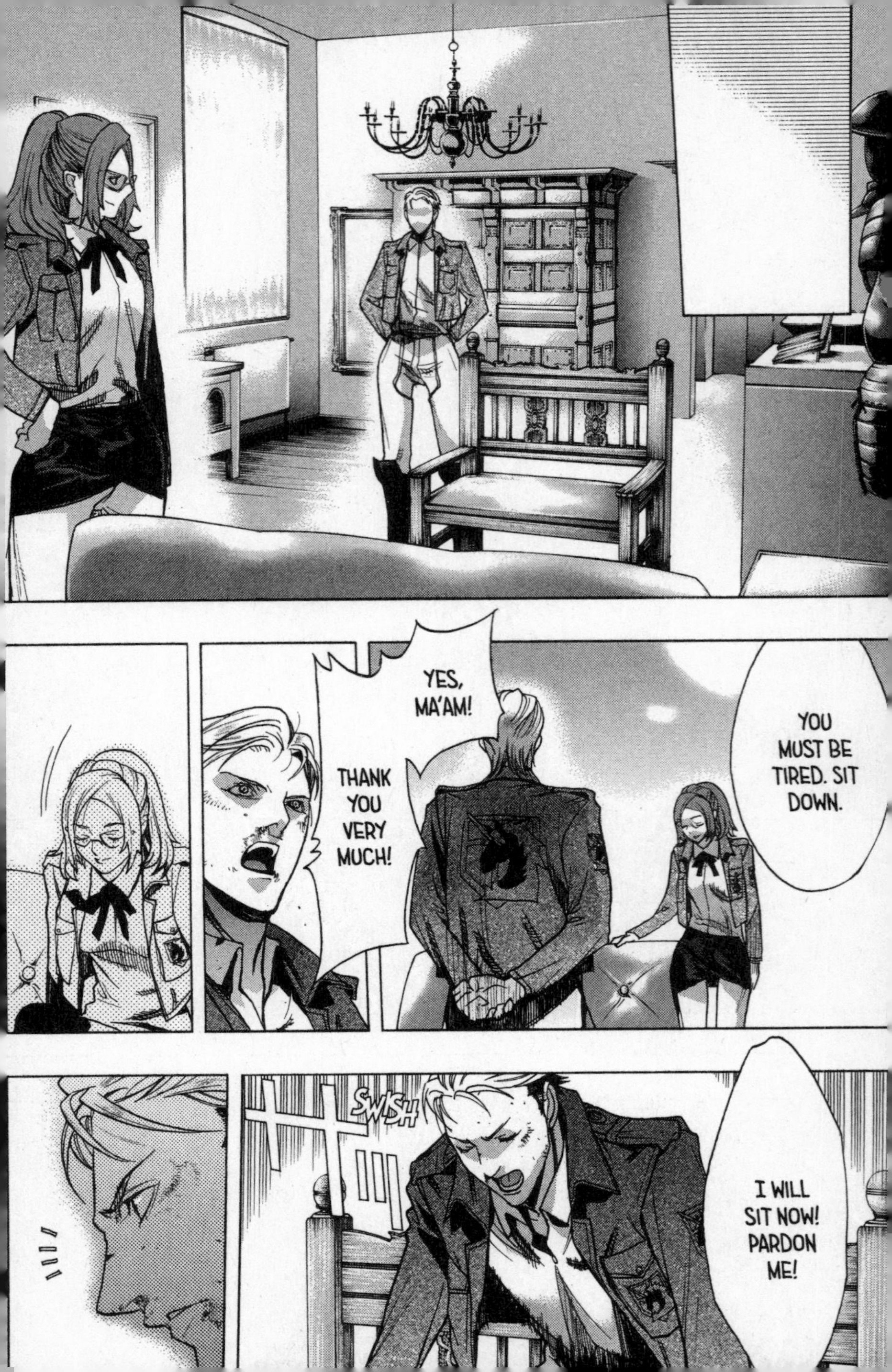
YOU MUST BE TIRED. SIT DOWN.
YES, MA'AM!
THANK YOU VERY MUCH!
I WILL SIT NOW! PARDON ME!
SWISH

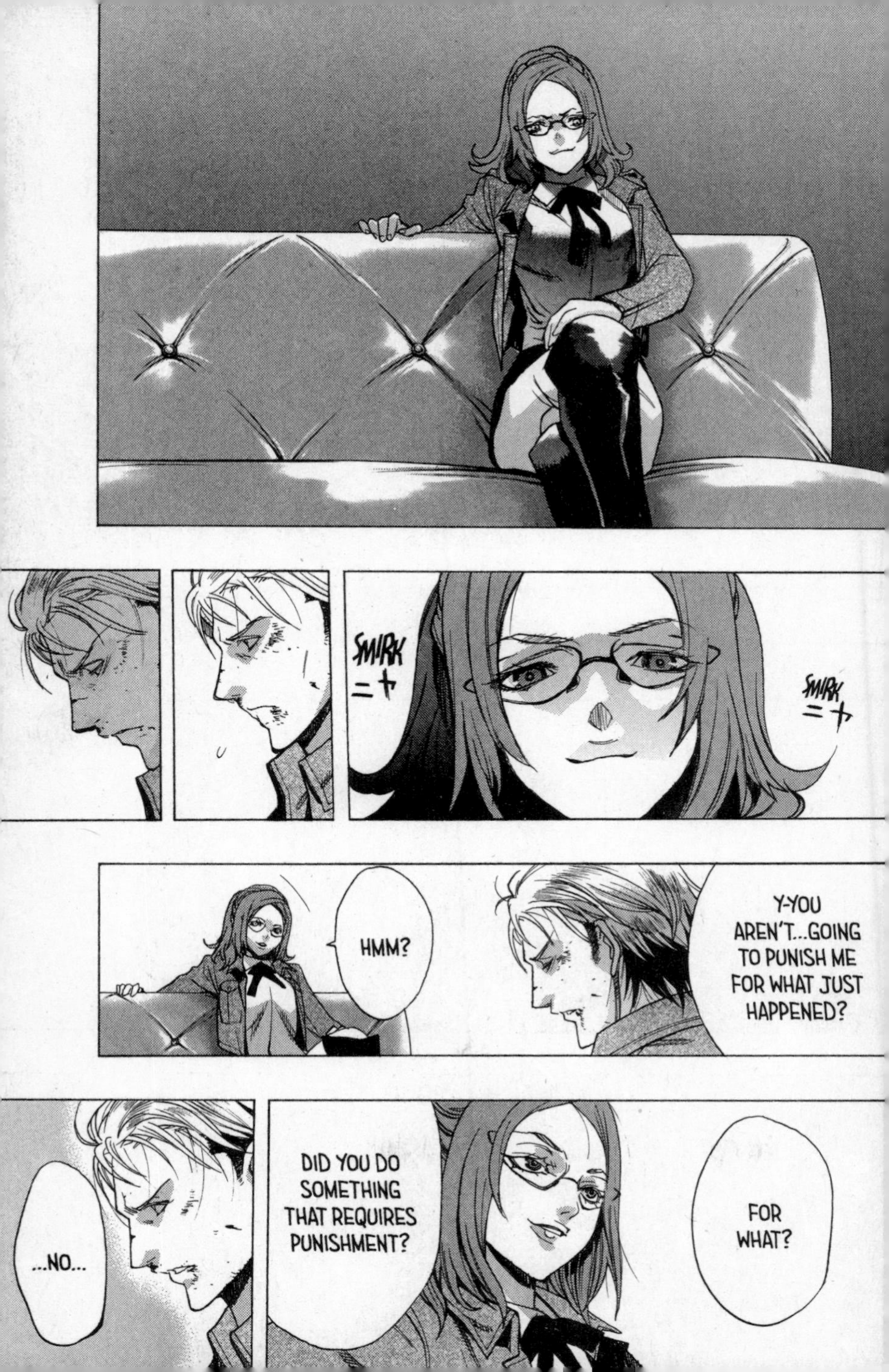
SMIRK
SMIRK
Y-YOU AREN'T...GOING TO PUNISH ME FOR WHAT JUST HAPPENED?
HMM?
FOR WHAT?
DID YOU DO SOMETHING THAT REQUIRES PUNISHMENT?
...NO...

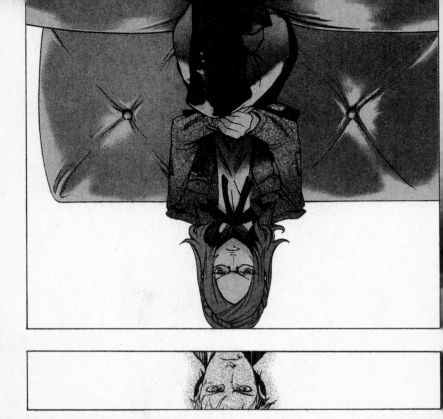

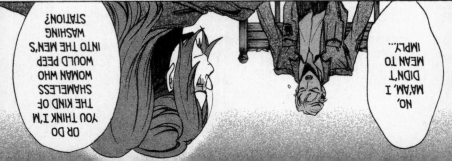

OR DO YOU THINK I'M THE KIND OF SHAMELESS WOMAN WHO WOULD PEEP INTO THE MEN'S WASHING STATION?

NO, MA'AM, I DIDN'T MEAN TO IMPLY...

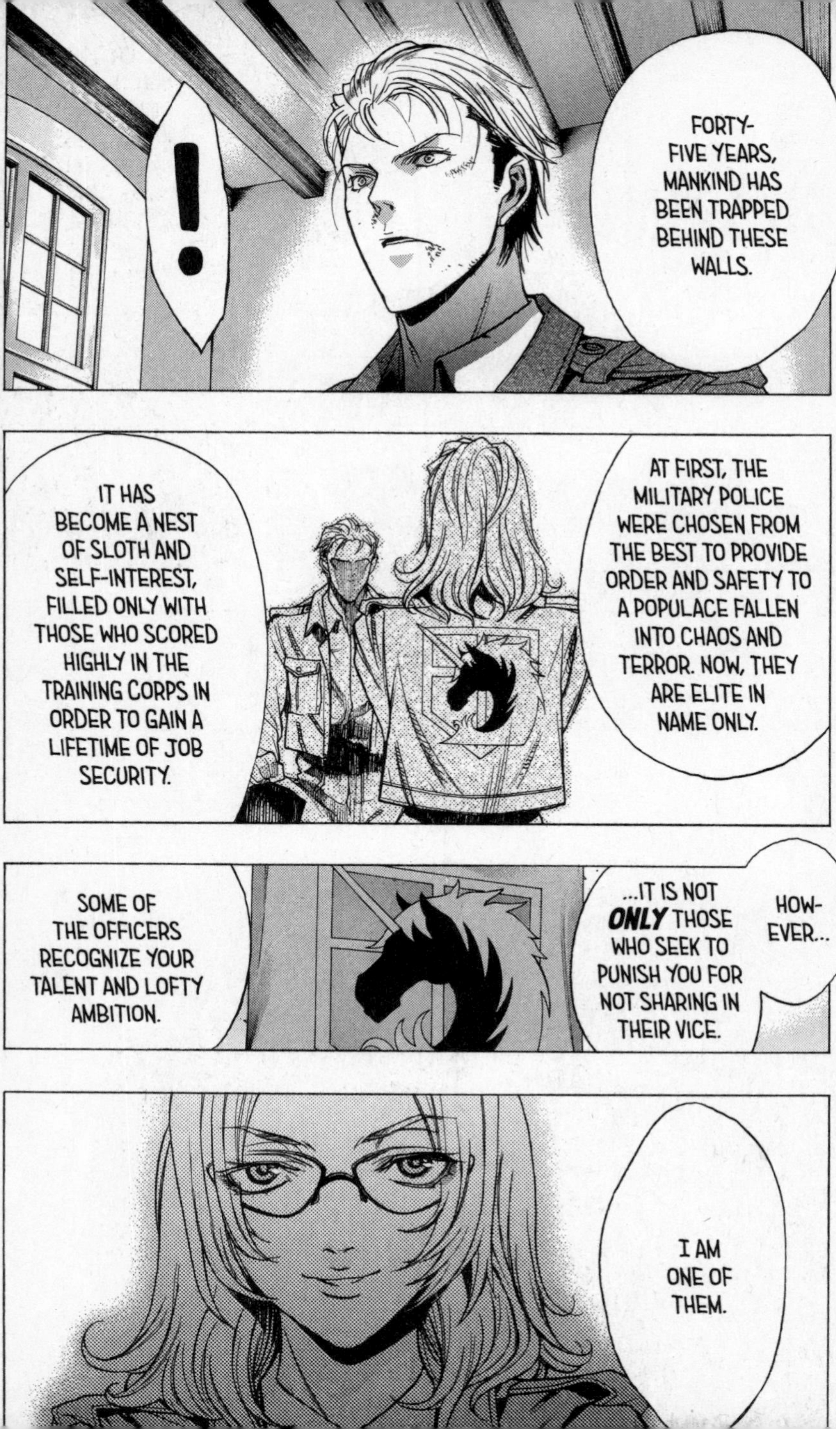
FORTY-FIVE YEARS, MANKIND HAS BEEN TRAPPED BEHIND THESE WALLS.
!
AT FIRST, THE MILITARY POLICE WERE CHOSEN FROM THE BEST TO PROVIDE ORDER AND SAFETY TO A POPULACE FALLEN INTO CHAOS AND TERROR. NOW, THEY ARE ELITE IN NAME ONLY.
IT HAS BECOME A NEST OF SLOTH AND SELF-INTEREST, FILLED ONLY WITH THOSE WHO SCORED HIGHLY IN THE TRAINING CORPS IN ORDER TO GAIN A LIFETIME OF JOB SECURITY.
HOW-EVER...
...IT IS NOT ***ONLY*** THOSE WHO SEEK TO PUNISH YOU FOR NOT SHARING IN THEIR VICE.
SOME OF THE OFFICERS RECOGNIZE YOUR TALENT AND LOFTY AMBITION.
I AM ONE OF THEM.

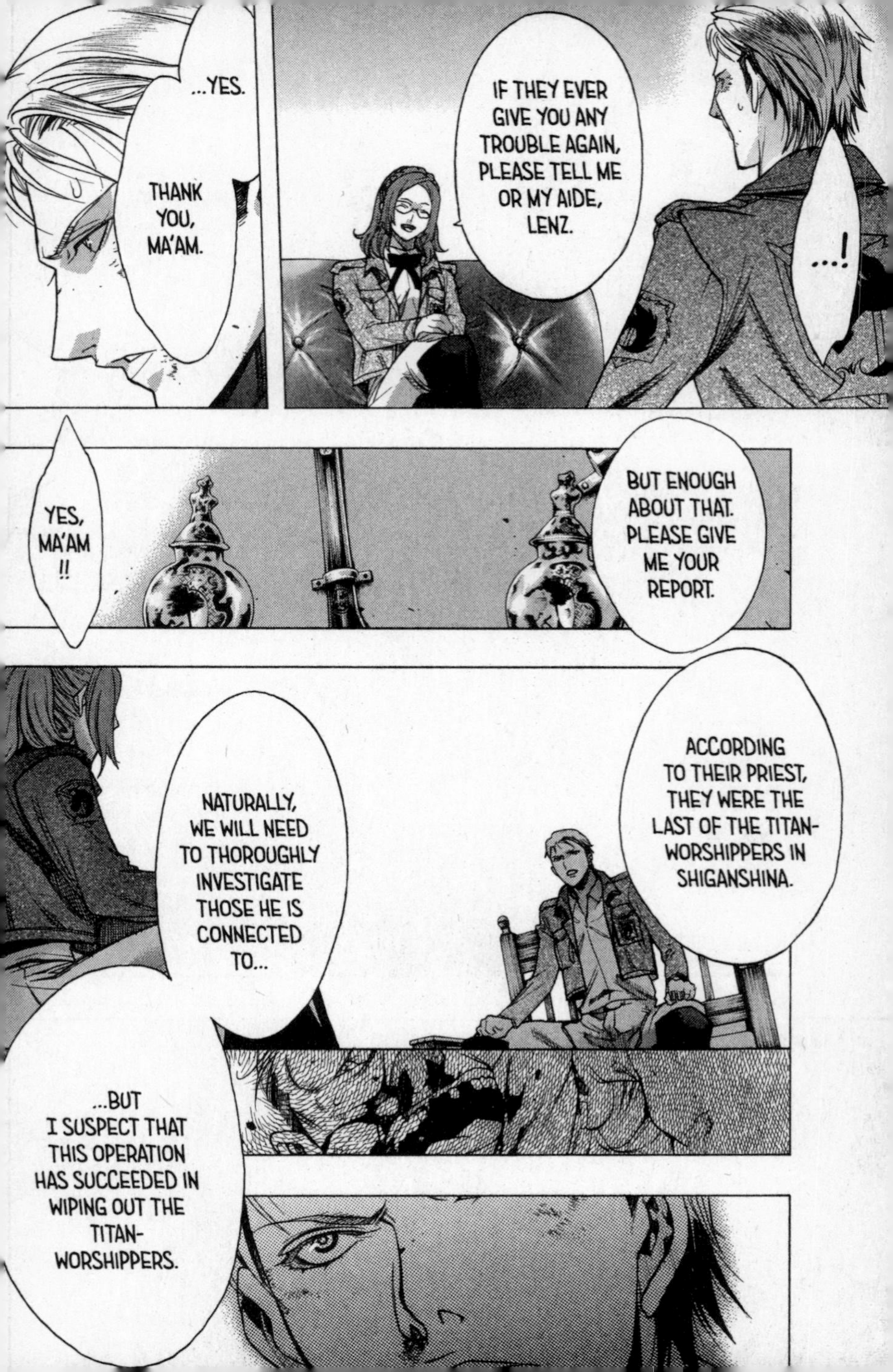
...!
IF THEY EVER GIVE YOU ANY TROUBLE AGAIN, PLEASE TELL ME OR MY AIDE, LENZ.
...YES.
THANK YOU, MA'AM.
BUT ENOUGH ABOUT THAT. PLEASE GIVE ME YOUR REPORT.
YES, MA'AM !!
ACCORDING TO THEIR PRIEST, THEY WERE THE LAST OF THE TITAN-WORSHIPPERS IN SHIGANSHINA.
NATURALLY, WE WILL NEED TO THOROUGHLY INVESTIGATE THOSE HE IS CONNECTED TO...
...BUT I SUSPECT THAT THIS OPERATION HAS SUCCEEDED IN WIPING OUT THE TITAN-WORSHIPPERS.

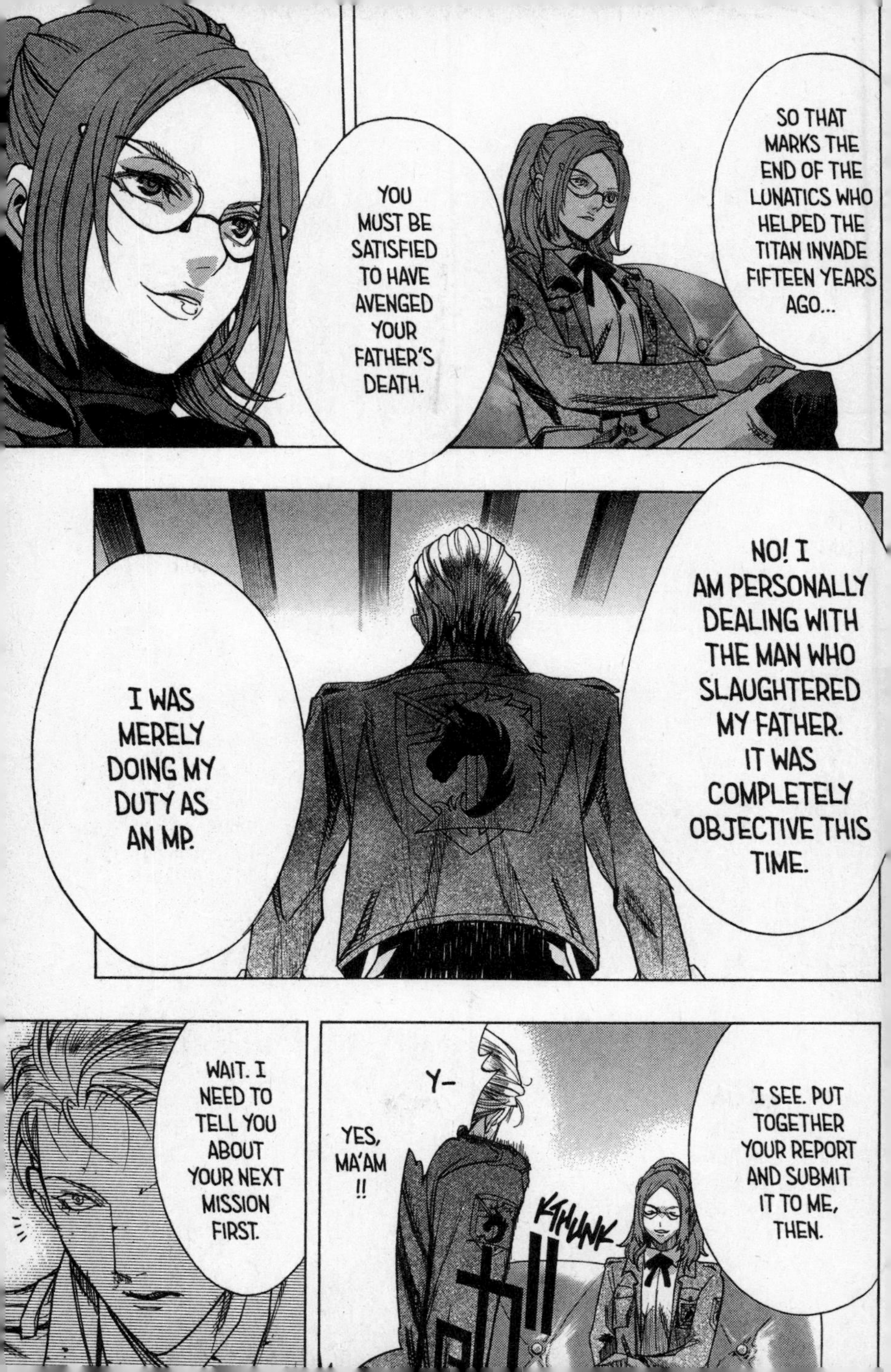
SO THAT MARKS THE END OF THE LUNATICS WHO HELPED THE TITAN INVADE FIFTEEN YEARS AGO...
YOU MUST BE SATISFIED TO HAVE AVENGED YOUR FATHER'S DEATH.
NO! I AM PERSONALLY DEALING WITH THE MAN WHO SLAUGHTERED MY FATHER. IT WAS COMPLETELY OBJECTIVE THIS TIME.
I WAS MERELY DOING MY DUTY AS AN MP.
I SEE. PUT TOGETHER YOUR REPORT AND SUBMIT IT TO ME, THEN.
KTHUNK
YES, MA'AM !!
Y-
WAIT. I NEED TO TELL YOU ABOUT YOUR NEXT MISSION FIRST.

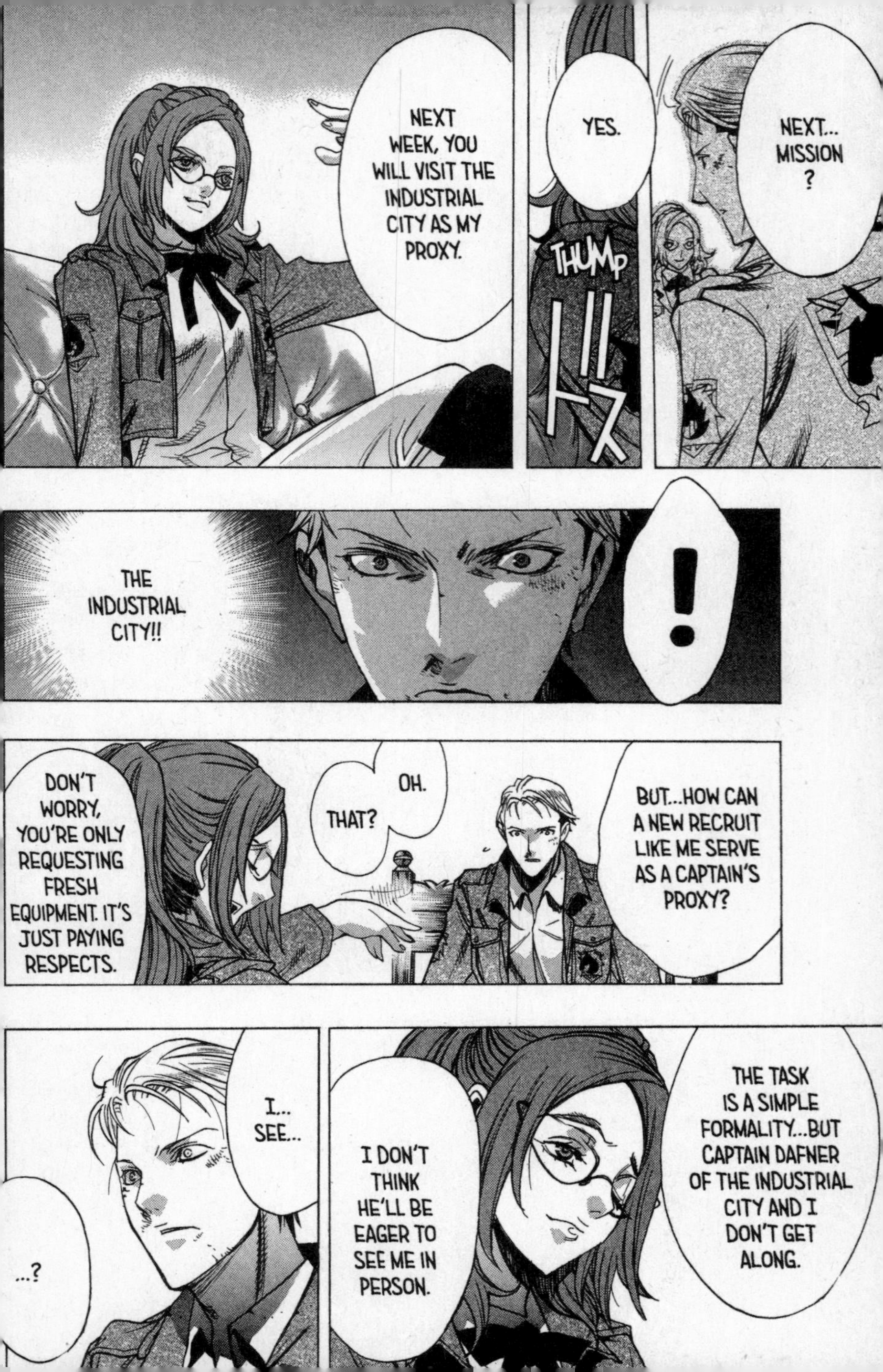
NEXT... MISSION ?
YES.
THUMP
NEXT WEEK, YOU WILL VISIT THE INDUSTRIAL CITY AS MY PROXY.
!
THE INDUSTRIAL CITY!!
BUT...HOW CAN A NEW RECRUIT LIKE ME SERVE AS A CAPTAIN'S PROXY?
OH. THAT?
DON'T WORRY, YOU'RE ONLY REQUESTING FRESH EQUIPMENT. IT'S JUST PAYING RESPECTS.
THE TASK IS A SIMPLE FORMALITY...BUT CAPTAIN DAFNER OF THE INDUSTRIAL CITY AND I DON'T GET ALONG.
I DON'T THINK HE'LL BE EAGER TO SEE ME IN PERSON.
I... SEE...
...?

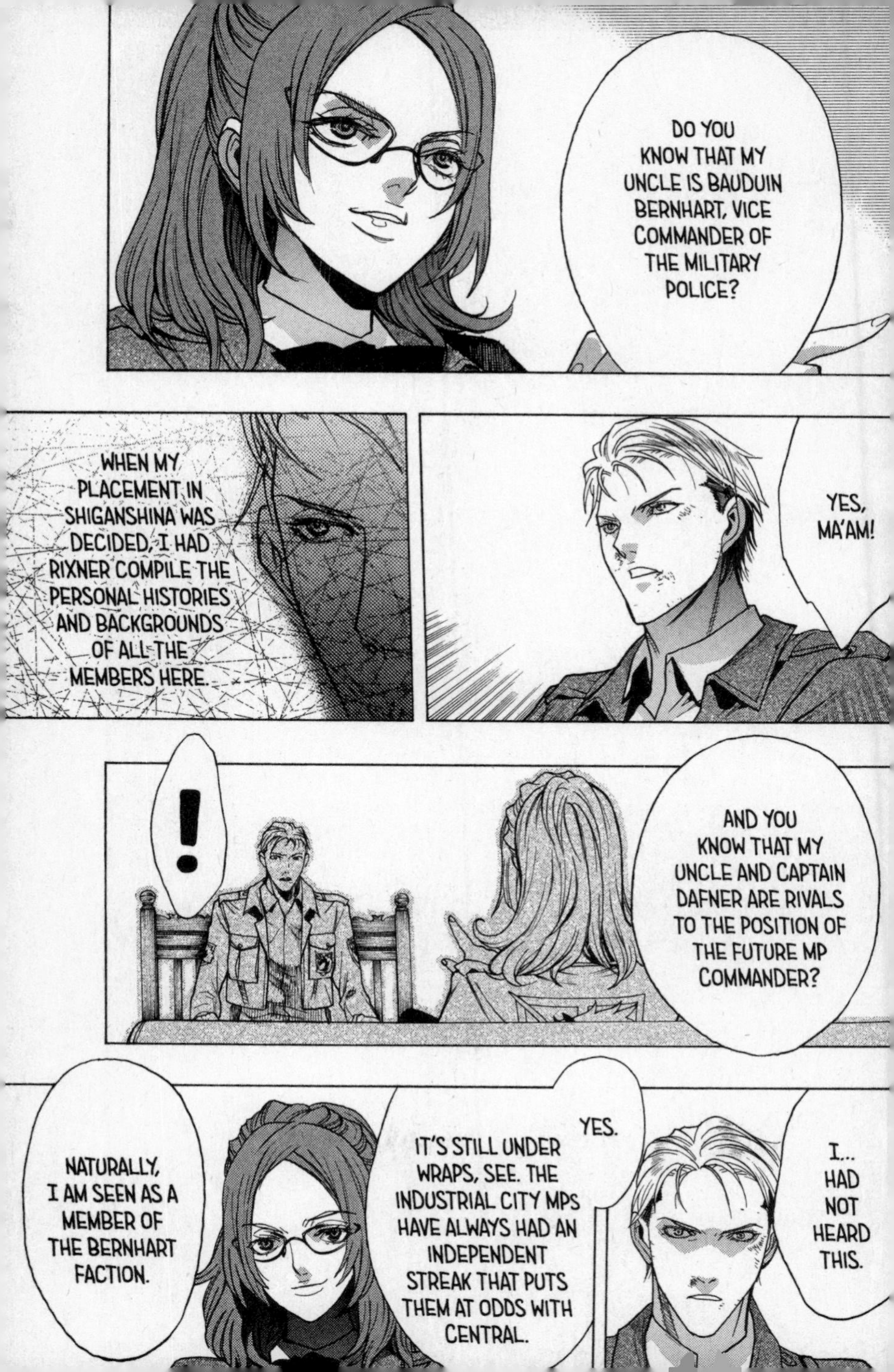
DO YOU KNOW THAT MY UNCLE IS BAUDUIN BERNHART, VICE COMMANDER OF THE MILITARY POLICE?
YES, MA'AM!
WHEN MY PLACEMENT IN SHIGANSHINA WAS DECIDED, I HAD RIXNER COMPILE THE PERSONAL HISTORIES AND BACKGROUNDS OF ALL THE MEMBERS HERE.
AND YOU KNOW THAT MY UNCLE AND CAPTAIN DAFNER ARE RIVALS TO THE POSITION OF THE FUTURE MP COMMANDER?
!
I... HAD NOT HEARD THIS.
YES.
IT'S STILL UNDER WRAPS, SEE. THE INDUSTRIAL CITY MPS HAVE ALWAYS HAD AN INDEPENDENT STREAK THAT PUTS THEM AT ODDS WITH CENTRAL.
NATURALLY, I AM SEEN AS A MEMBER OF THE BERNHART FACTION.

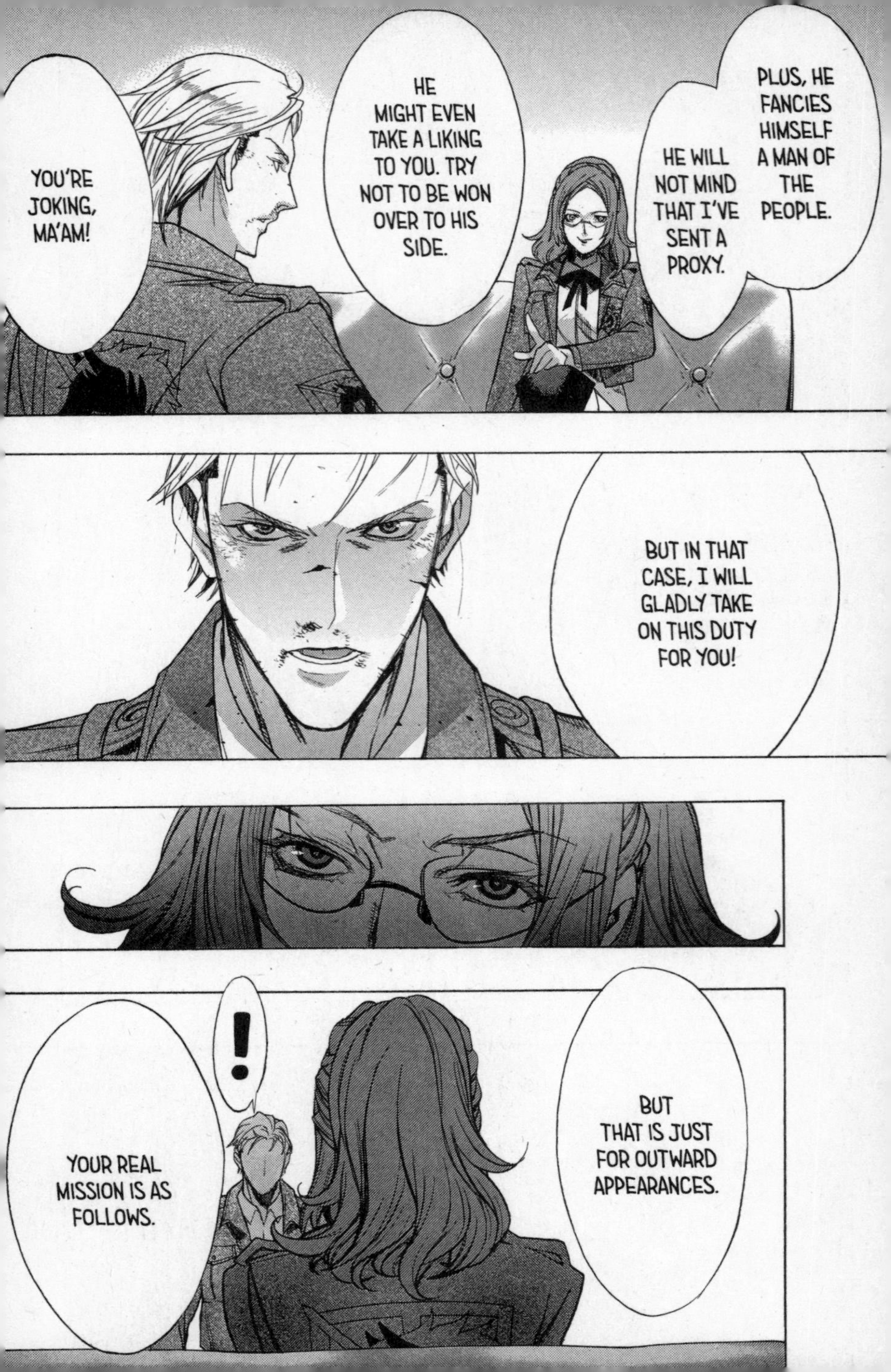
PLUS, HE FANCIES HIMSELF A MAN OF THE PEOPLE.
HE WILL NOT MIND THAT I'VE SENT A PROXY.
HE MIGHT EVEN TAKE A LIKING TO YOU. TRY NOT TO BE WON OVER TO HIS SIDE.
YOU'RE JOKING, MA'AM!
BUT IN THAT CASE, I WILL GLADLY TAKE ON THIS DUTY FOR YOU!
BUT THAT IS JUST FOR OUTWARD APPEARANCES.
!
YOUR REAL MISSION IS AS FOLLOWS.

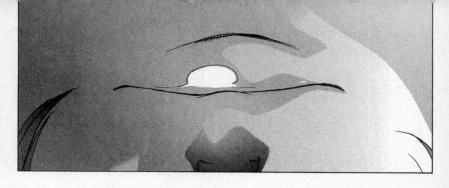

KNOWING YOUR TALENTS, XAVI, I HAVE A REQUEST OF YOU.

MURMUR 壬エニ」 壬エニ」 MURMUR

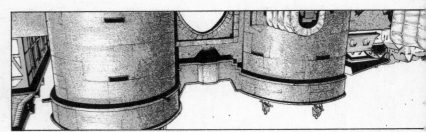

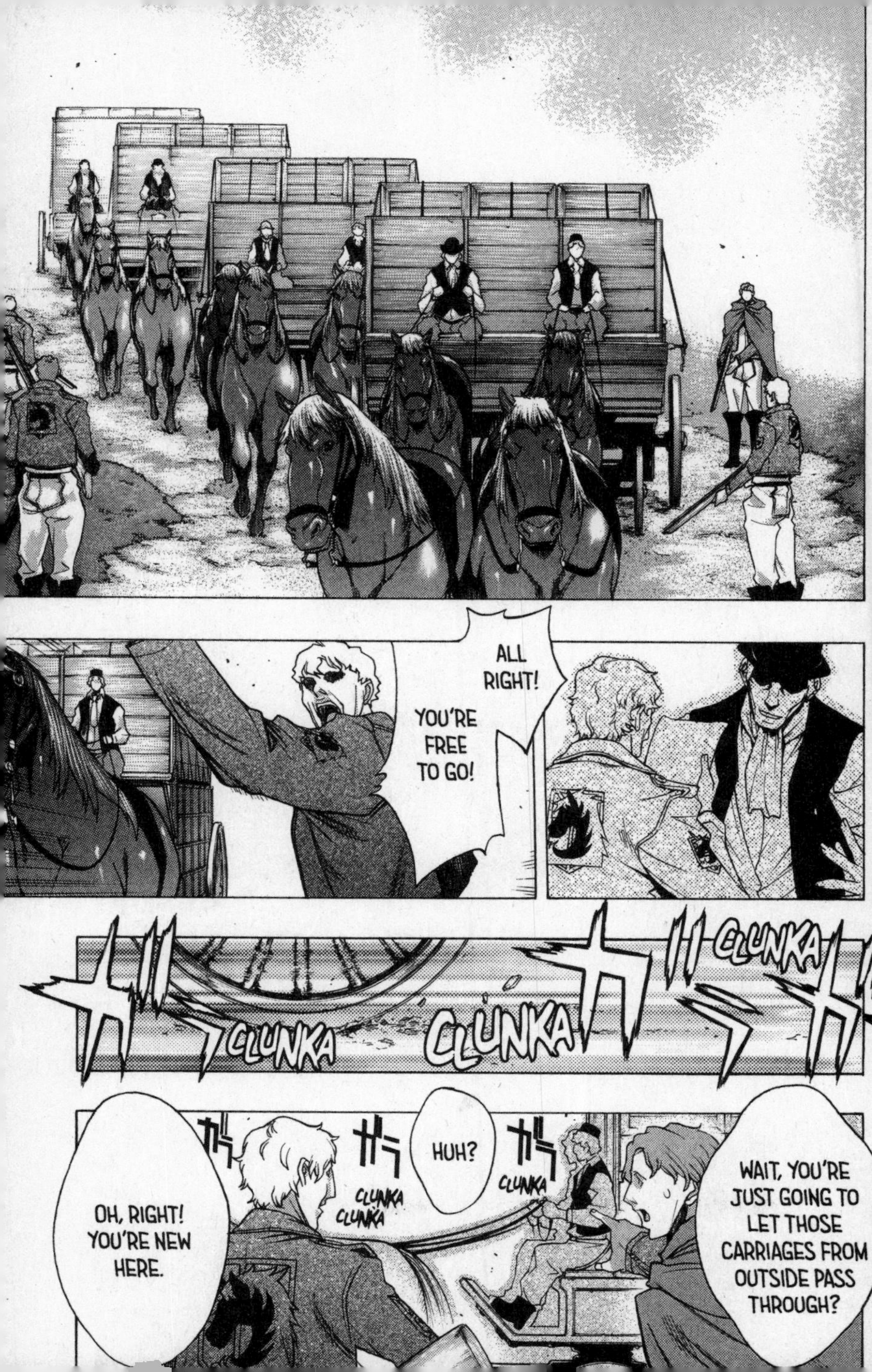
ALL RIGHT!
YOU'RE FREE TO GO!
CLUNKA
CLUNKA
CLUNKA
WAIT, YOU'RE JUST GOING TO LET THOSE CARRIAGES FROM OUTSIDE PASS THROUGH?
CLUNKA
HUH?
CLUNKA CLUNKA
OH, RIGHT! YOU'RE NEW HERE.

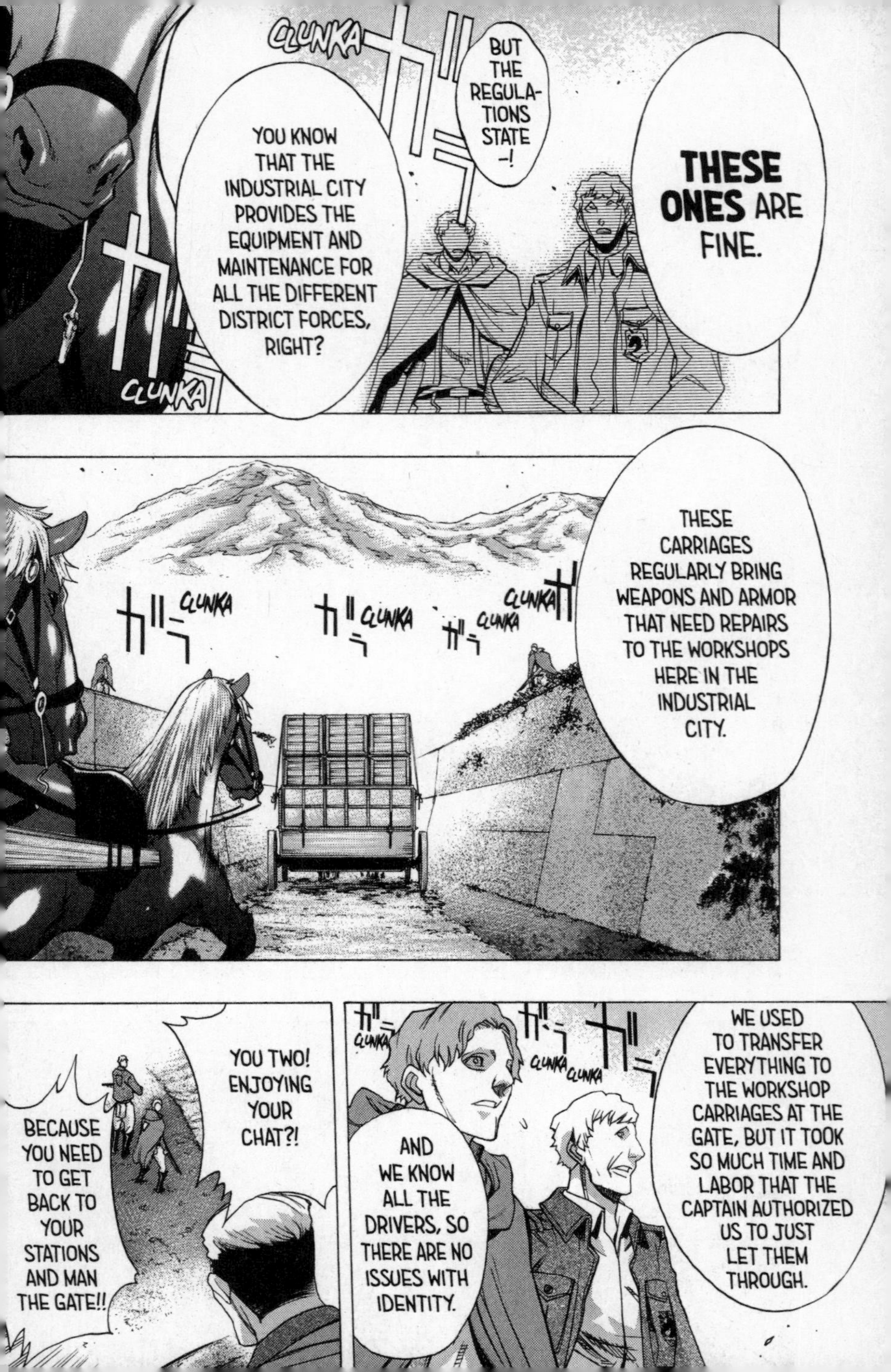
THESE ONES ARE FINE.
BUT THE REGULATIONS STATE—!
CLUNKA
YOU KNOW THAT THE INDUSTRIAL CITY PROVIDES THE EQUIPMENT AND MAINTENANCE FOR ALL THE DIFFERENT DISTRICT FORCES, RIGHT?
CLUNKA
THESE CARRIAGES REGULARLY BRING WEAPONS AND ARMOR THAT NEED REPAIRS TO THE WORKSHOPS HERE IN THE INDUSTRIAL CITY.
CLUNKA
CLUNKA
CLUNKA
CLUNKA
WE USED TO TRANSFER EVERYTHING TO THE WORKSHOP CARRIAGES AT THE GATE, BUT IT TOOK SO MUCH TIME AND LABOR THAT THE CAPTAIN AUTHORIZED US TO JUST LET THEM THROUGH.
CLUNKA
CLUNKA
CLUNKA
AND WE KNOW ALL THE DRIVERS, SO THERE ARE NO ISSUES WITH IDENTITY.
YOU TWO! ENJOYING YOUR CHAT?!
BECAUSE YOU NEED TO GET BACK TO YOUR STATIONS AND MAN THE GATE!!

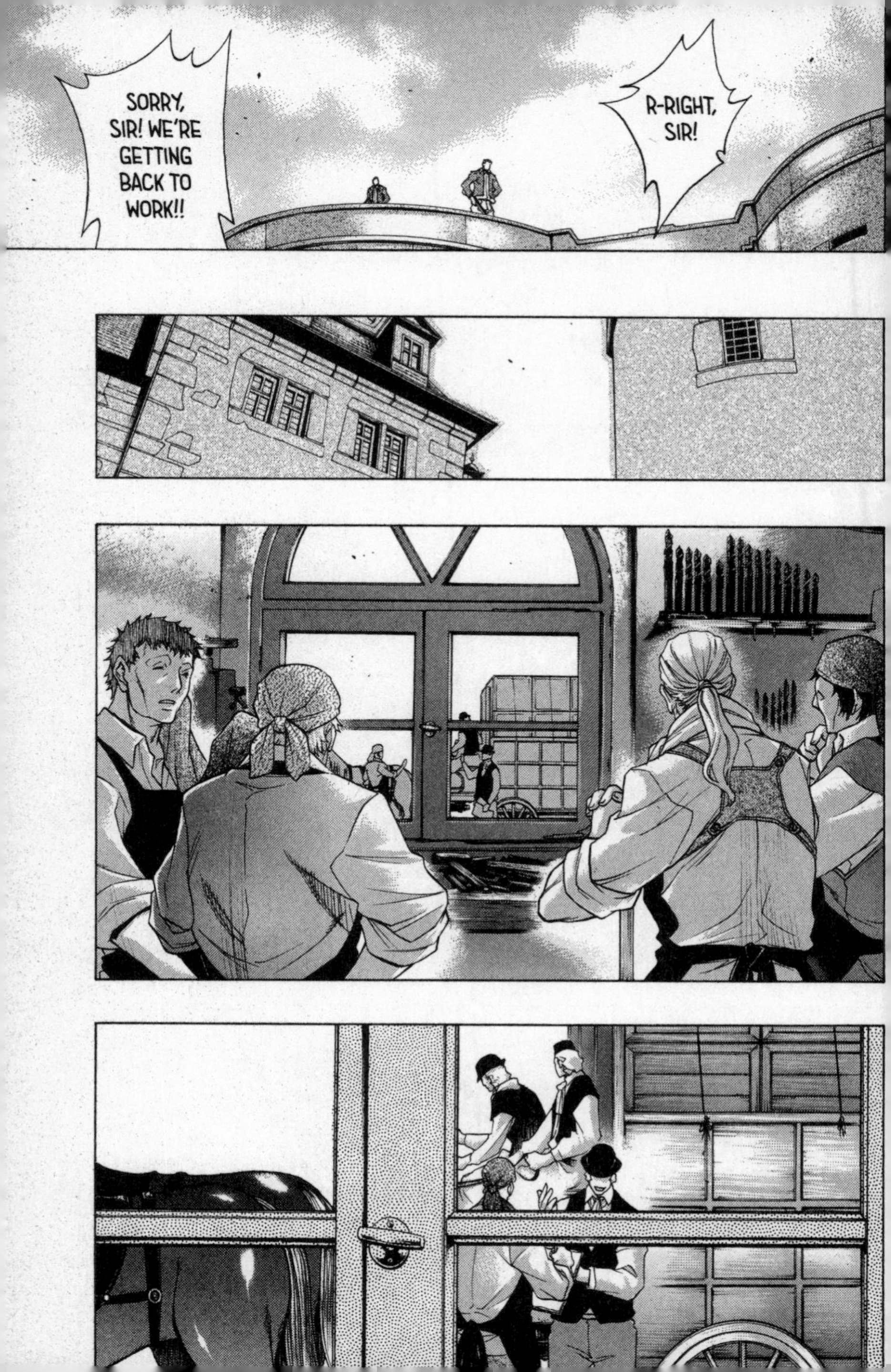
R-RIGHT, SIR!
SORRY, SIR! WE'RE GETTING BACK TO WORK!!

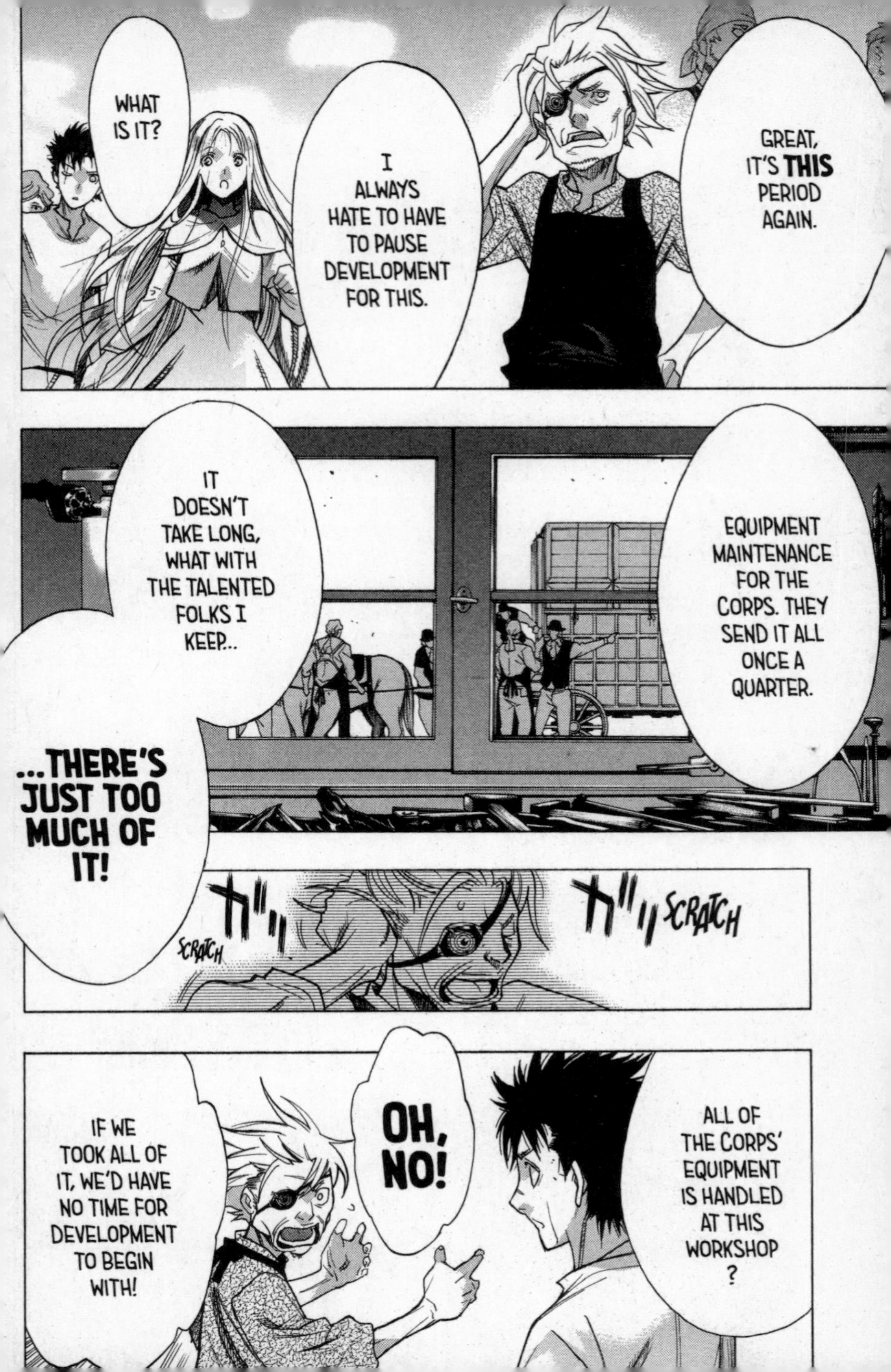
GREAT, IT'S **THIS** PERIOD AGAIN.
I ALWAYS HATE TO HAVE TO PAUSE DEVELOPMENT FOR THIS.
WHAT IS IT?
EQUIPMENT MAINTENANCE FOR THE CORPS. THEY SEND IT ALL ONCE A QUARTER.
IT DOESN'T TAKE LONG, WHAT WITH THE TALENTED FOLKS I KEEP...
...THERE'S JUST TOO MUCH OF IT!
SCRATCH
SCRATCH
ALL OF THE CORPS' EQUIPMENT IS HANDLED AT THIS WORKSHOP ?
OH, NO!
IF WE TOOK ALL OF IT, WE'D HAVE NO TIME FOR DEVELOPMENT TO BEGIN WITH!

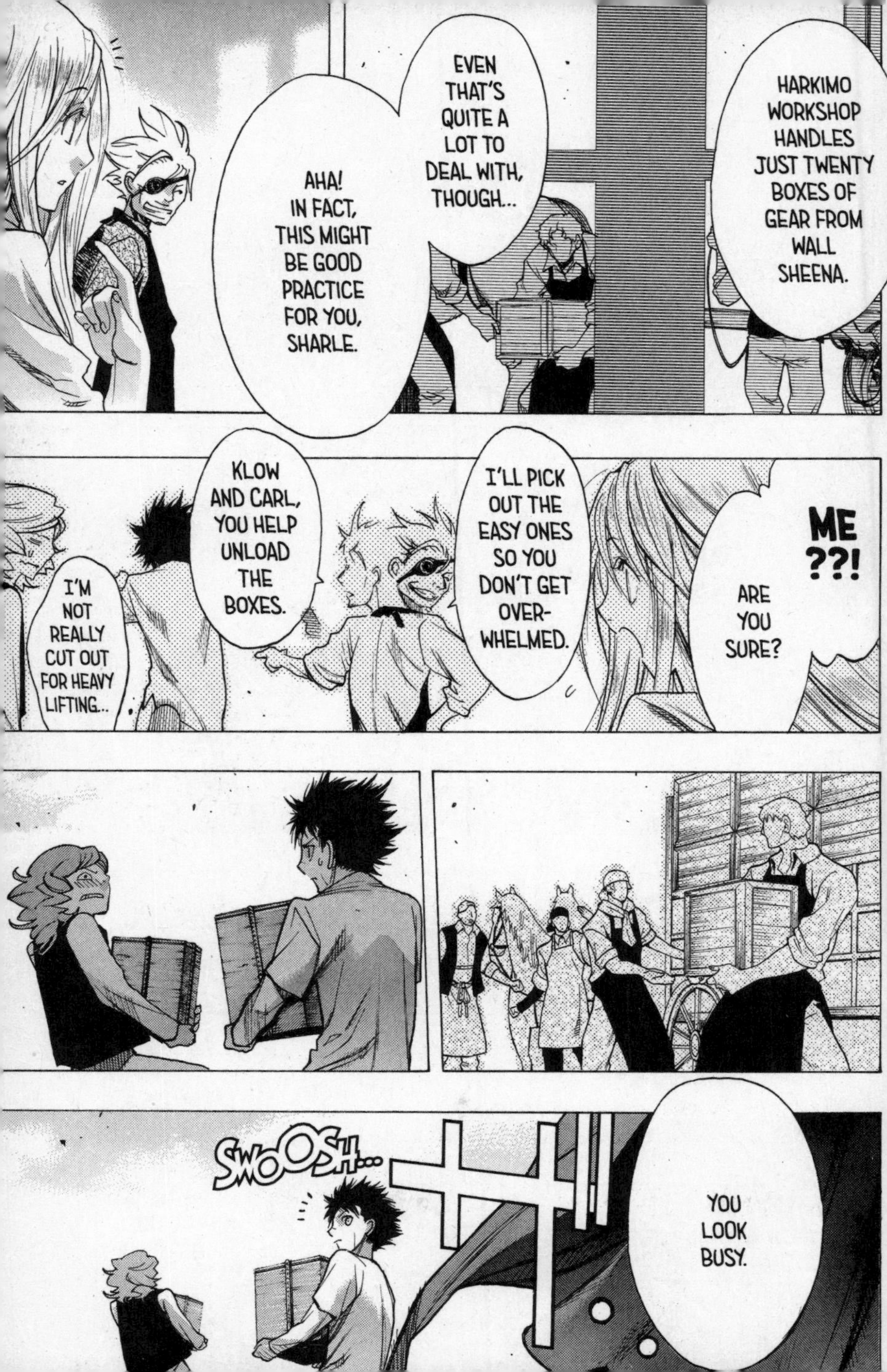
HARKIMO WORKSHOP HANDLES JUST TWENTY BOXES OF GEAR FROM WALL SHEENA.
EVEN THAT'S QUITE A LOT TO DEAL WITH, THOUGH...
AHA! IN FACT, THIS MIGHT BE GOOD PRACTICE FOR YOU, SHARLE.
ME ??!
ARE YOU SURE?
I'LL PICK OUT THE EASY ONES SO YOU DON'T GET OVER-WHELMED.
KLOW AND CARL, YOU HELP UNLOAD THE BOXES.
I'M NOT REALLY CUT OUT FOR HEAVY LIFTING...
YOU LOOK BUSY.
SWOOSH...

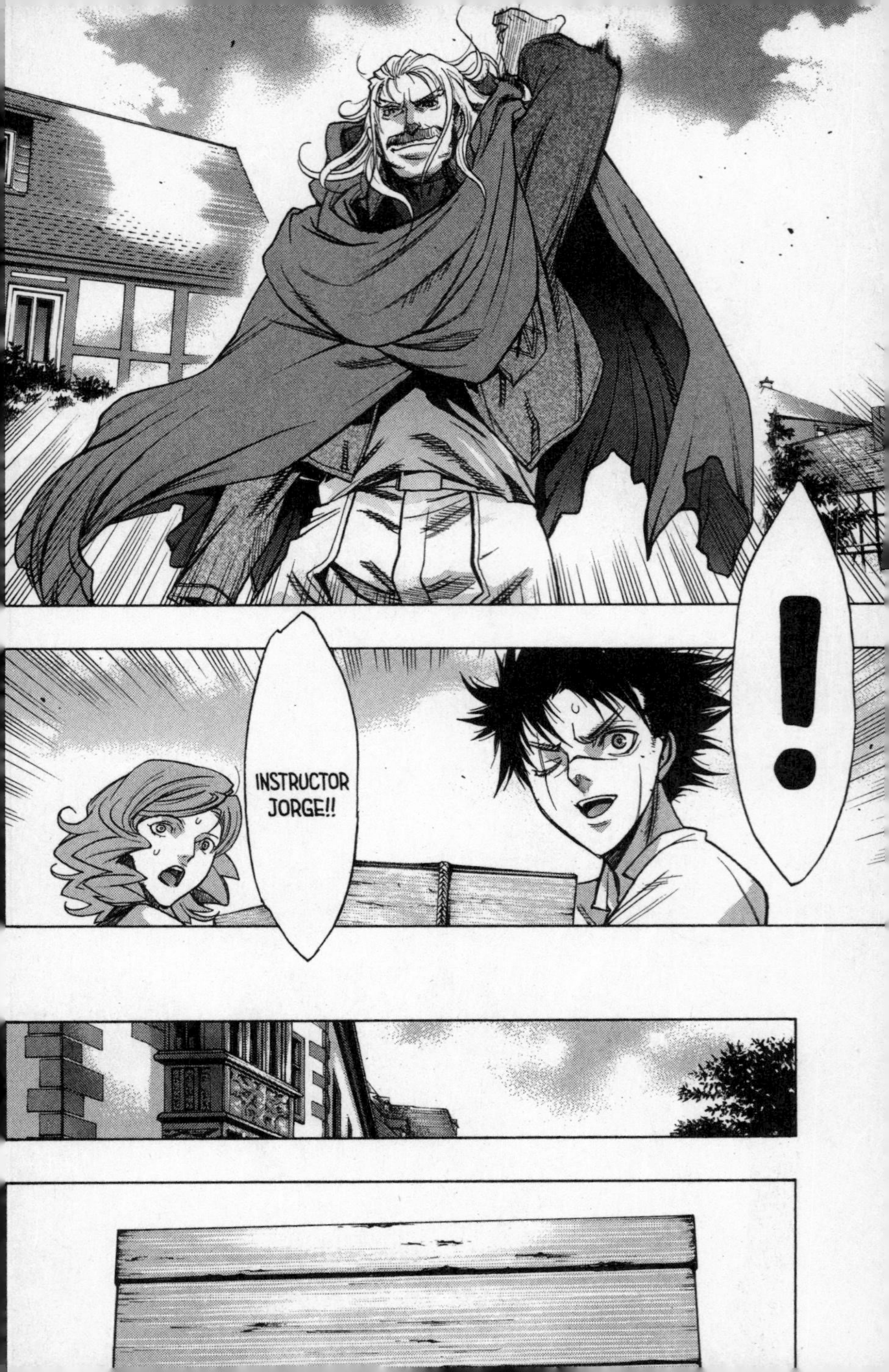
!
INSTRUCTOR JORGE!!

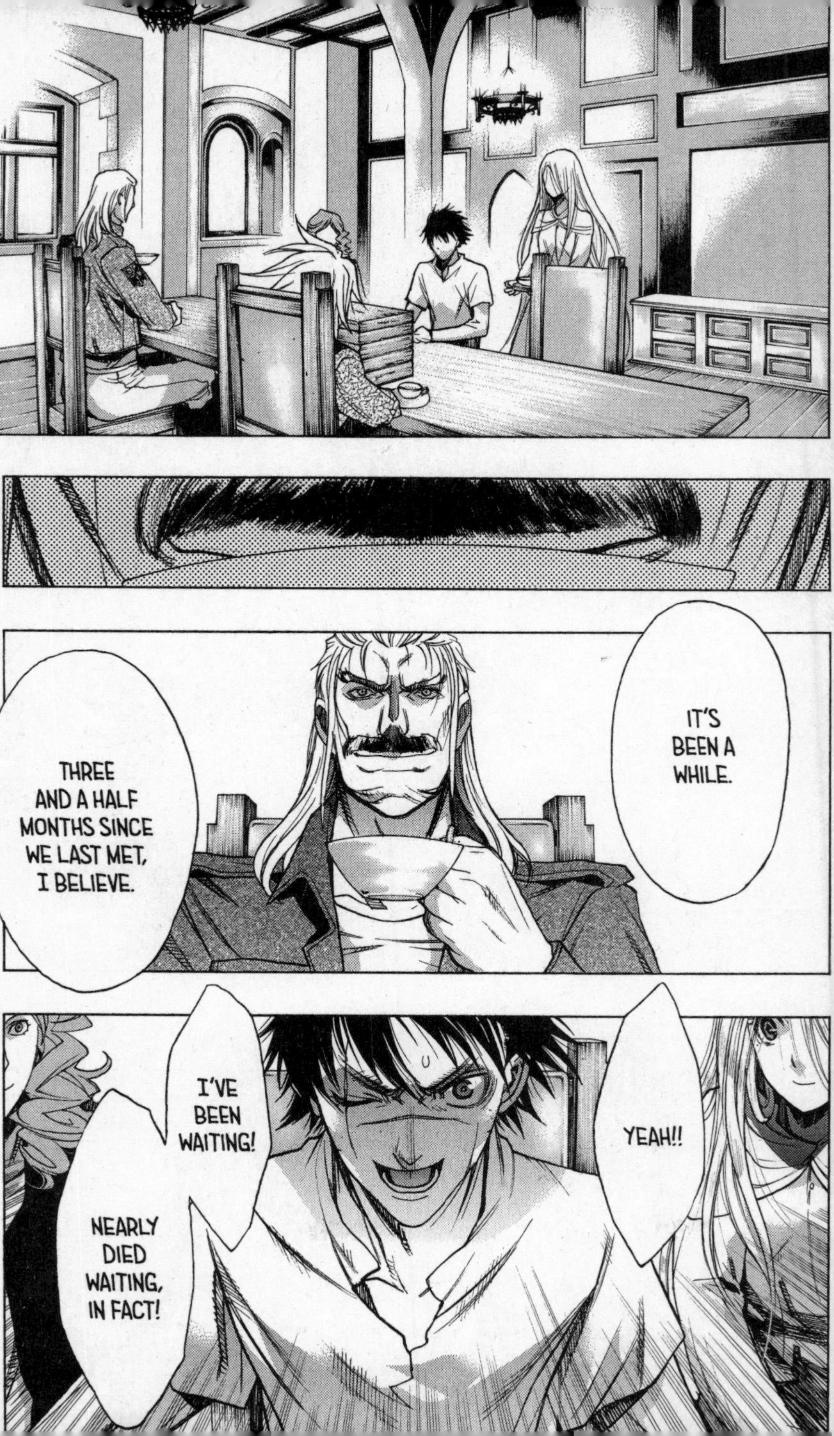
IT'S BEEN A WHILE.
THREE AND A HALF MONTHS SINCE WE LAST MET, I BELIEVE.
YEAH!!
I'VE BEEN WAITING!
NEARLY DIED WAITING, IN FACT!

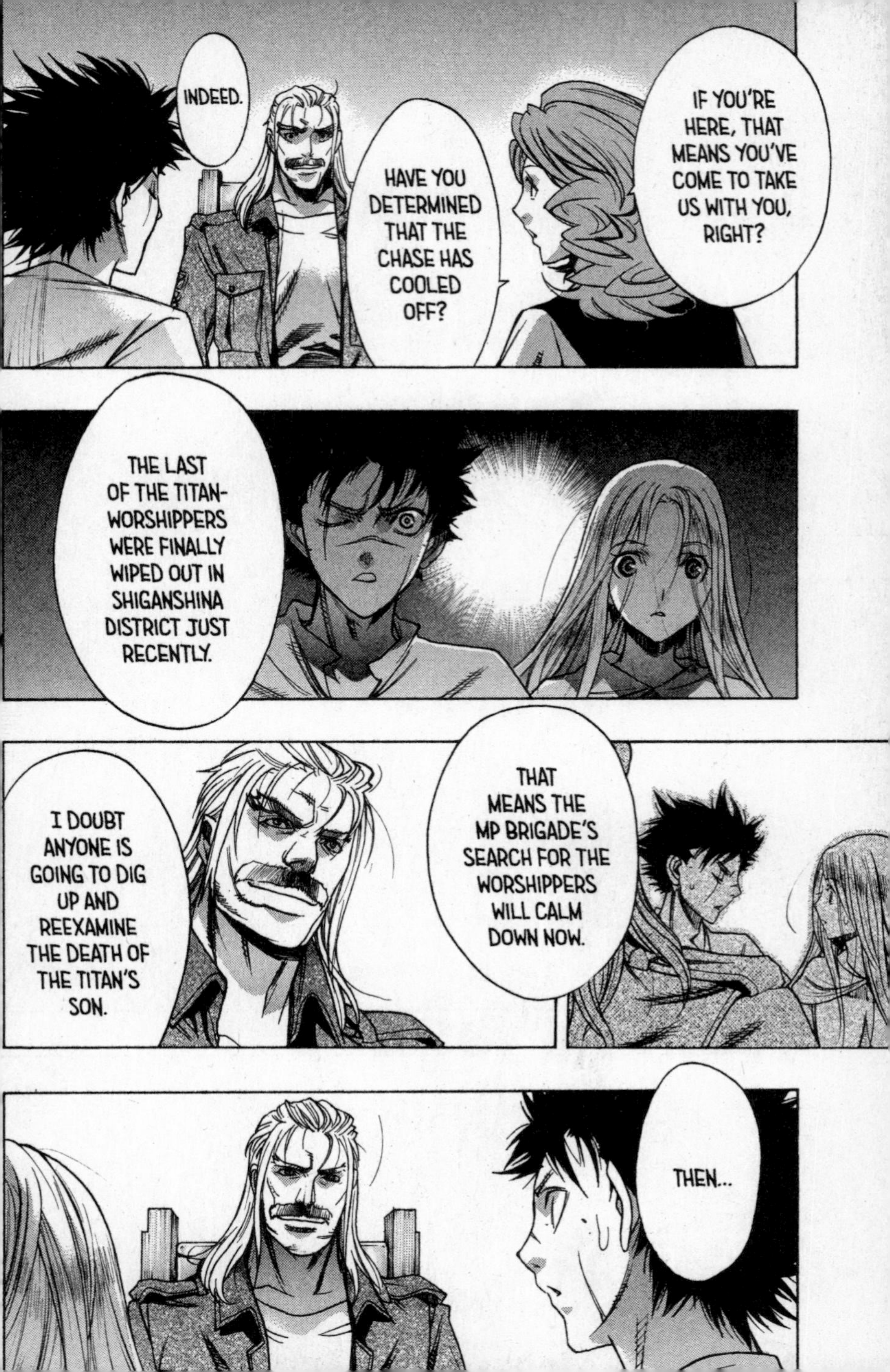
IF YOU'RE HERE, THAT MEANS YOU'VE COME TO TAKE US WITH YOU, RIGHT?
HAVE YOU DETERMINED THAT THE CHASE HAS COOLED OFF?
INDEED.
THE LAST OF THE TITAN-WORSHIPPERS WERE FINALLY WIPED OUT IN SHIGANSHINA DISTRICT JUST RECENTLY.
THAT MEANS THE MP BRIGADE'S SEARCH FOR THE WORSHIPPERS WILL CALM DOWN NOW.
I DOUBT ANYONE IS GOING TO DIG UP AND REEXAMINE THE DEATH OF THE TITAN'S SON.
THEN...

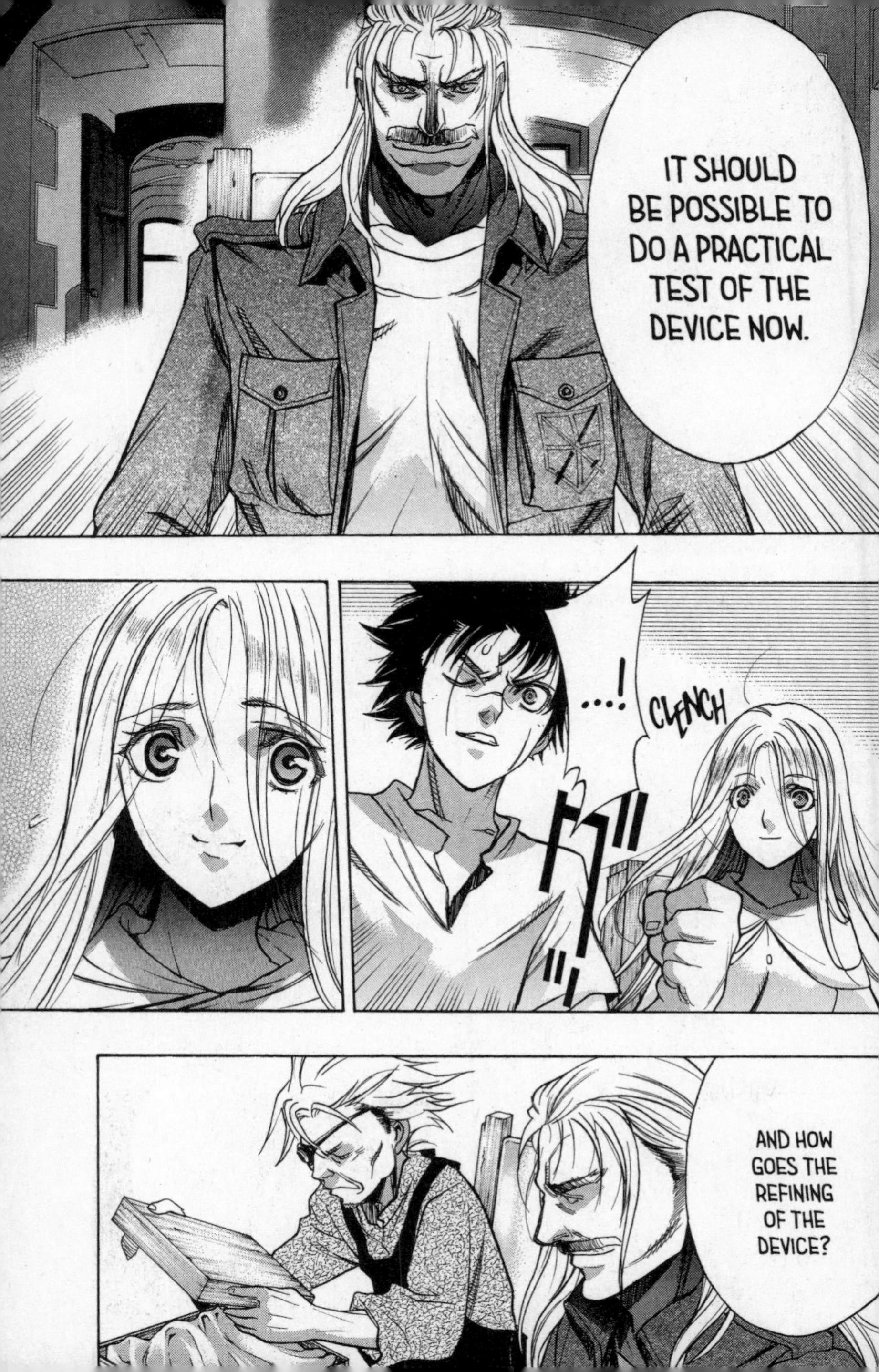

IT SHOULD BE POSSIBLE TO DO A PRACTICAL TEST OF THE DEVICE NOW.
...!
CLENCH
AND HOW GOES THE REFINING OF THE DEVICE?

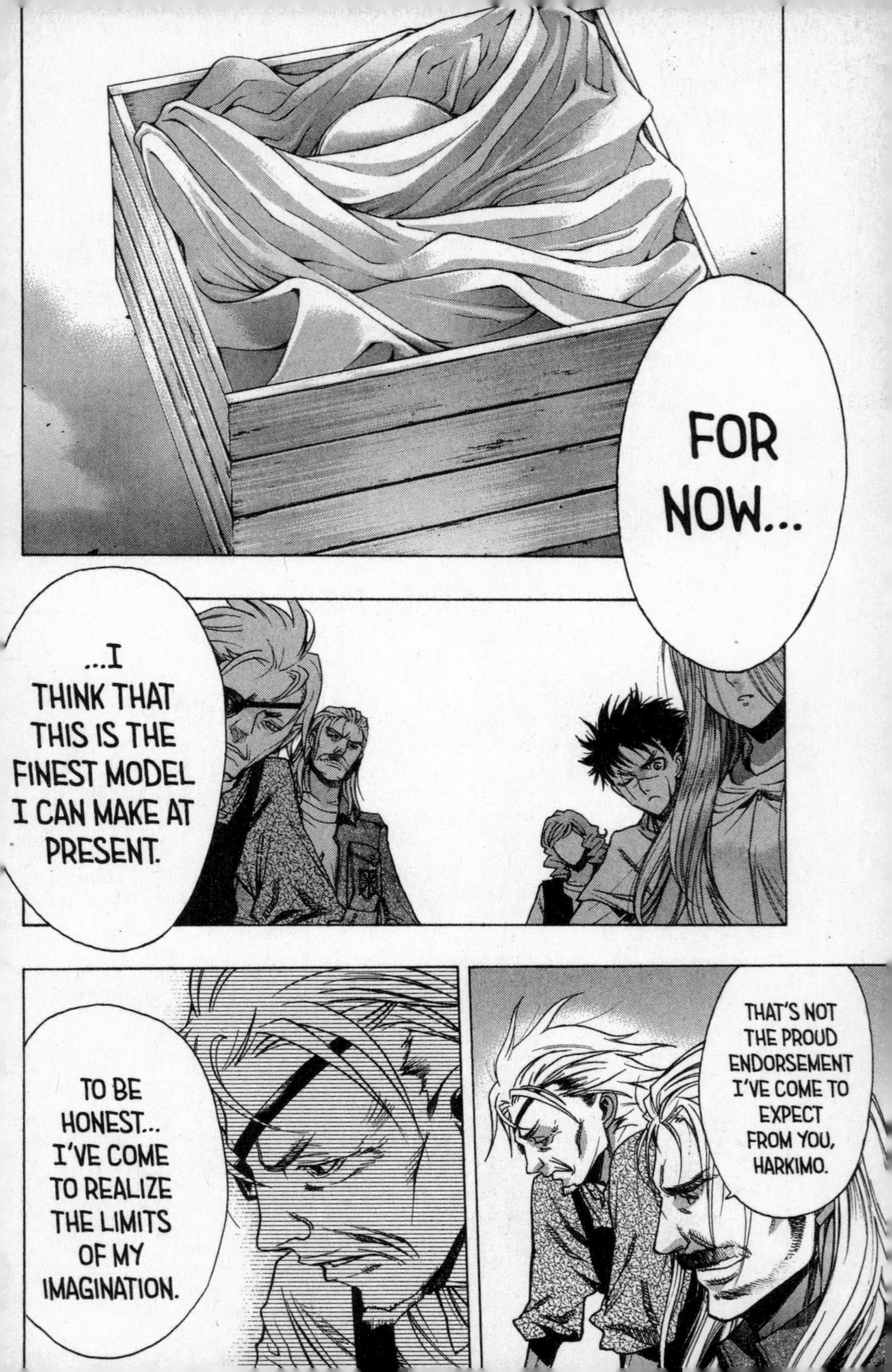
FOR NOW...
...I THINK THAT THIS IS THE FINEST MODEL I CAN MAKE AT PRESENT.
THAT'S NOT THE PROUD ENDORSEMENT I'VE COME TO EXPECT FROM YOU, HARKIMO.
TO BE HONEST... I'VE COME TO REALIZE THE LIMITS OF MY IMAGINATION.

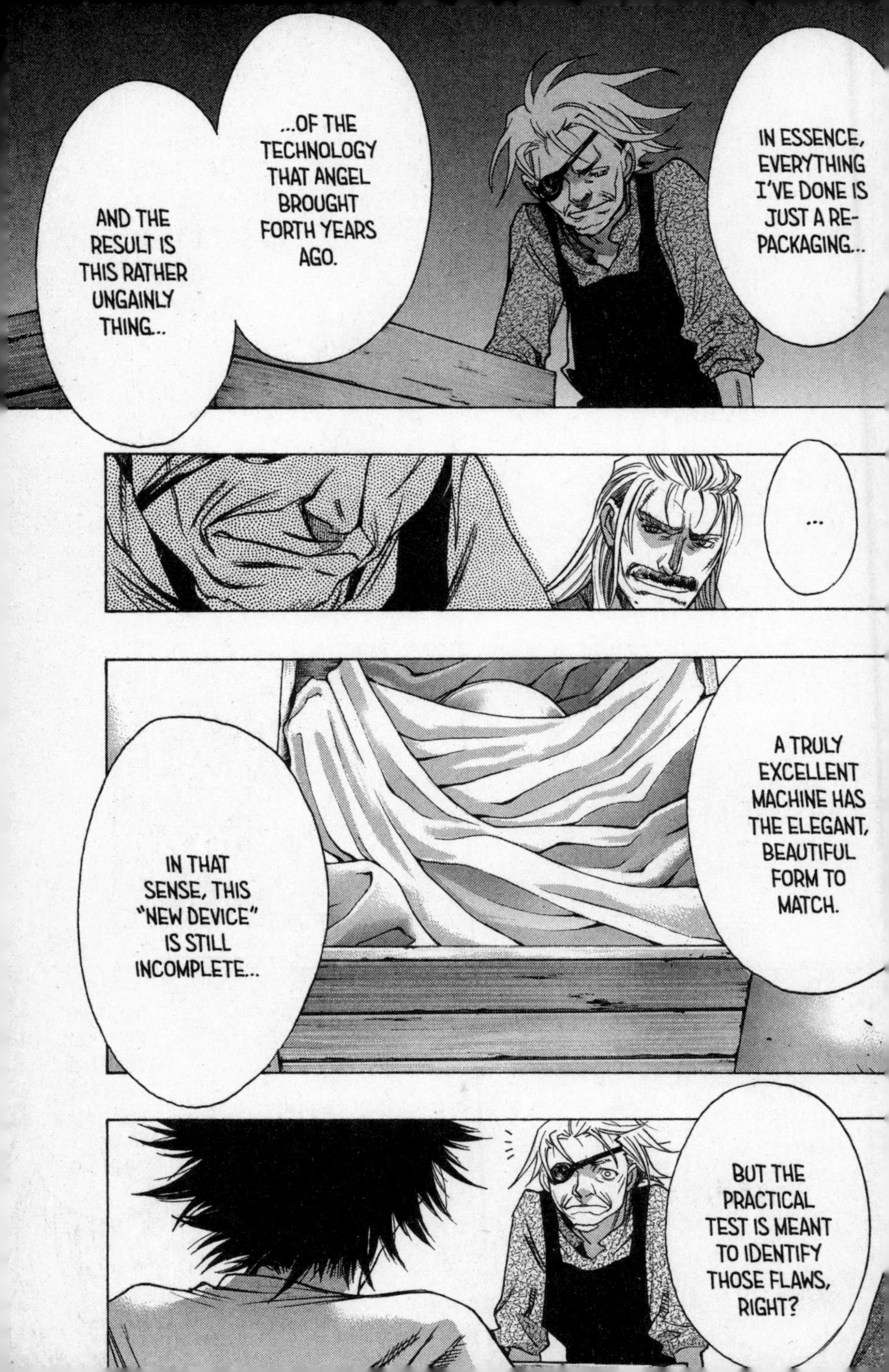
IN ESSENCE, EVERYTHING I'VE DONE IS JUST A RE-PACKAGING...
...OF THE TECHNOLOGY THAT ANGEL BROUGHT FORTH YEARS AGO.
AND THE RESULT IS THIS RATHER UNGAINLY THING...
...
A TRULY EXCELLENT MACHINE HAS THE ELEGANT, BEAUTIFUL FORM TO MATCH.
IN THAT SENSE, THIS "NEW DEVICE" IS STILL INCOMPLETE...
BUT THE PRACTICAL TEST IS MEANT TO IDENTIFY THOSE FLAWS, RIGHT?

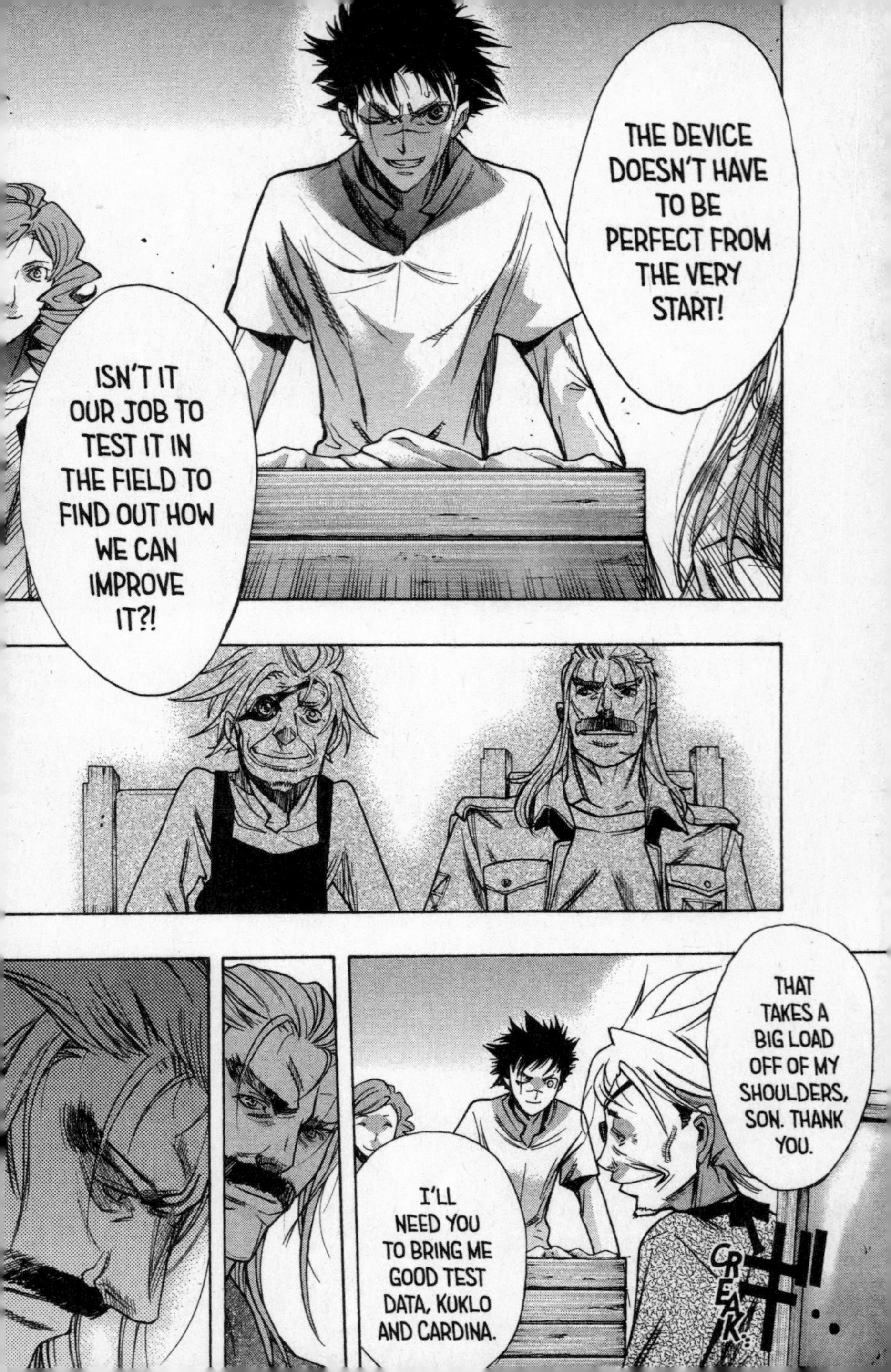
THE DEVICE DOESN'T HAVE TO BE PERFECT FROM THE VERY START!
ISN'T IT OUR JOB TO TEST IT IN THE FIELD TO FIND OUT HOW WE CAN IMPROVE IT?!
THAT TAKES A BIG LOAD OFF OF MY SHOULDERS, SON. THANK YOU.
I'LL NEED YOU TO BRING ME GOOD TEST DATA, KUKLO AND CARDINA.
CREAK...

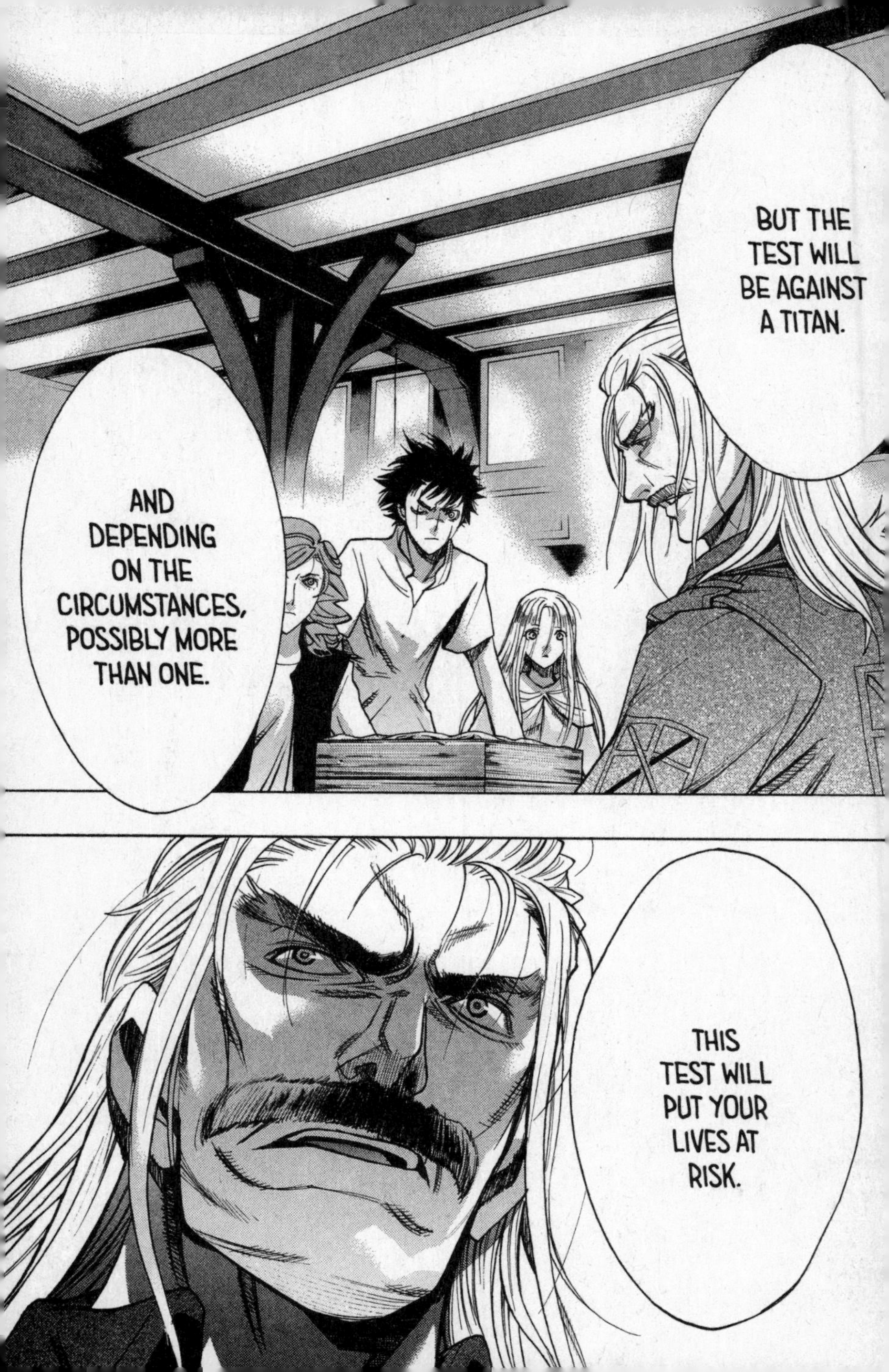
BUT THE TEST WILL BE AGAINST A TITAN.
AND DEPENDING ON THE CIRCUMSTANCES, POSSIBLY MORE THAN ONE.
THIS TEST WILL PUT YOUR LIVES AT RISK.

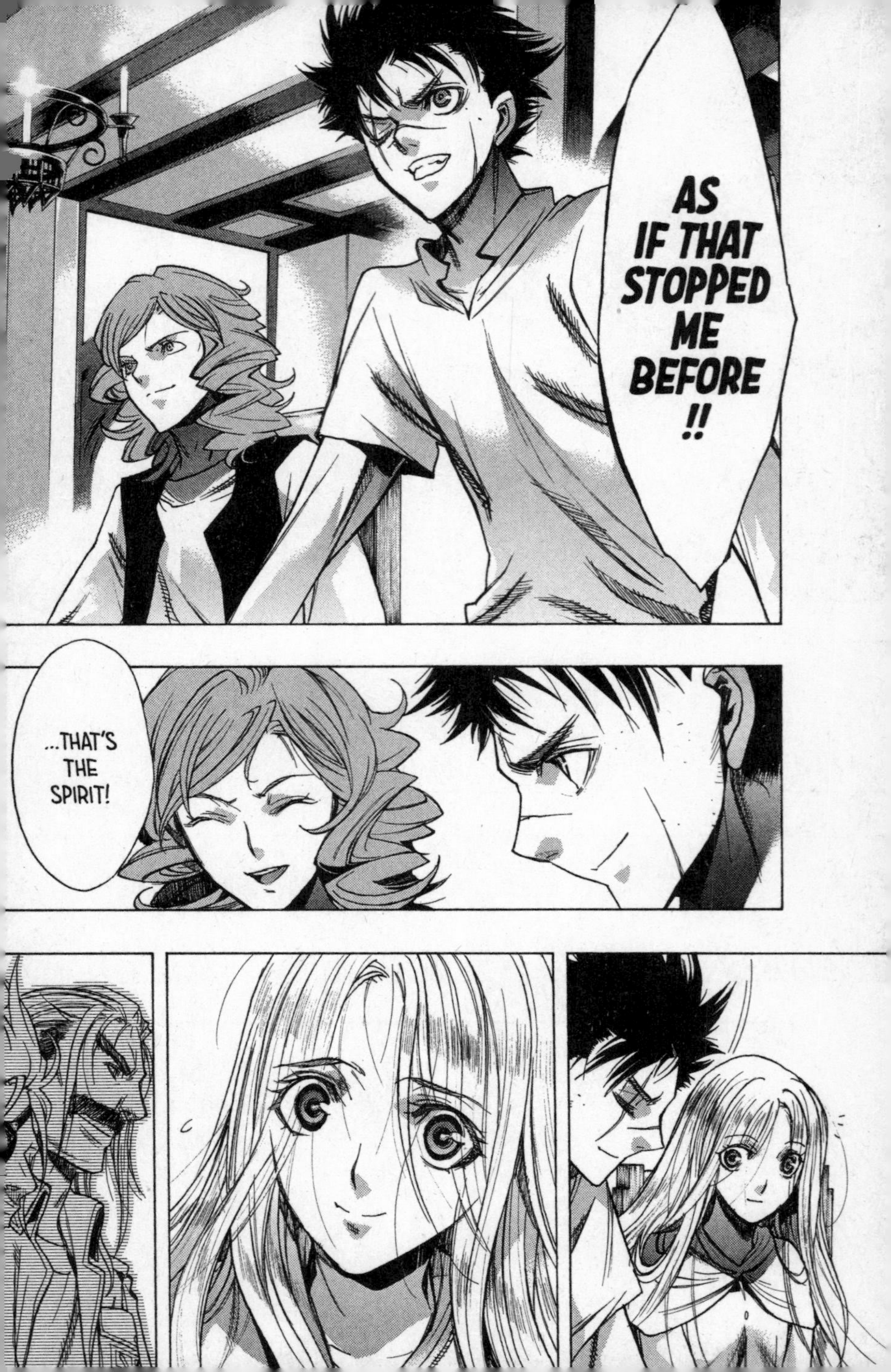
AS IF THAT STOPPED ME BEFORE !!
...THAT'S THE SPIRIT!

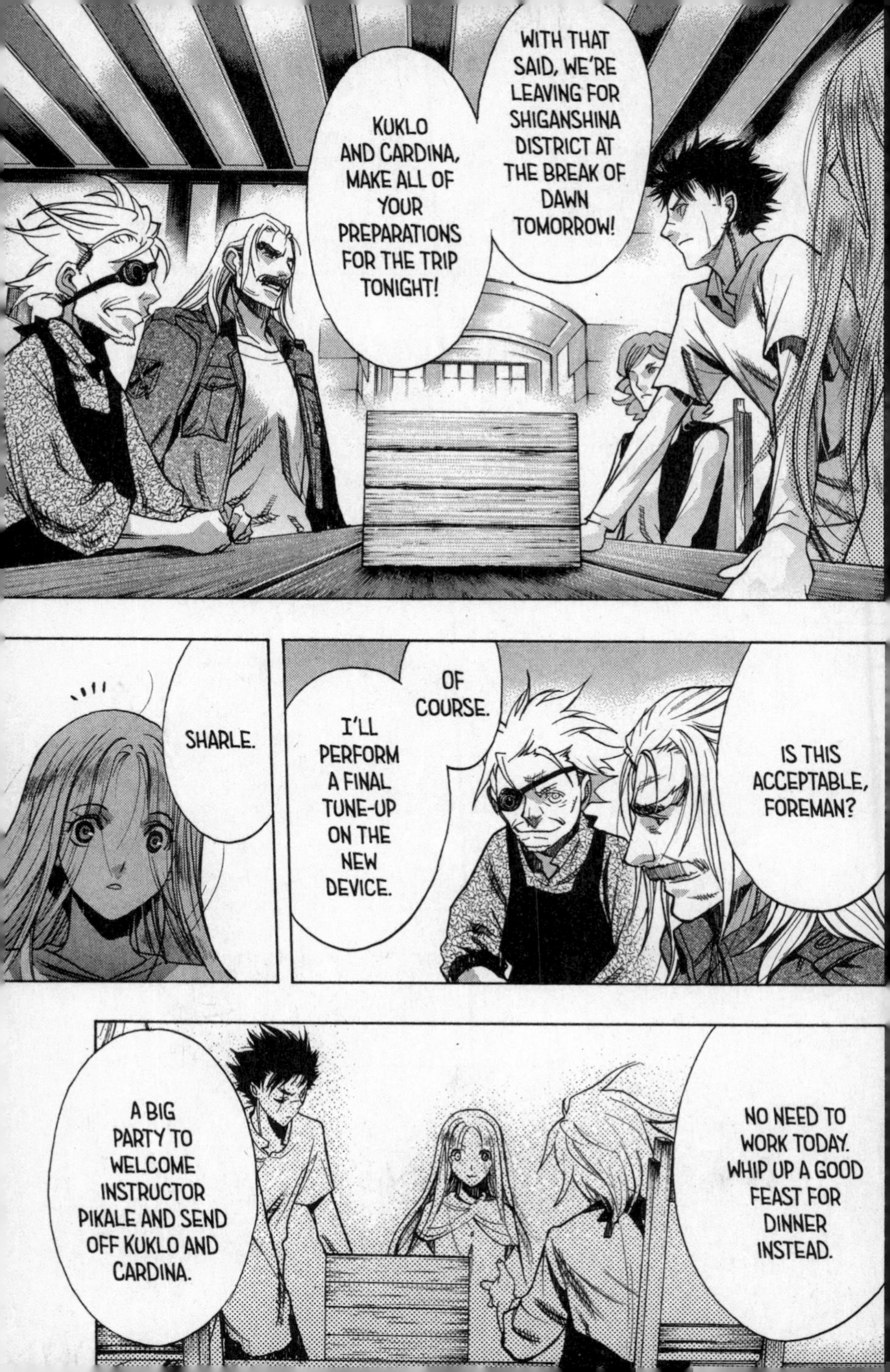
WITH THAT SAID, WE'RE LEAVING FOR SHIGANSHINA DISTRICT AT THE BREAK OF DAWN TOMORROW!
KUKLO AND CARDINA, MAKE ALL OF YOUR PREPARATIONS FOR THE TRIP TONIGHT!
IS THIS ACCEPTABLE, FOREMAN?
OF COURSE.
I'LL PERFORM A FINAL TUNE-UP ON THE NEW DEVICE.
SHARLE.
NO NEED TO WORK TODAY. WHIP UP A GOOD FEAST FOR DINNER INSTEAD.
A BIG PARTY TO WELCOME INSTRUCTOR PIKALE AND SEND OFF KUKLO AND CARDINA.

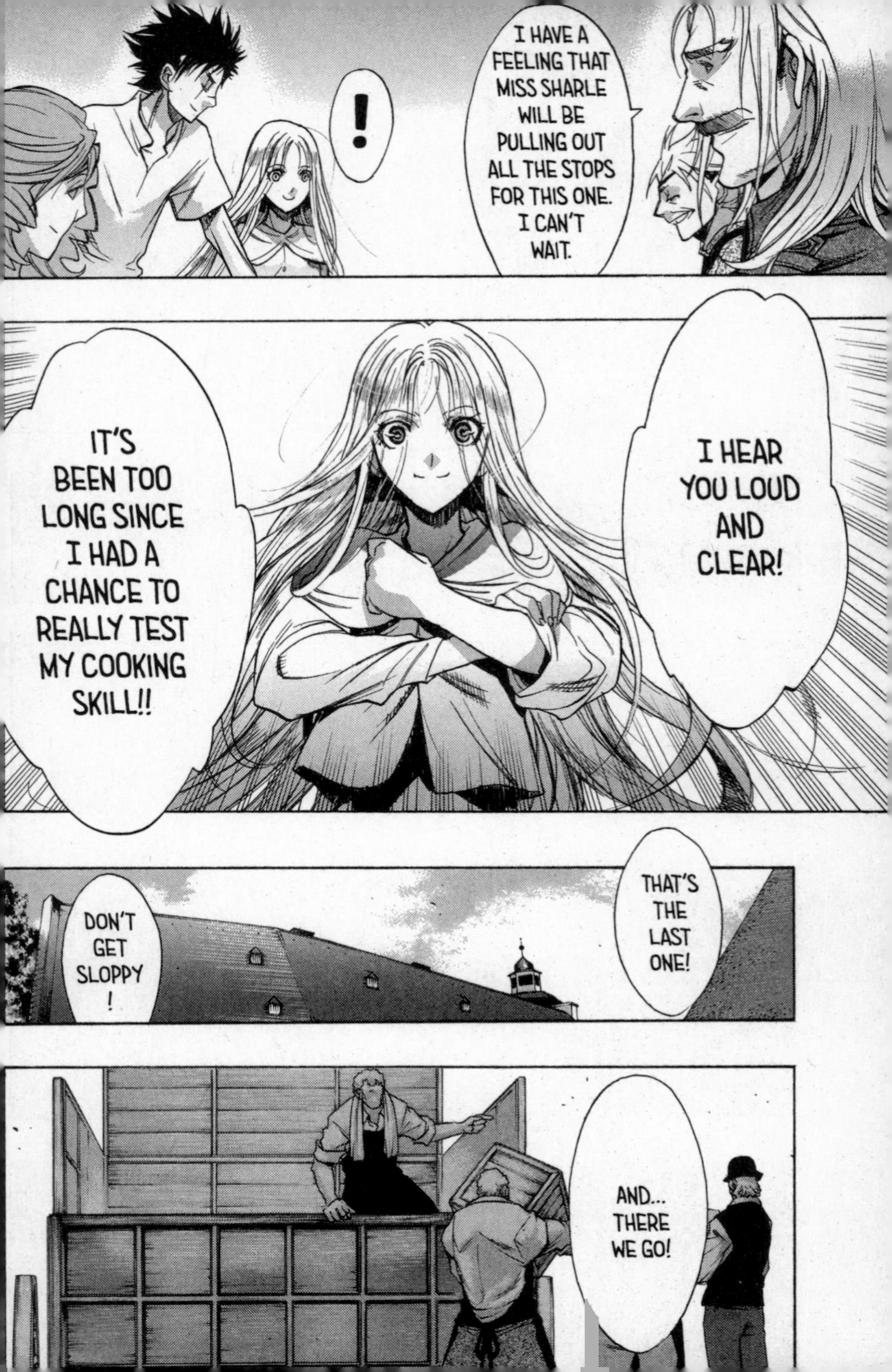
I HAVE A FEELING THAT MISS SHARLE WILL BE PULLING OUT ALL THE STOPS FOR THIS ONE. I CAN'T WAIT.
!
I HEAR YOU LOUD AND CLEAR!
IT'S BEEN TOO LONG SINCE I HAD A CHANCE TO REALLY TEST MY COOKING SKILL!!
THAT'S THE LAST ONE!
DON'T GET SLOPPY!
AND... THERE WE GO!

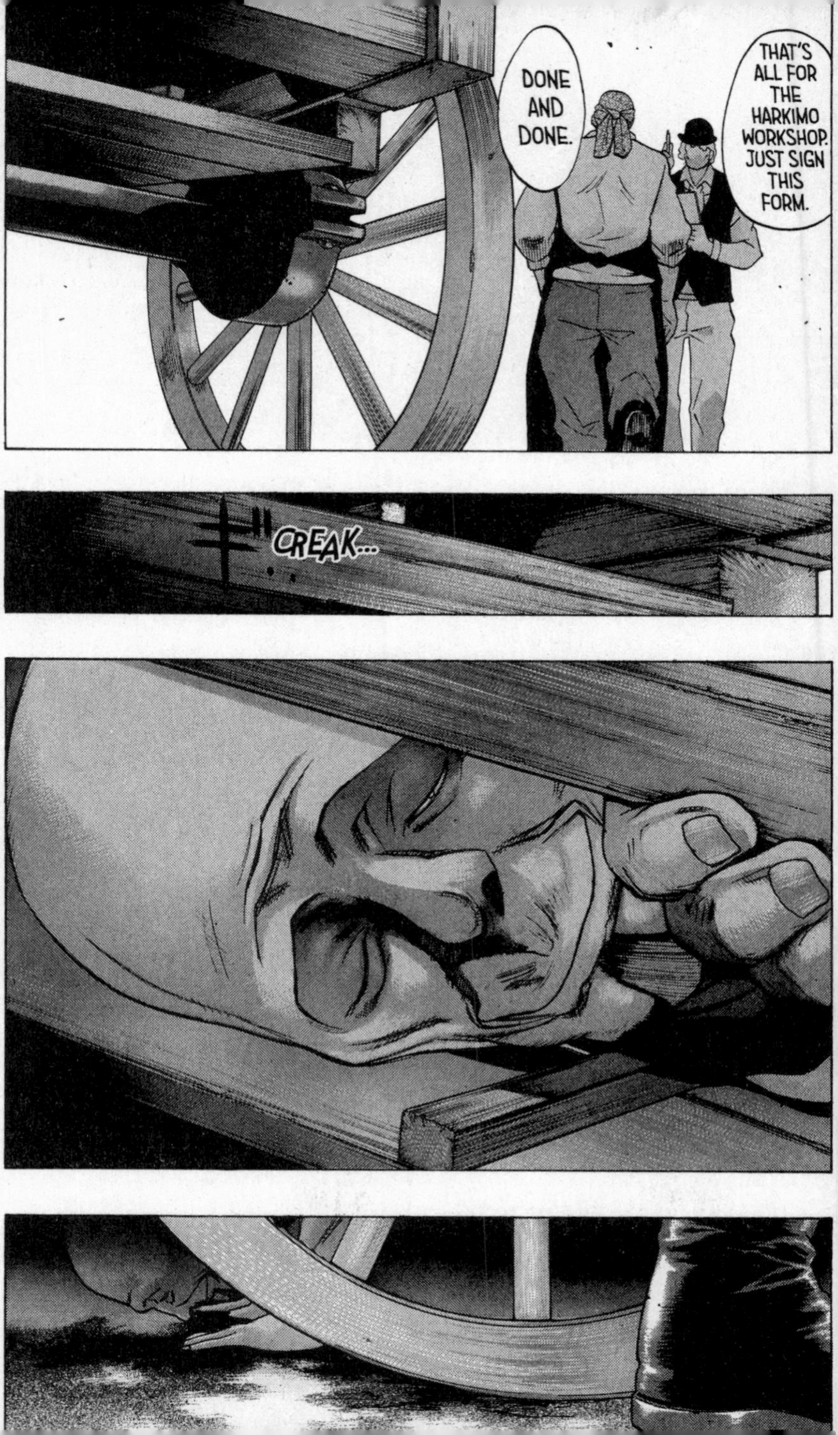
THAT'S ALL FOR THE HARKIMO WORKSHOP. JUST SIGN THIS FORM.
DONE AND DONE.
CREAK...

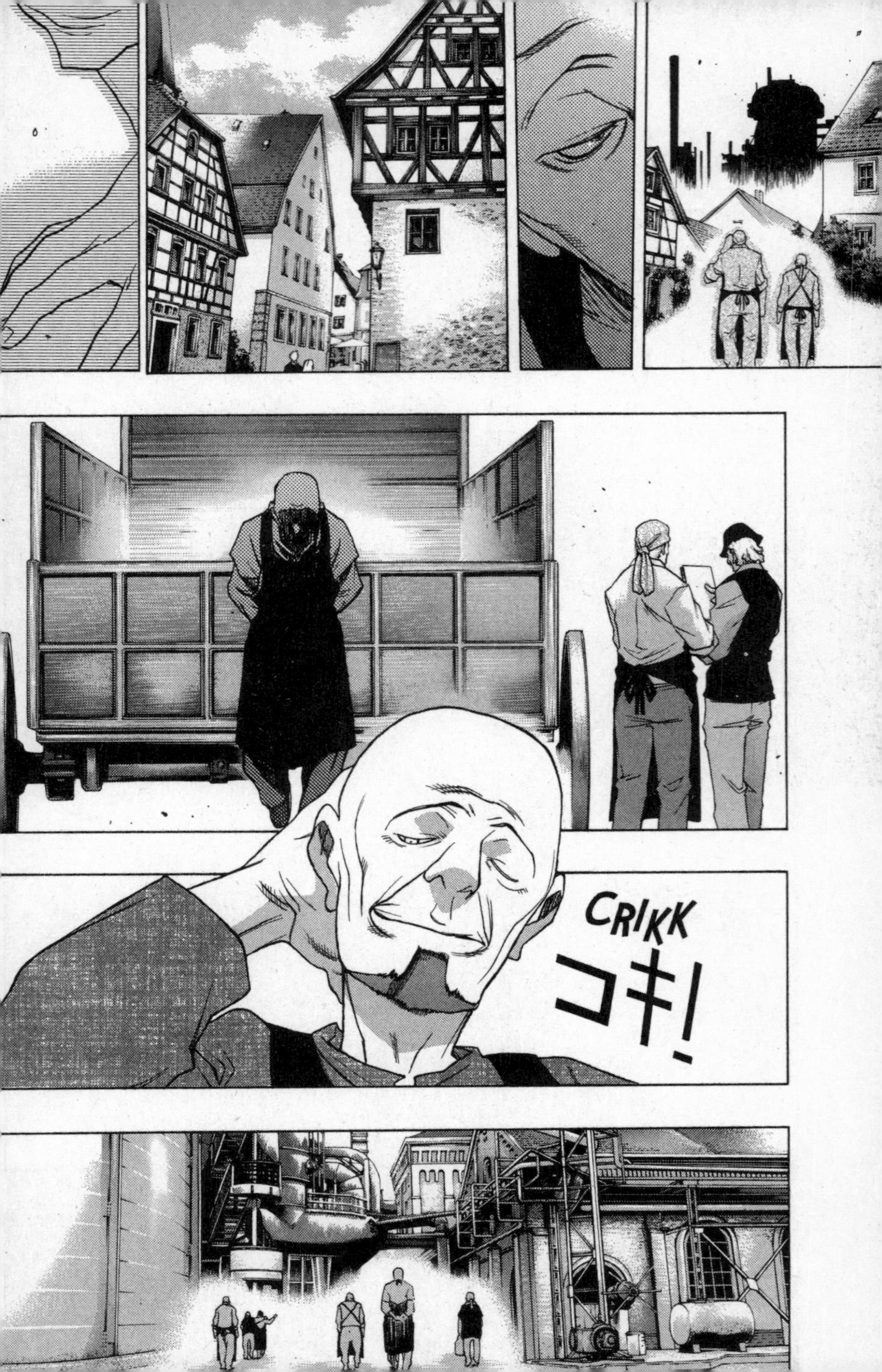
CRIKK
コキ!

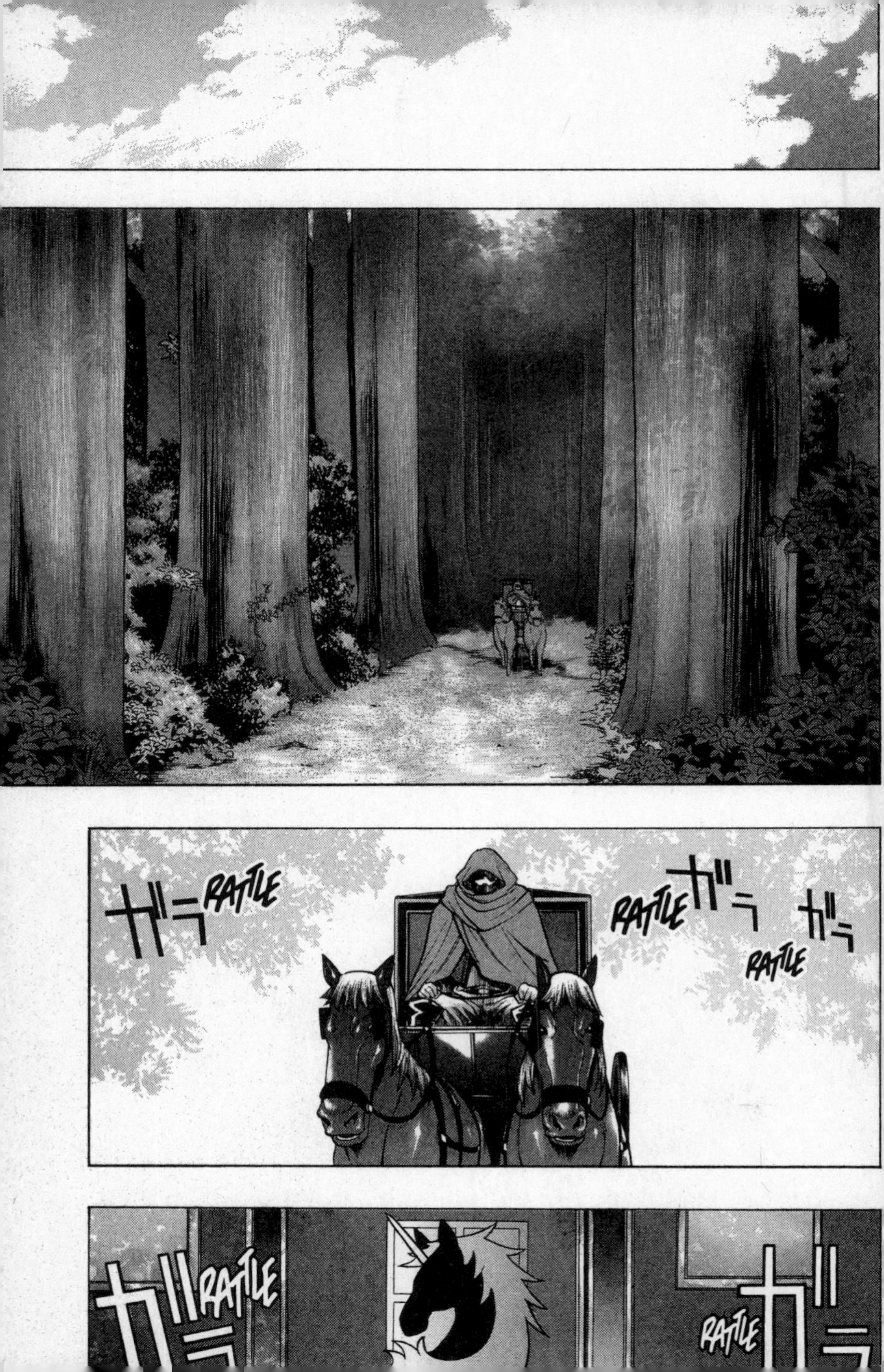

ガラ RATTLE
ガラ RATTLE
ガラ RATTLE
ガラ RATTLE
ガラ RATTLE
ガラ RATTLE

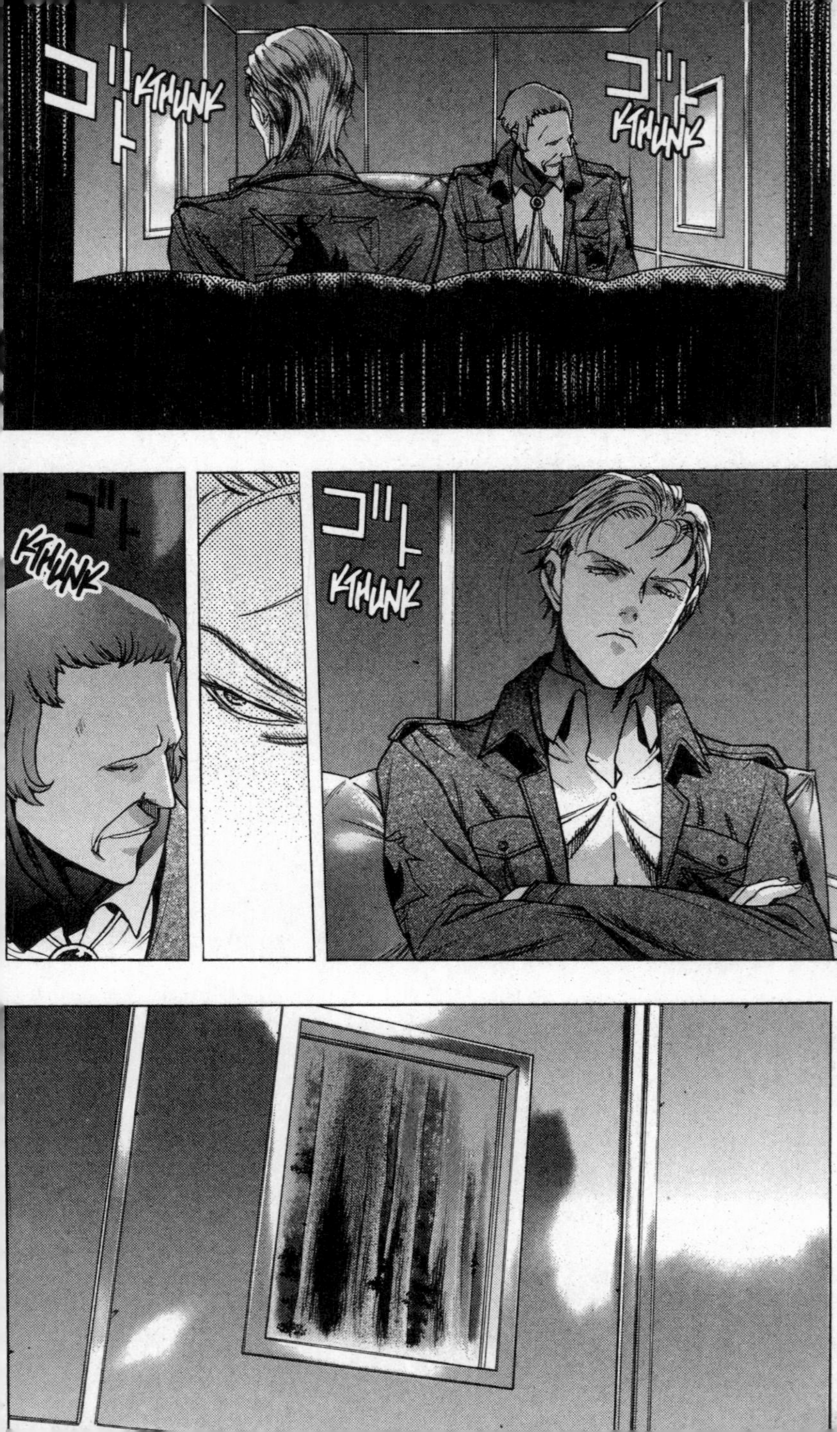
ゴト
KTHUNK
ゴト
KTHUNK
ゴト
KTHUNK
ゴト
KTHUNK

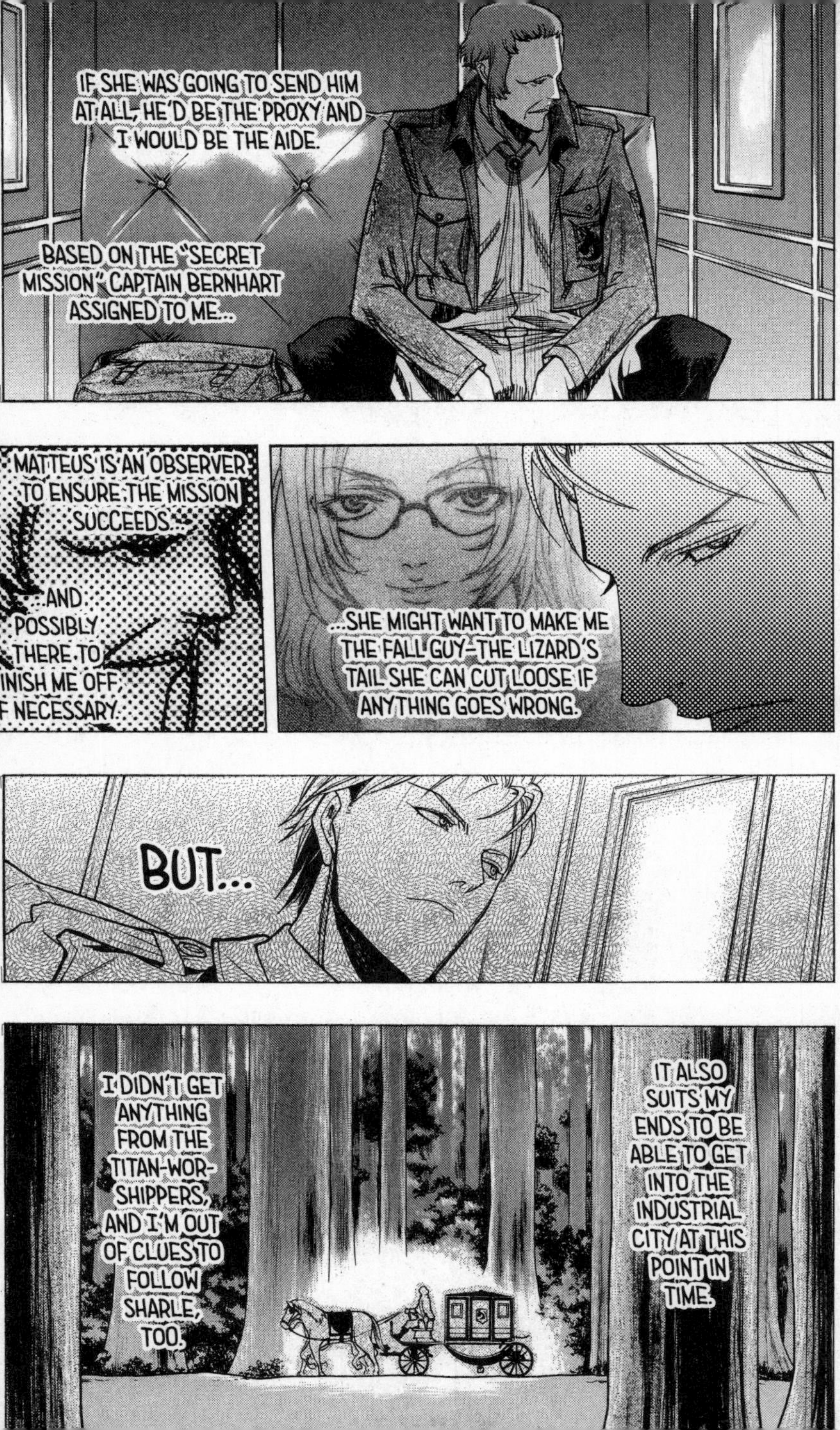
IF SHE WAS GOING TO SEND HIM AT ALL, HE'D BE THE PROXY AND I WOULD BE THE AIDE.
BASED ON THE "SECRET MISSION" CAPTAIN BERNHART ASSIGNED TO ME...
...SHE MIGHT WANT TO MAKE ME THE FALL GUY—THE LIZARD'S TAIL SHE CAN CUT LOOSE IF ANYTHING GOES WRONG.
MATTEUS IS AN OBSERVER TO ENSURE THE MISSION SUCCEEDS...
...AND POSSIBLY THERE TO FINISH ME OFF, IF NECESSARY.
BUT...
IT ALSO SUITS MY ENDS TO BE ABLE TO GET INTO THE INDUSTRIAL CITY AT THIS POINT IN TIME.
I DIDN'T GET ANYTHING FROM THE TITAN-WORSHIPPERS, AND I'M OUT OF CLUES TO FOLLOW SHARLE, TOO.

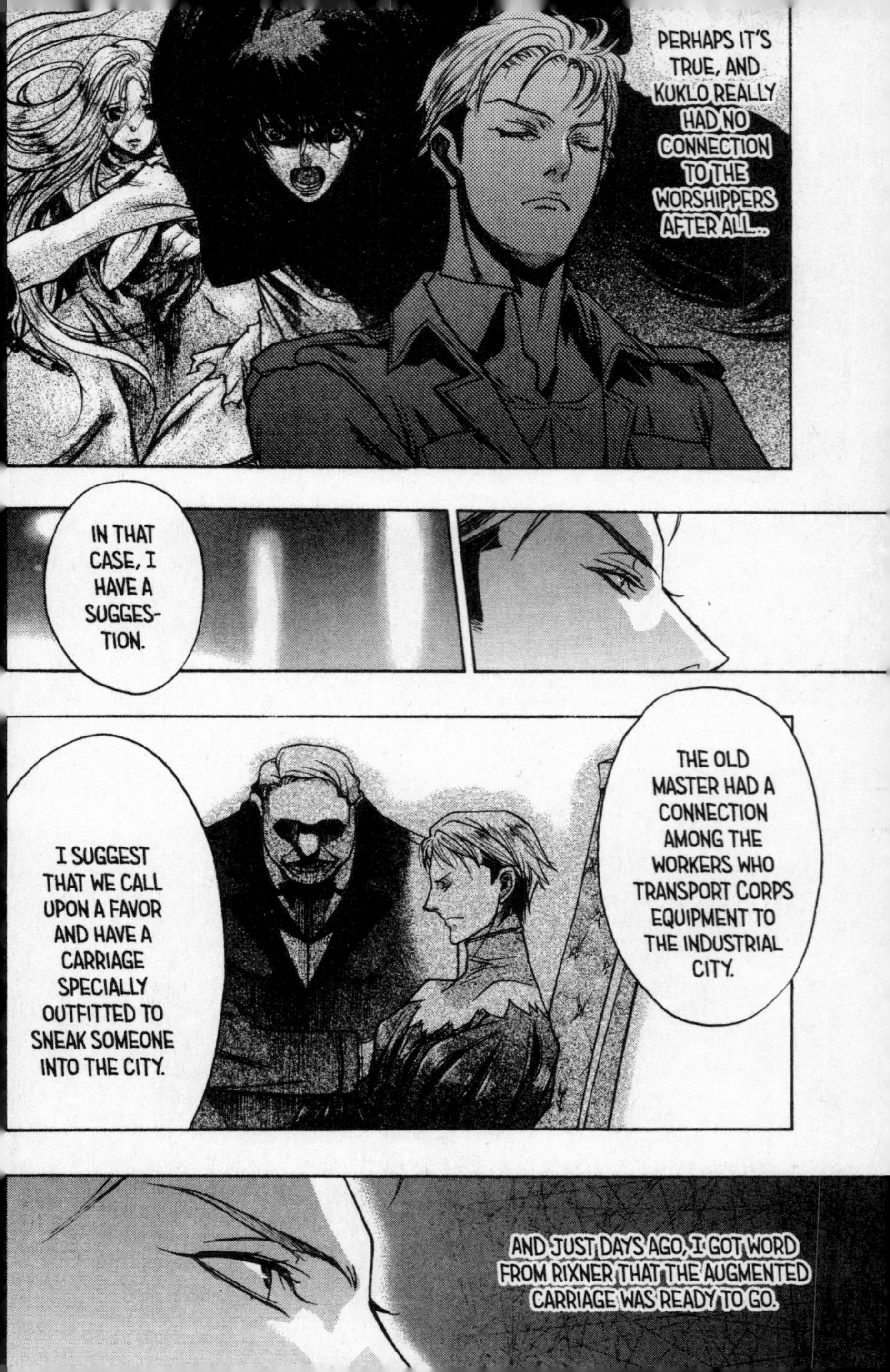
PERHAPS IT'S TRUE, AND KUKLO REALLY HAD NO CONNECTION TO THE WORSHIPPERS AFTER ALL...
IN THAT CASE, I HAVE A SUGGES-TION.
THE OLD MASTER HAD A CONNECTION AMONG THE WORKERS WHO TRANSPORT CORPS EQUIPMENT TO THE INDUSTRIAL CITY.
I SUGGEST THAT WE CALL UPON A FAVOR AND HAVE A CARRIAGE SPECIALLY OUTFITTED TO SNEAK SOMEONE INTO THE CITY.
AND JUST DAYS AGO, I GOT WORD FROM RIXNER THAT THE AUGMENTED CARRIAGE WAS READY TO GO.

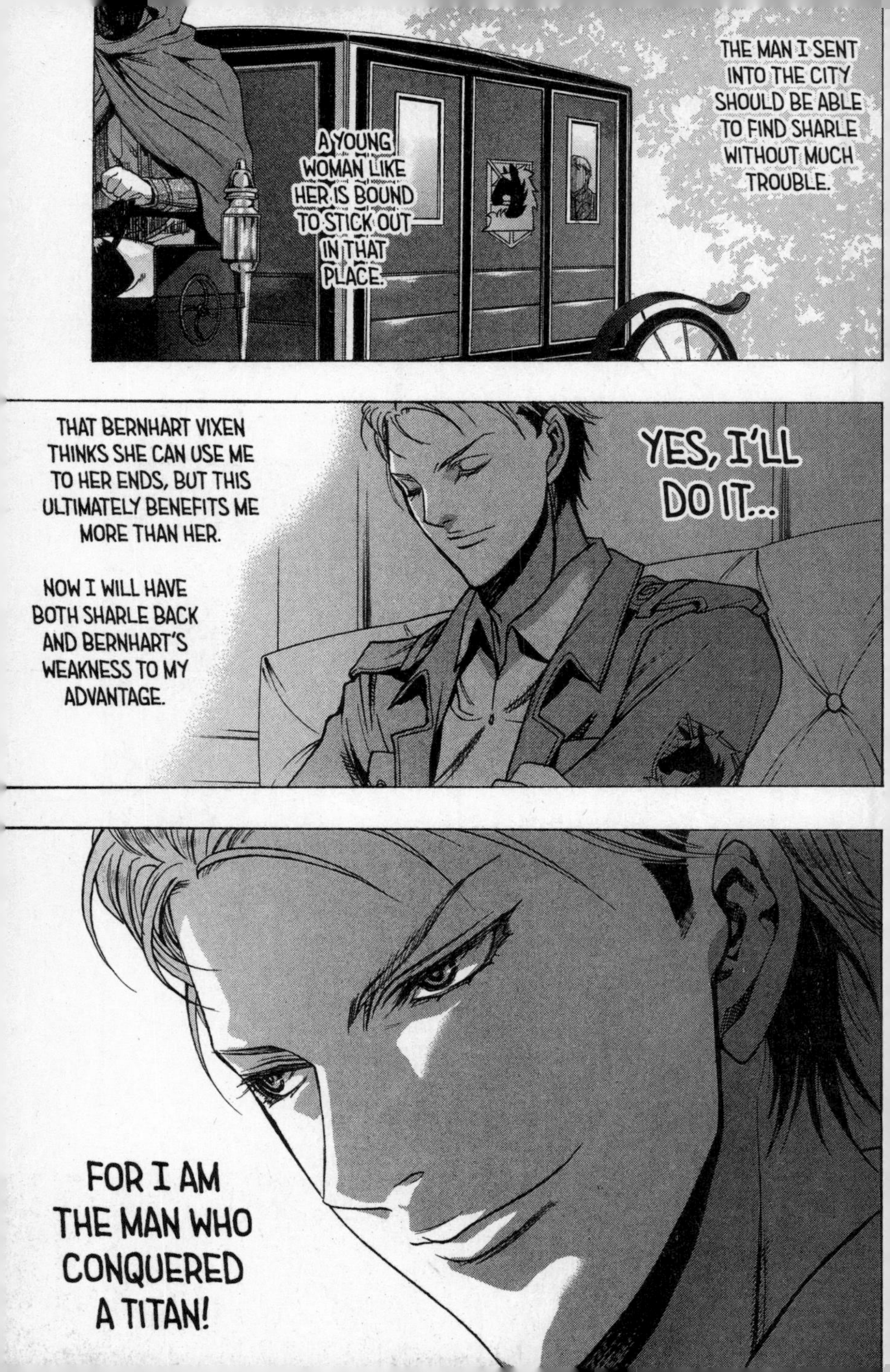
THE MAN I SENT INTO THE CITY SHOULD BE ABLE TO FIND SHARLE WITHOUT MUCH TROUBLE.
A YOUNG WOMAN LIKE HER IS BOUND TO STICK OUT IN THAT PLACE.
YES, I'LL DO IT...
THAT BERNHART VIXEN THINKS SHE CAN USE ME TO HER ENDS, BUT THIS ULTIMATELY BENEFITS ME MORE THAN HER.
NOW I WILL HAVE BOTH SHARLE BACK AND BERNHART'S WEAKNESS TO MY ADVANTAGE.
FOR I AM THE MAN WHO CONQUERED A TITAN!

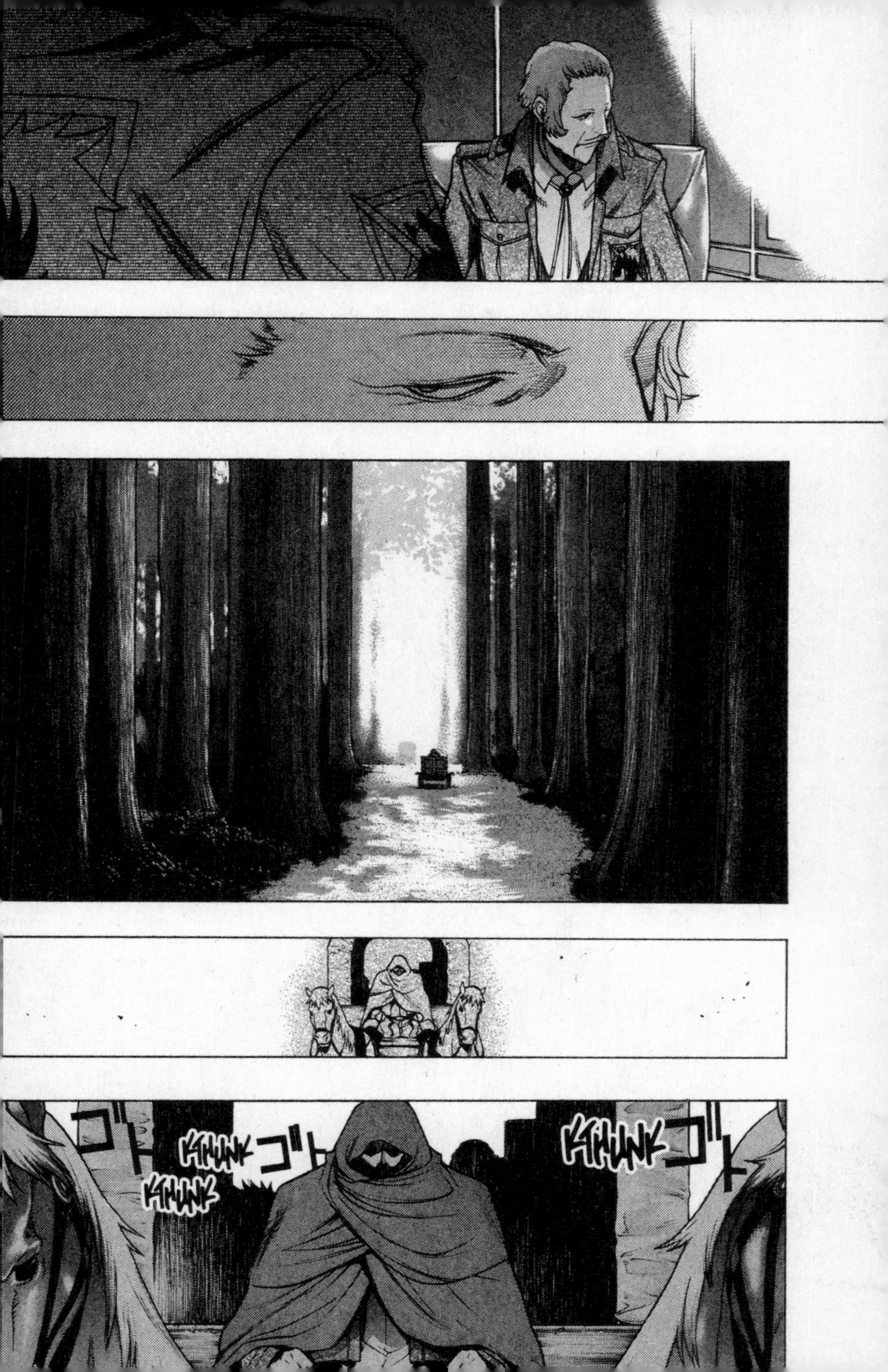
KCHUNK
ゴト
KCHUNK
ゴト
KCHUNK
ゴト

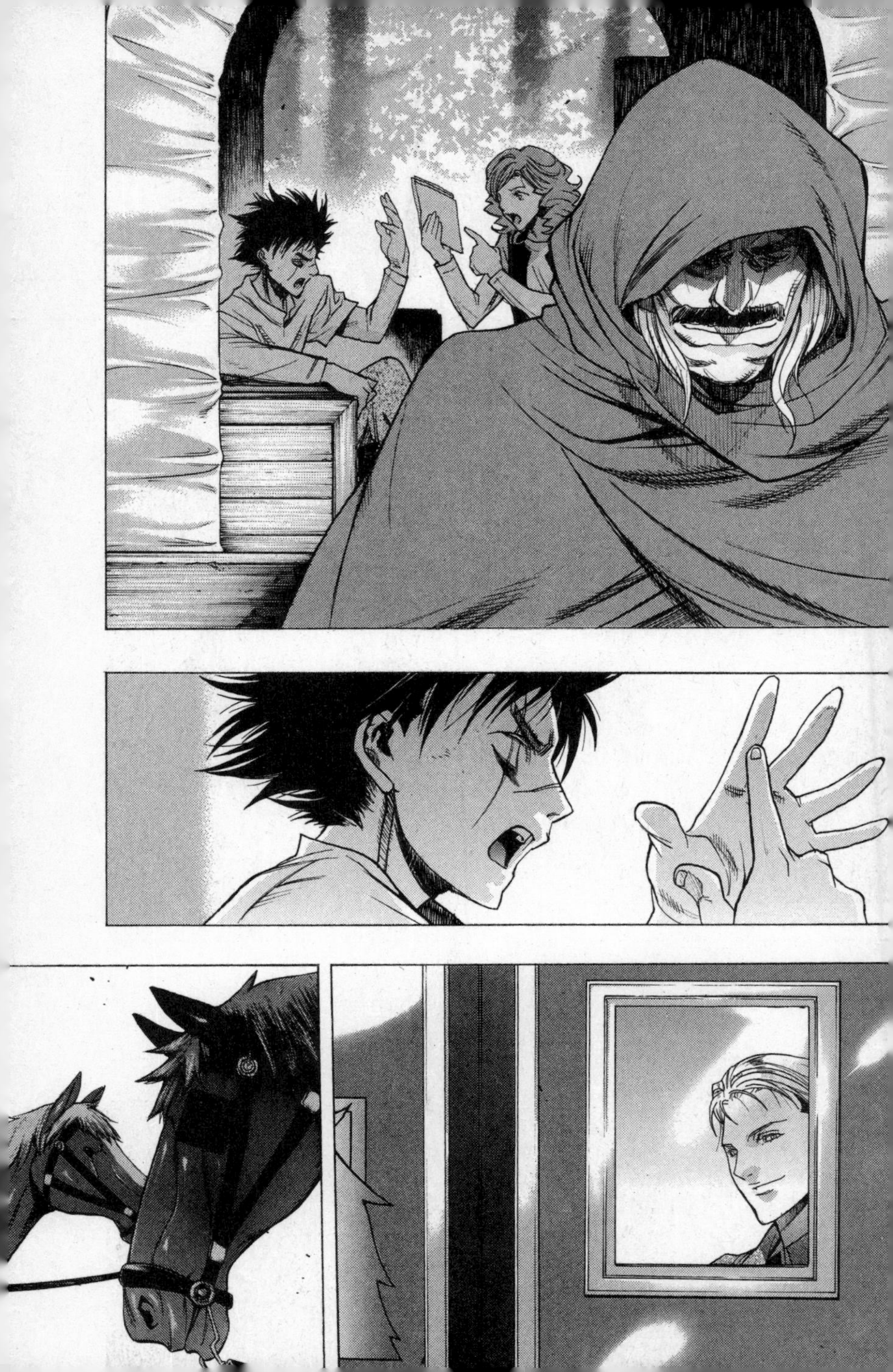

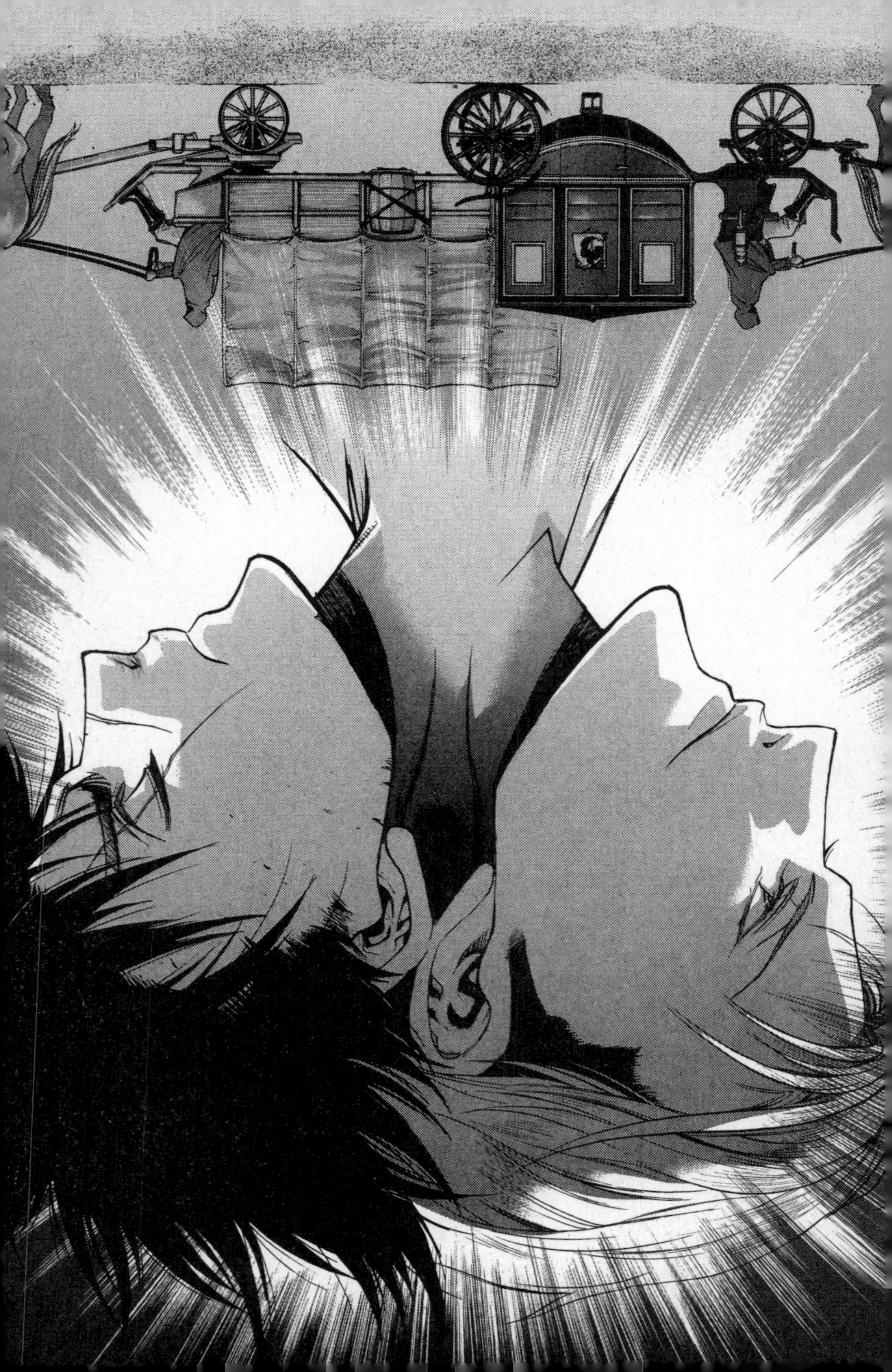

Chapter 21: Den of Treachery · End

ATTACK on TITAN

BEFORE THE FALL

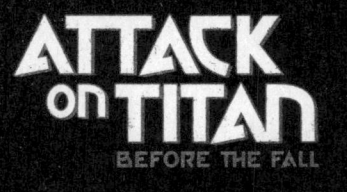

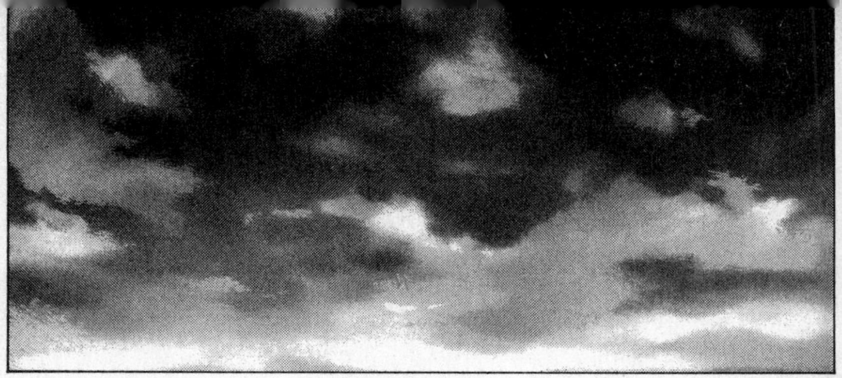

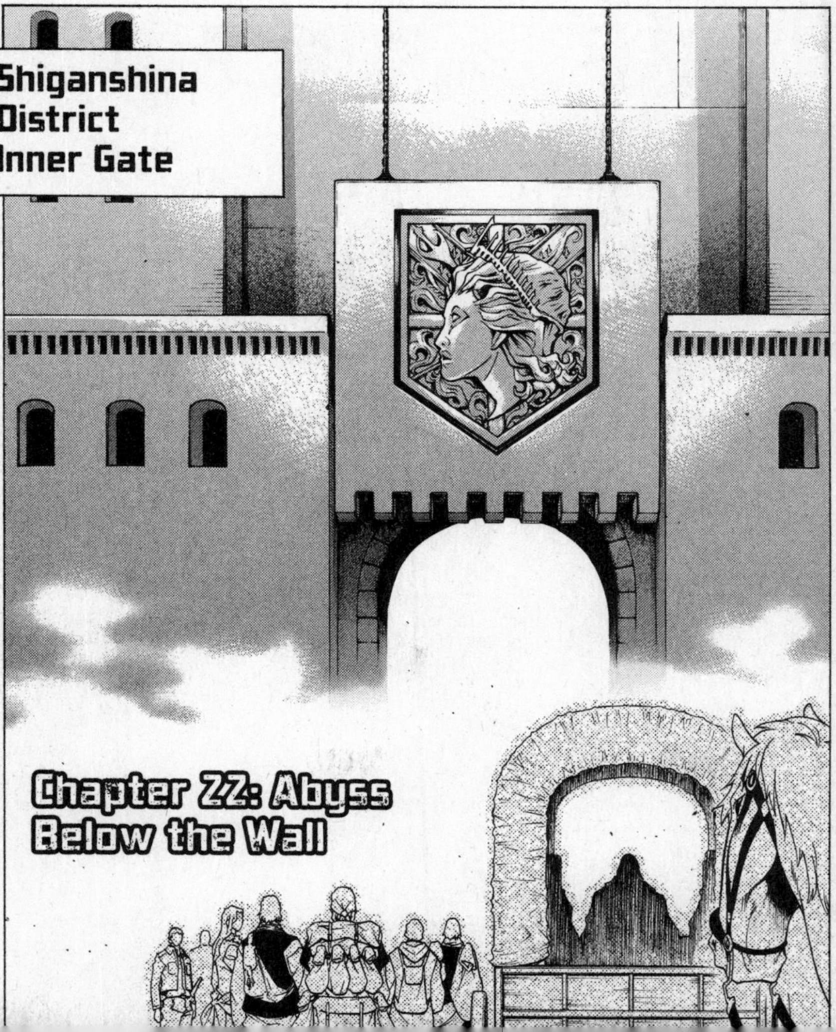
Shiganshina
District
Inner Gate
Chapter 22: Abyss
Below the Wall

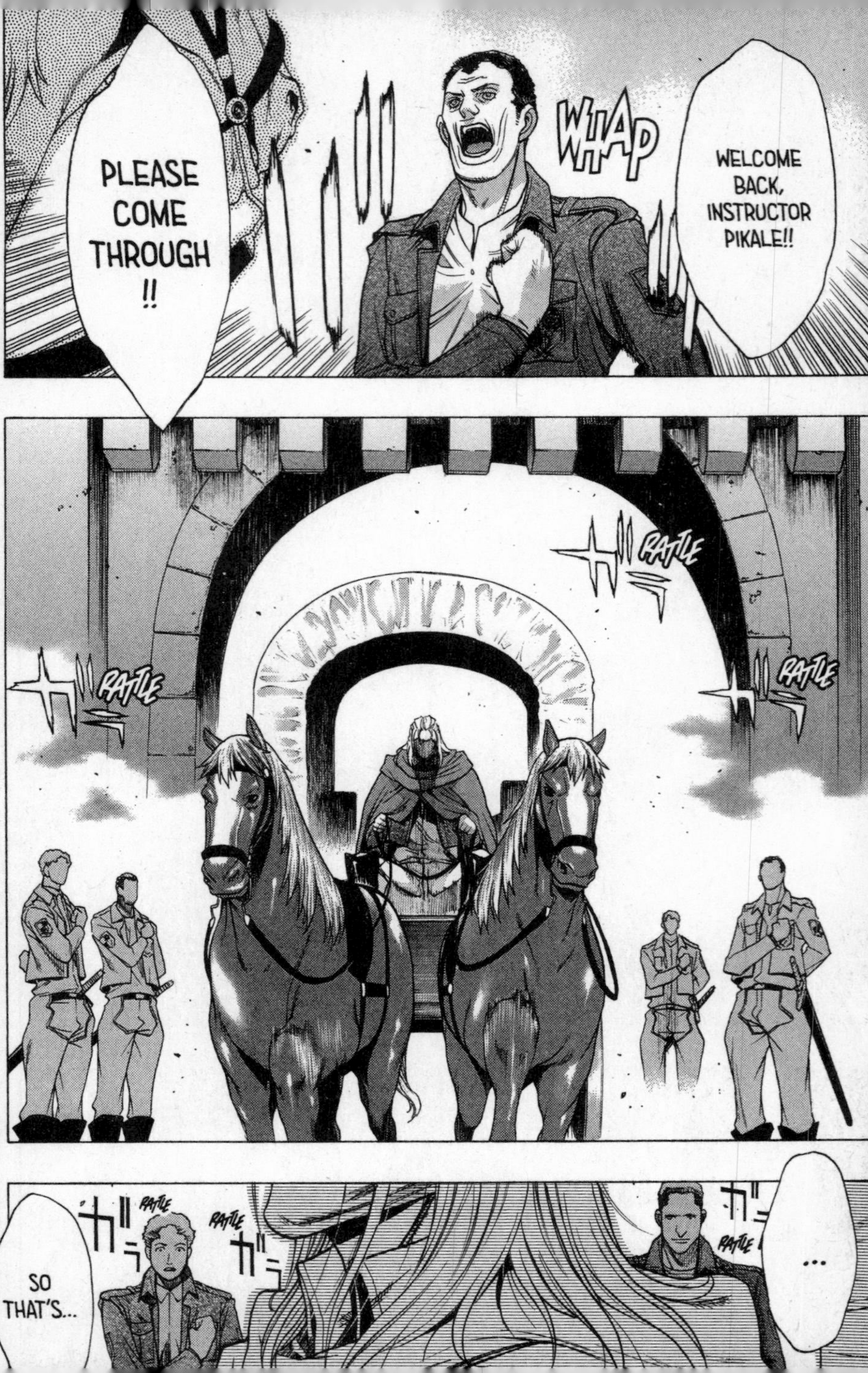
WELCOME BACK, INSTRUCTOR PIKALE!!
WHAP
PLEASE COME THROUGH !!
RATTLE
RATTLE
RATTLE
...
RATTLE
RATTLE
RATTLE
SO THAT'S...

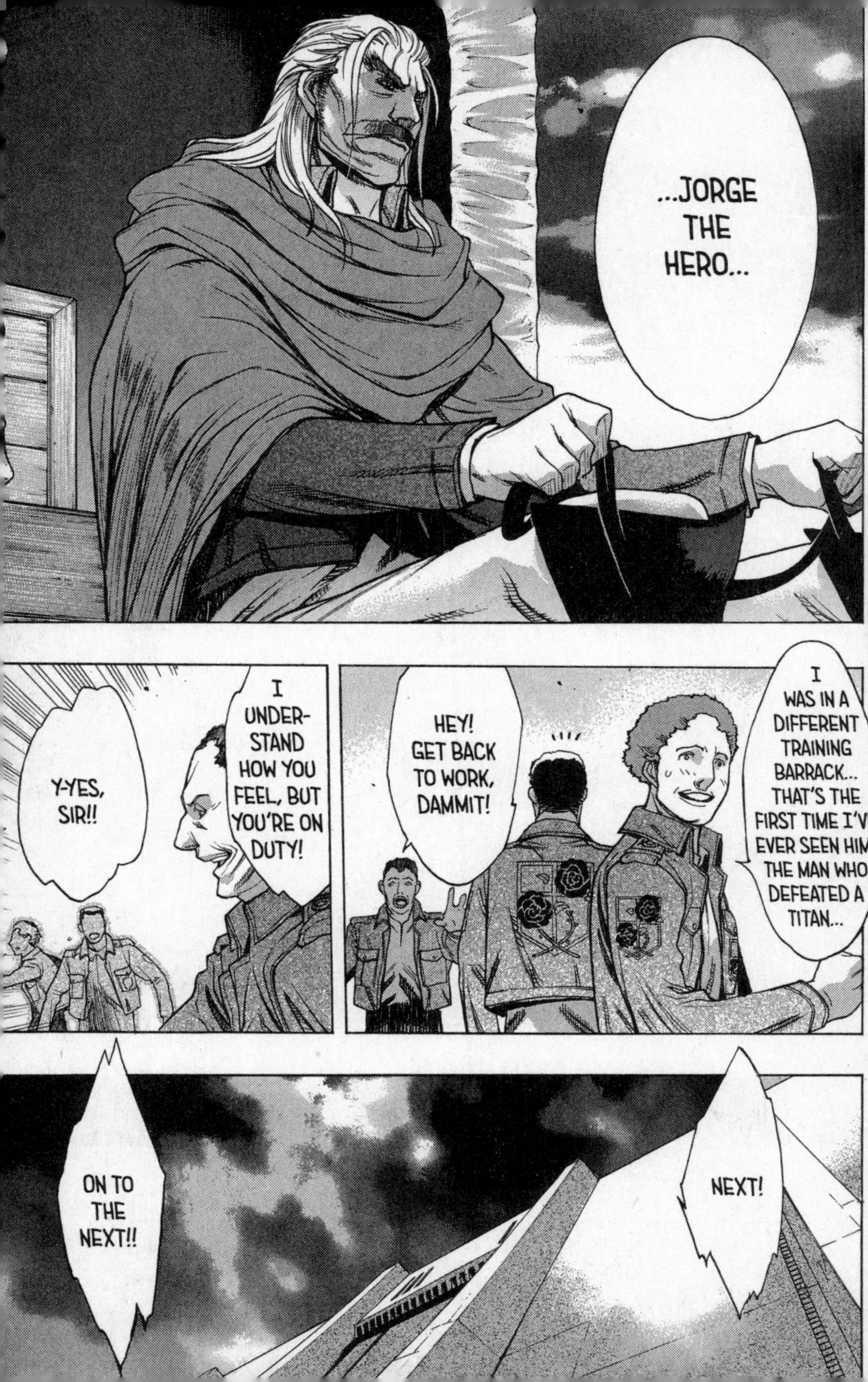
...JORGE THE HERO...
I WAS IN A DIFFERENT TRAINING BARRACK... THAT'S THE FIRST TIME I'VE EVER SEEN HIM! THE MAN WHO DEFEATED A TITAN...
HEY! GET BACK TO WORK, DAMMIT!
I UNDER-STAND HOW YOU FEEL, BUT YOU'RE ON DUTY!
Y-YES, SIR!!
NEXT!
ON TO THE NEXT!!

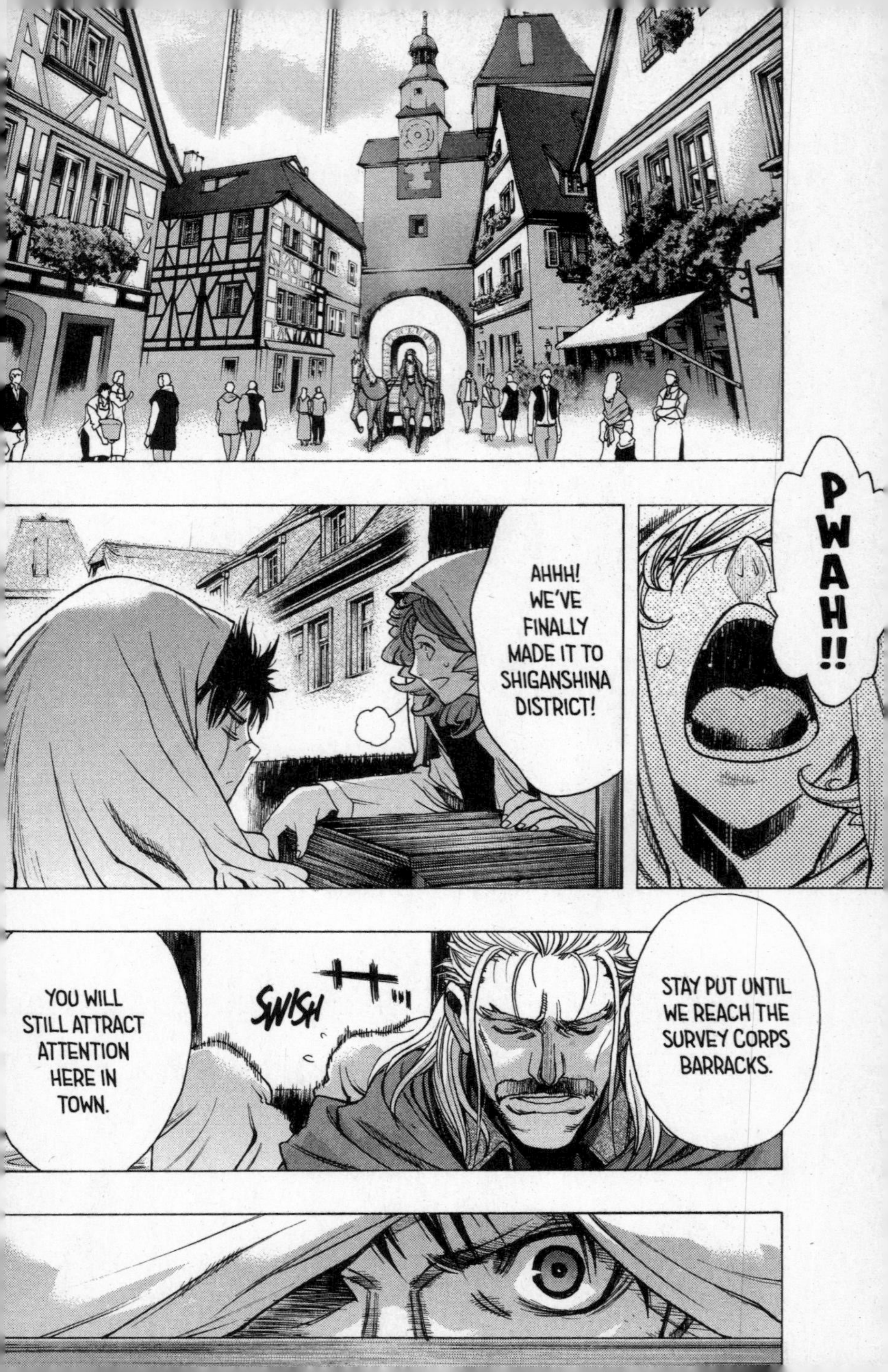
PWAH!!
AHHH! WE'VE FINALLY MADE IT TO SHIGANSHINA DISTRICT!
STAY PUT UNTIL WE REACH THE SURVEY CORPS BARRACKS.
SWISH
YOU WILL STILL ATTRACT ATTENTION HERE IN TOWN.

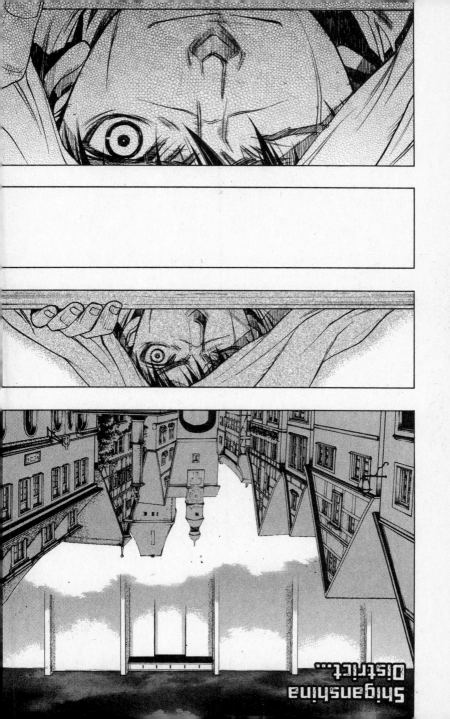

Shiganshina
District....

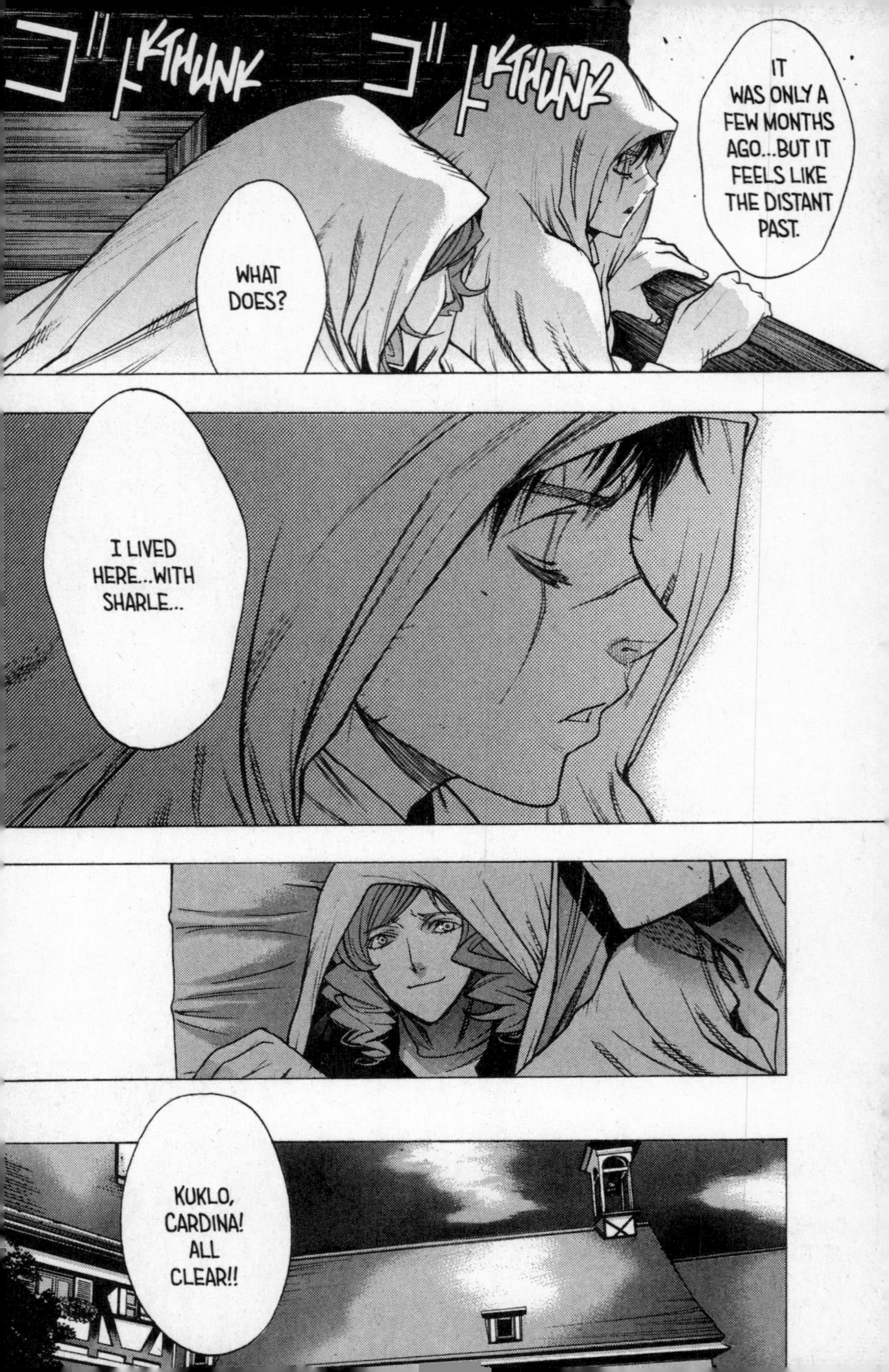

ゴトKTHUNK
ゴトKTHUNK
IT WAS ONLY A FEW MONTHS AGO...BUT IT FEELS LIKE THE DISTANT PAST.
WHAT DOES?
I LIVED HERE...WITH SHARLE...
KUKLO, CARDINA! ALL CLEAR!!

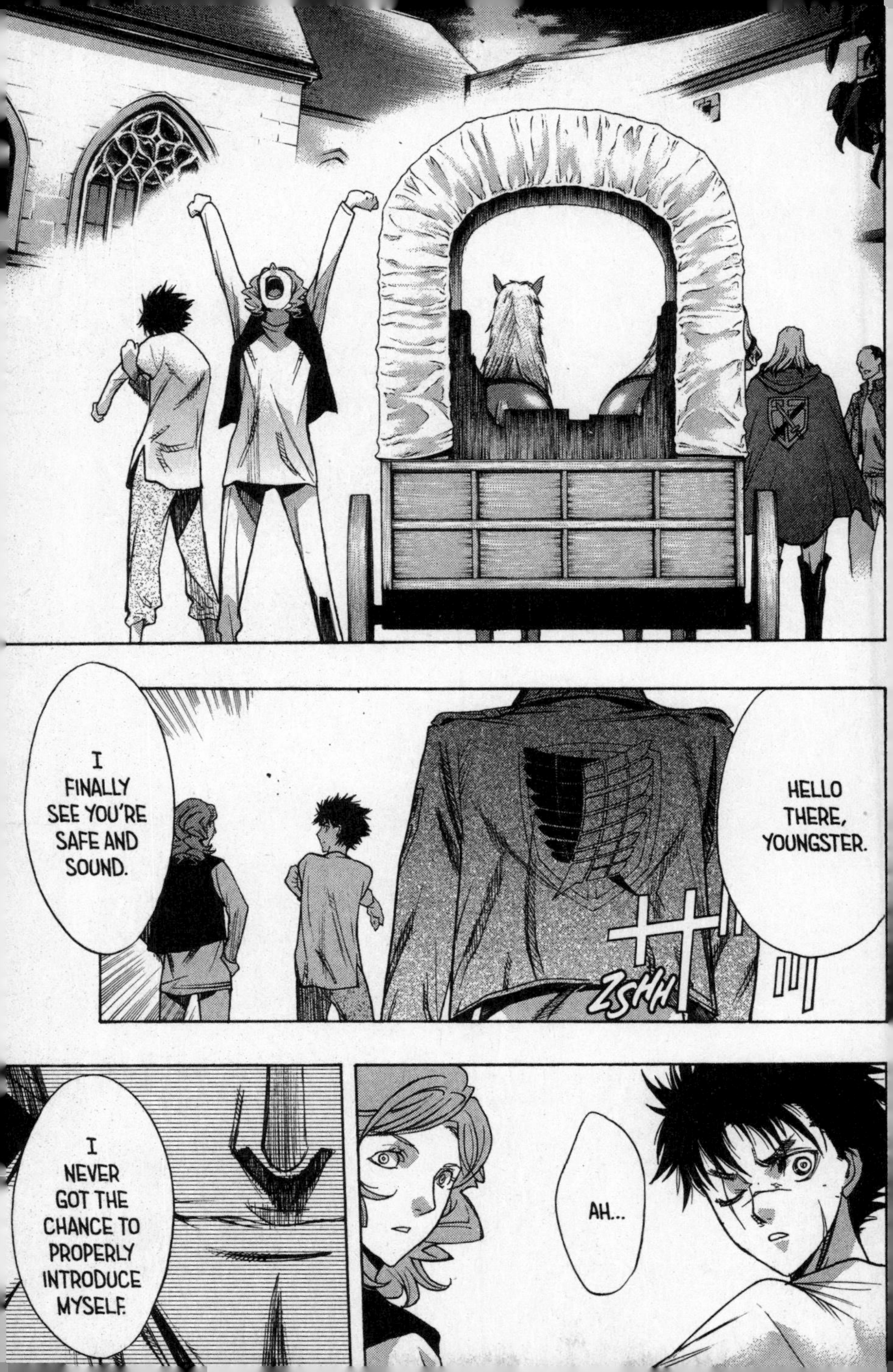
HELLO THERE, YOUNGSTER.
ZSHH
I FINALLY SEE YOU'RE SAFE AND SOUND.
AH...
I NEVER GOT THE CHANCE TO PROPERLY INTRODUCE MYSELF.

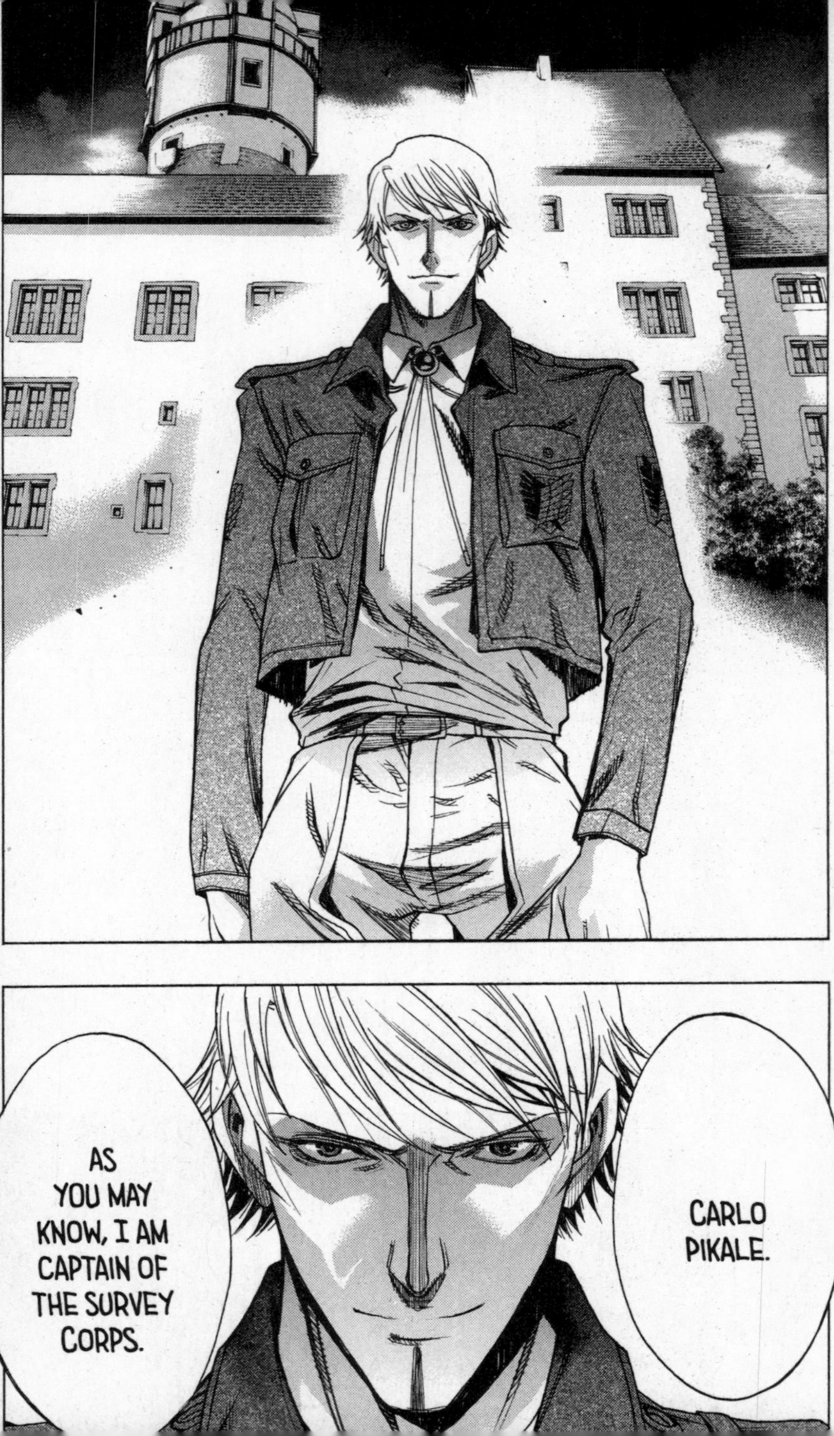
CARLO PIKALE.
AS YOU MAY KNOW, I AM CAPTAIN OF THE SURVEY CORPS.

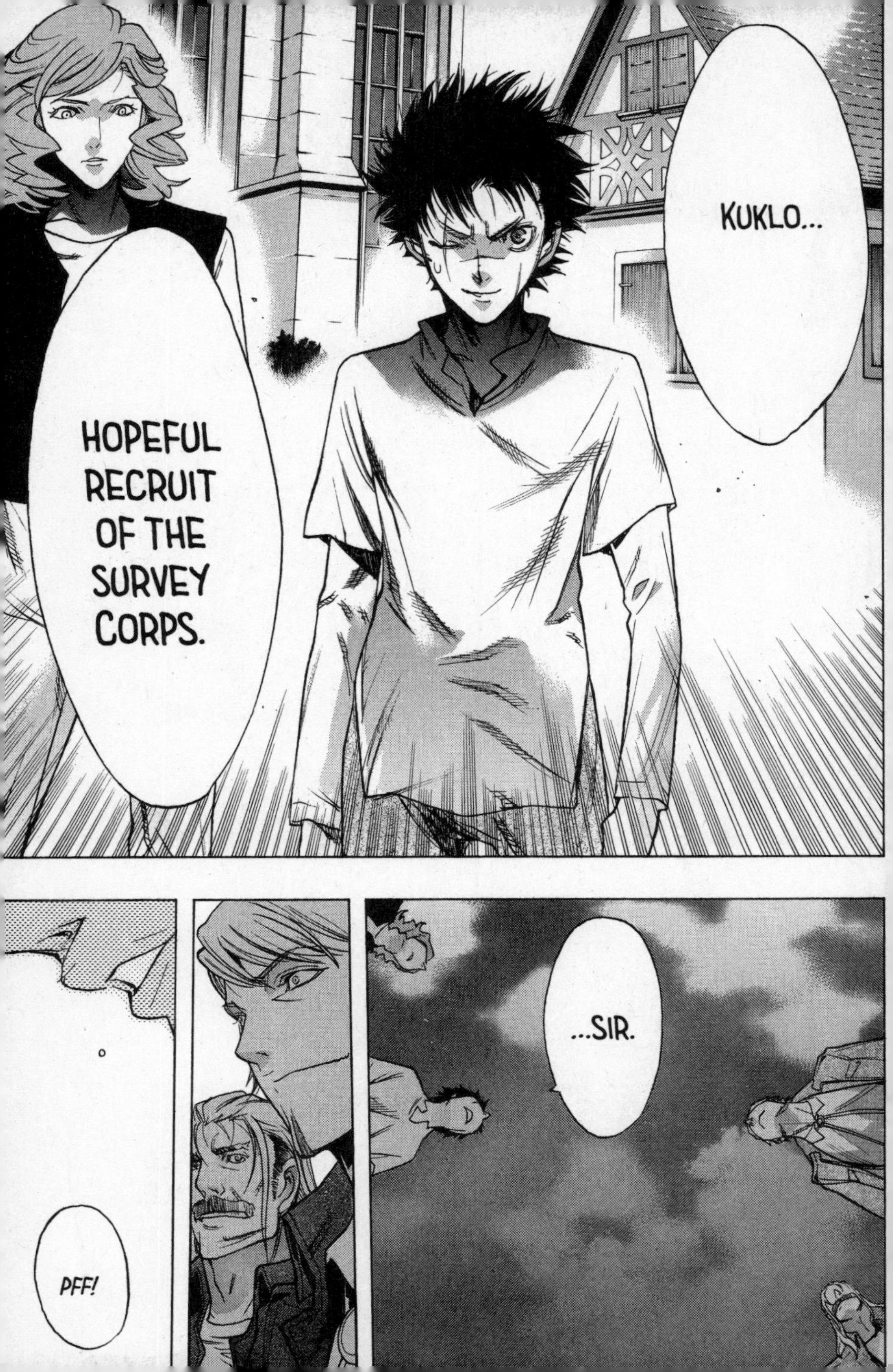
KUKLO...
HOPEFUL RECRUIT OF THE SURVEY CORPS.
...SIR.
PFF!

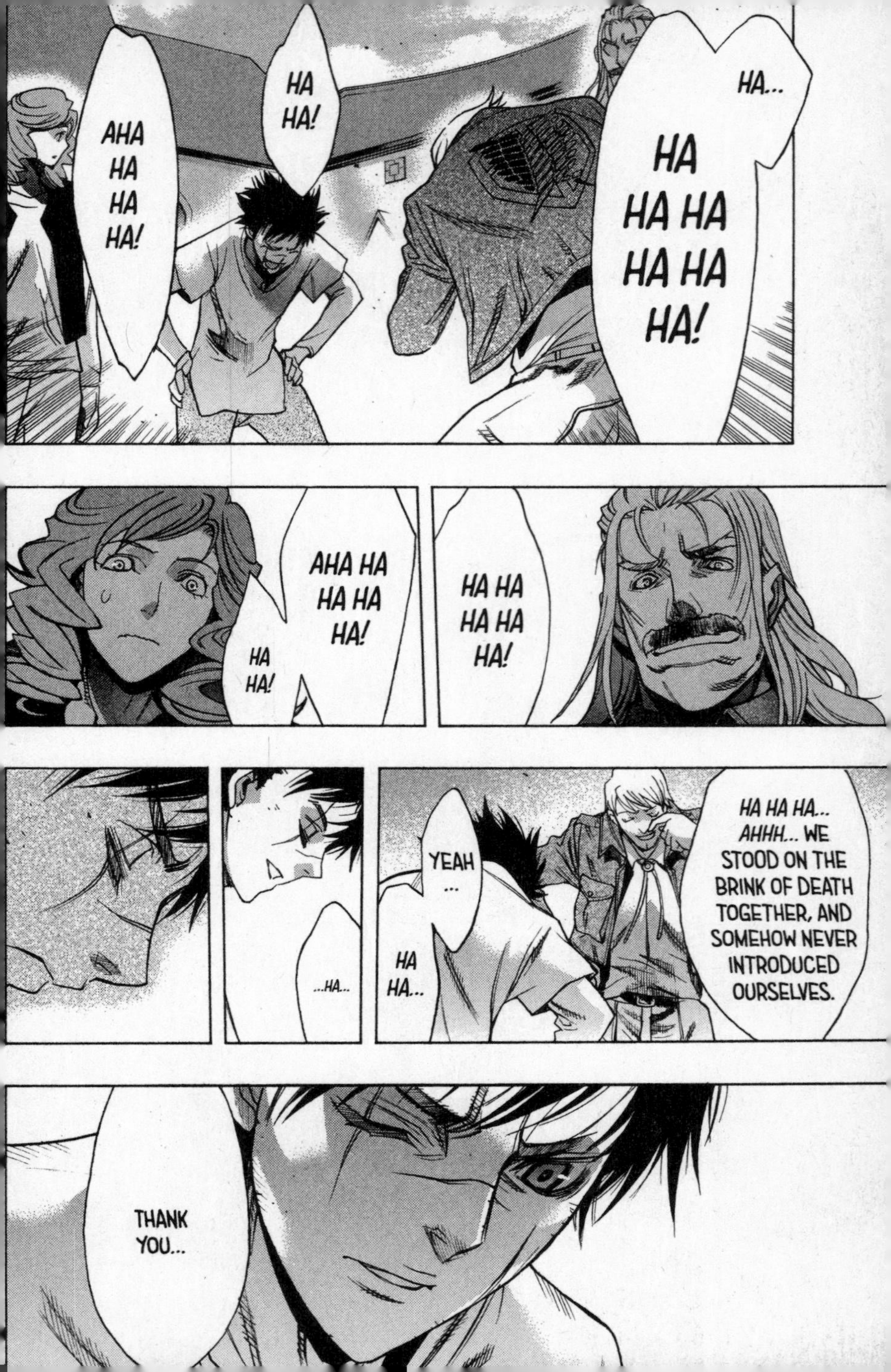
HA...
HA HA HA HA HA HA!
HA HA!
AHA HA HA HA!
HA HA HA HA HA!
AHA HA HA HA HA!
HA HA!
HA HA HA... AHHH... WE STOOD ON THE BRINK OF DEATH TOGETHER, AND SOMEHOW NEVER INTRODUCED OURSELVES.
YEAH ...
HA HA...
...HA...
THANK YOU...

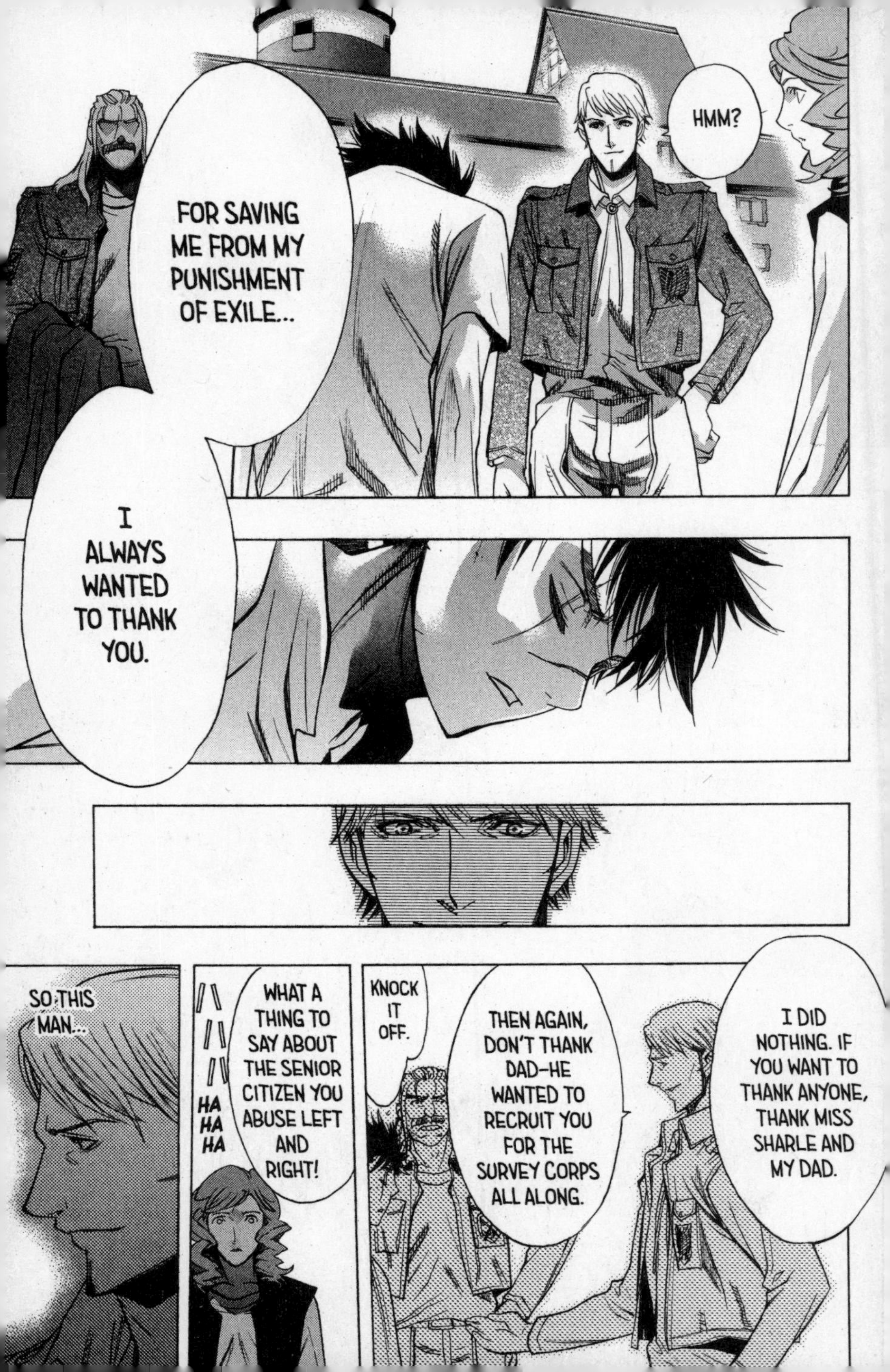
HMM?
FOR SAVING ME FROM MY PUNISHMENT OF EXILE...
I ALWAYS WANTED TO THANK YOU.
I DID NOTHING. IF YOU WANT TO THANK ANYONE, THANK MISS SHARLE AND MY DAD.
THEN AGAIN, DON'T THANK DAD—HE WANTED TO RECRUIT YOU FOR THE SURVEY CORPS ALL ALONG.
KNOCK IT OFF.
WHAT A THING TO SAY ABOUT THE SENIOR CITIZEN YOU ABUSE LEFT AND RIGHT!
HA HA HA
SO THIS MAN...

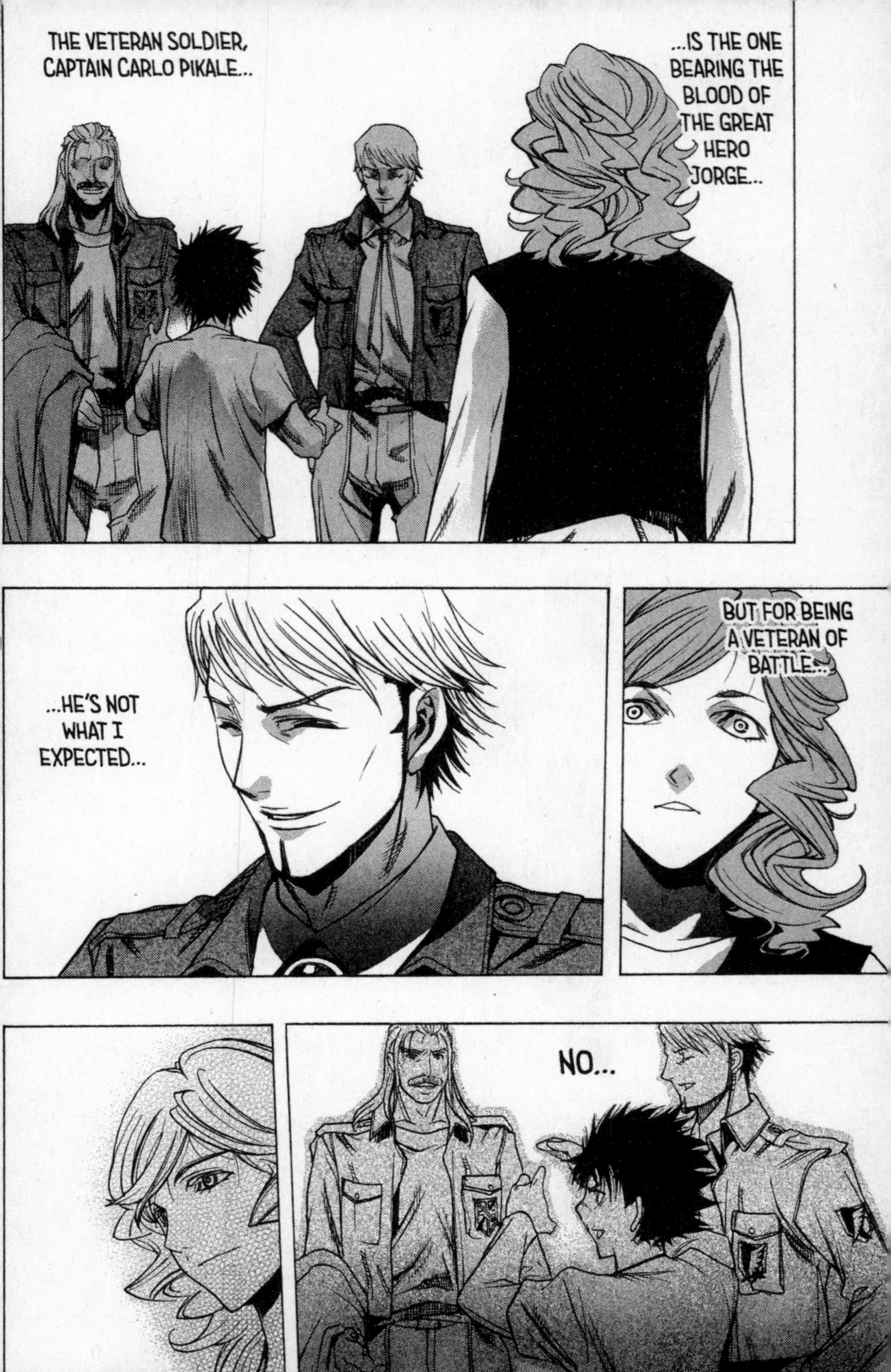
THE VETERAN SOLDIER, CAPTAIN CARLO PIKALE...
...IS THE ONE BEARING THE BLOOD OF THE GREAT HERO JORGE...
BUT FOR BEING A VETERAN OF BATTLE...
...HE'S NOT WHAT I EXPECTED...
NO...

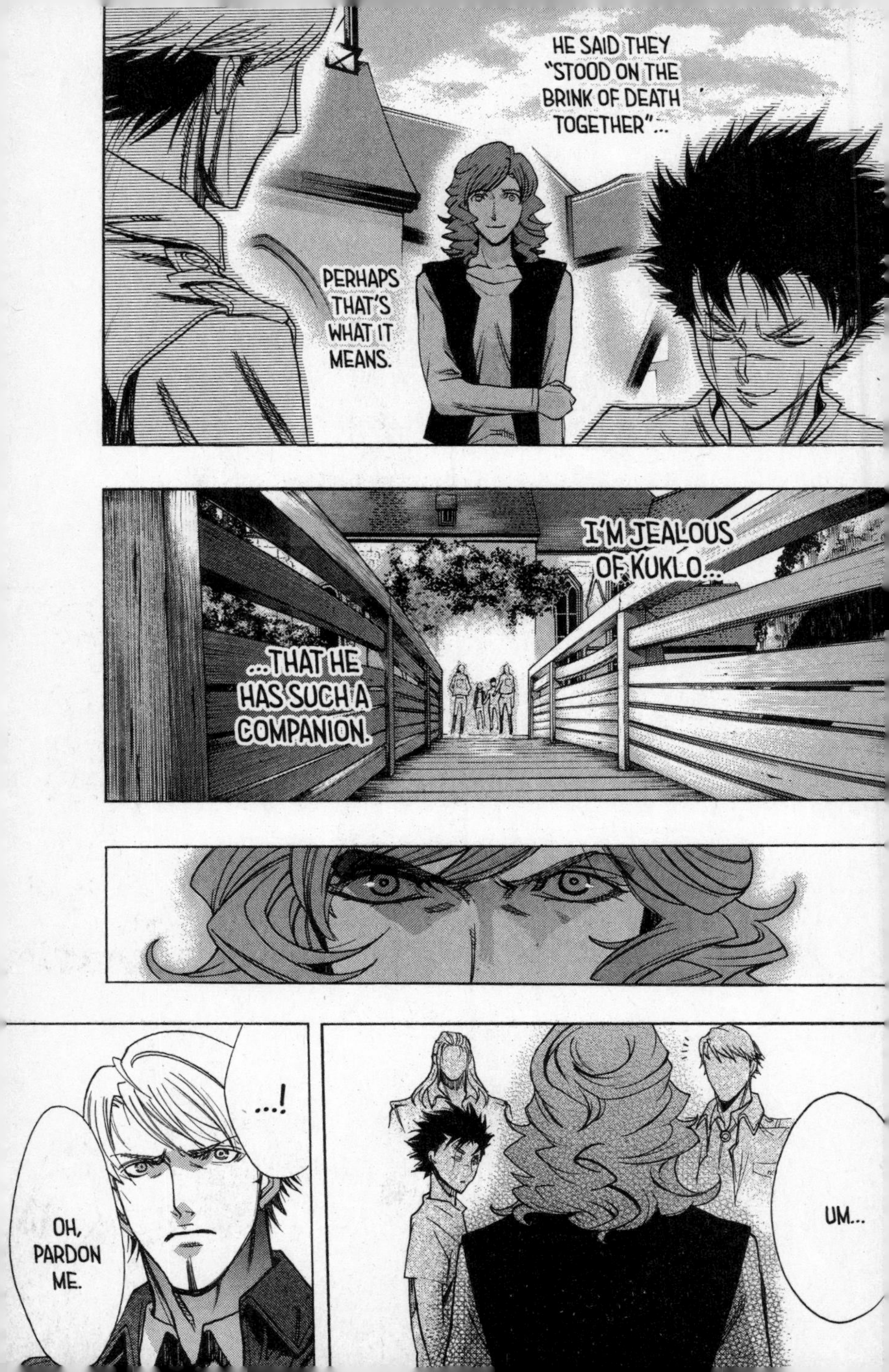
HE SAID THEY "STOOD ON THE BRINK OF DEATH TOGETHER"...
PERHAPS THAT'S WHAT IT MEANS.
I'M JEALOUS OF KUKLO...
...THAT HE HAS SUCH A COMPANION.
UM...
...!
OH, PARDON ME.

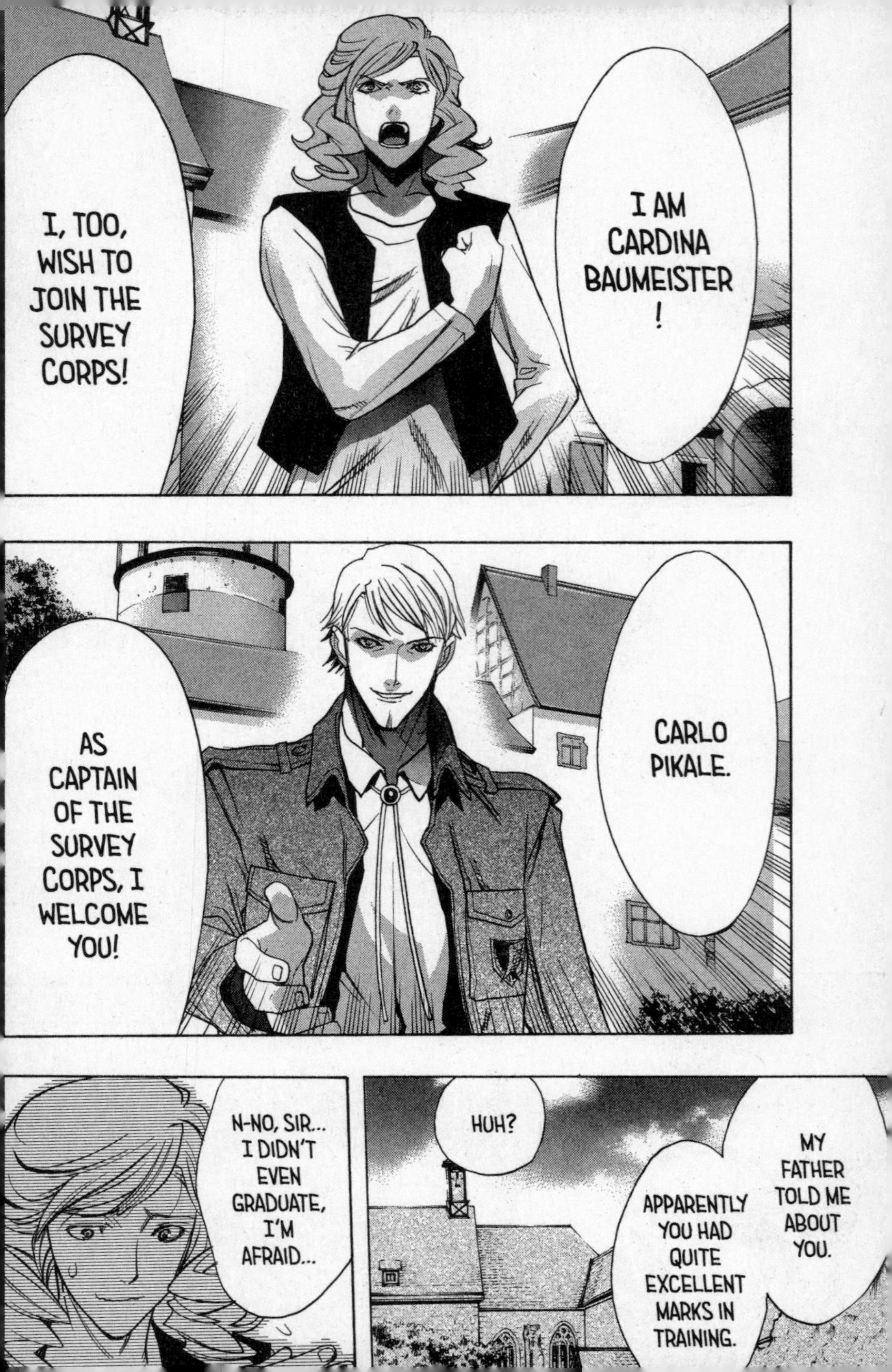
I AM CARDINA BAUMEISTER!
I, TOO, WISH TO JOIN THE SURVEY CORPS!
CARLO PIKALE.
AS CAPTAIN OF THE SURVEY CORPS, I WELCOME YOU!
MY FATHER TOLD ME ABOUT YOU.
APPARENTLY YOU HAD QUITE EXCELLENT MARKS IN TRAINING.
HUH?
N-NO, SIR... I DIDN'T EVEN GRADUATE, I'M AFRAID...

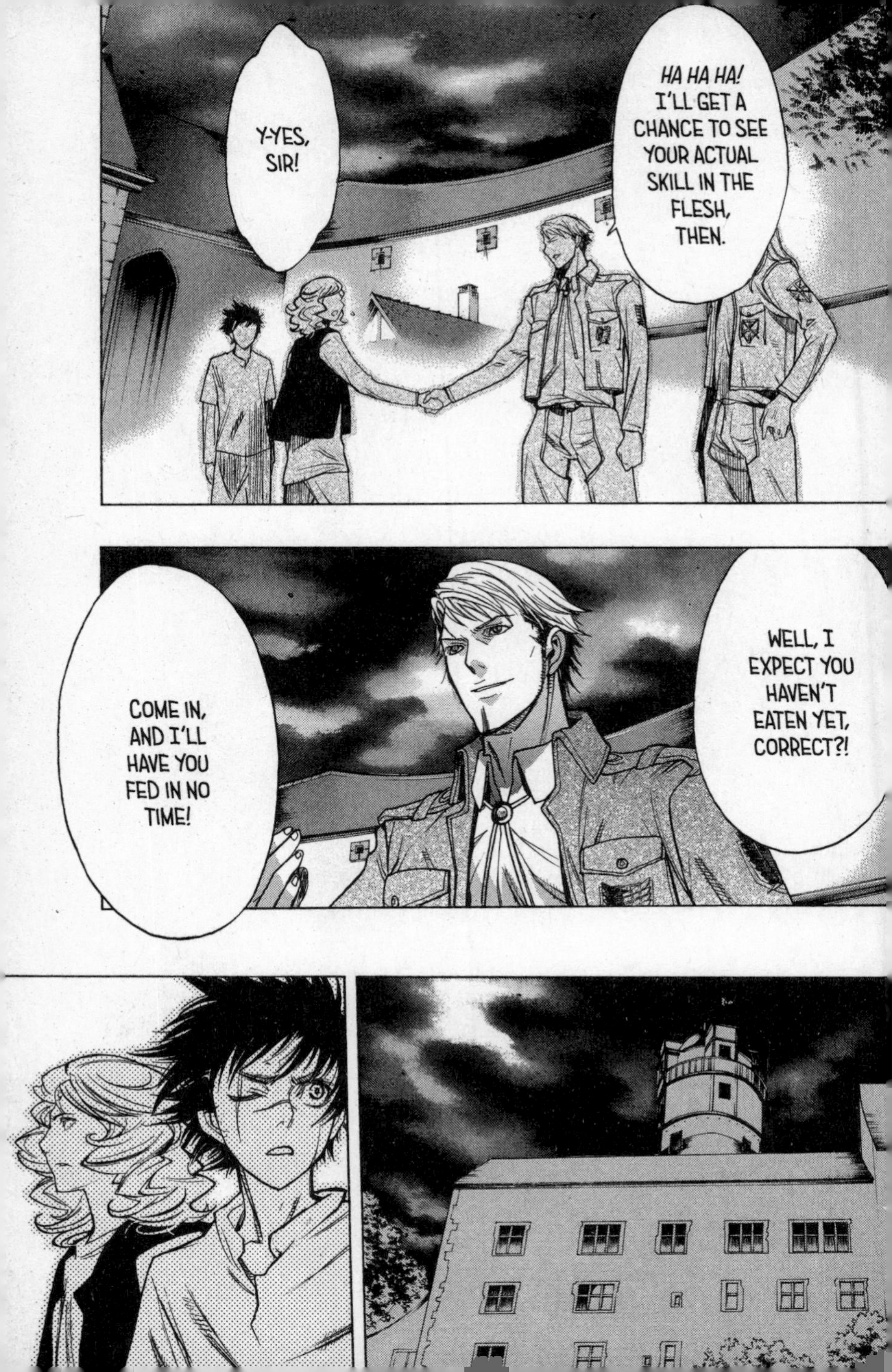
HA HA HA! I'LL GET A CHANCE TO SEE YOUR ACTUAL SKILL IN THE FLESH, THEN.
Y-YES, SIR!
WELL, I EXPECT YOU HAVEN'T EATEN YET, CORRECT?!
COME IN, AND I'LL HAVE YOU FED IN NO TIME!

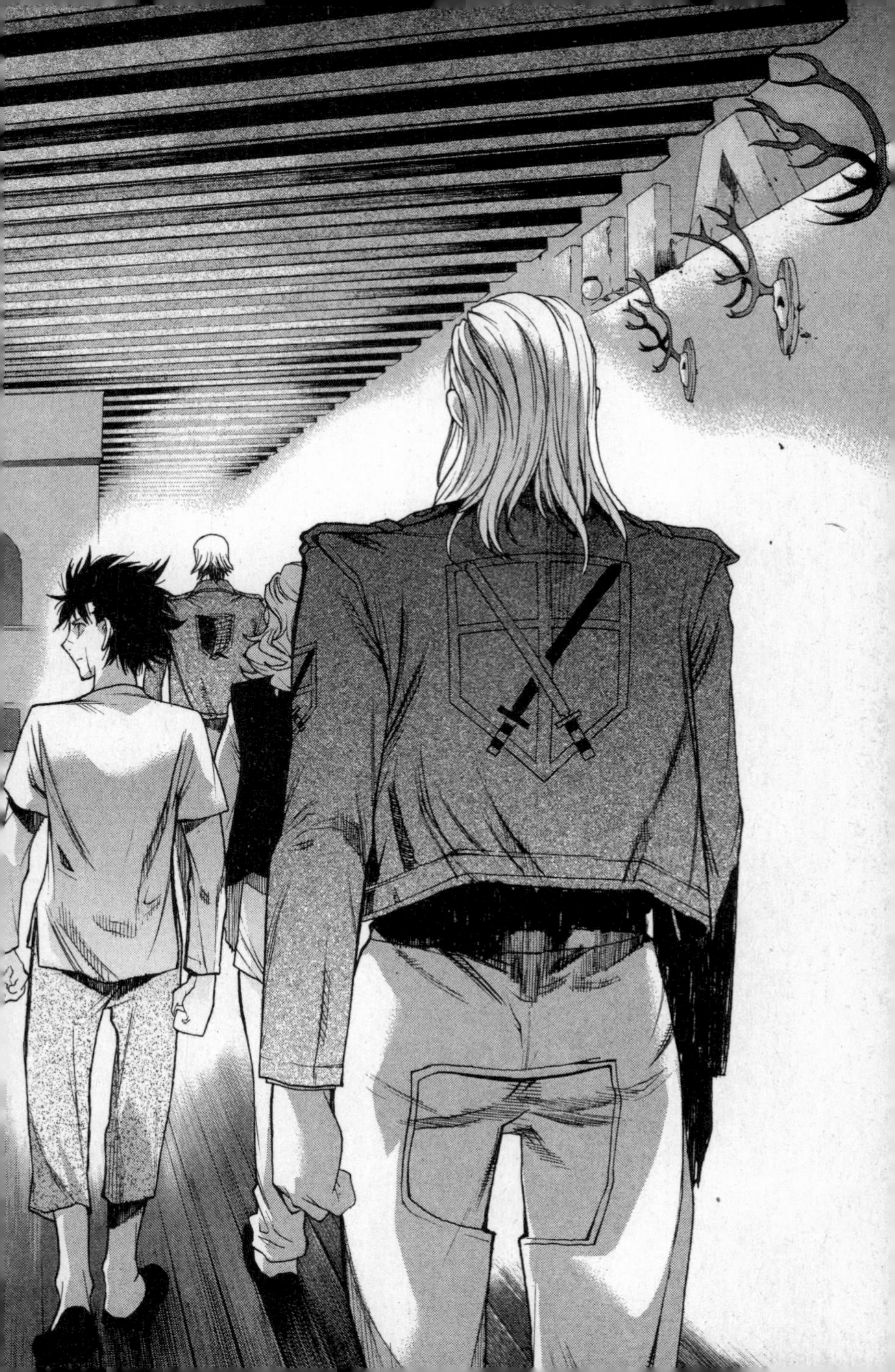

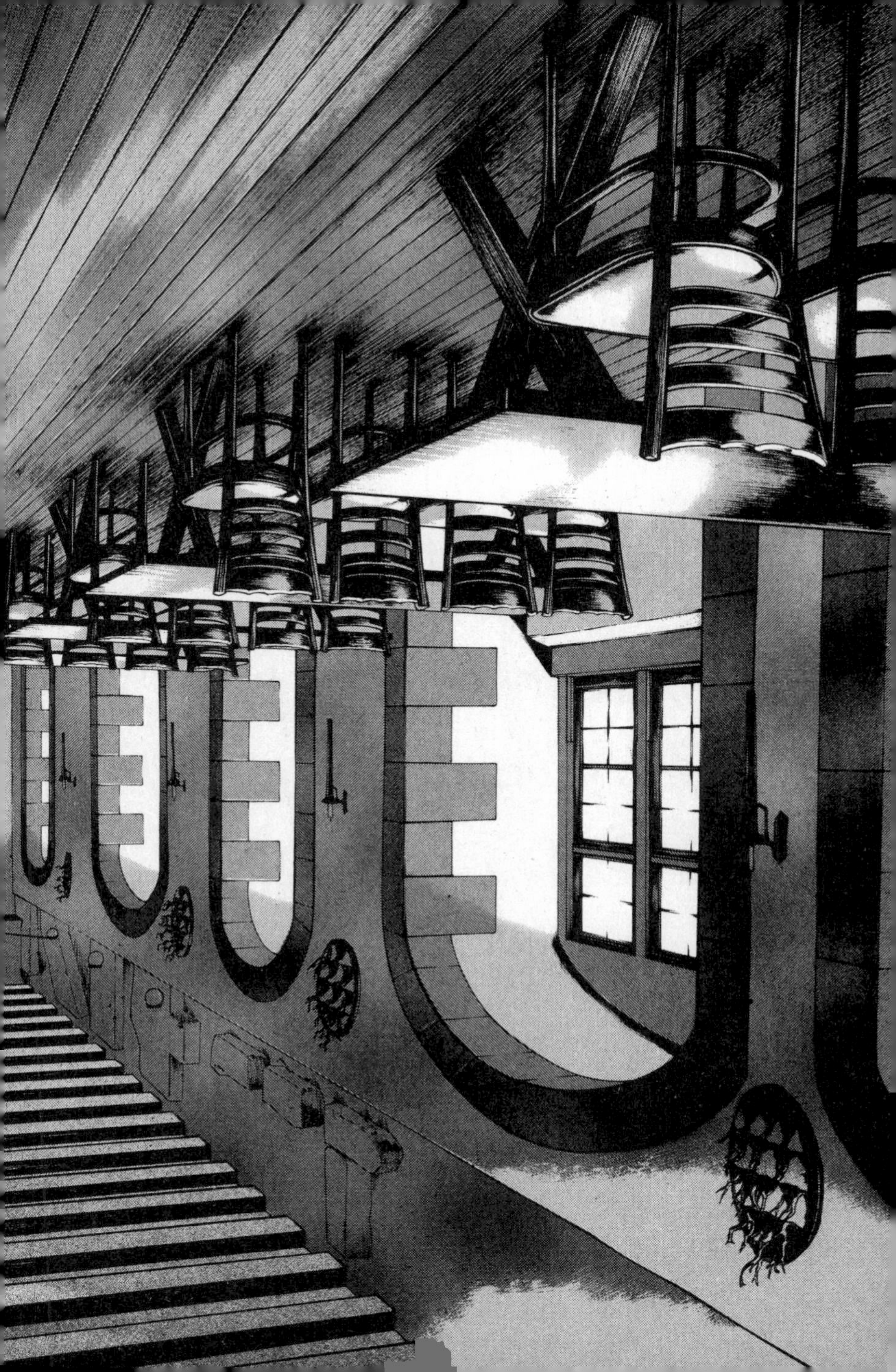

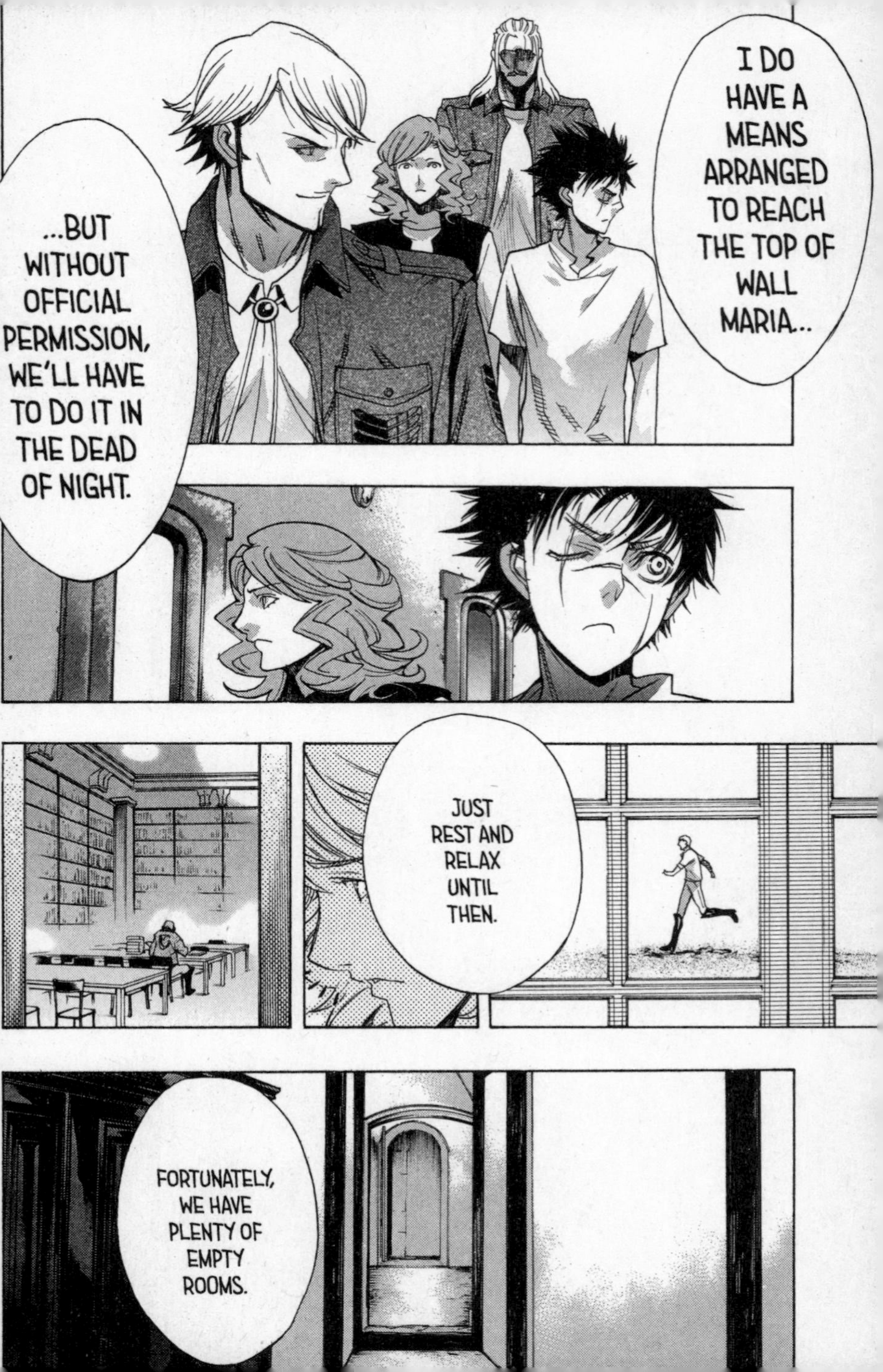
I DO HAVE A MEANS ARRANGED TO REACH THE TOP OF WALL MARIA...
...BUT WITHOUT OFFICIAL PERMISSION, WE'LL HAVE TO DO IT IN THE DEAD OF NIGHT.
JUST REST AND RELAX UNTIL THEN.
FORTUNATELY, WE HAVE PLENTY OF EMPTY ROOMS.

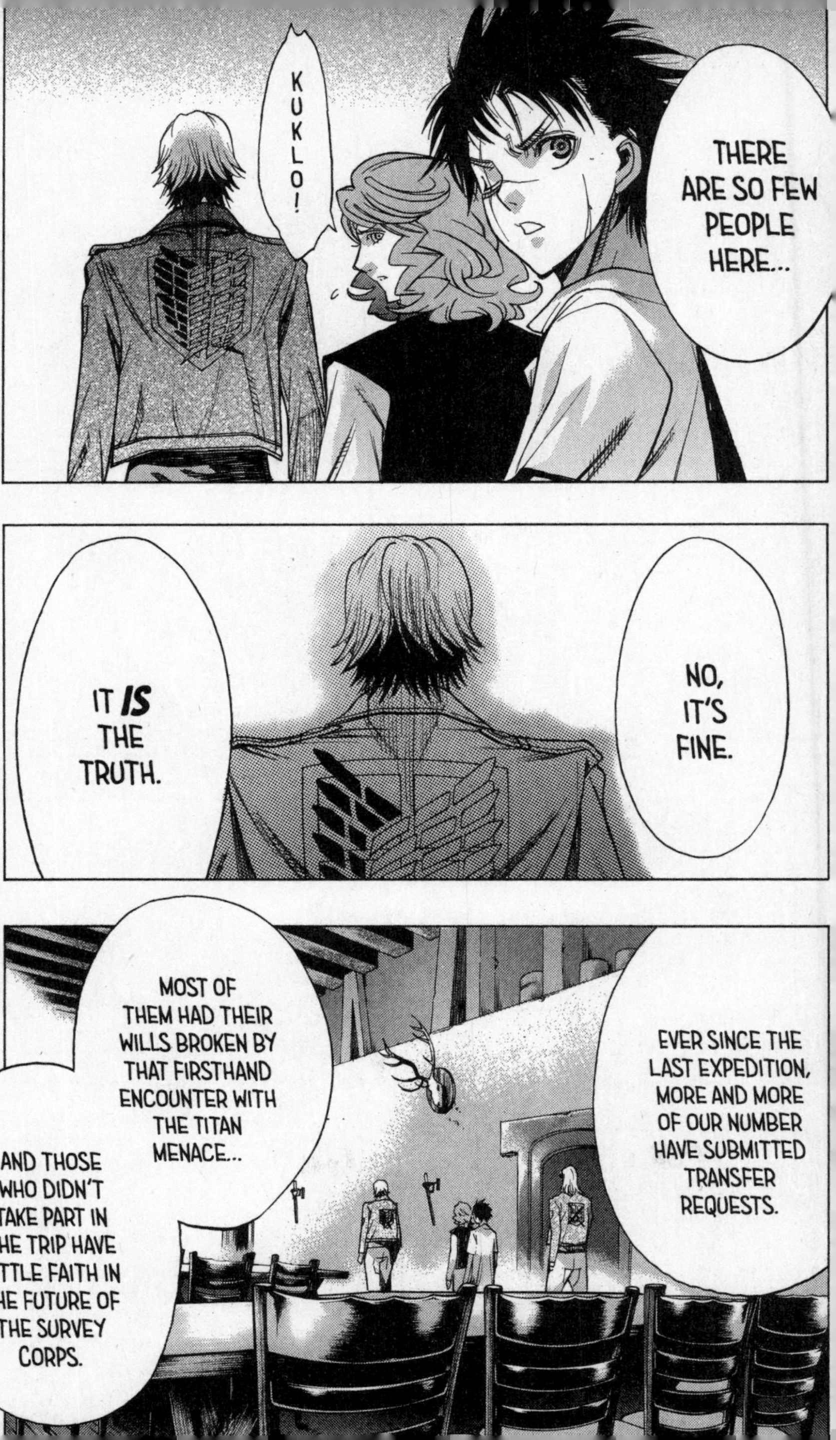
THERE ARE SO FEW PEOPLE HERE...
KUKLO!
NO, IT'S FINE.
IT *IS* THE TRUTH.
EVER SINCE THE LAST EXPEDITION, MORE AND MORE OF OUR NUMBER HAVE SUBMITTED TRANSFER REQUESTS.
MOST OF THEM HAD THEIR WILLS BROKEN BY THAT FIRSTHAND ENCOUNTER WITH THE TITAN MENACE...
AND THOSE WHO DIDN'T TAKE PART IN THE TRIP HAVE LITTLE FAITH IN THE FUTURE OF THE SURVEY CORPS.

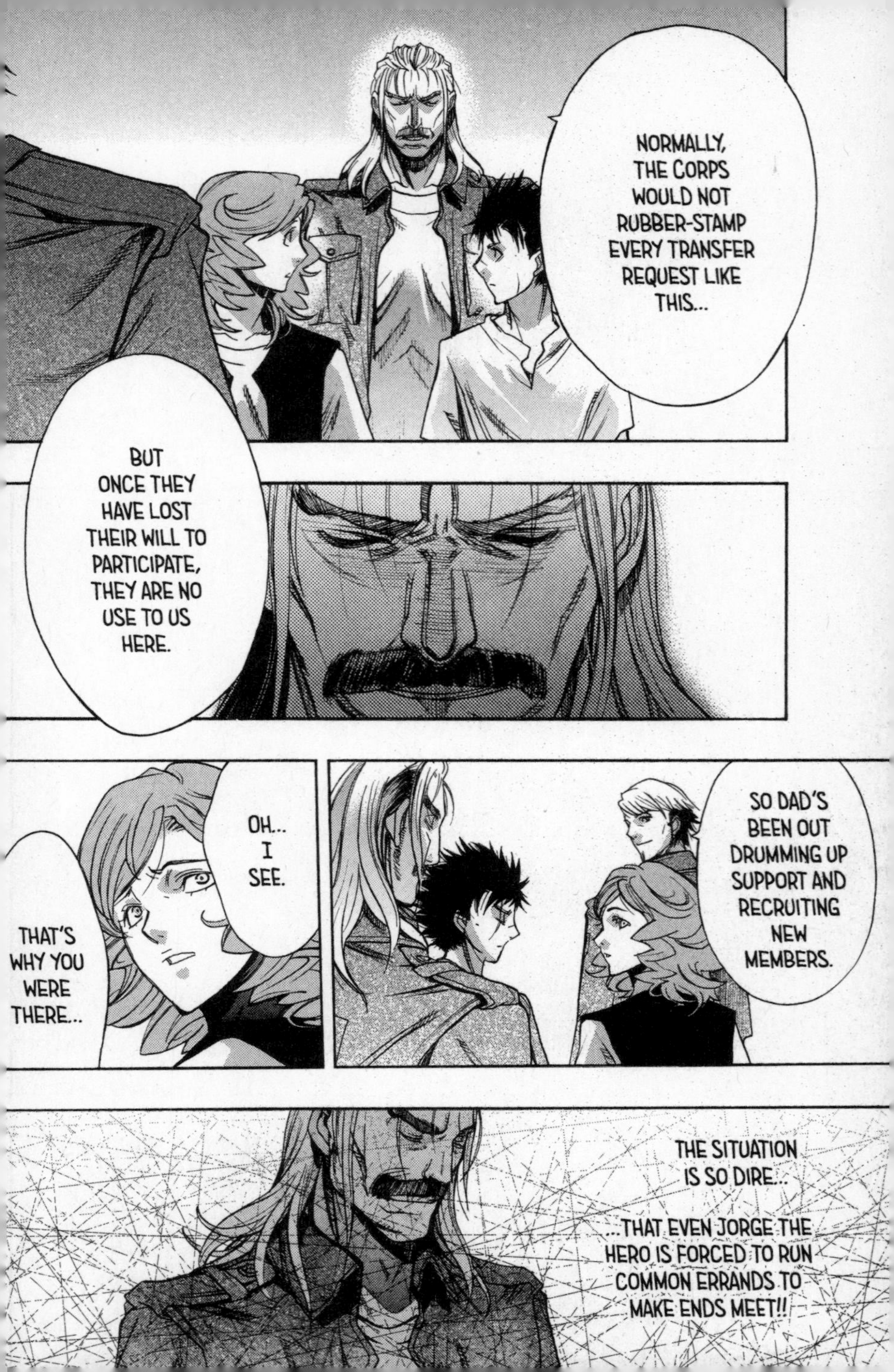
NORMALLY, THE CORPS WOULD NOT RUBBER-STAMP EVERY TRANSFER REQUEST LIKE THIS...
BUT ONCE THEY HAVE LOST THEIR WILL TO PARTICIPATE, THEY ARE NO USE TO US HERE.
SO DAD'S BEEN OUT DRUMMING UP SUPPORT AND RECRUITING NEW MEMBERS.
OH... I SEE.
THAT'S WHY YOU WERE THERE...
THE SITUATION IS SO DIRE...
...THAT EVEN JORGE THE HERO IS FORCED TO RUN COMMON ERRANDS TO MAKE ENDS MEET!!

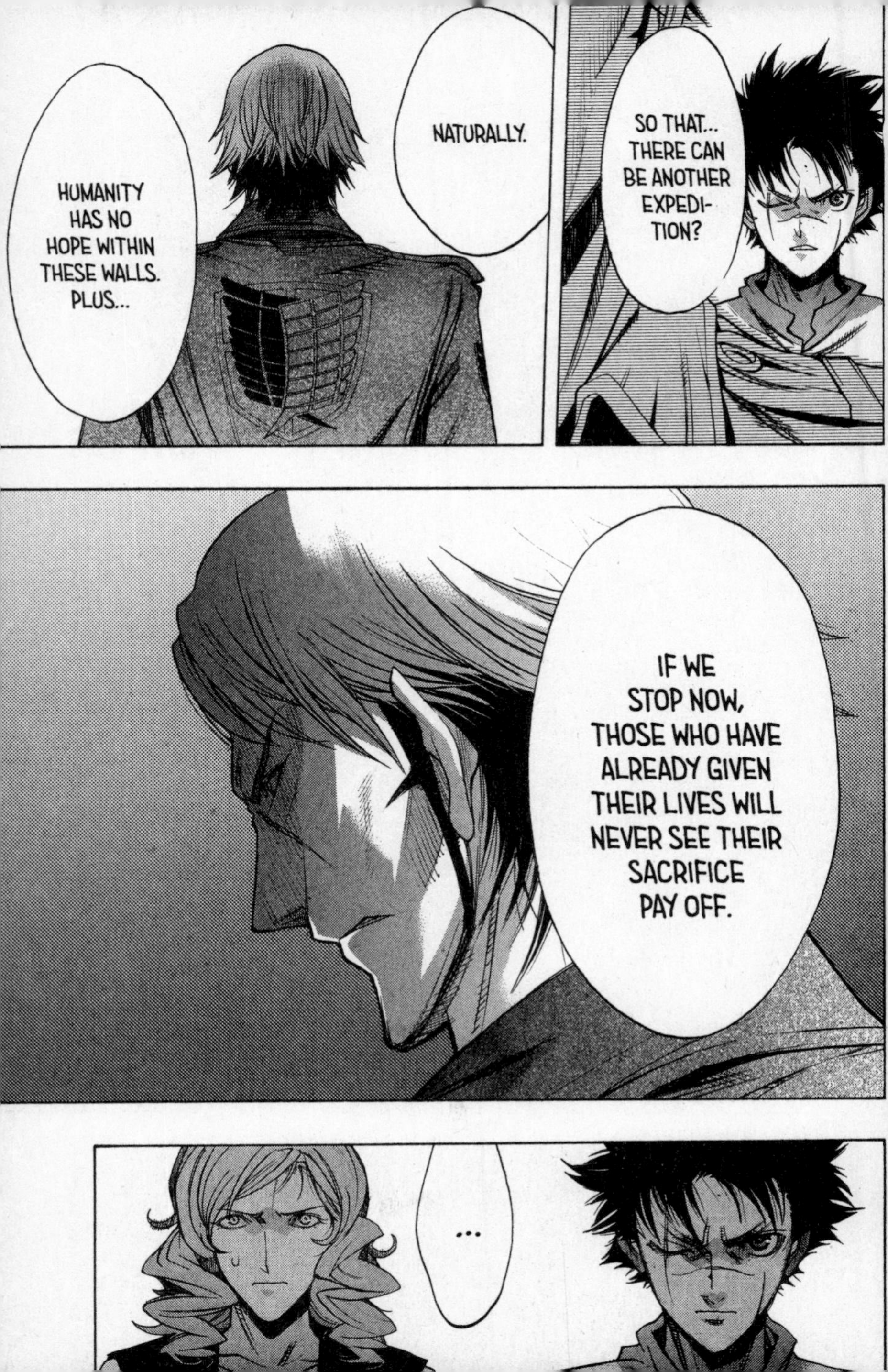
SO THAT... THERE CAN BE ANOTHER EXPEDI- TION?
NATURALLY.
HUMANITY HAS NO HOPE WITHIN THESE WALLS. PLUS...
IF WE STOP NOW, THOSE WHO HAVE ALREADY GIVEN THEIR LIVES WILL NEVER SEE THEIR SACRIFICE PAY OFF.
...

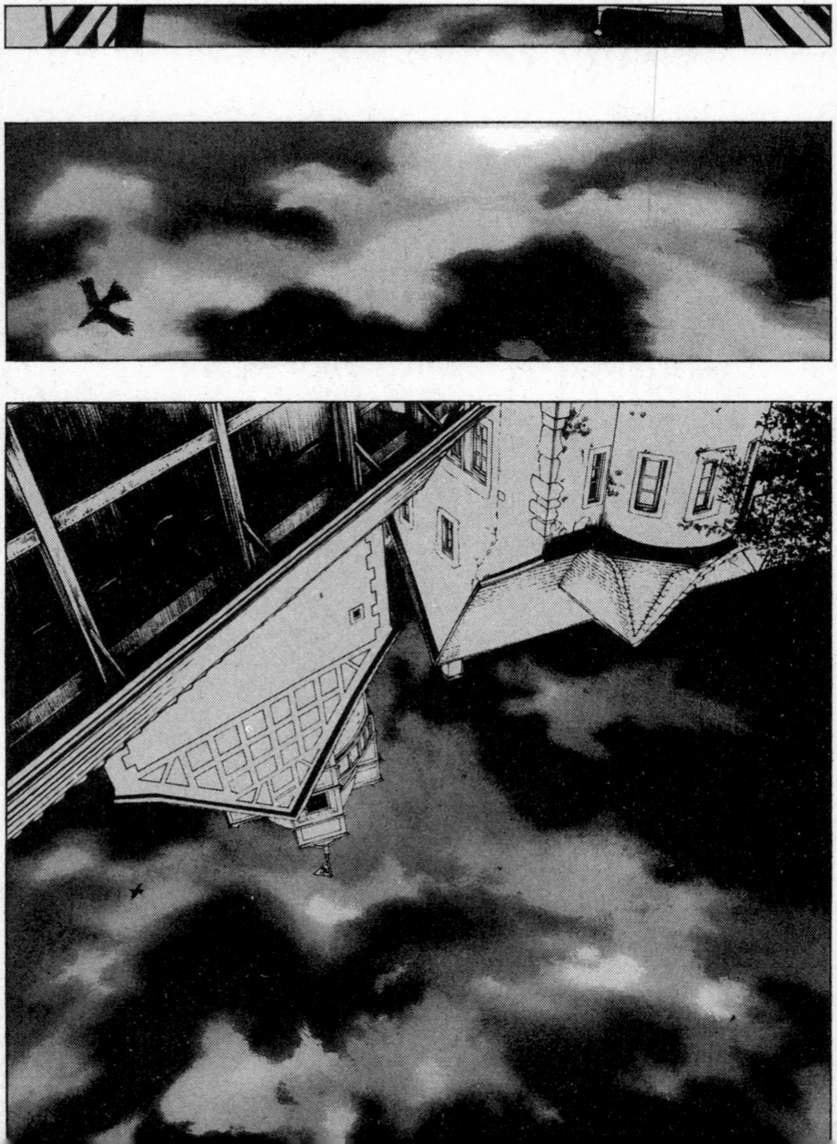

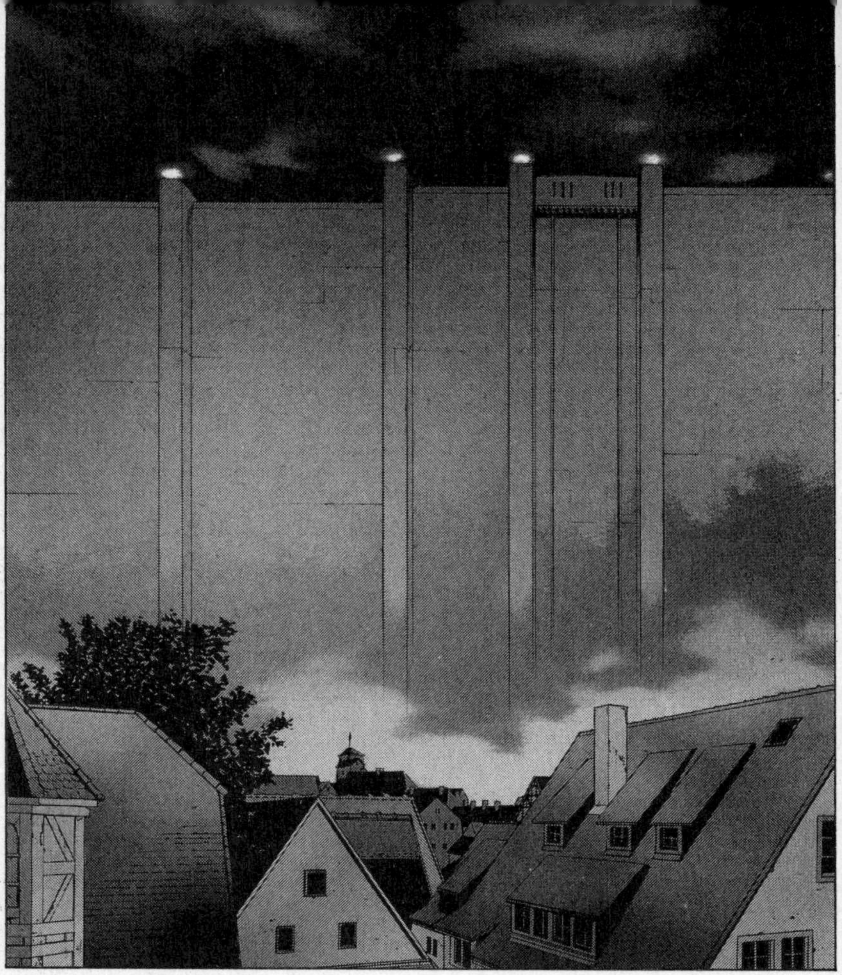

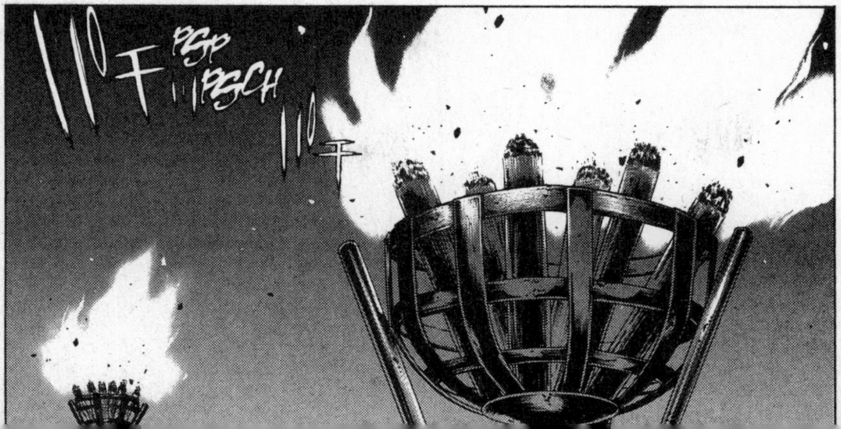
PSP
PSCH

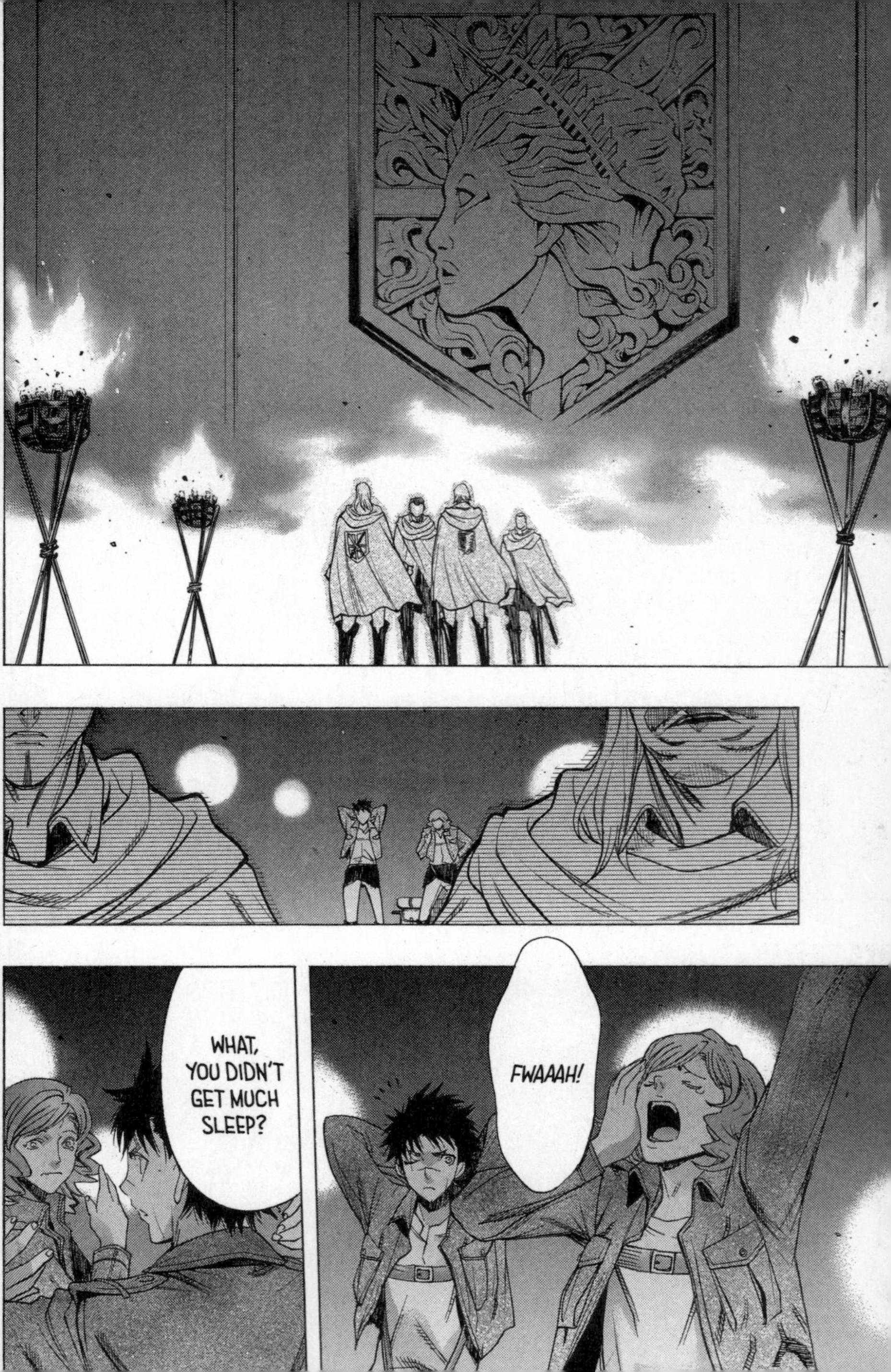
FWAAAH!
WHAT, YOU DIDN'T GET MUCH SLEEP?

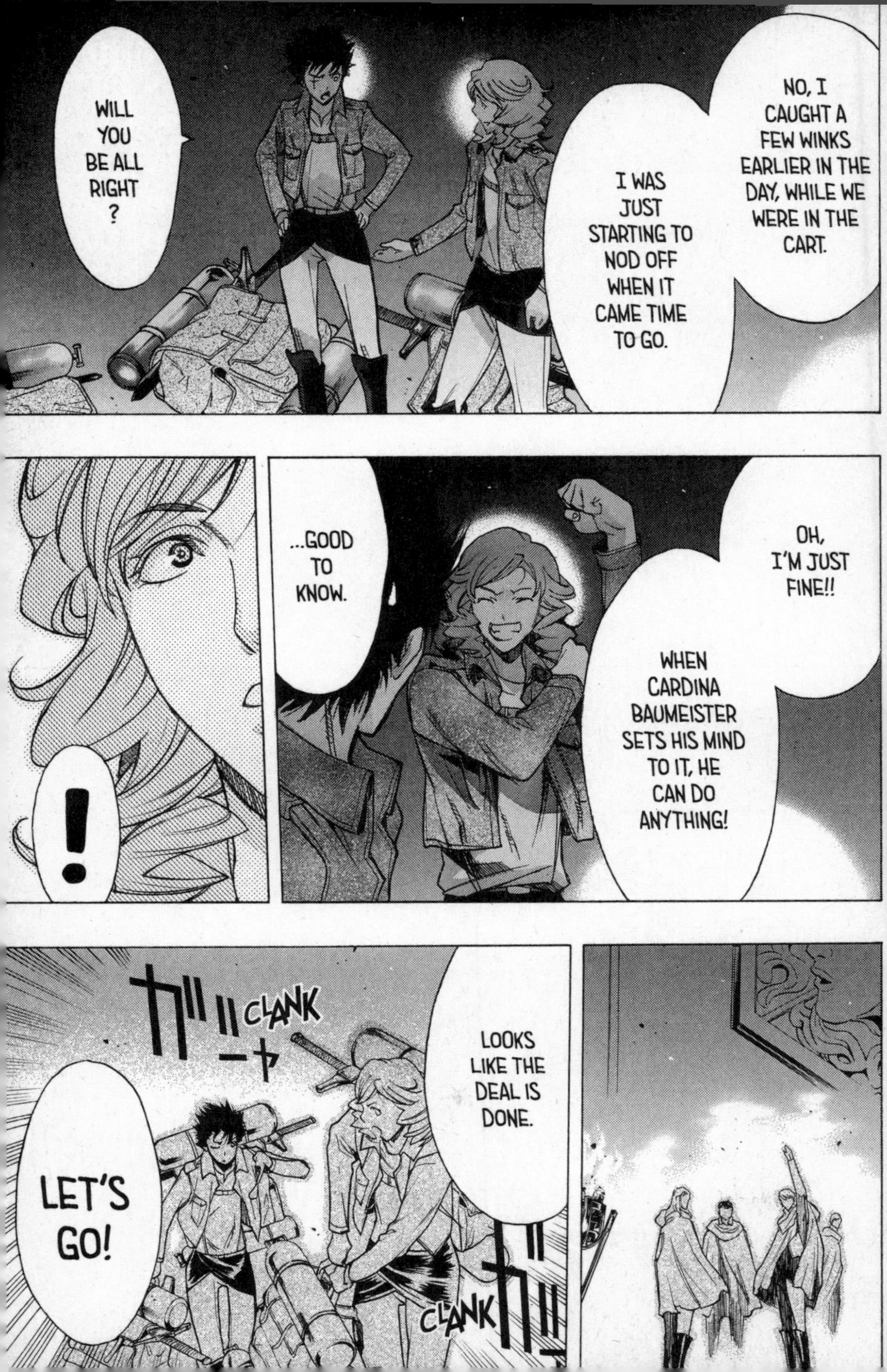
NO, I CAUGHT A FEW WINKS EARLIER IN THE DAY, WHILE WE WERE IN THE CART.
I WAS JUST STARTING TO NOD OFF WHEN IT CAME TIME TO GO.
WILL YOU BE ALL RIGHT?
OH, I'M JUST FINE!!
WHEN CARDINA BAUMEISTER SETS HIS MIND TO IT, HE CAN DO ANYTHING!
...GOOD TO KNOW.
!
LOOKS LIKE THE DEAL IS DONE.
CLANK
LET'S GO!
CLANK

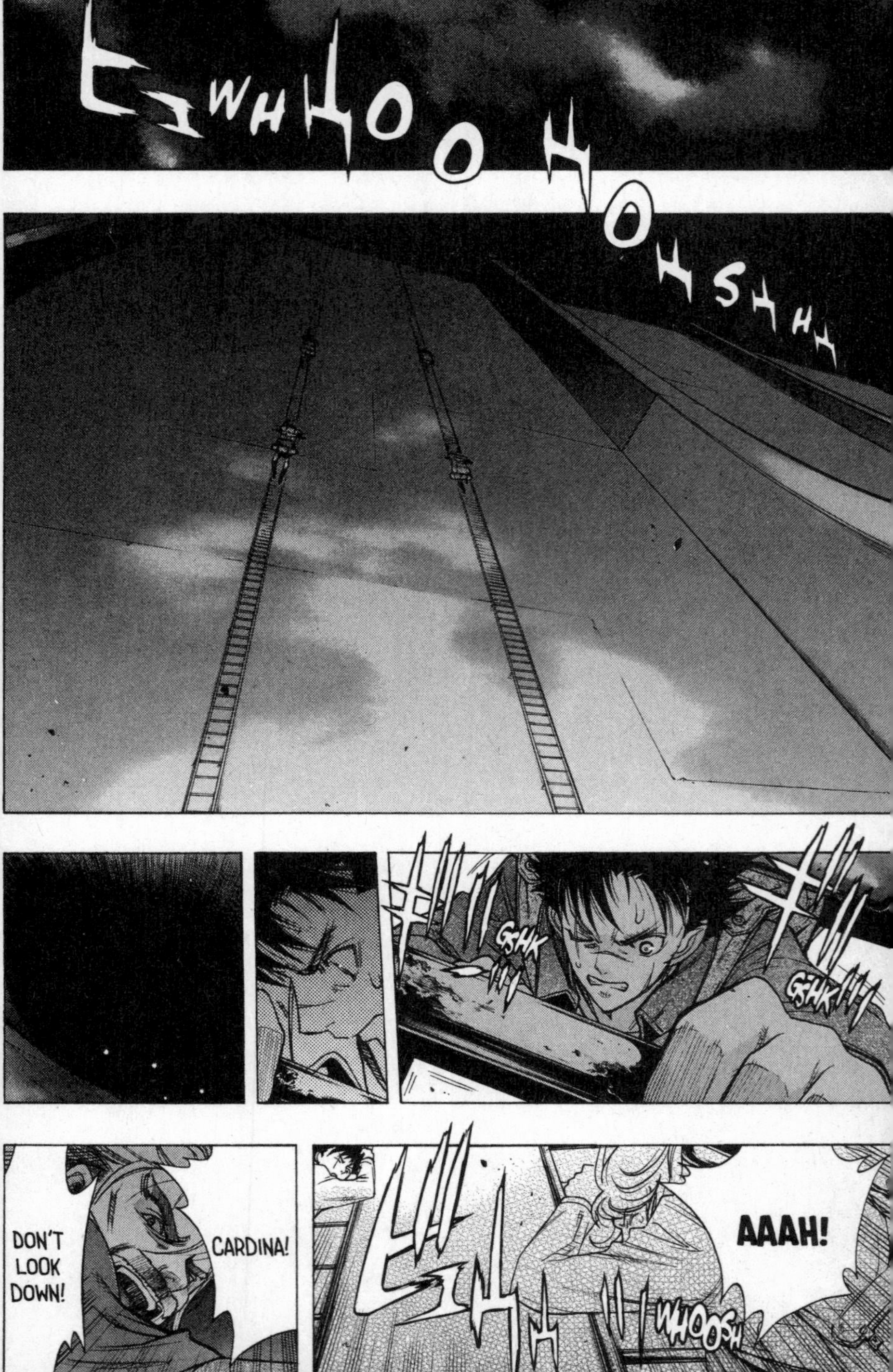
WHOOOSHHH
GSHK
GSHK
AAAH!
WHOOSH
CARDINA!
DON'T LOOK DOWN!

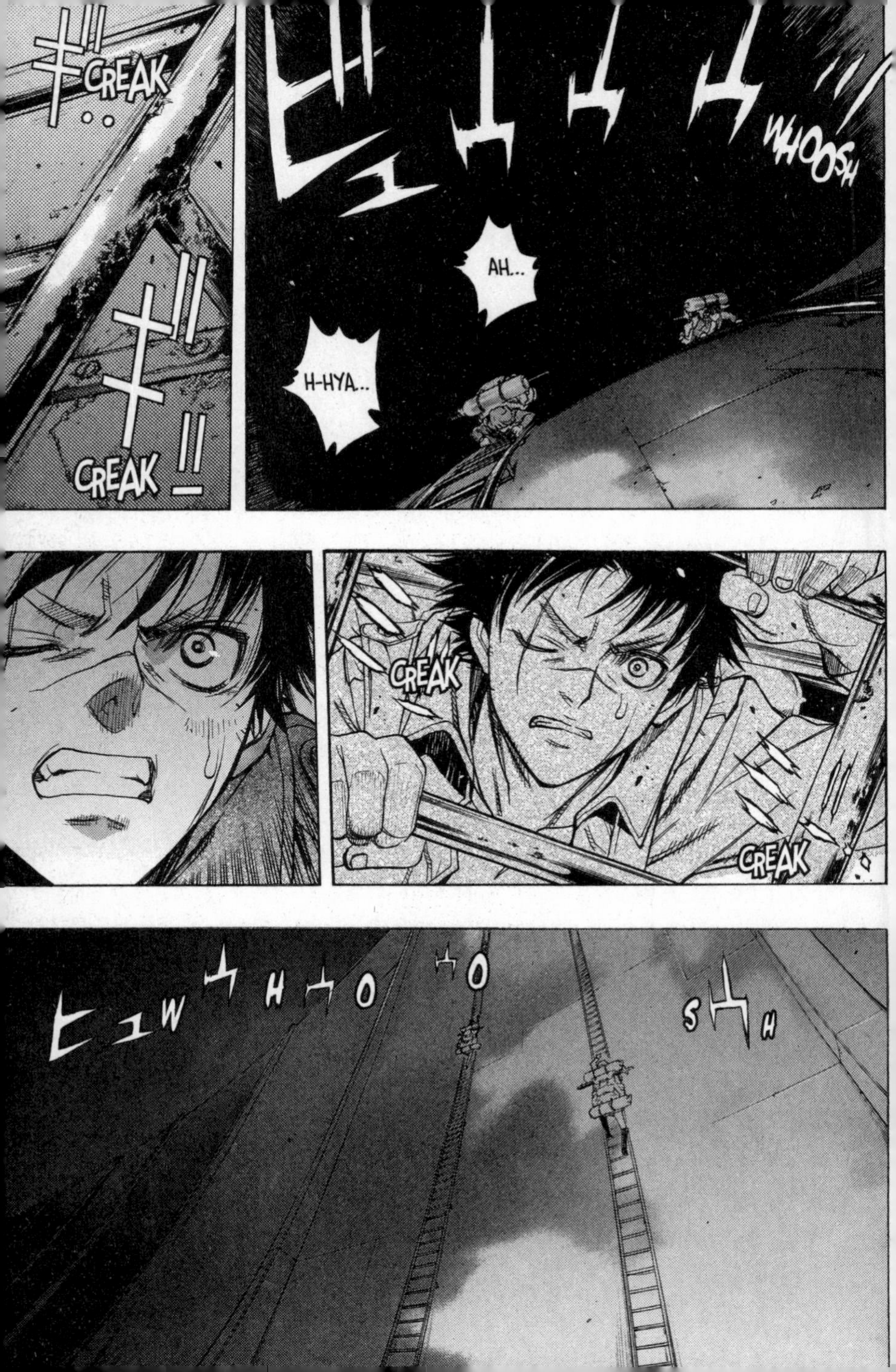
WHOOSH
AH...
H-HYA...
CREAK...
CREAK!!
CREAK
CREAK
WHOOSH

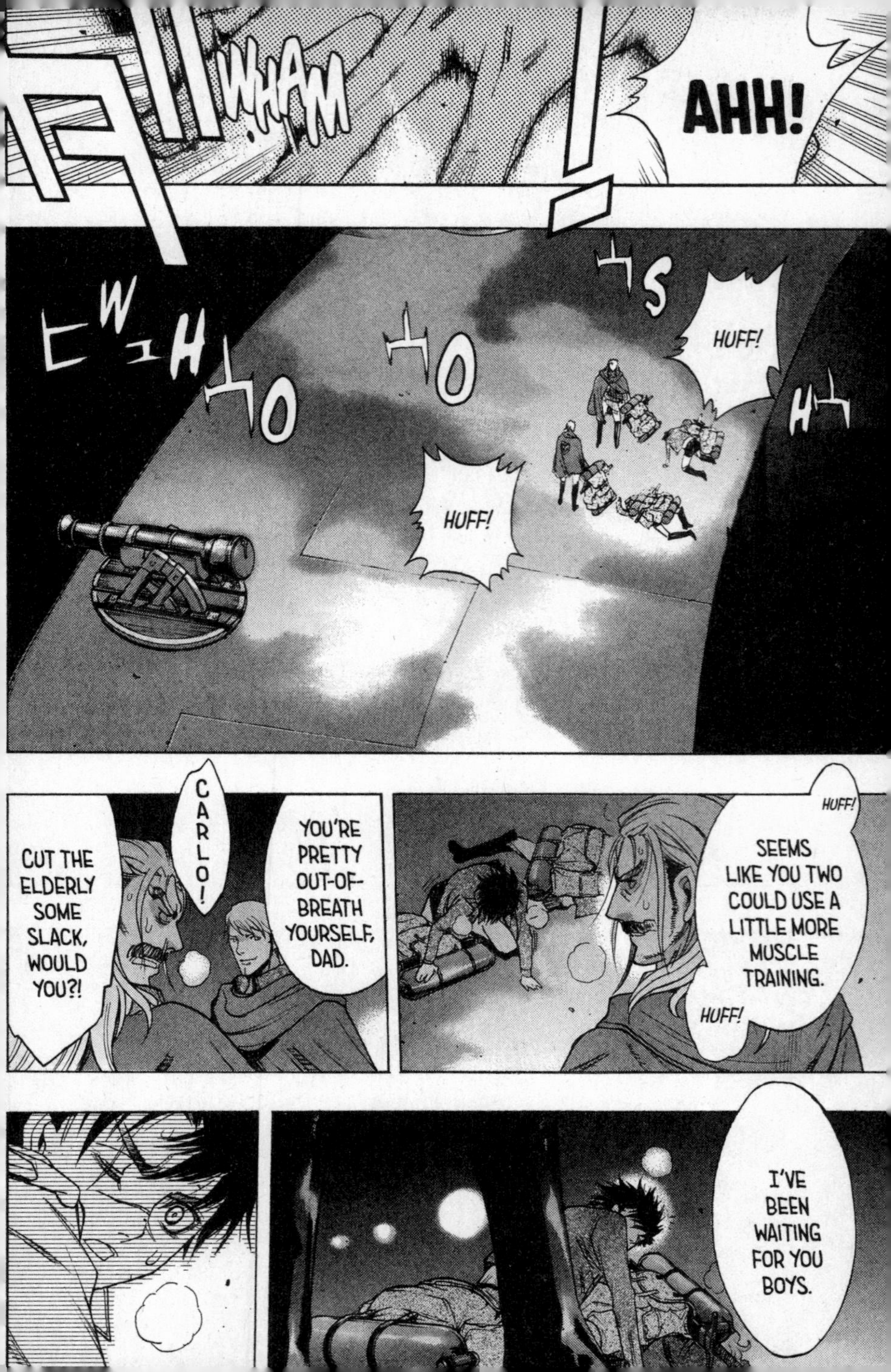
AHH!
WHAM
SHHH
WHOOOSH
HUFF!
HUFF!
HUFF!
SEEMS LIKE YOU TWO COULD USE A LITTLE MORE MUSCLE TRAINING.
HUFF!
YOU'RE PRETTY OUT-OF-BREATH YOURSELF, DAD.
CARLO!
CUT THE ELDERLY SOME SLACK, WOULD YOU?!
I'VE BEEN WAITING FOR YOU BOYS.

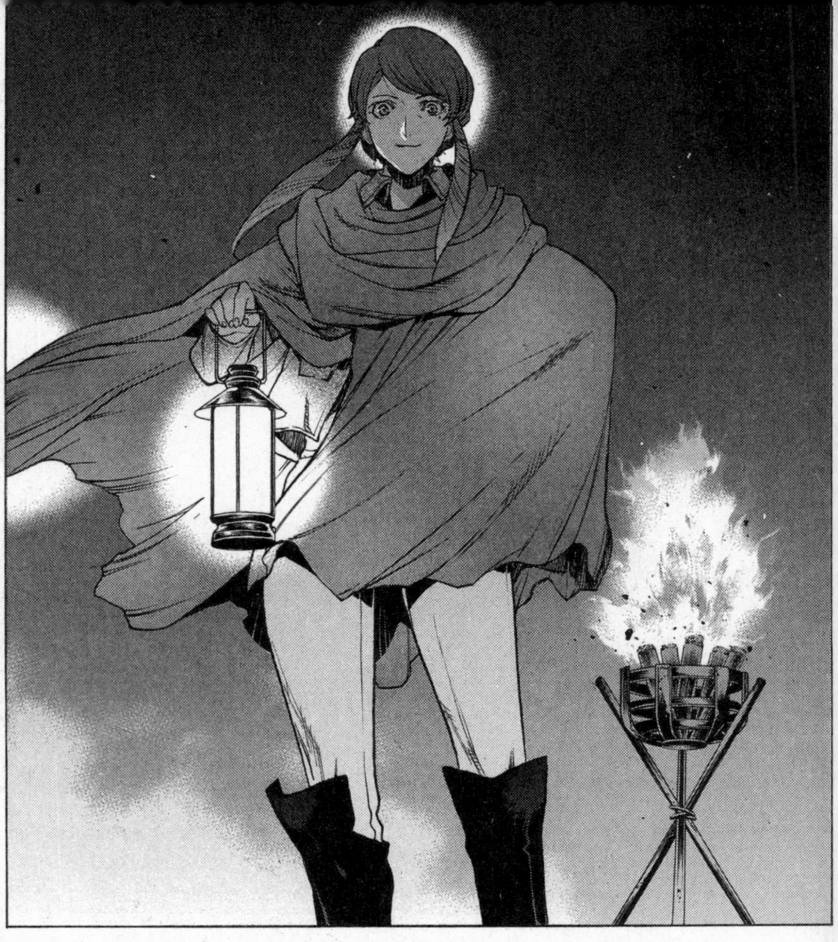

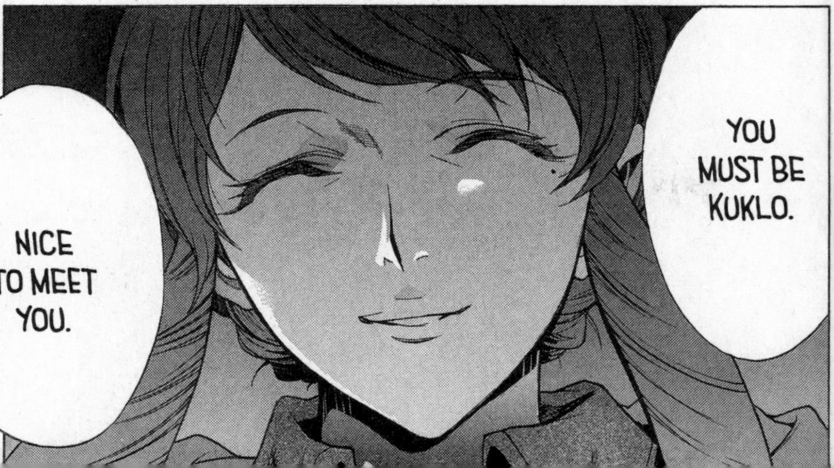
YOU MUST BE KUKLO.
NICE TO MEET YOU.

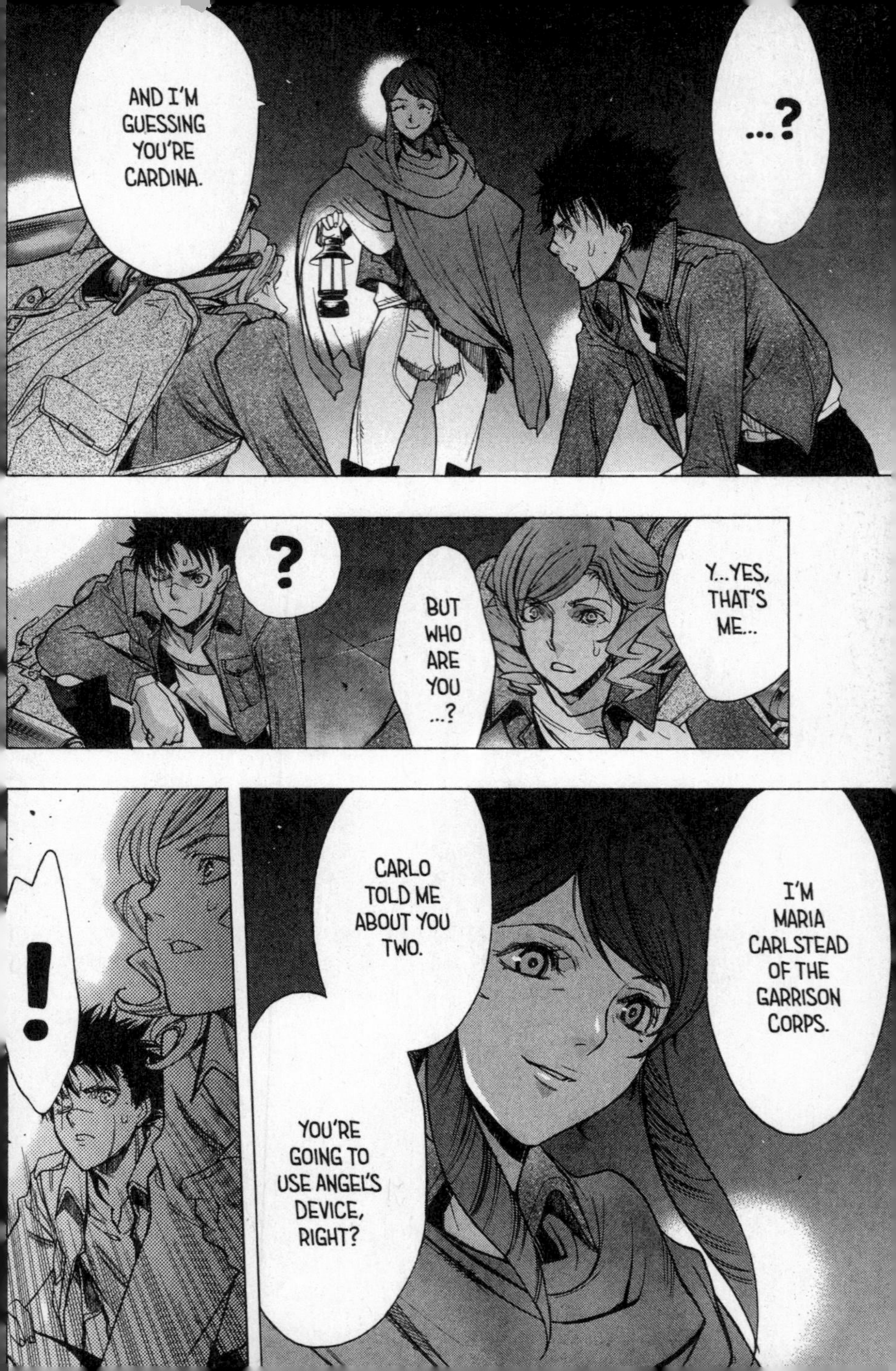
...?
AND I'M GUESSING YOU'RE CARDINA.
Y...YES, THAT'S ME...
BUT WHO ARE YOU ...?
?
I'M MARIA CARLSTEAD OF THE GARRISON CORPS.
CARLO TOLD ME ABOUT YOU TWO.
YOU'RE GOING TO USE ANGEL'S DEVICE, RIGHT?
!

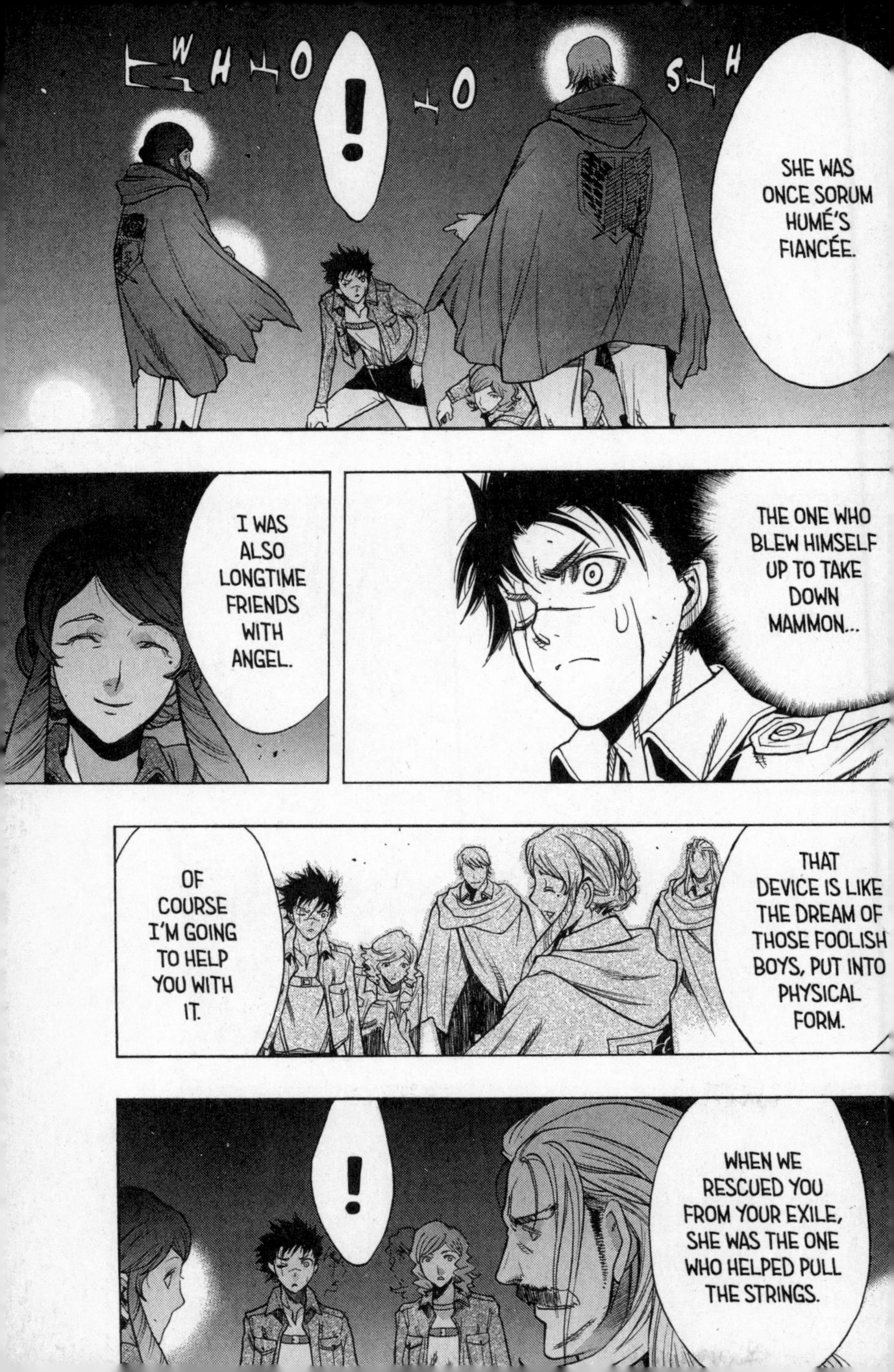
SHE WAS ONCE SORUM HUMÉ'S FIANCÉE.
!
THE ONE WHO BLEW HIMSELF UP TO TAKE DOWN MAMMON...
I WAS ALSO LONGTIME FRIENDS WITH ANGEL.
THAT DEVICE IS LIKE THE DREAM OF THOSE FOOLISH BOYS, PUT INTO PHYSICAL FORM.
OF COURSE I'M GOING TO HELP YOU WITH IT.
WHEN WE RESCUED YOU FROM YOUR EXILE, SHE WAS THE ONE WHO HELPED PULL THE STRINGS.
!

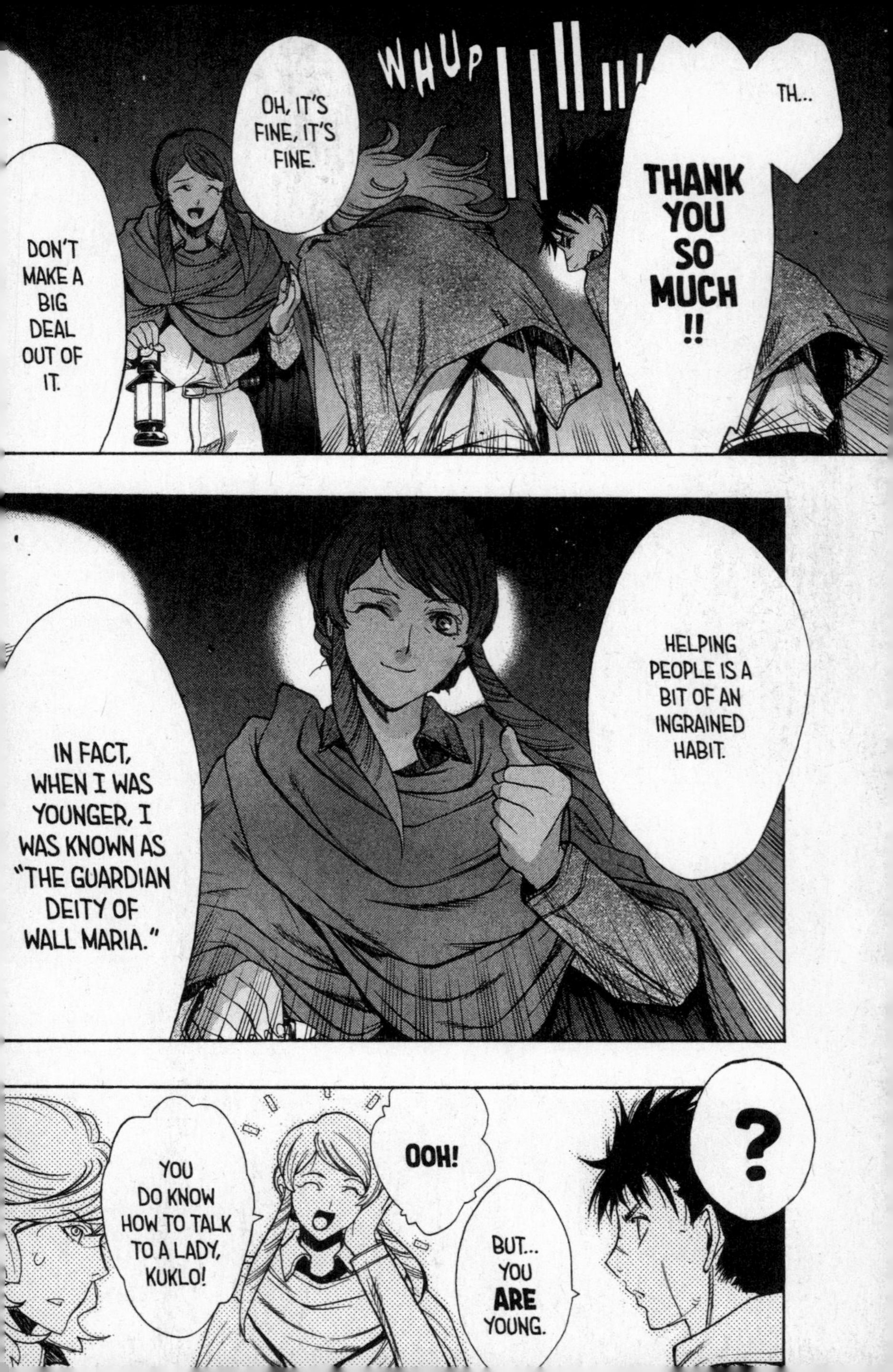
TH...
THANK YOU SO MUCH!!
WHUP
OH, IT'S FINE, IT'S FINE.
DON'T MAKE A BIG DEAL OUT OF IT.
HELPING PEOPLE IS A BIT OF AN INGRAINED HABIT.
IN FACT, WHEN I WAS YOUNGER, I WAS KNOWN AS "THE GUARDIAN DEITY OF WALL MARIA."
?
BUT... YOU **ARE** YOUNG.
OOH!
YOU DO KNOW HOW TO TALK TO A LADY, KUKLO!

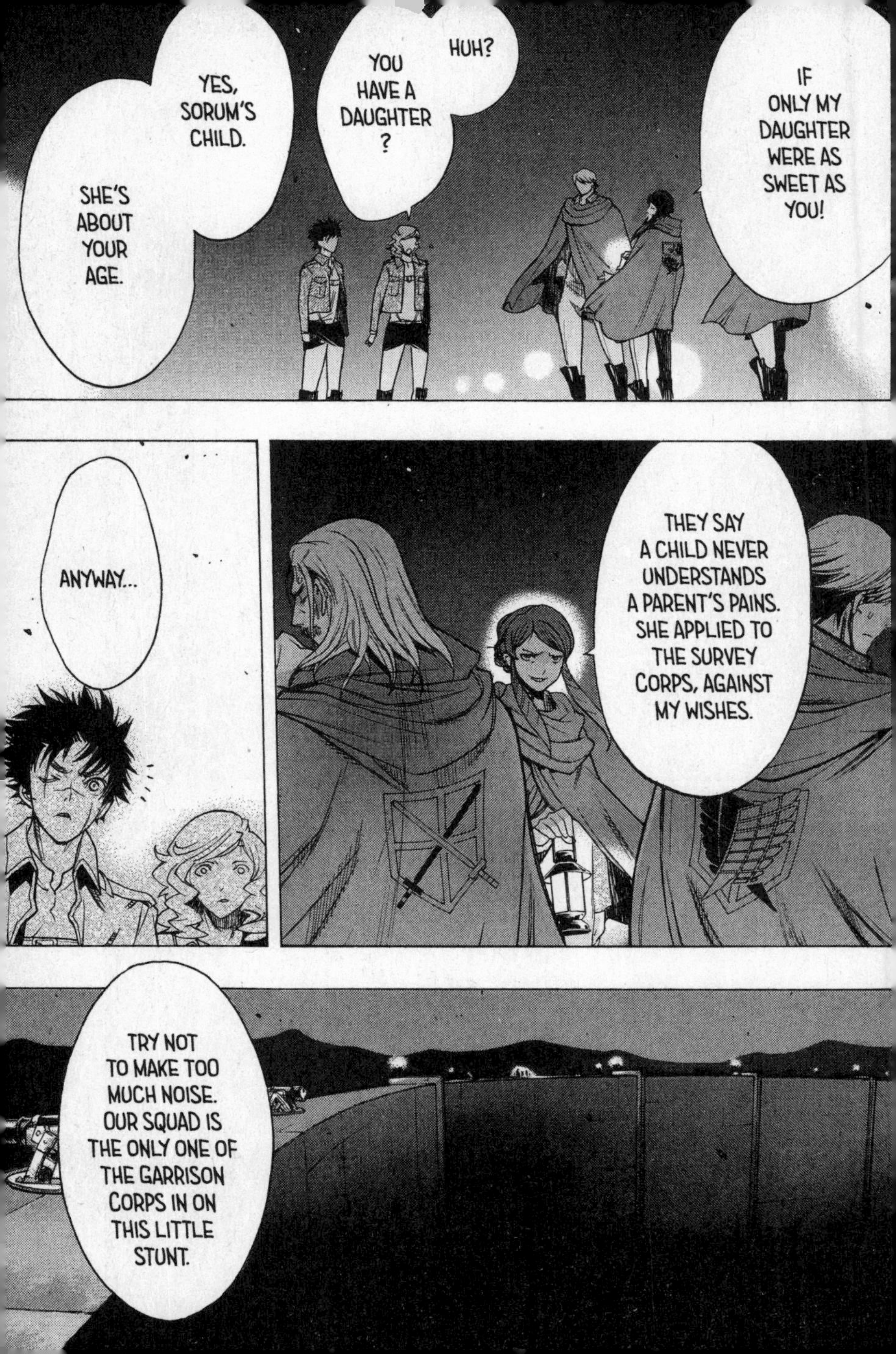
IF ONLY MY DAUGHTER WERE AS SWEET AS YOU!
HUH?
YOU HAVE A DAUGHTER ?
YES, SORUM'S CHILD.
SHE'S ABOUT YOUR AGE.
THEY SAY A CHILD NEVER UNDERSTANDS A PARENT'S PAINS. SHE APPLIED TO THE SURVEY CORPS, AGAINST MY WISHES.
ANYWAY...
TRY NOT TO MAKE TOO MUCH NOISE. OUR SQUAD IS THE ONLY ONE OF THE GARRISON CORPS IN ON THIS LITTLE STUNT.

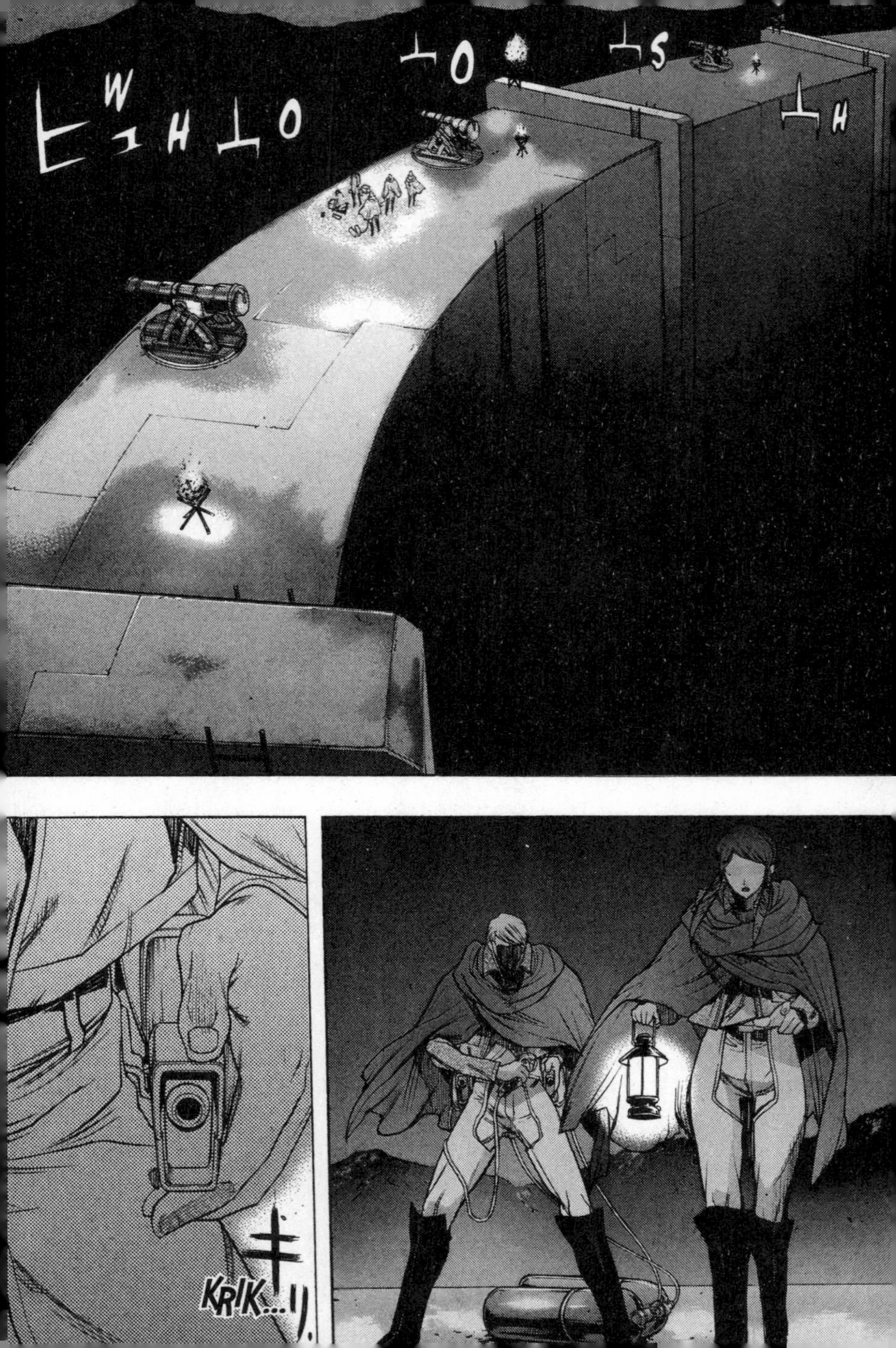
KRIK...!!

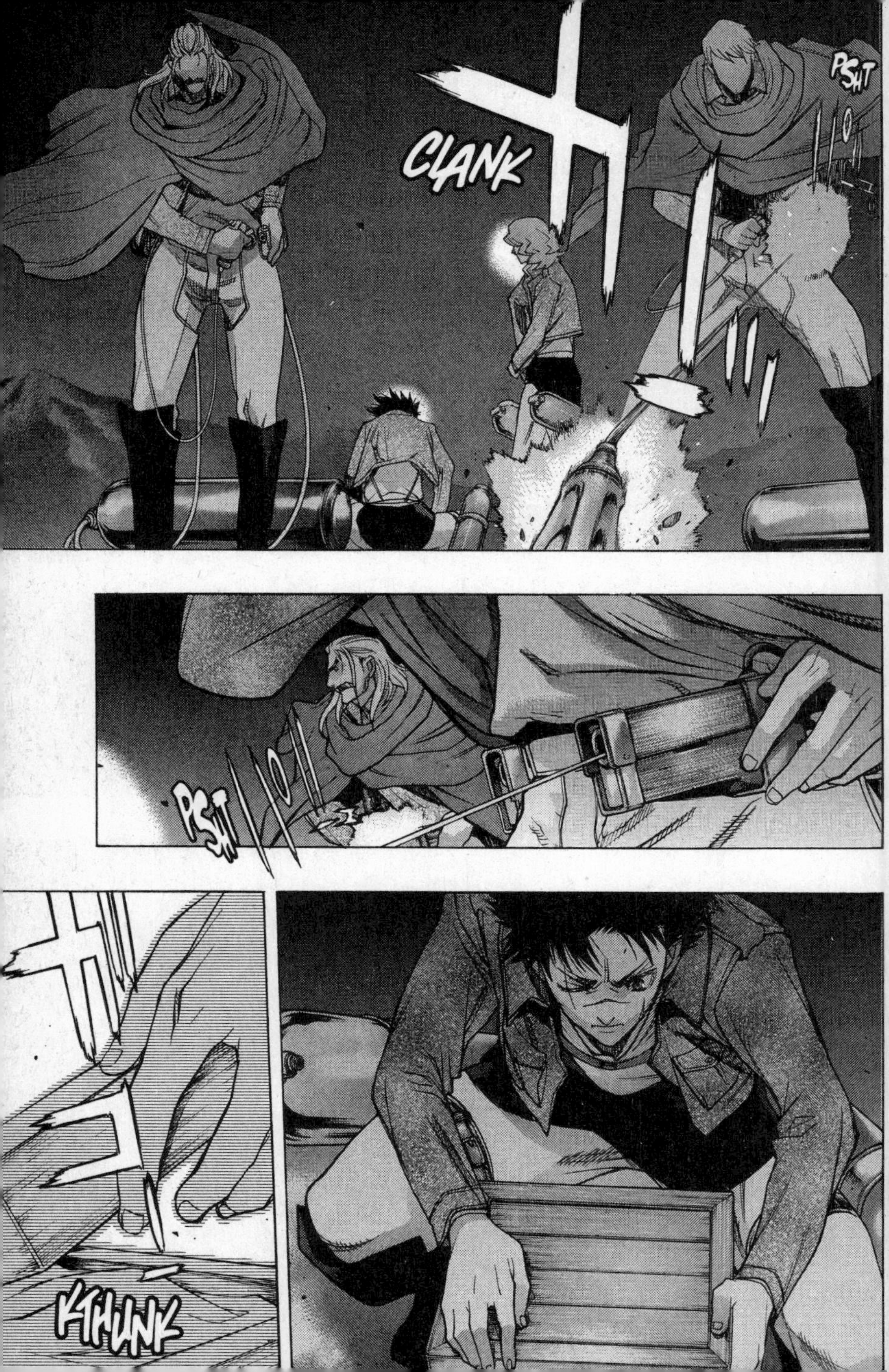
PSHT
CLANK
PSHT
KTHUNK

IS IT...
A NEW
MODEL?

LOOK
AT
THAT!

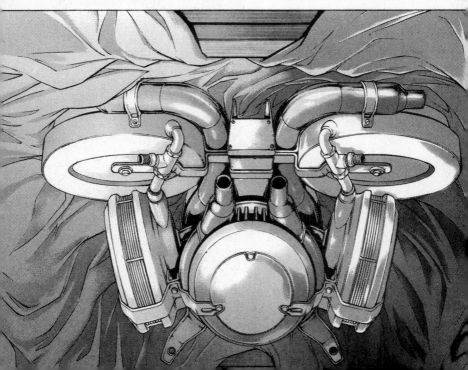

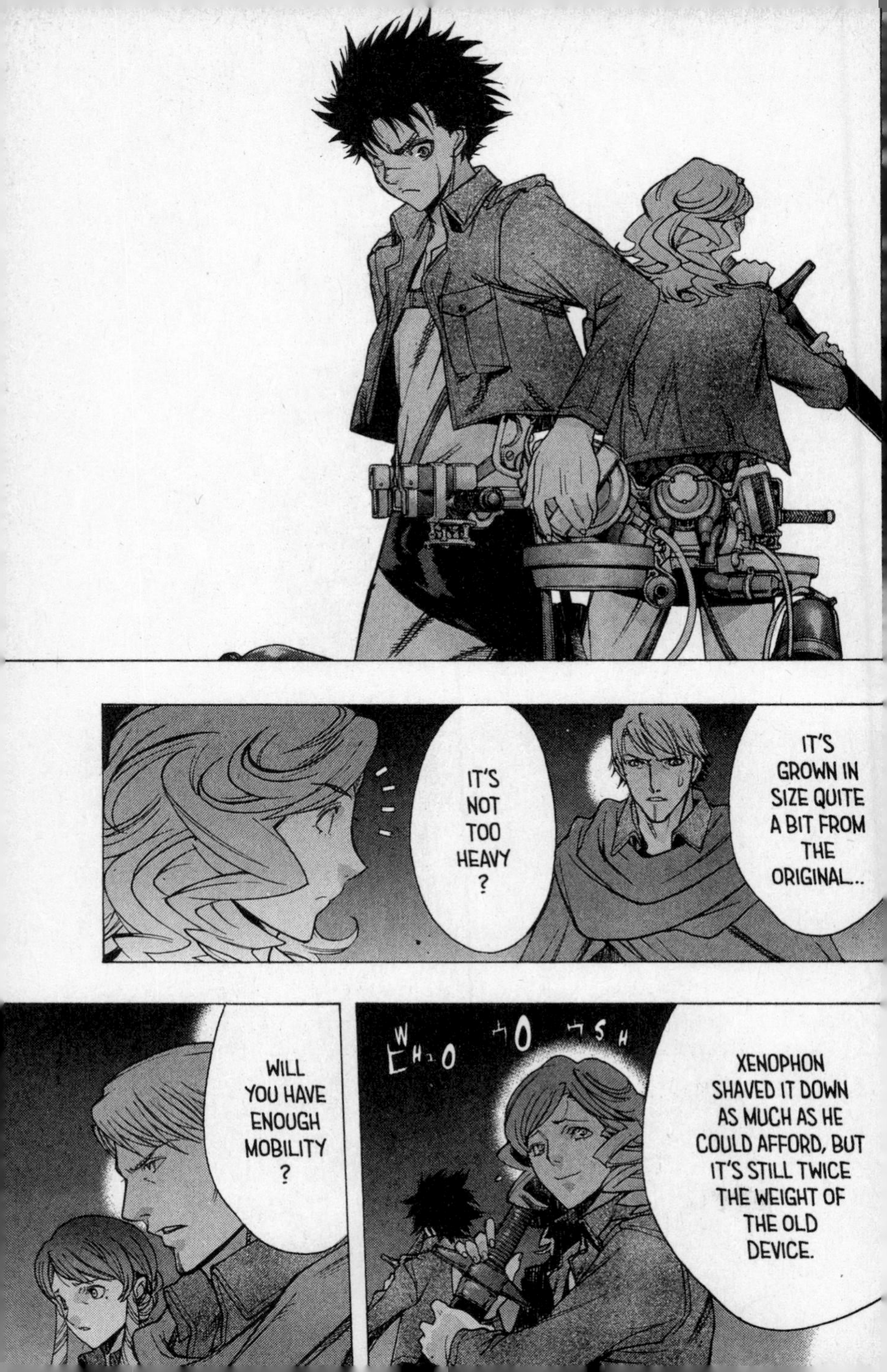
IT'S GROWN IN SIZE QUITE A BIT FROM THE ORIGINAL...
IT'S NOT TOO HEAVY ?
XENOPHON SHAVED IT DOWN AS MUCH AS HE COULD AFFORD, BUT IT'S STILL TWICE THE WEIGHT OF THE OLD DEVICE.
WILL YOU HAVE ENOUGH MOBILITY ?

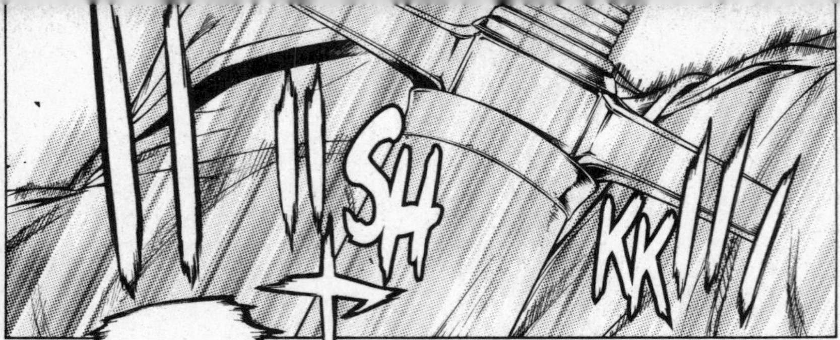
SHKK

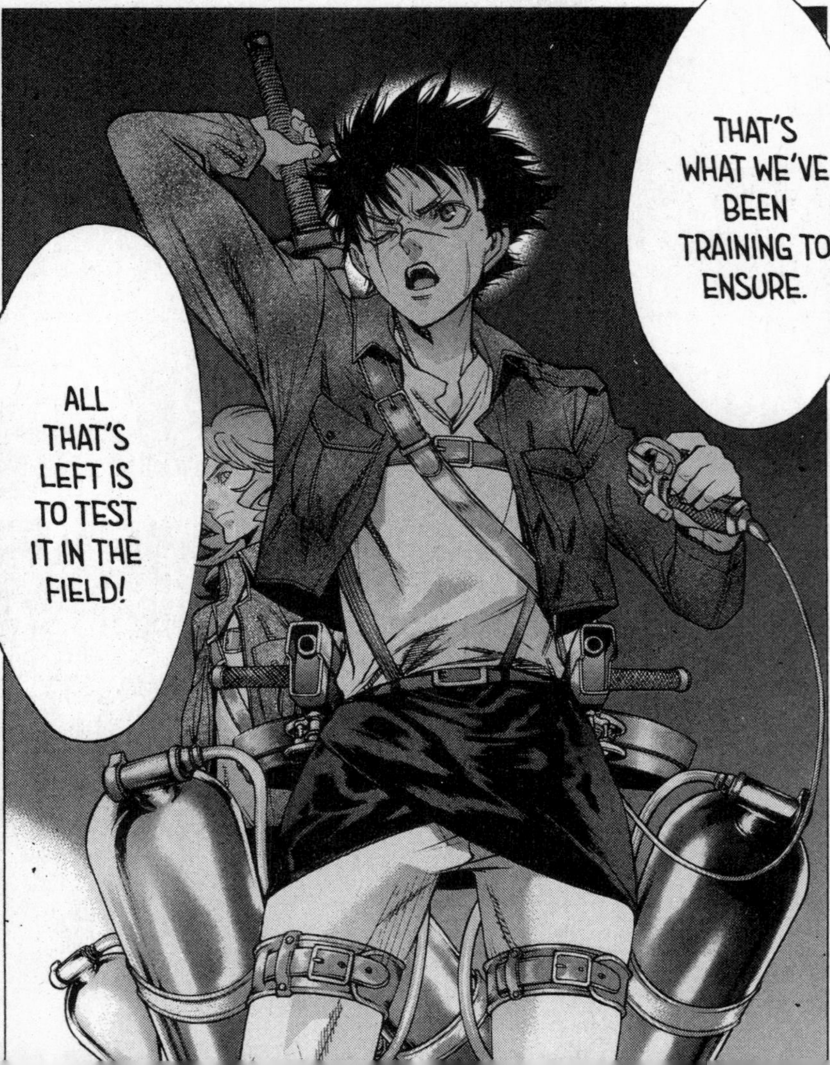
THAT'S WHAT WE'VE BEEN TRAINING TO ENSURE.
ALL THAT'S LEFT IS TO TEST IT IN THE FIELD!

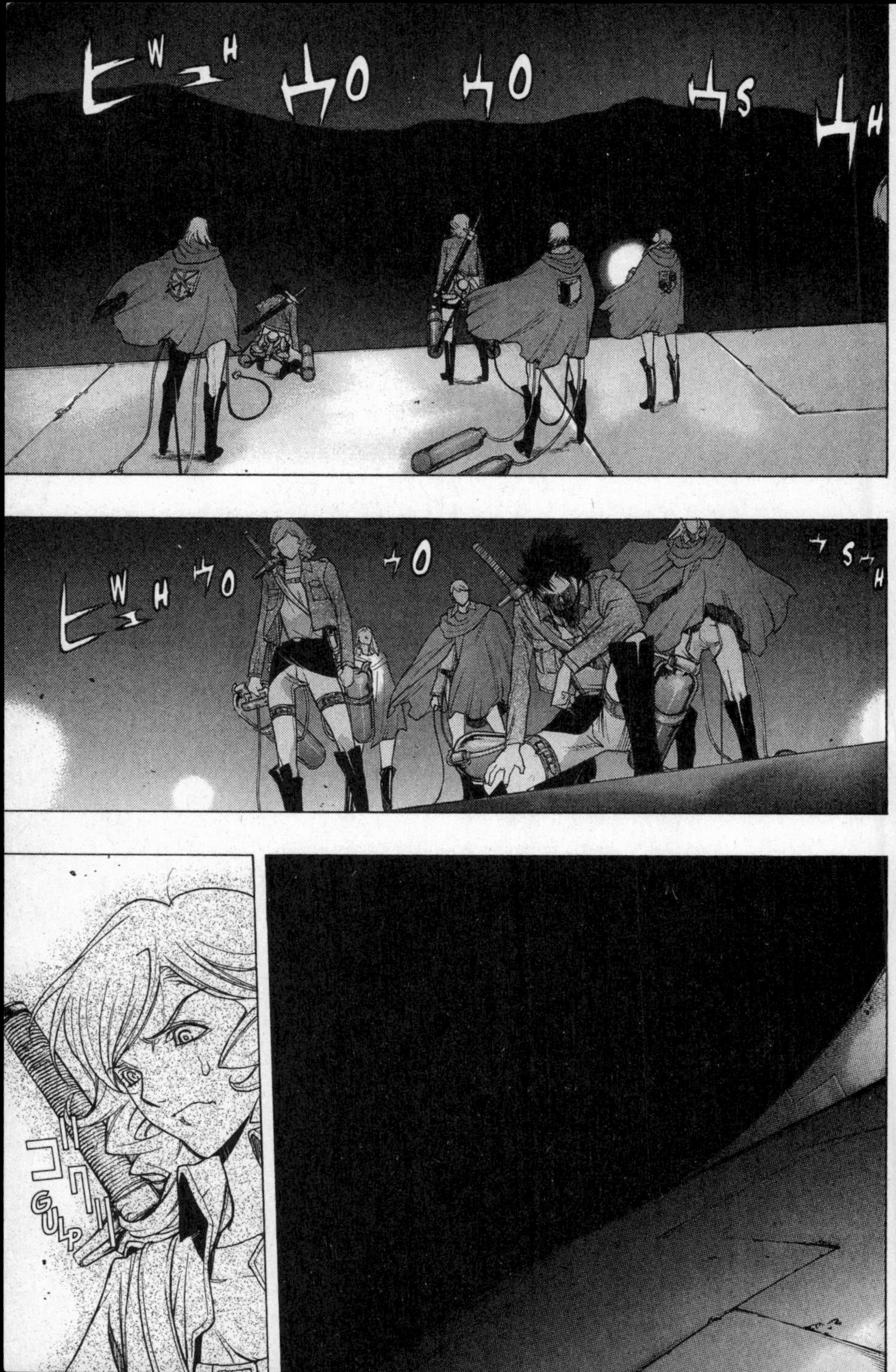
WHOOSH
WHOOSH
GULP

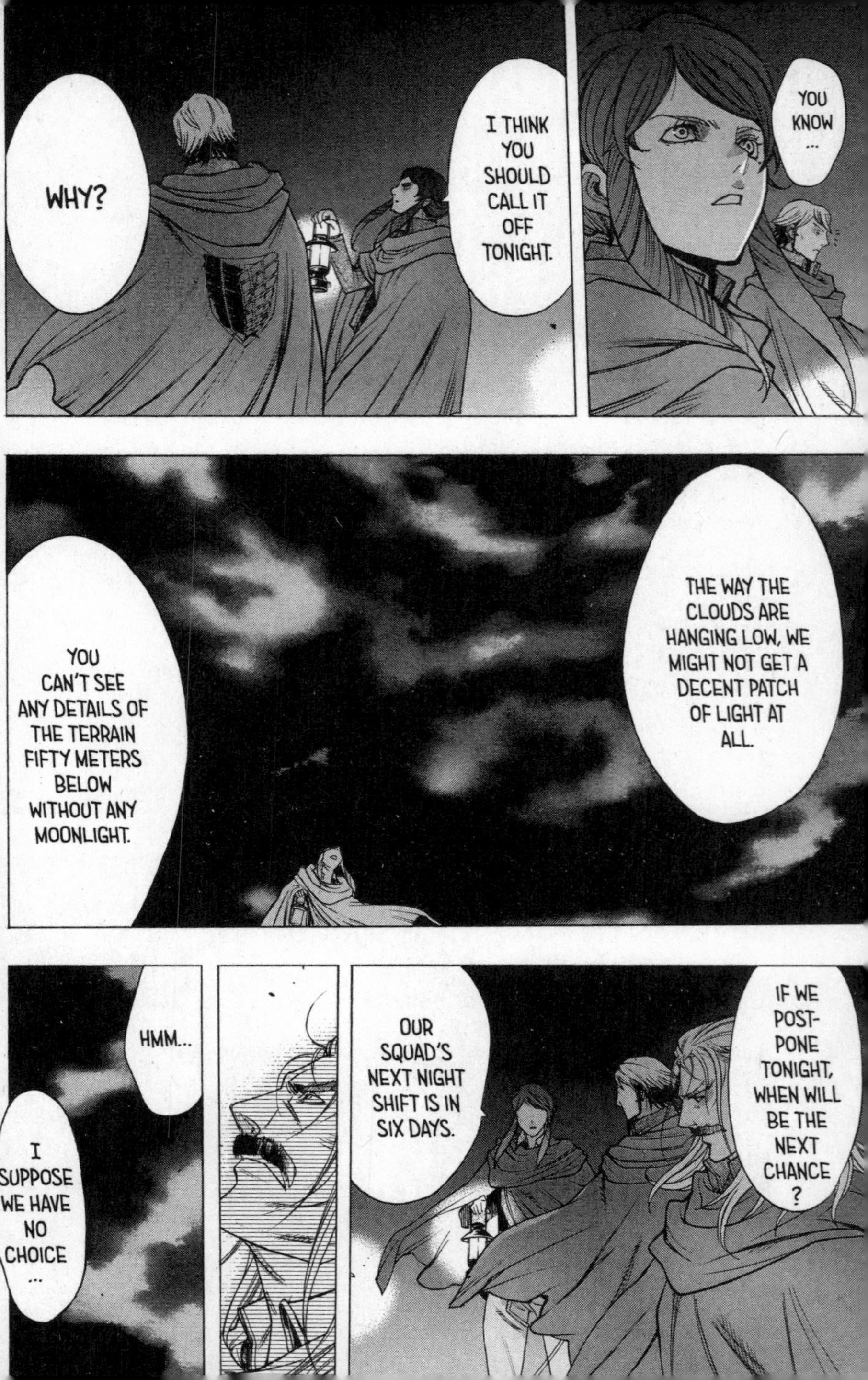
YOU KNOW ...
I THINK YOU SHOULD CALL IT OFF TONIGHT.
WHY?
THE WAY THE CLOUDS ARE HANGING LOW, WE MIGHT NOT GET A DECENT PATCH OF LIGHT AT ALL.
YOU CAN'T SEE ANY DETAILS OF THE TERRAIN FIFTY METERS BELOW WITHOUT ANY MOONLIGHT.
IF WE POST-PONE TONIGHT, WHEN WILL BE THE NEXT CHANCE ?
OUR SQUAD'S NEXT NIGHT SHIFT IS IN SIX DAYS.
HMM...
I SUPPOSE WE HAVE NO CHOICE ...

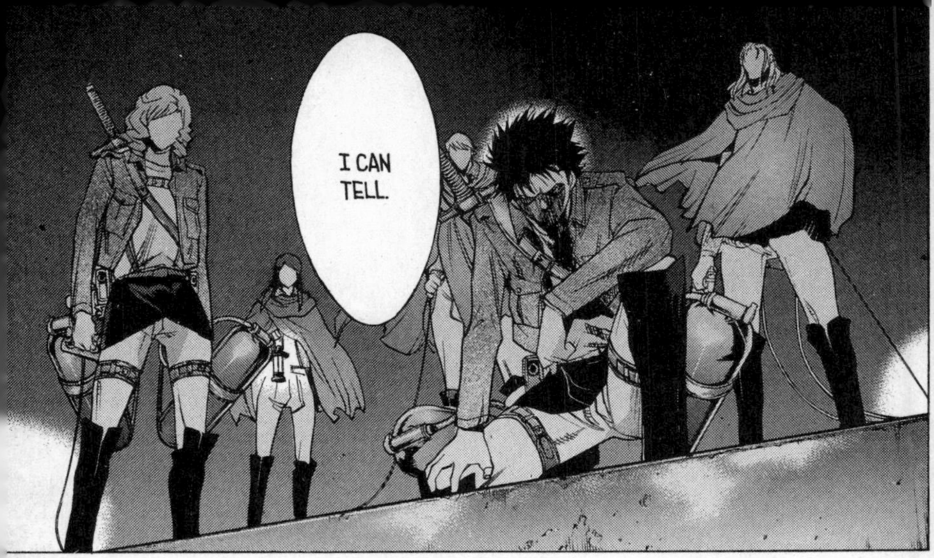
I CAN TELL.
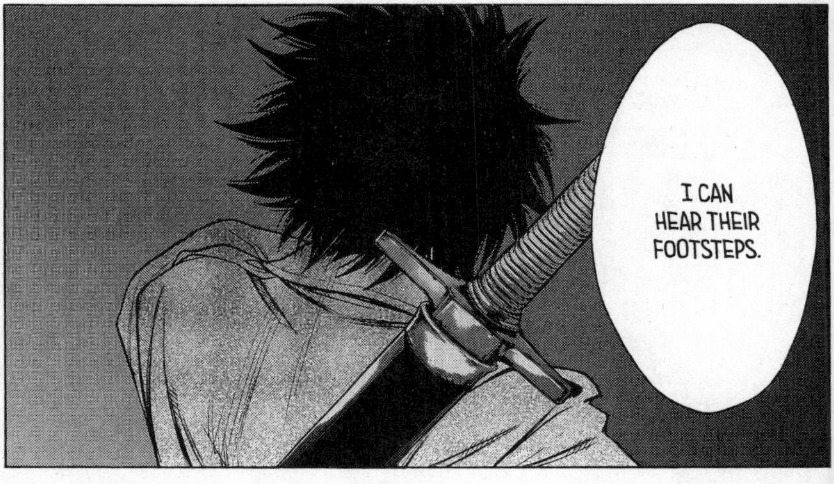
I CAN HEAR THEIR FOOTSTEPS.
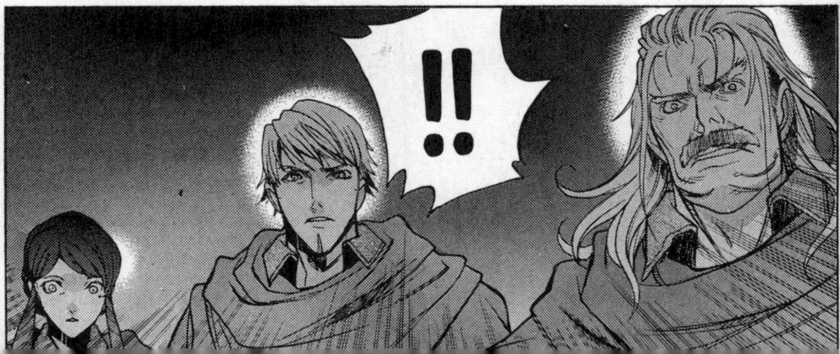
!!

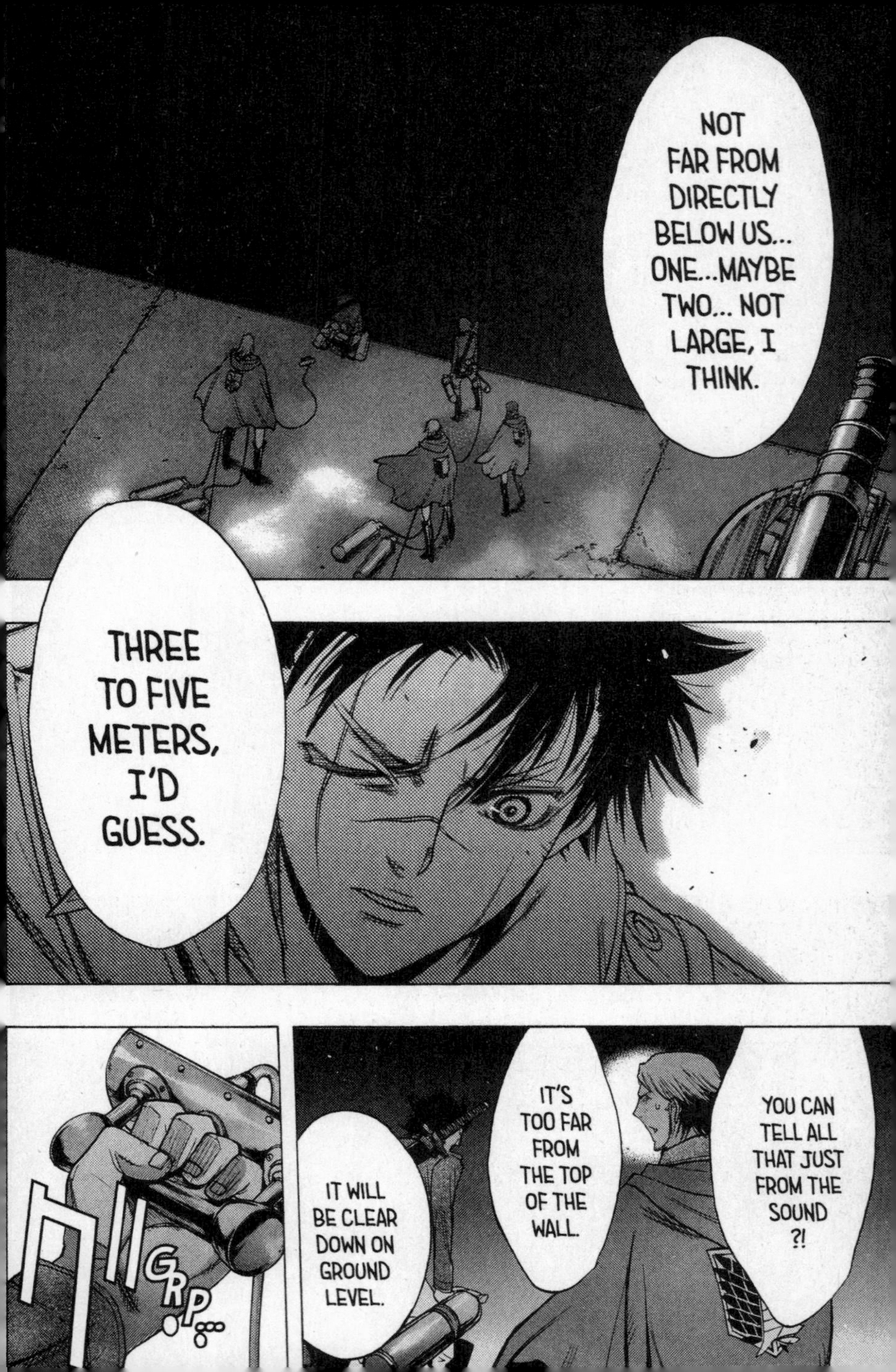
NOT FAR FROM DIRECTLY BELOW US... ONE...MAYBE TWO... NOT LARGE, I THINK.
THREE TO FIVE METERS, I'D GUESS.
YOU CAN TELL ALL THAT JUST FROM THE SOUND ?!
IT'S TOO FAR FROM THE TOP OF THE WALL.
IT WILL BE CLEAR DOWN ON GROUND LEVEL.
GRP...

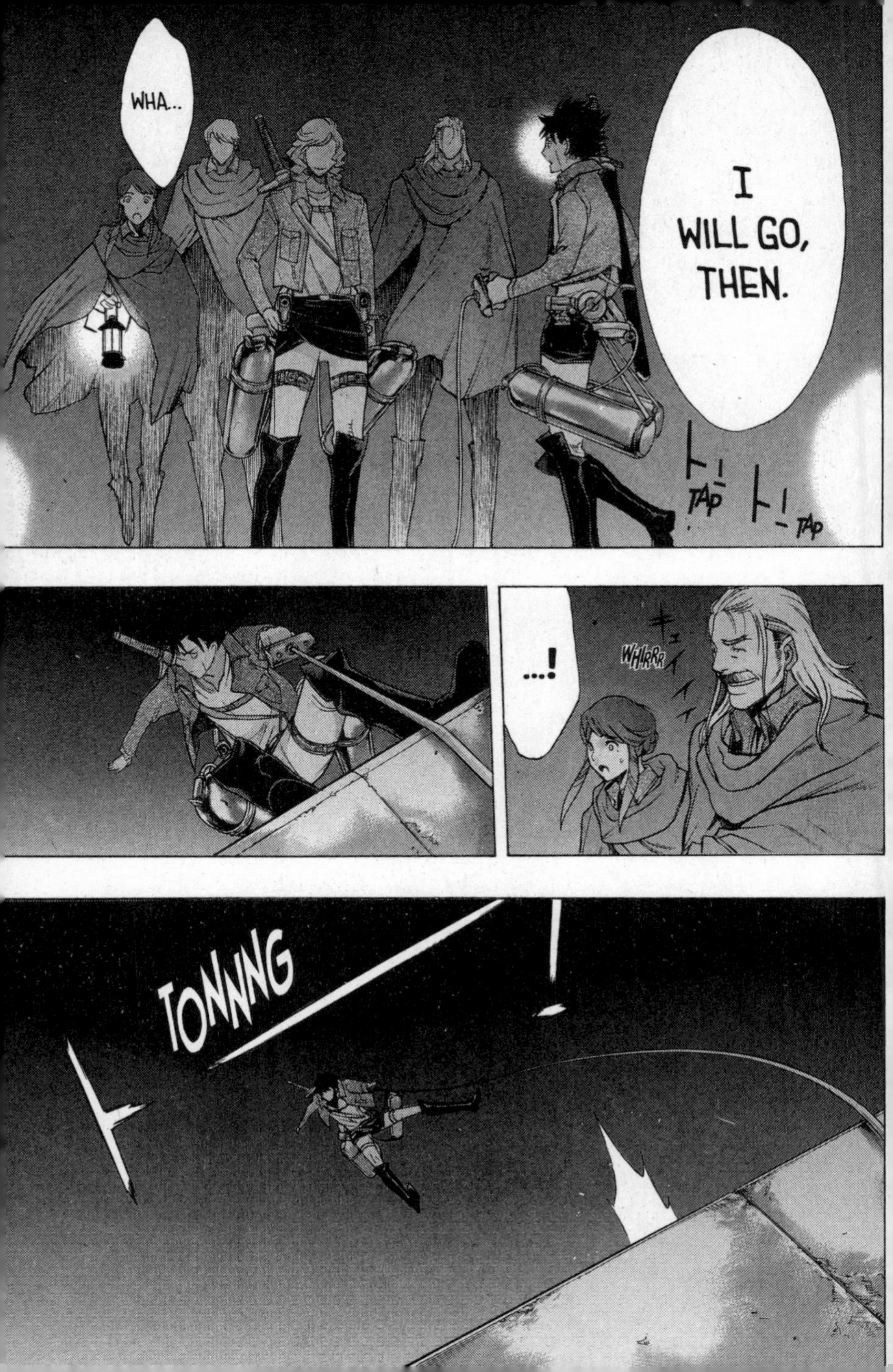
I WILL GO, THEN.
TAP TAP
WHA...
WHIRRR
...!
TONNNG

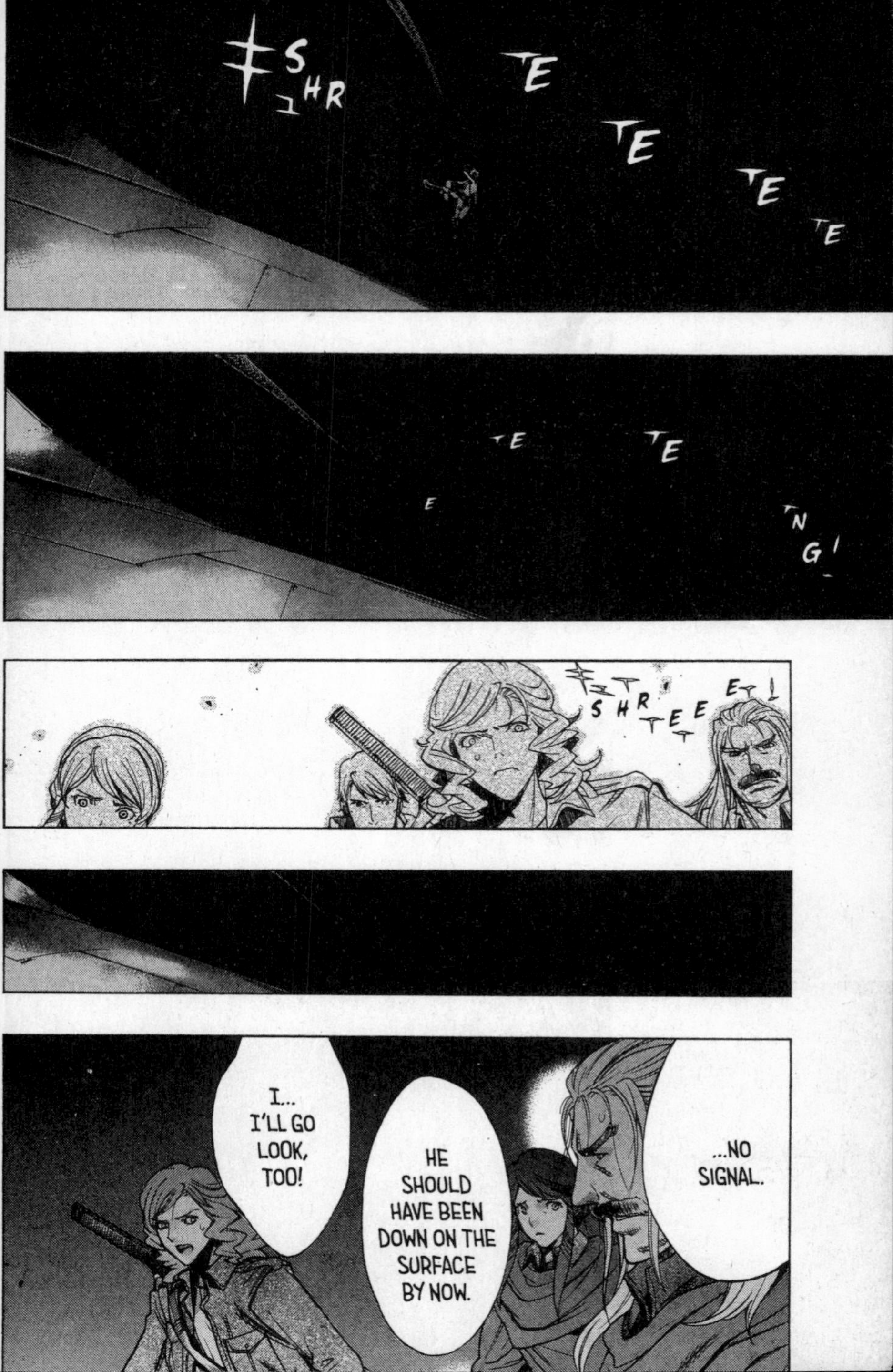
SHRTETETETE
TETEENG!
SHRTEEEE!
...NO SIGNAL.
HE SHOULD HAVE BEEN DOWN ON THE SURFACE BY NOW.
I... I'LL GO LOOK, TOO!

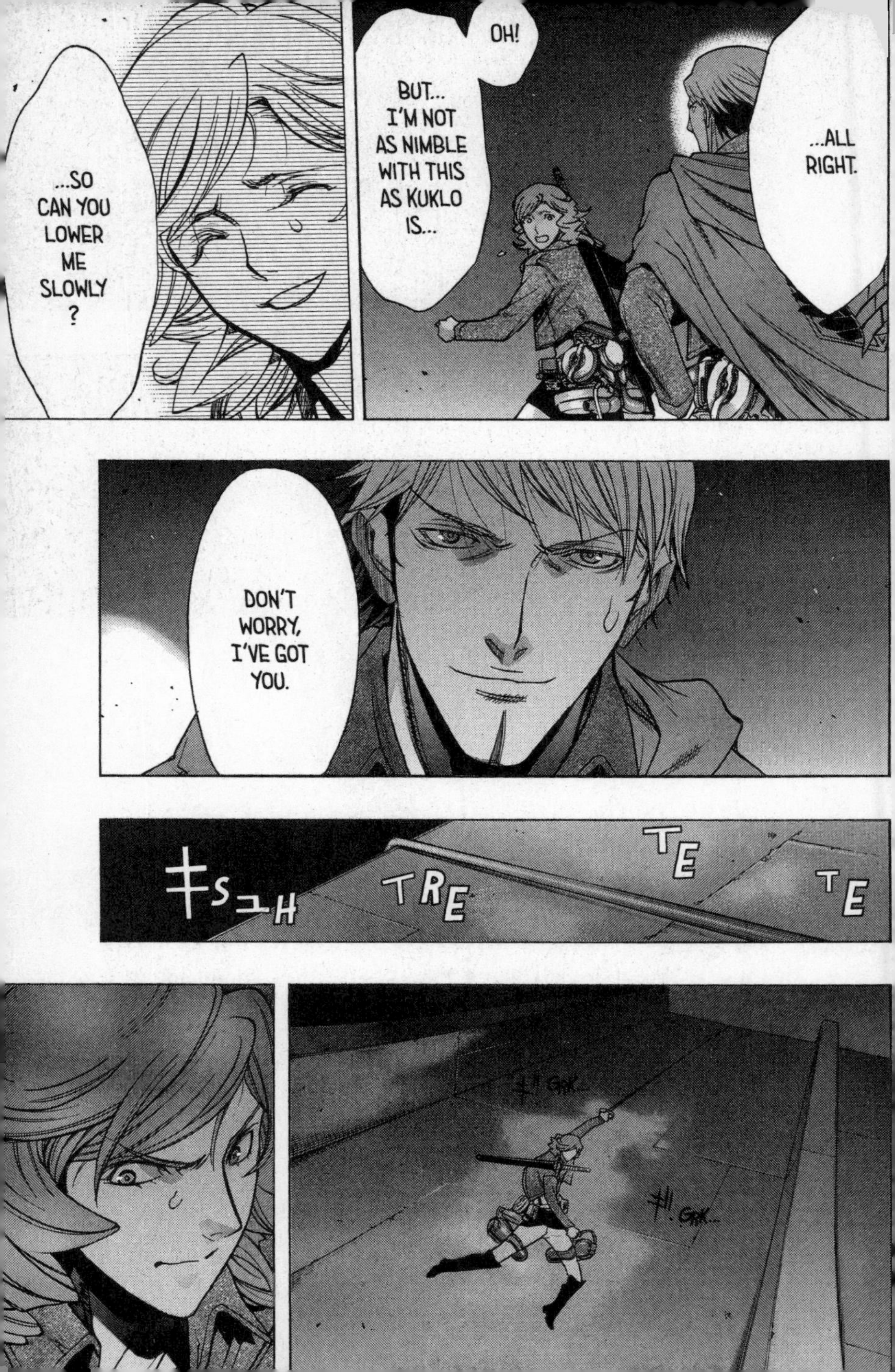
...ALL RIGHT.
OH!
BUT... I'M NOT AS NIMBLE WITH THIS AS KUKLO IS...
...SO CAN YOU LOWER ME SLOWLY ?
DON'T WORRY, I'VE GOT YOU.
TE
TE
TRE
GRK...
GRK...

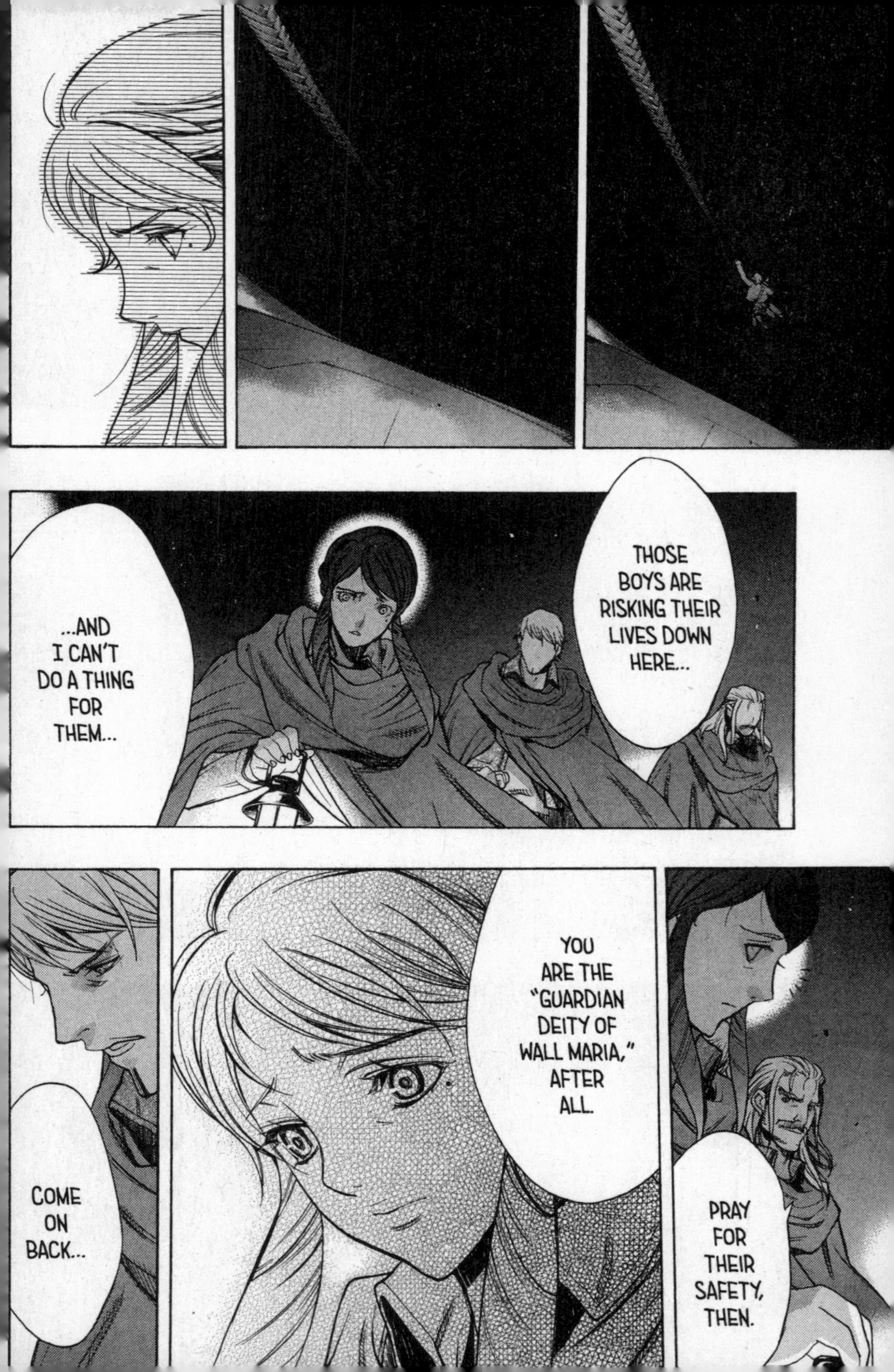
THOSE BOYS ARE RISKING THEIR LIVES DOWN HERE...
...AND I CAN'T DO A THING FOR THEM...
PRAY FOR THEIR SAFETY, THEN.
YOU ARE THE "GUARDIAN DEITY OF WALL MARIA," AFTER ALL.
COME ON BACK...

YOU ARE BOTH FULL-FLEDGED SOLDIERS OF THE SURVEY CORPS NOW.
CRIK
CRIK...
CRIK...
I THINK I MUST BE TWO-THIRDS OF THE WAY DOWN...
KUKLO...
IF YOU'RE NOT ABLE TO SEND A SIGNAL, IT MUST MEAN...
FWUF

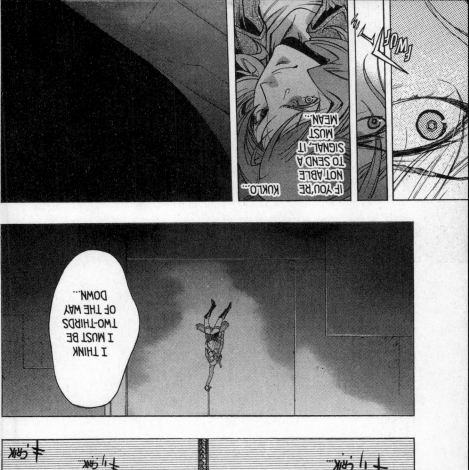

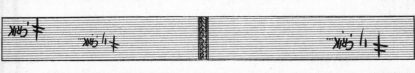

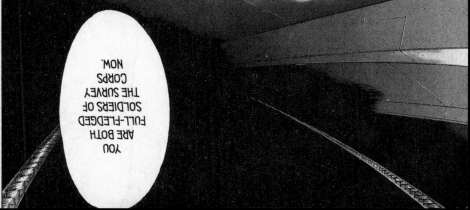

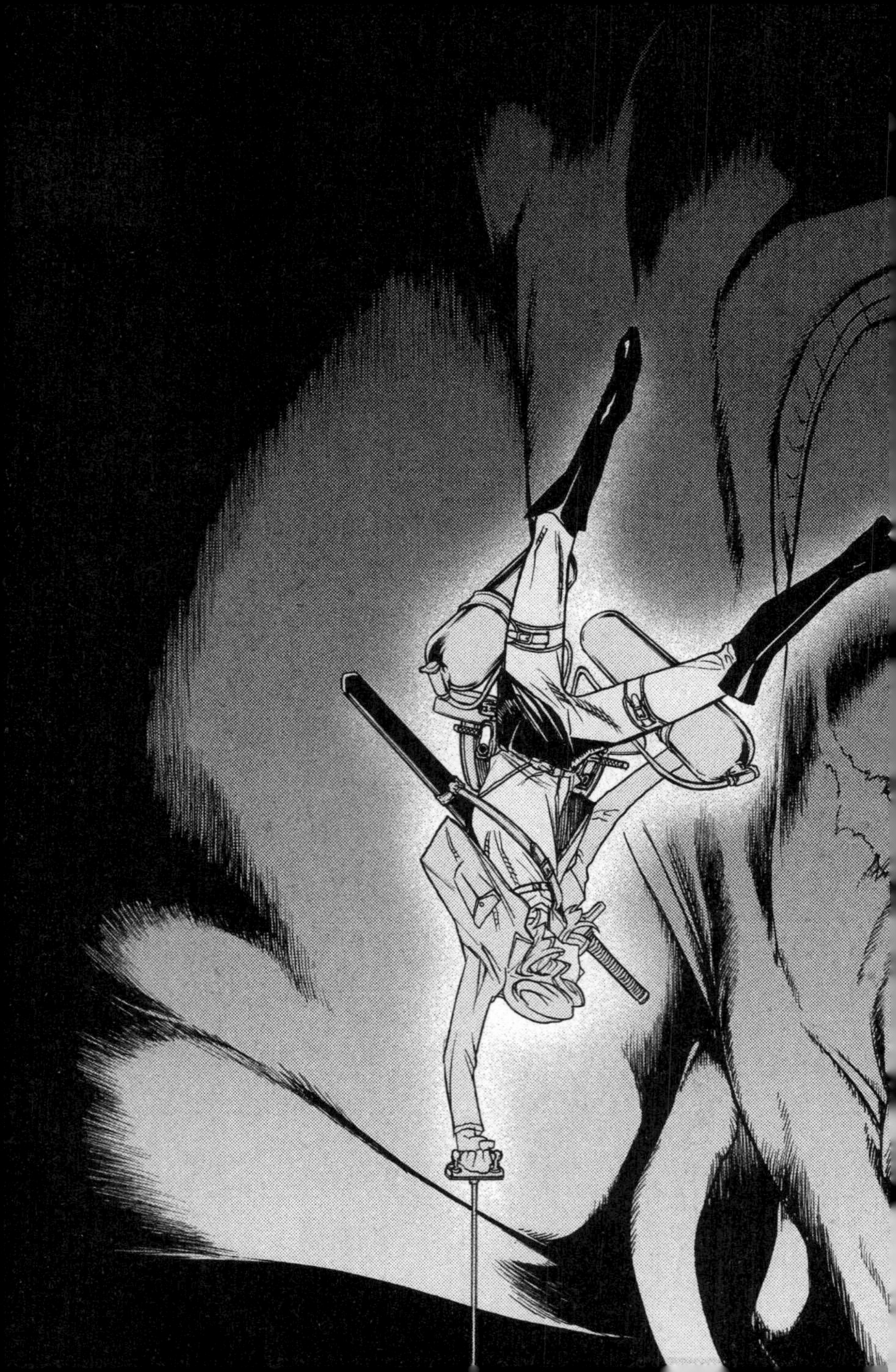

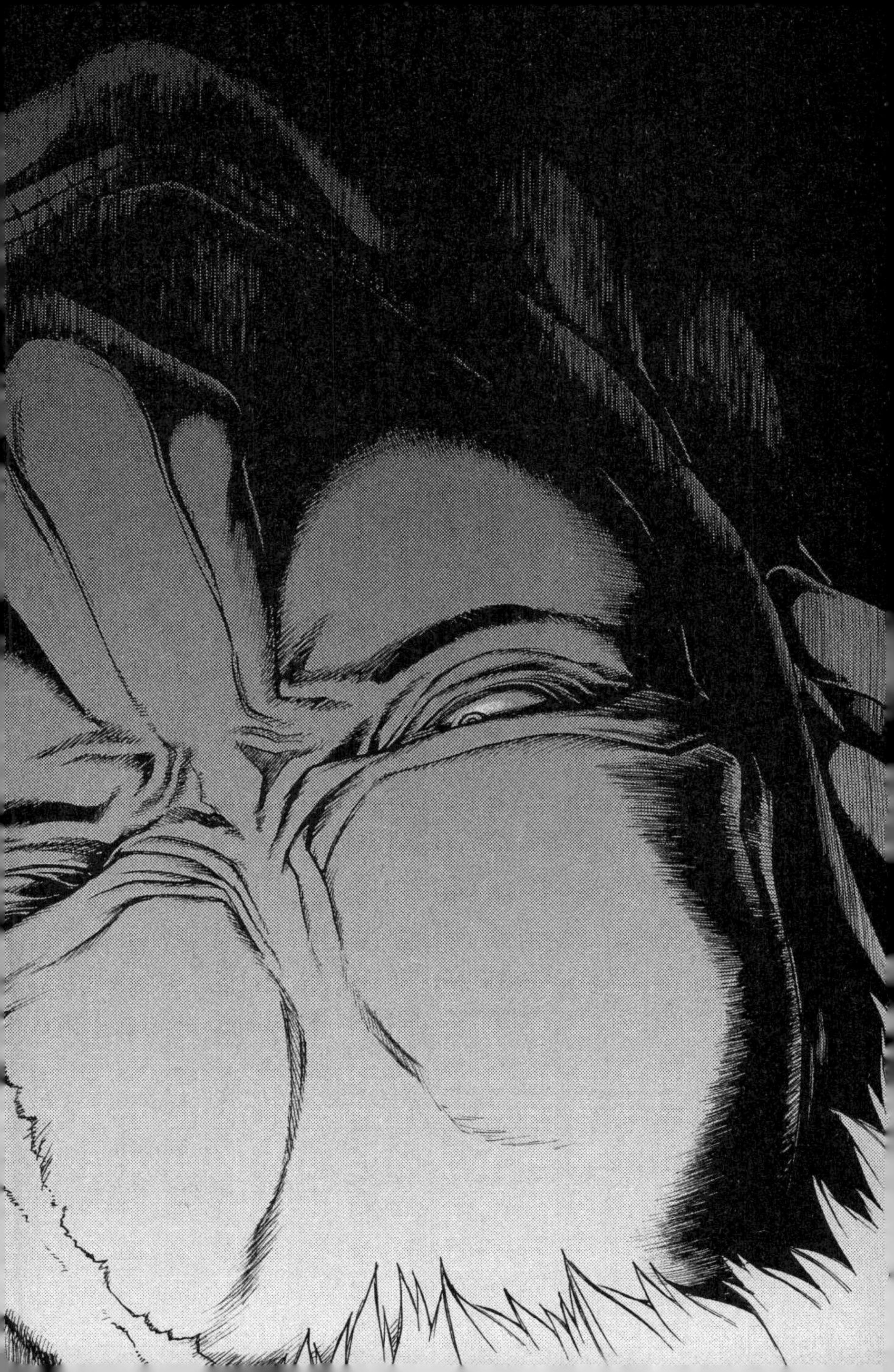

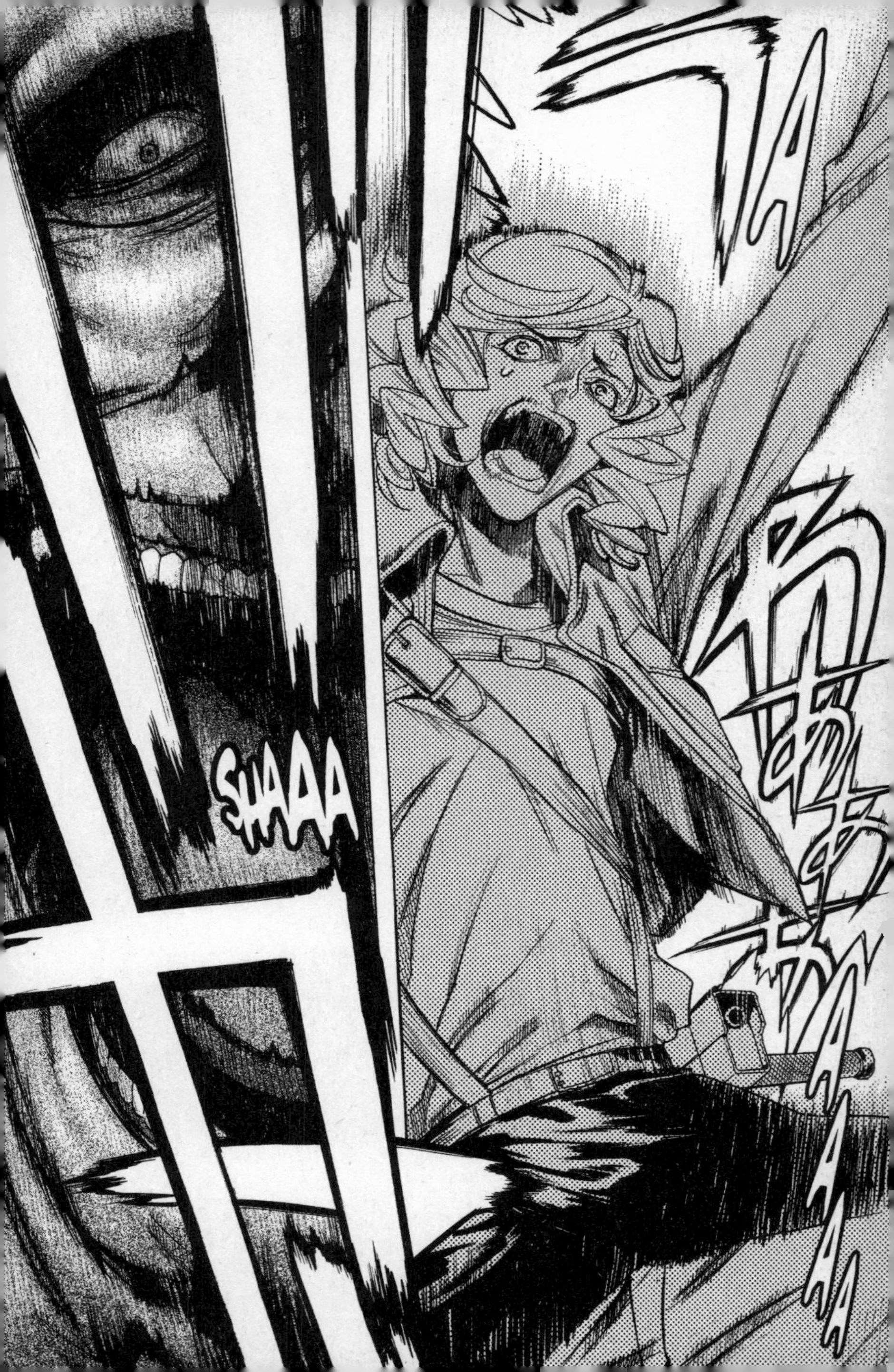
SHAAA

Chapter 22: Abyss Below the Wall · End

ATTACK on TITAN

BEFORE THE FALL

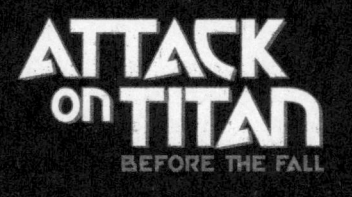

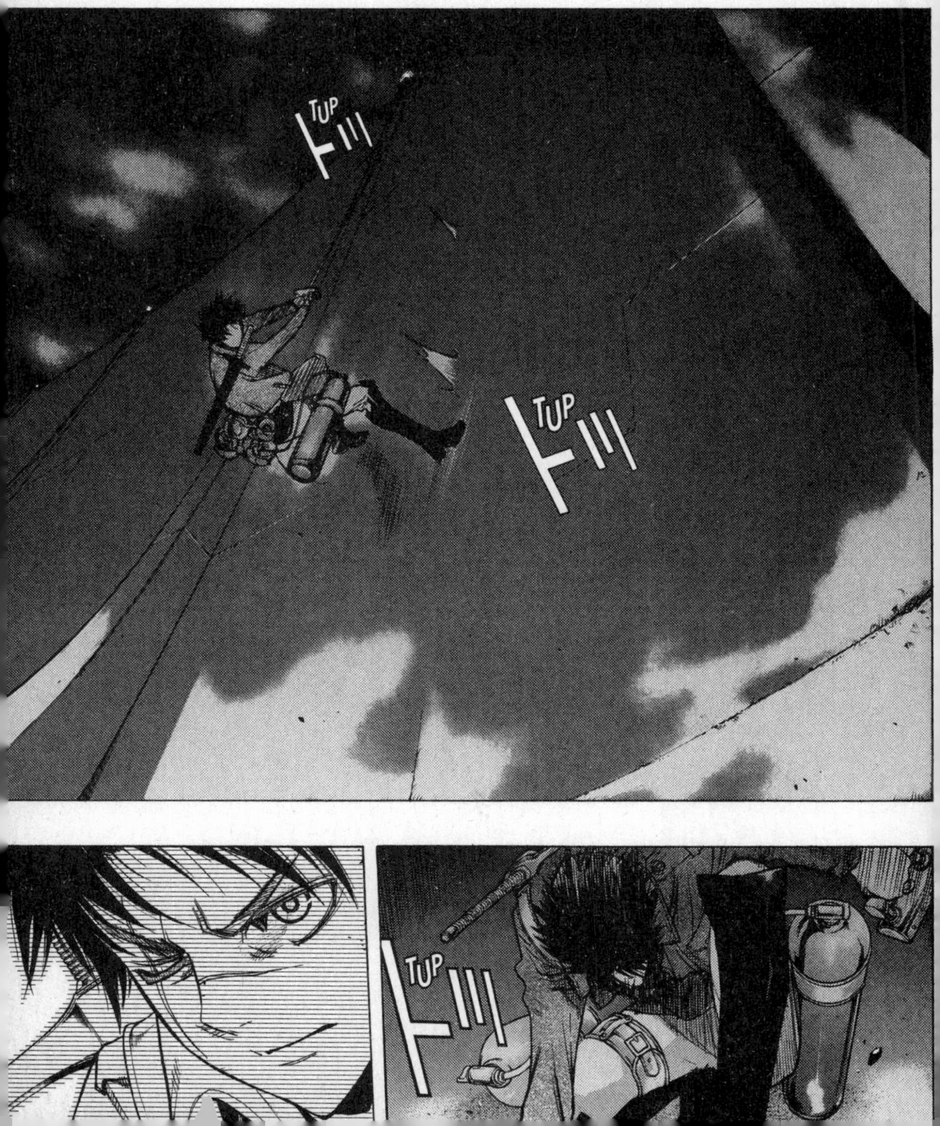
TUP
TUP
TUP

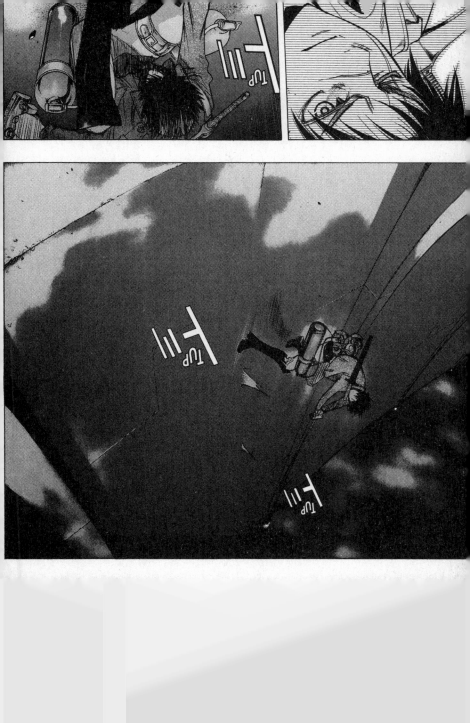

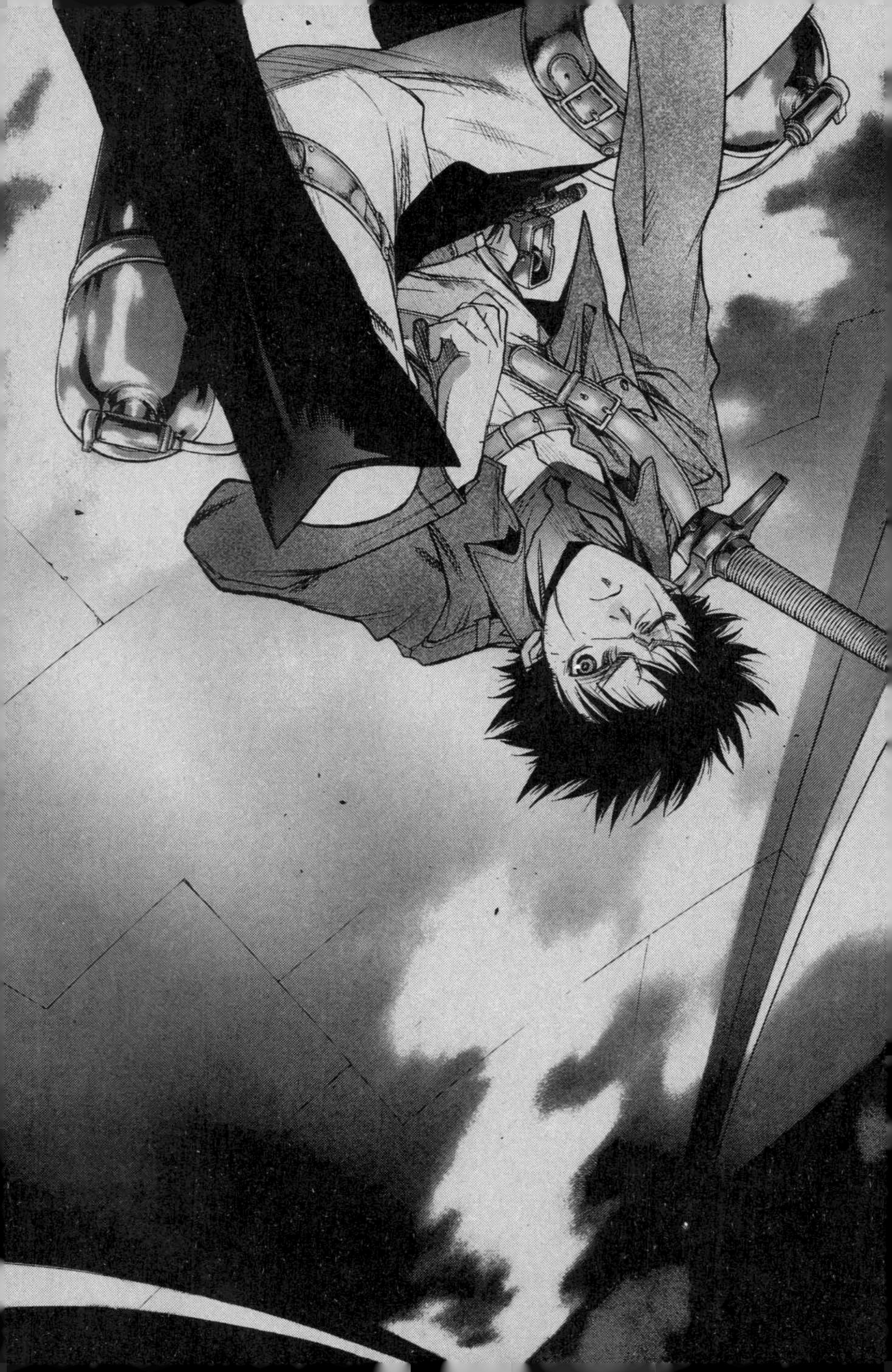

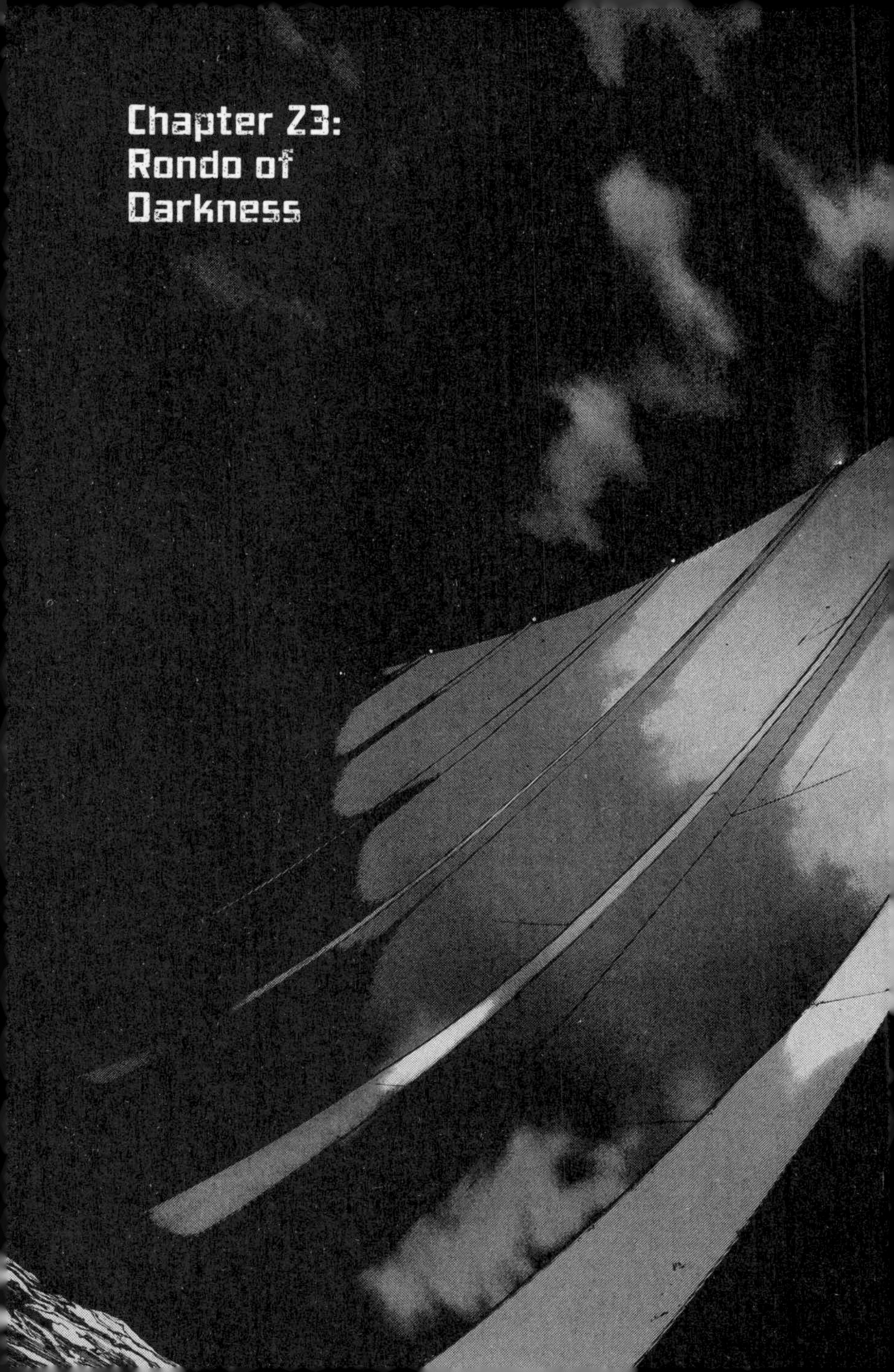
Chapter 23:
Rondo of
Darkness

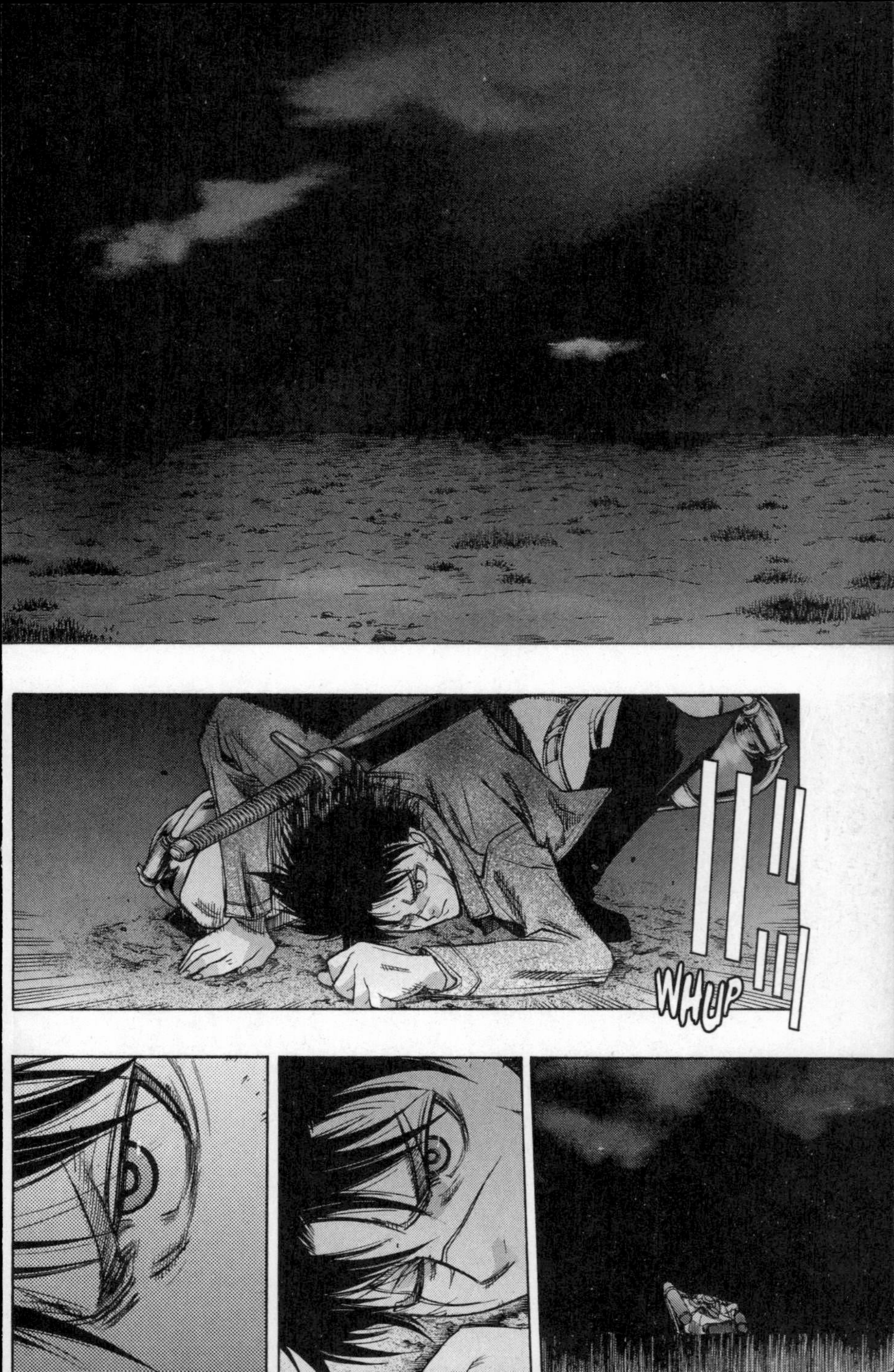
WHUP

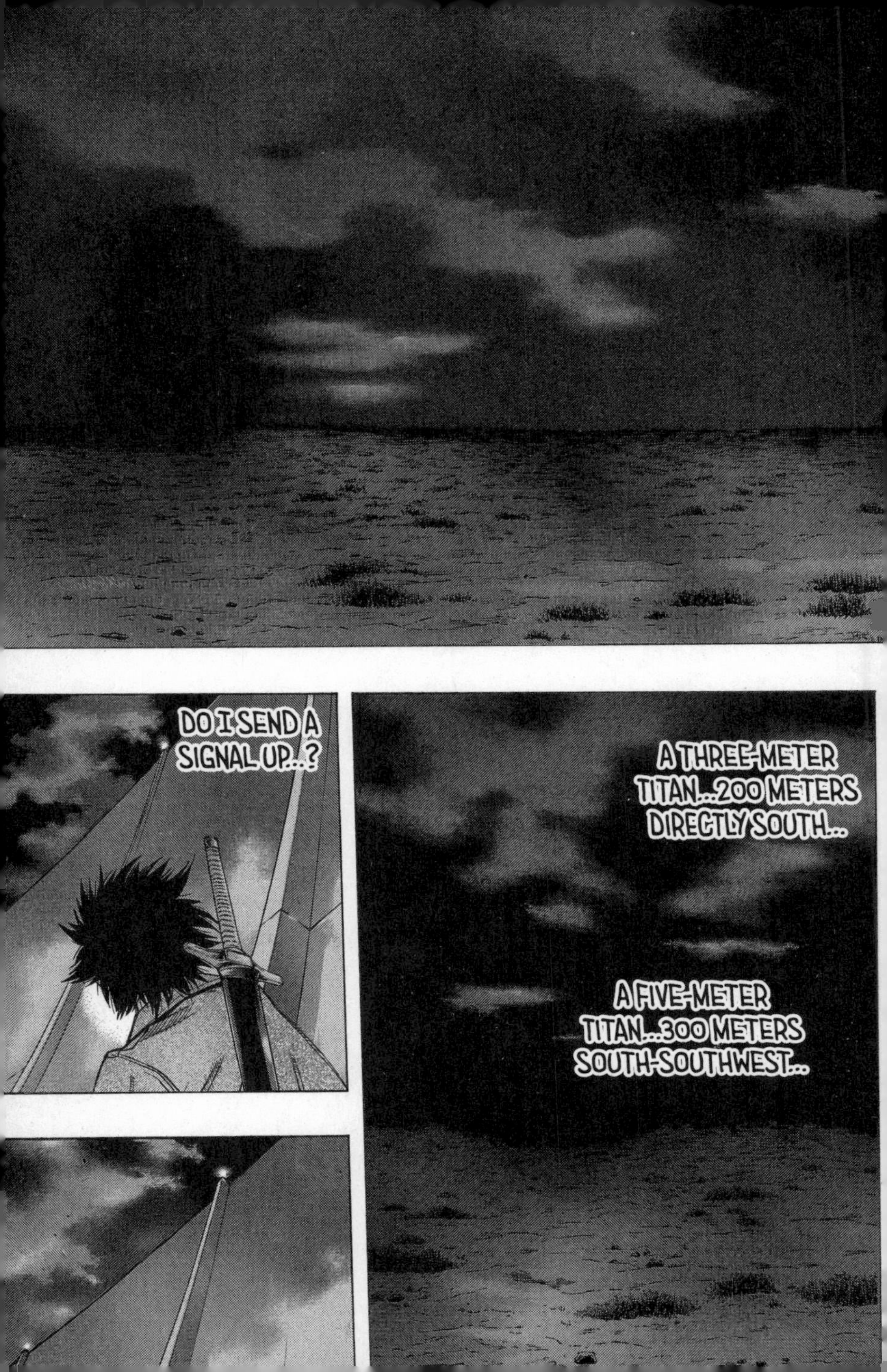
A THREE-METER TITAN...200 METERS DIRECTLY SOUTH...
A FIVE-METER TITAN...300 METERS SOUTH-SOUTHWEST...
DO I SEND A SIGNAL UP...?

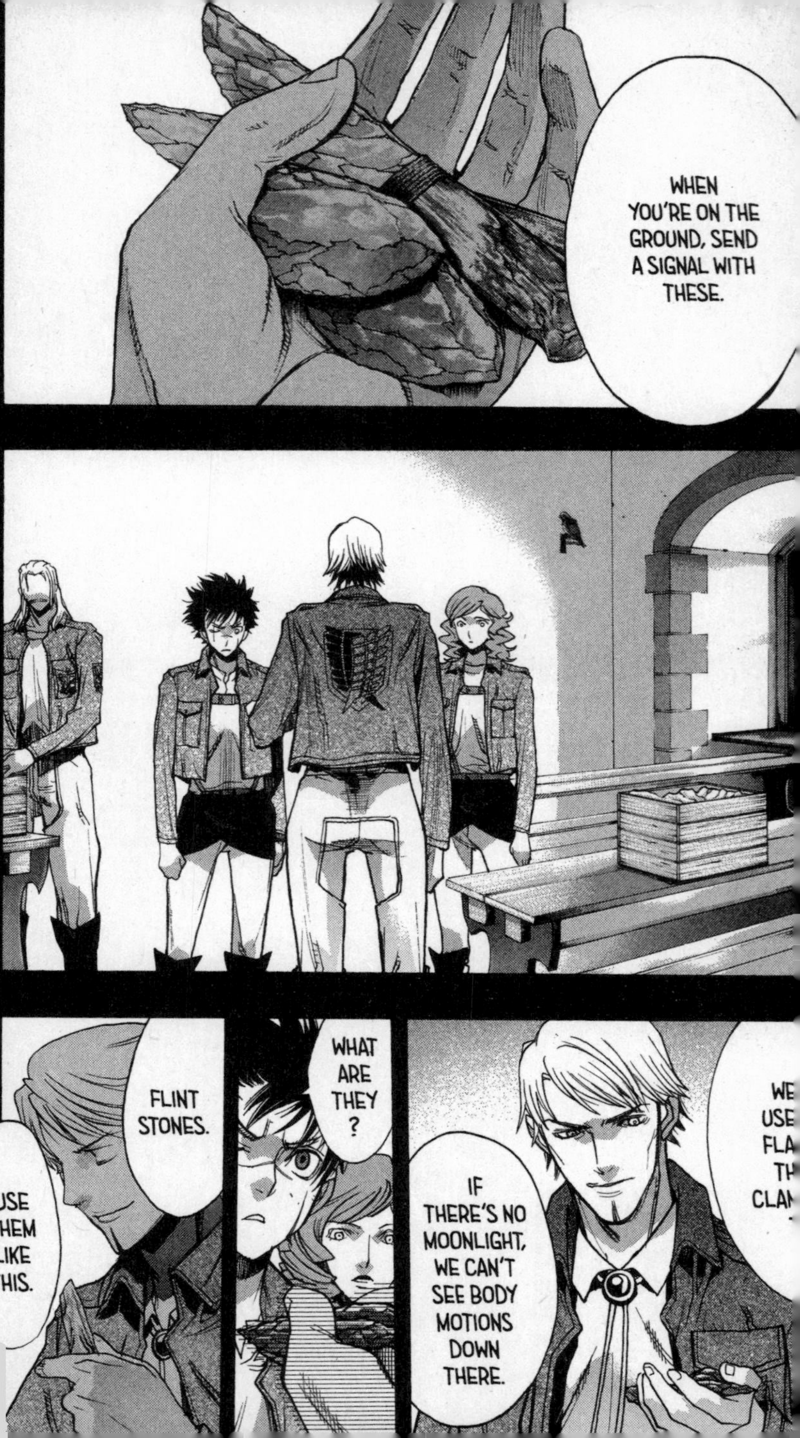
WHEN YOU'RE ON THE GROUND, SEND A SIGNAL WITH THESE.
IF THERE'S NO MOONLIGHT, WE CAN'T SEE BODY MOTIONS DOWN THERE.
WHAT ARE THEY ?
FLINT STONES.
USE THEM LIKE THIS.

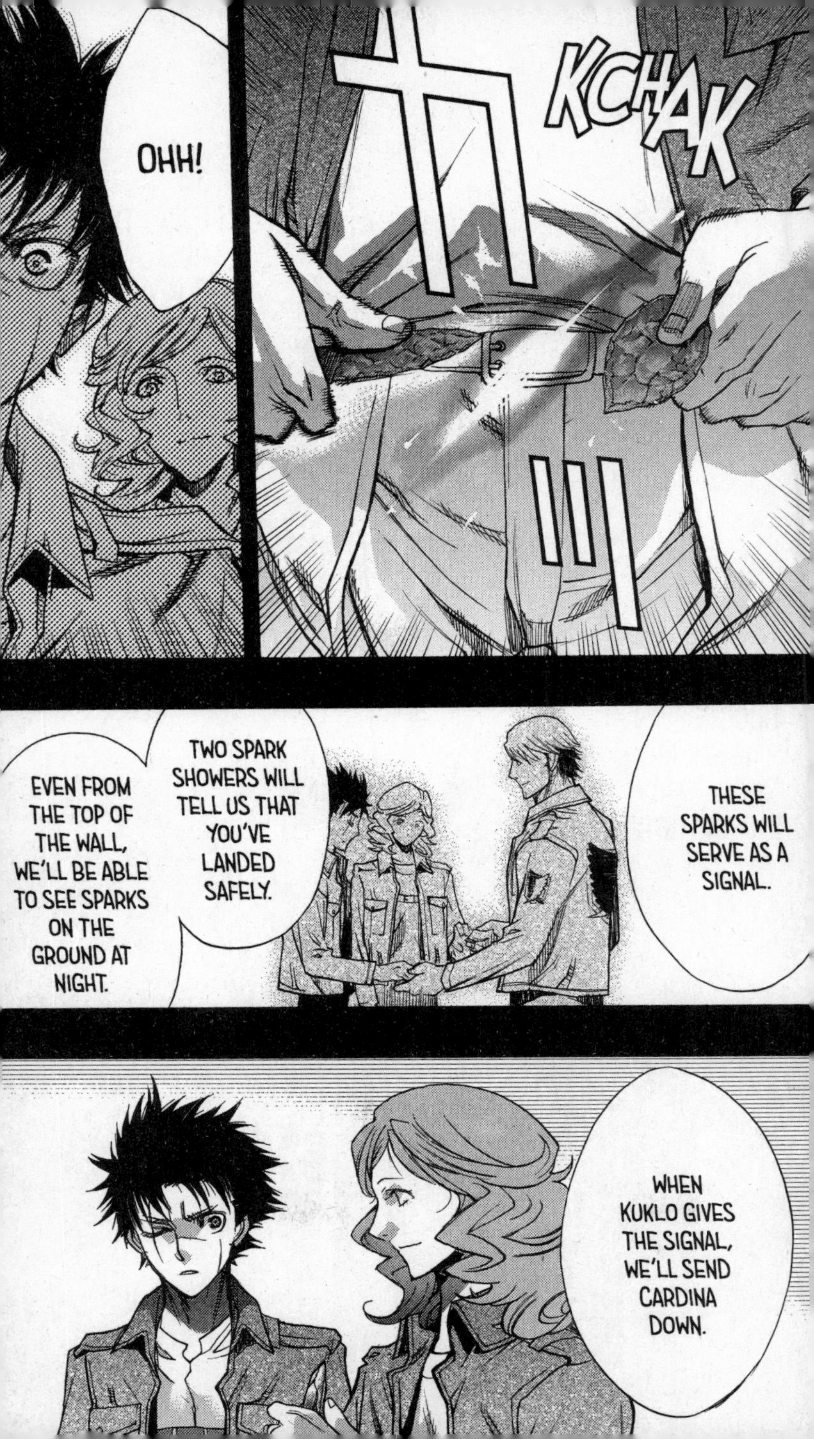
KCHAK
OHH!
THESE SPARKS WILL SERVE AS A SIGNAL.
TWO SPARK SHOWERS WILL TELL US THAT YOU'VE LANDED SAFELY.
EVEN FROM THE TOP OF THE WALL, WE'LL BE ABLE TO SEE SPARKS ON THE GROUND AT NIGHT.
WHEN KUKLO GIVES THE SIGNAL, WE'LL SEND CARDINA DOWN.

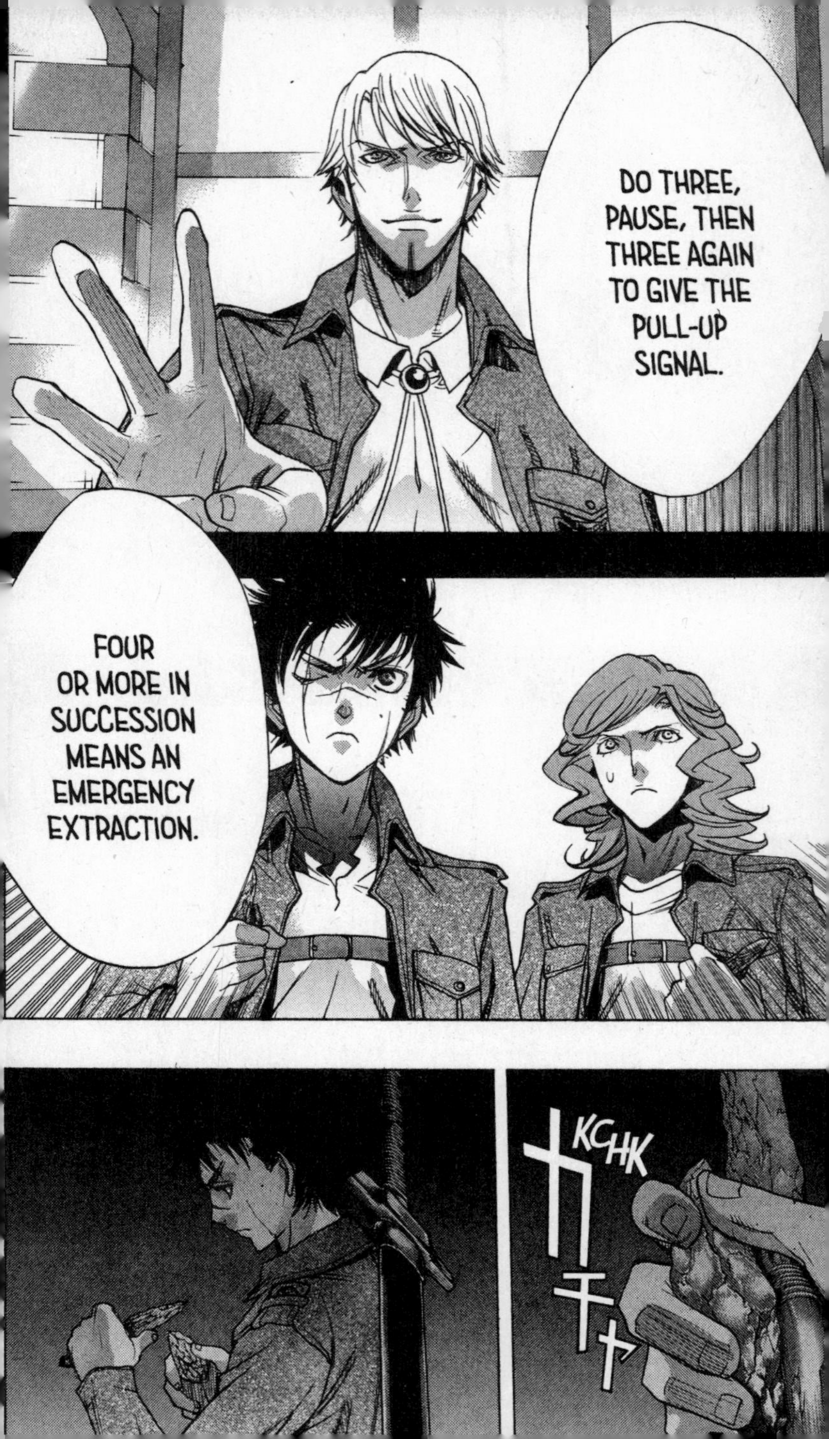
DO THREE, PAUSE, THEN THREE AGAIN TO GIVE THE PULL-UP SIGNAL.
FOUR OR MORE IN SUCCESSION MEANS AN EMERGENCY EXTRACTION.
KCHK
カチャ

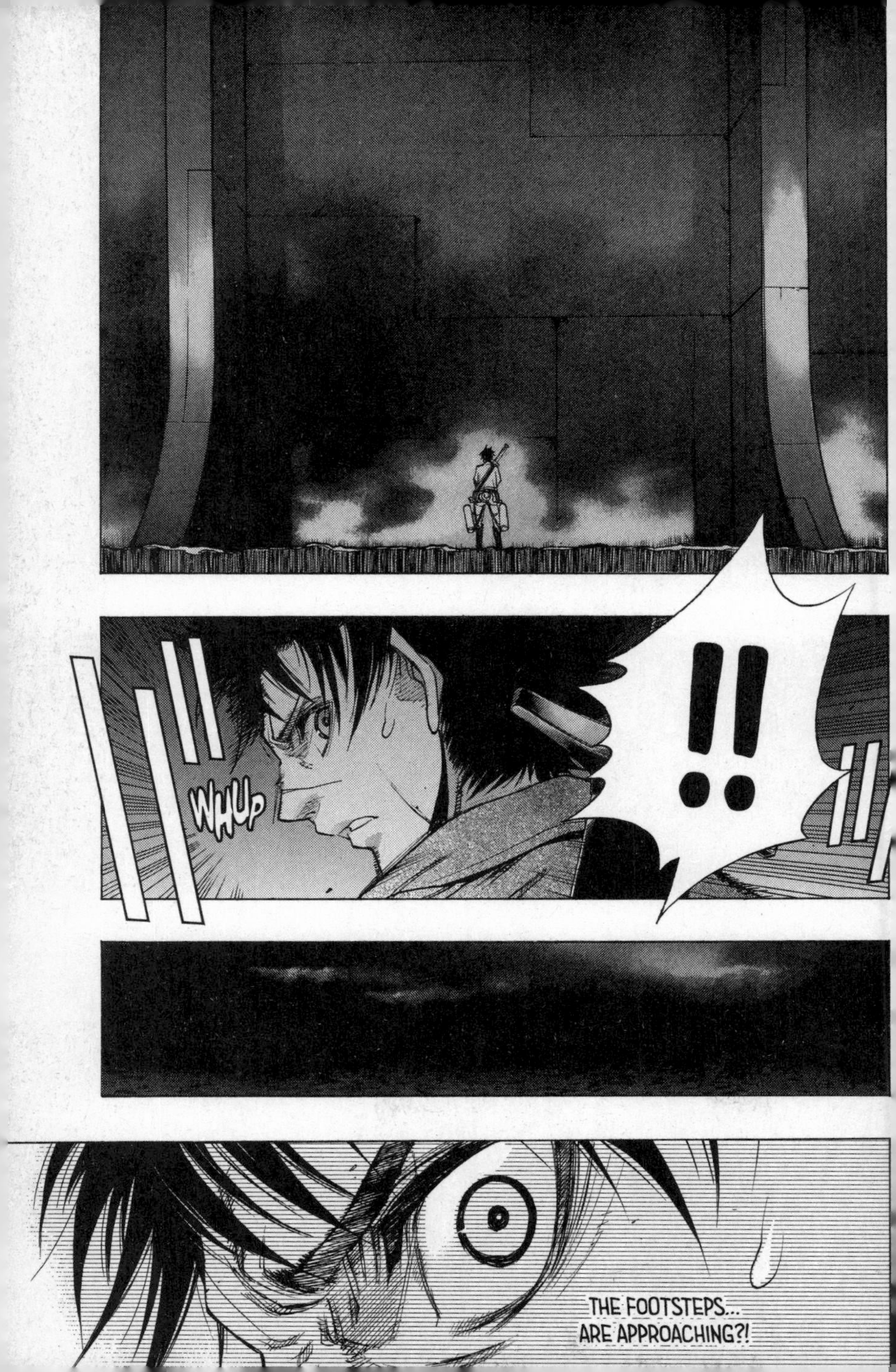
!!
WHUP
THE FOOTSTEPS... ARE APPROACHING?!

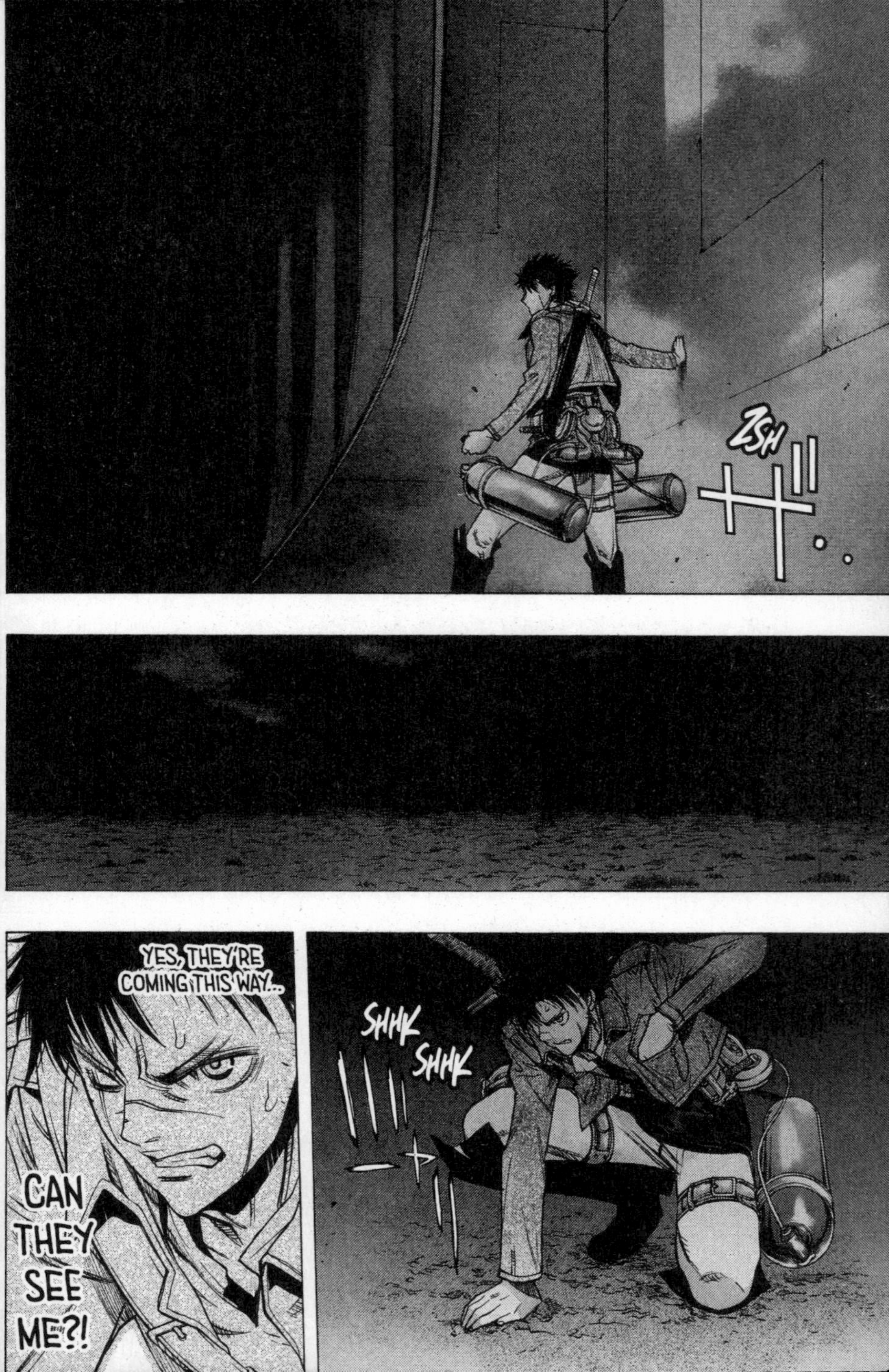
ZSH
SHHK
SHHK
YES, THEY'RE COMING THIS WAY...
CAN THEY SEE ME?!

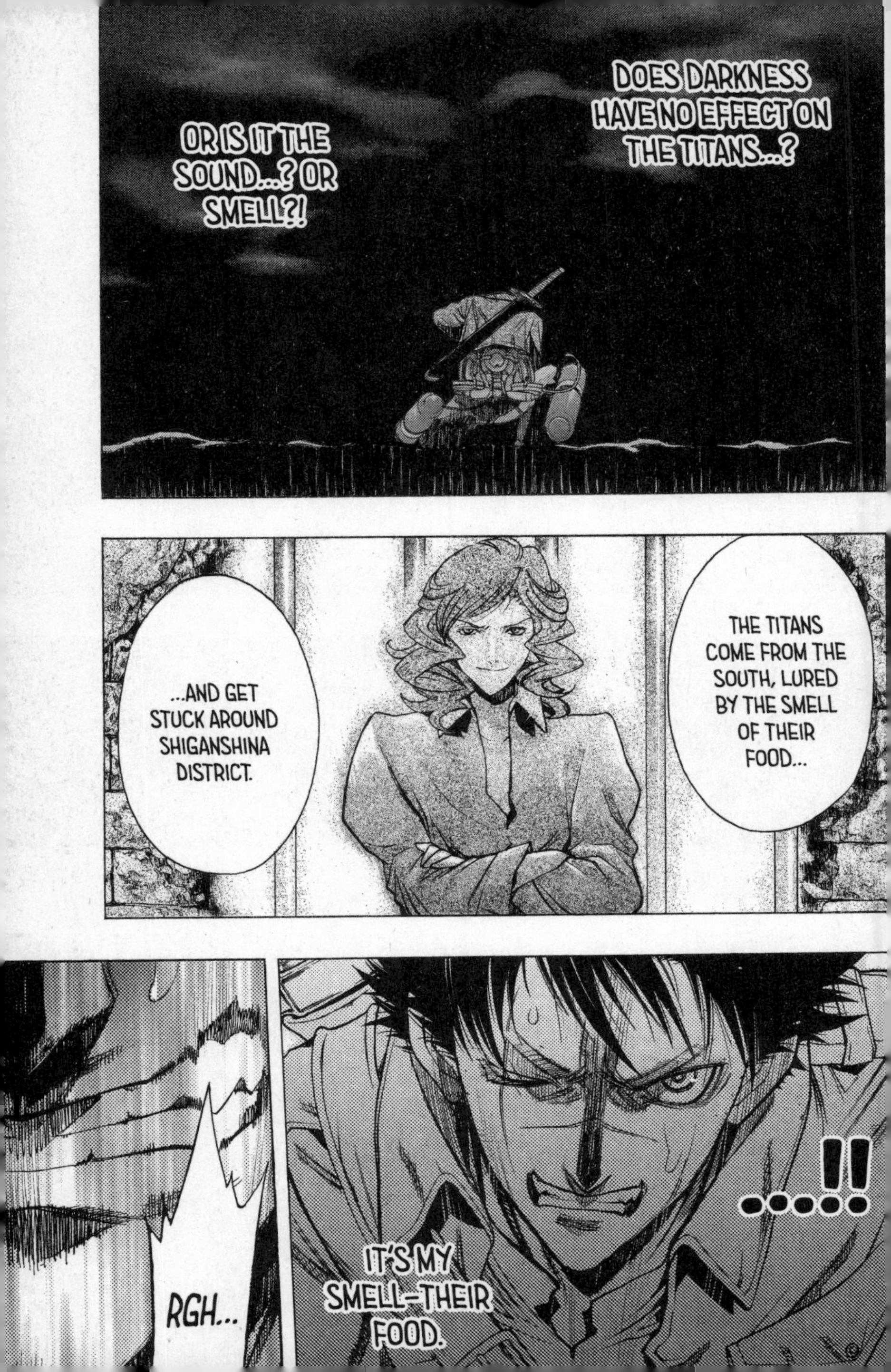
DOES DARKNESS HAVE NO EFFECT ON THE TITANS...?
OR IS IT THE SOUND...? OR SMELL?!
THE TITANS COME FROM THE SOUTH, LURED BY THE SMELL OF THEIR FOOD...
...AND GET STUCK AROUND SHIGANSHINA DISTRICT.
...!!
IT'S MY SMELL–THEIR FOOD.
RGH...

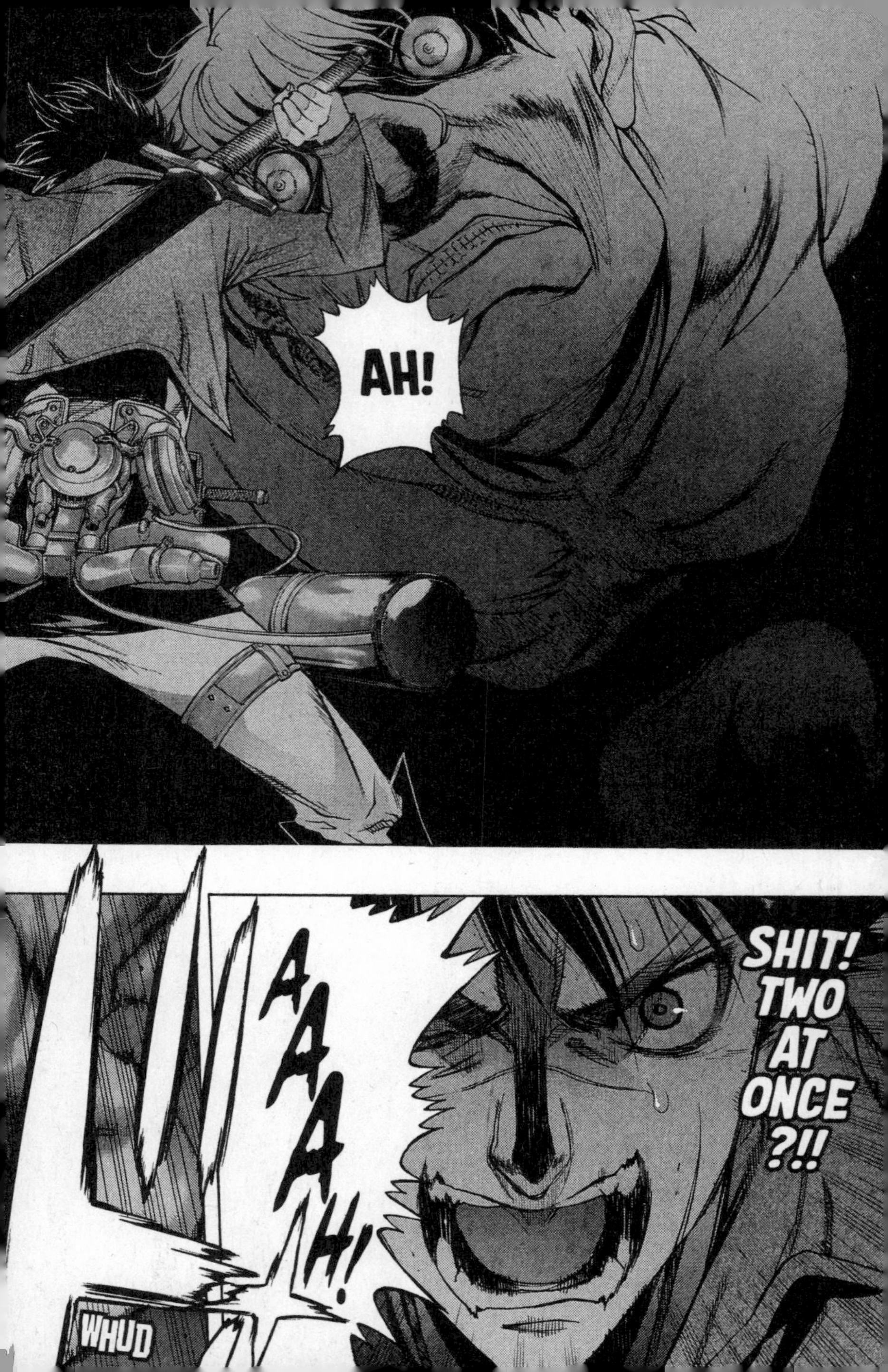
AH!
SHIT! TWO AT ONCE ?!!
AAAAH!
WHUD

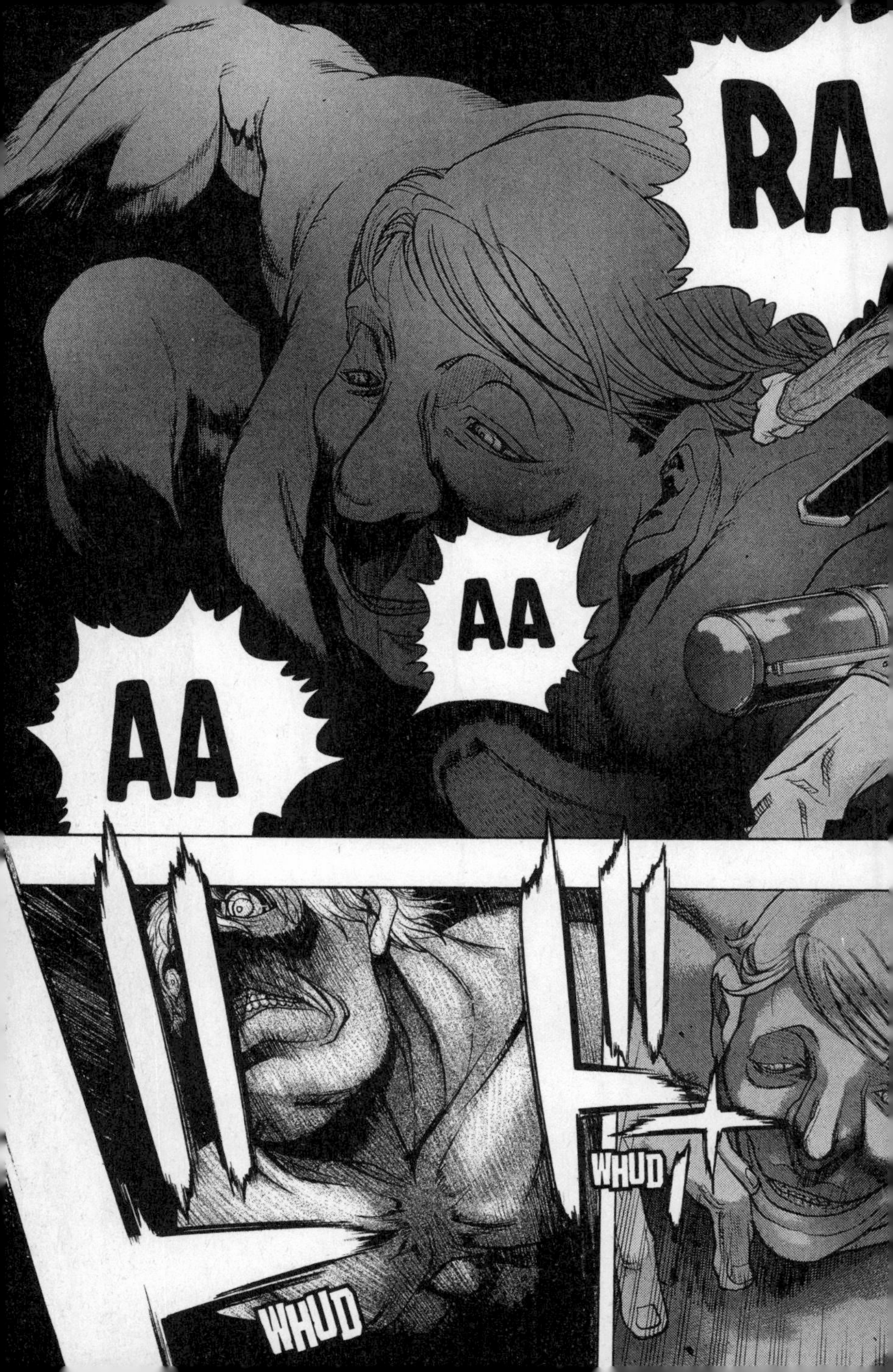
RA
AA
AA
WHUD
WHUD

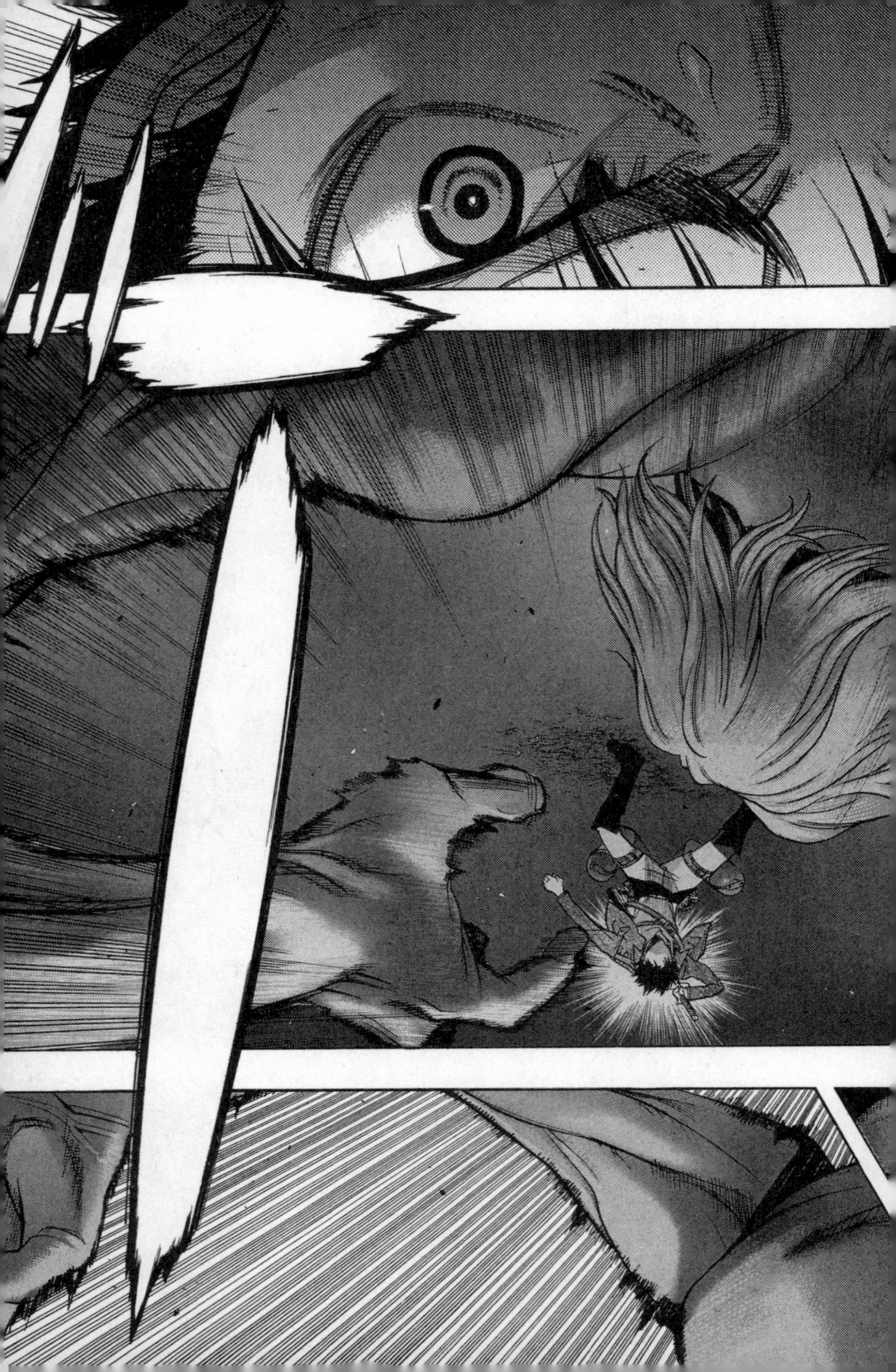

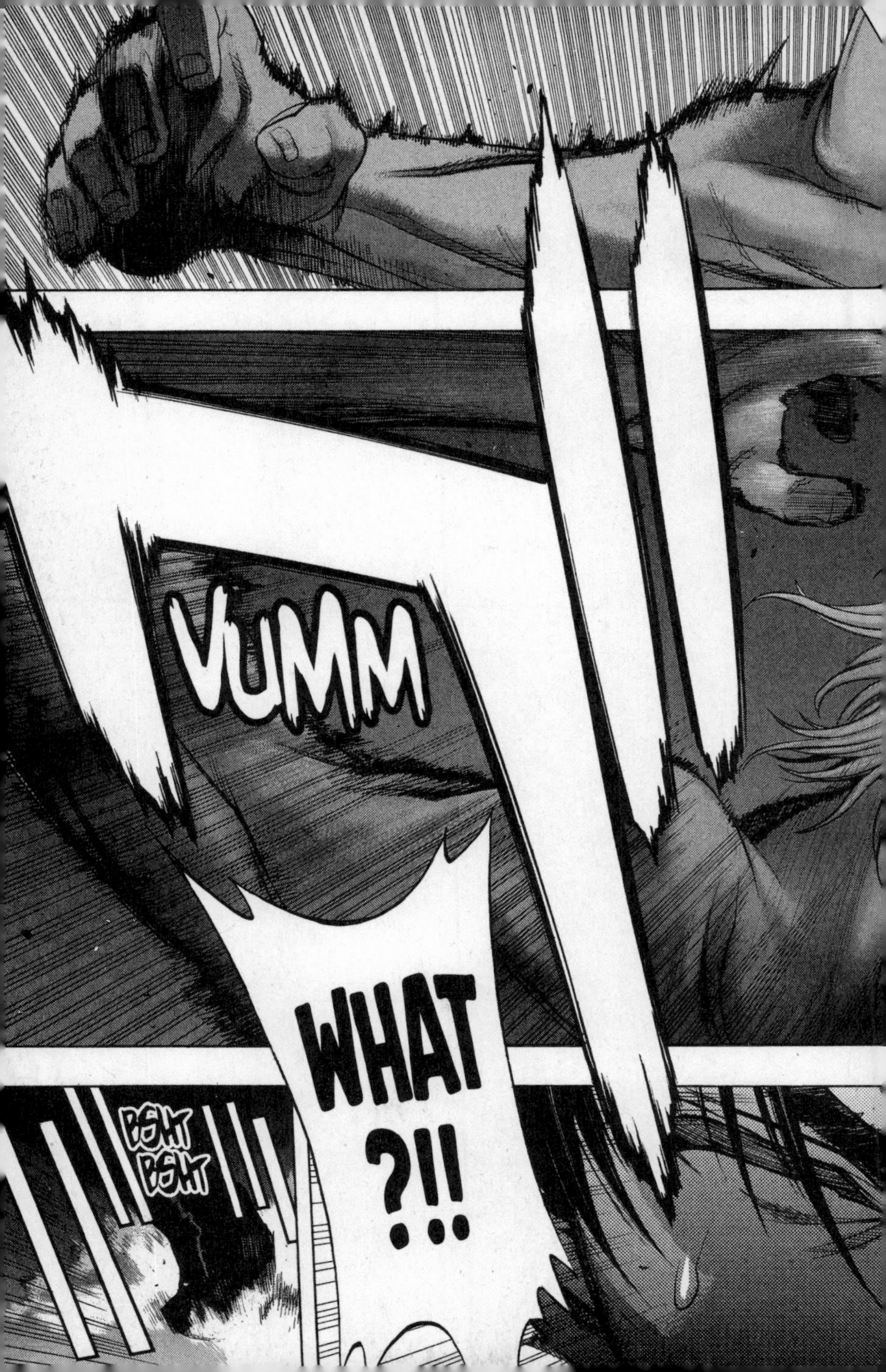
VUMM
WHAT ?!!
BSHT BSHT

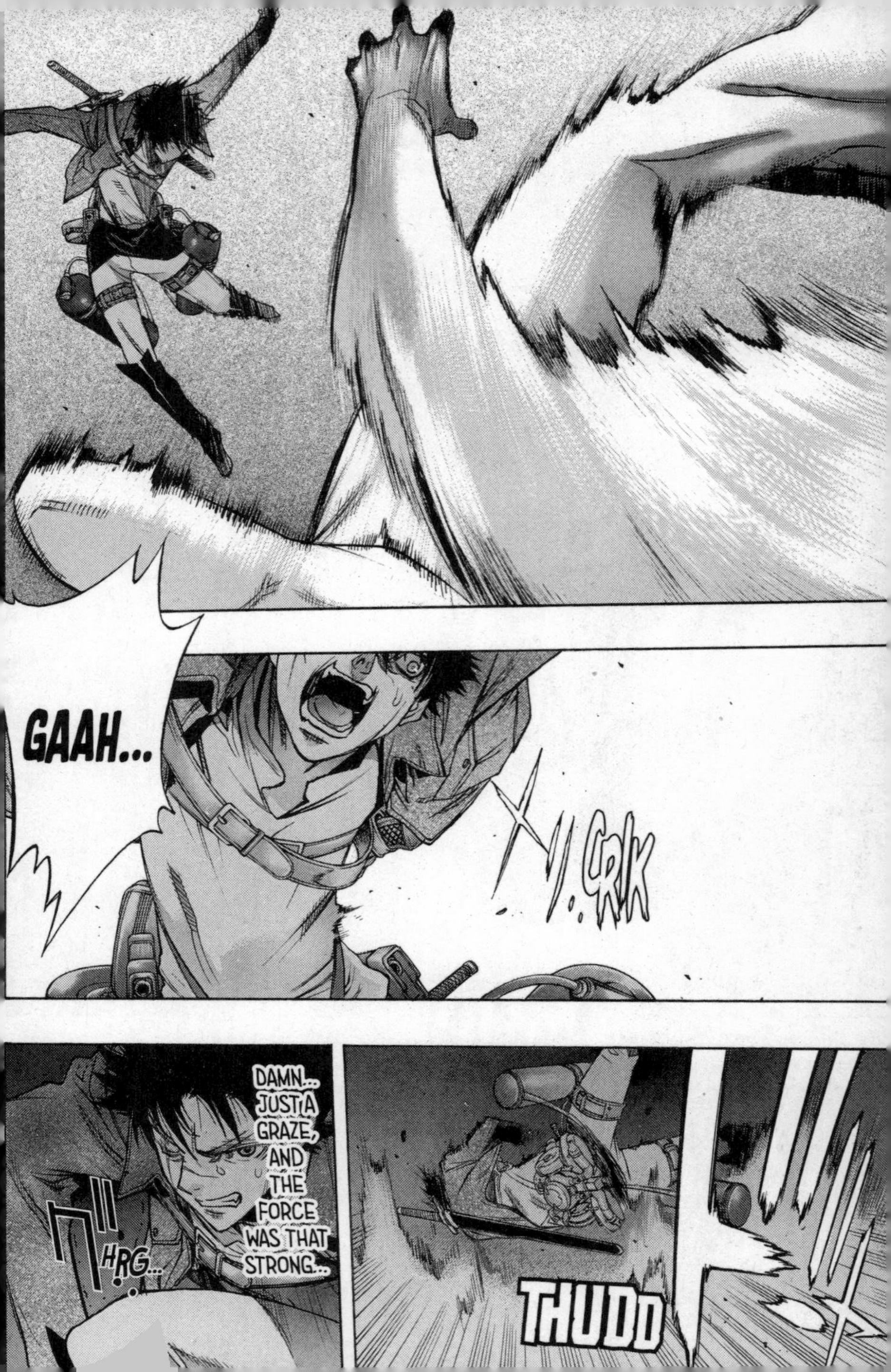
GAAH...
CRIK
THUDD
HRG...
DAMN... JUST A GRAZE, AND THE FORCE WAS THAT STRONG...

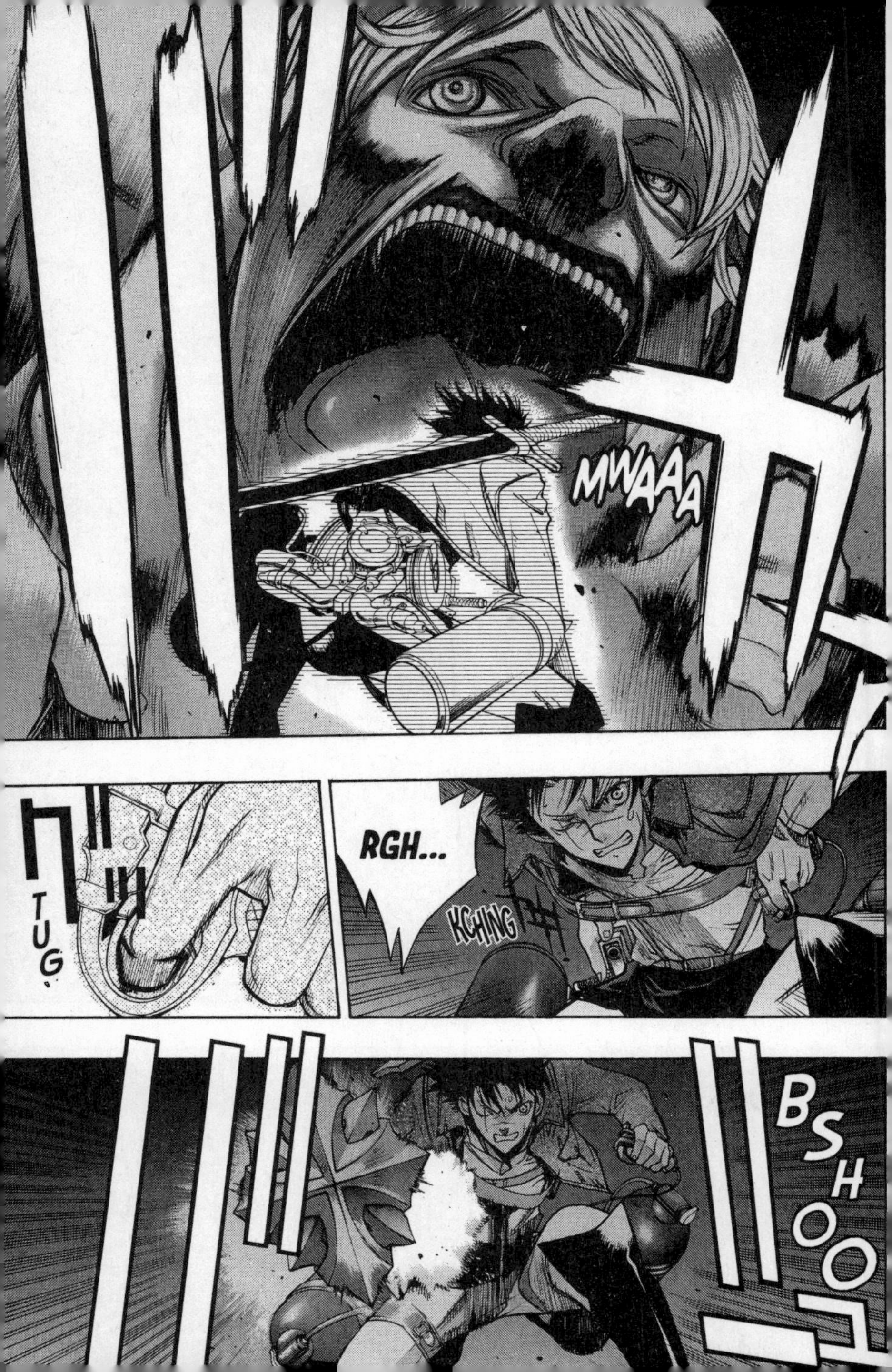
MWAAA
RGH...
KCHING
TUG
BSHOOM

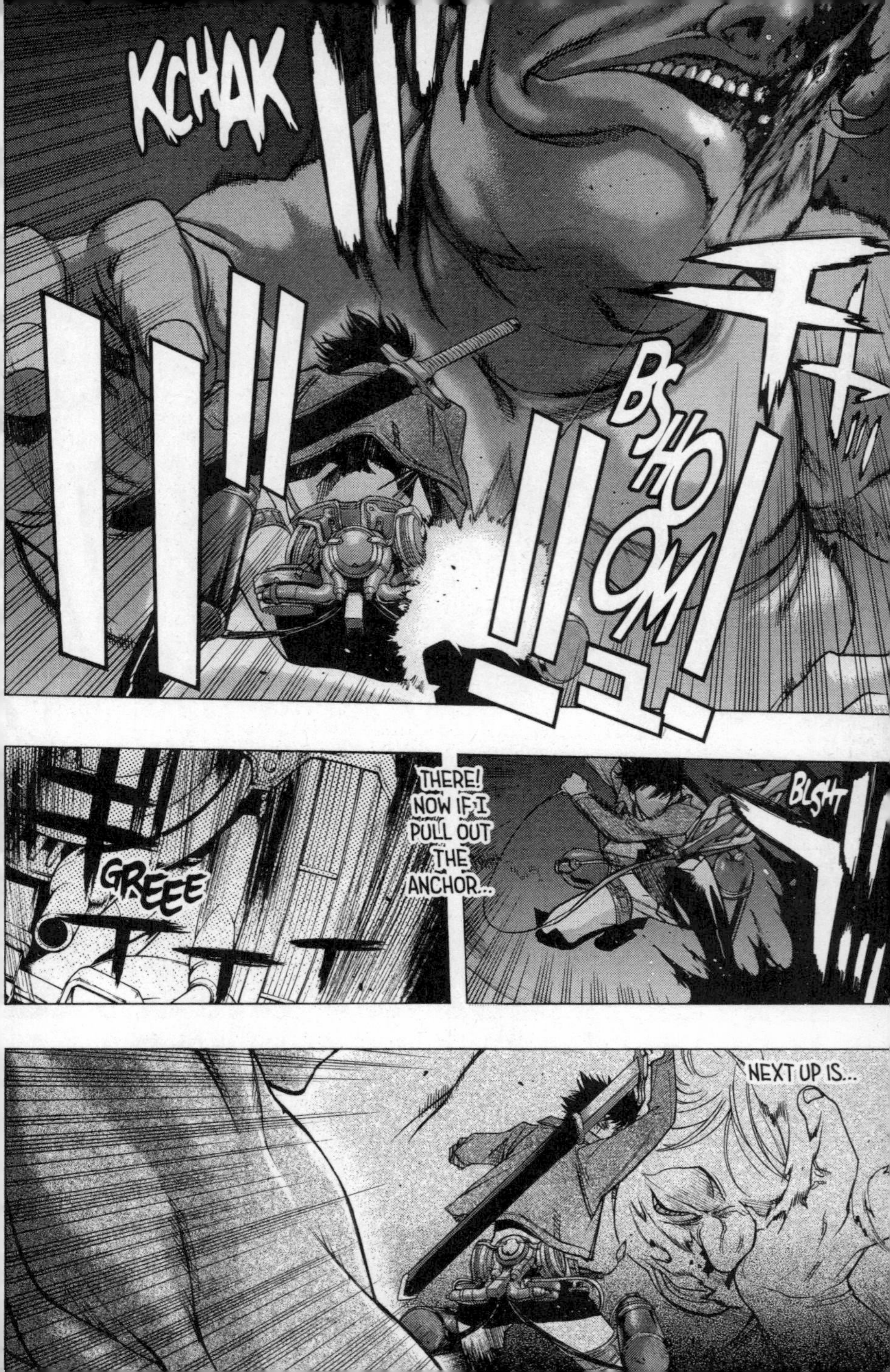
KCHAK
BSHOOM
BLSHT
THERE! NOW IF I PULL OUT THE ANCHOR...
GREEE
NEXT UP IS...

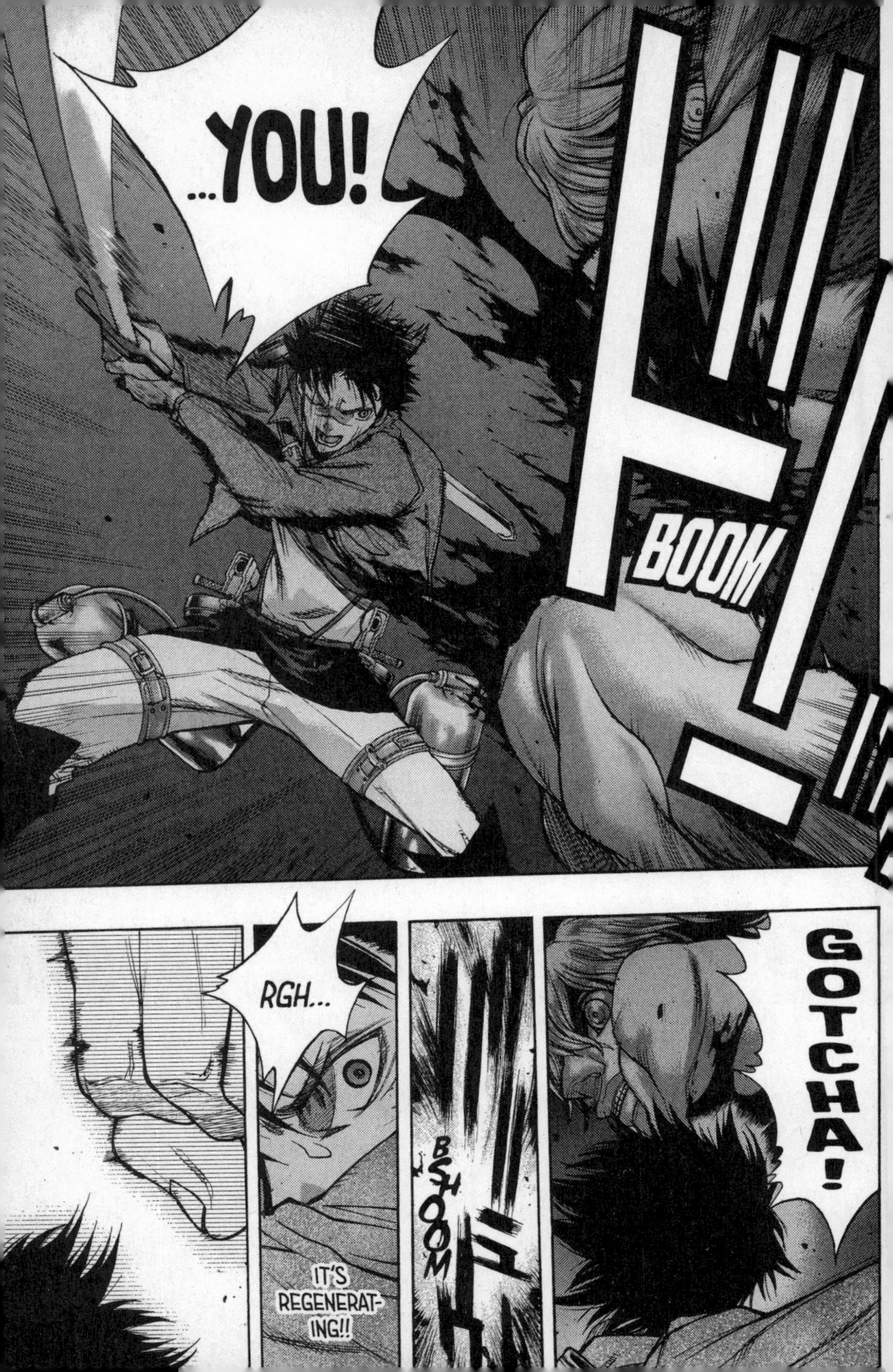
...YOU!
BOOM
GOTCHA!
BSHOOM
RGH...
IT'S REGENERAT-ING!!

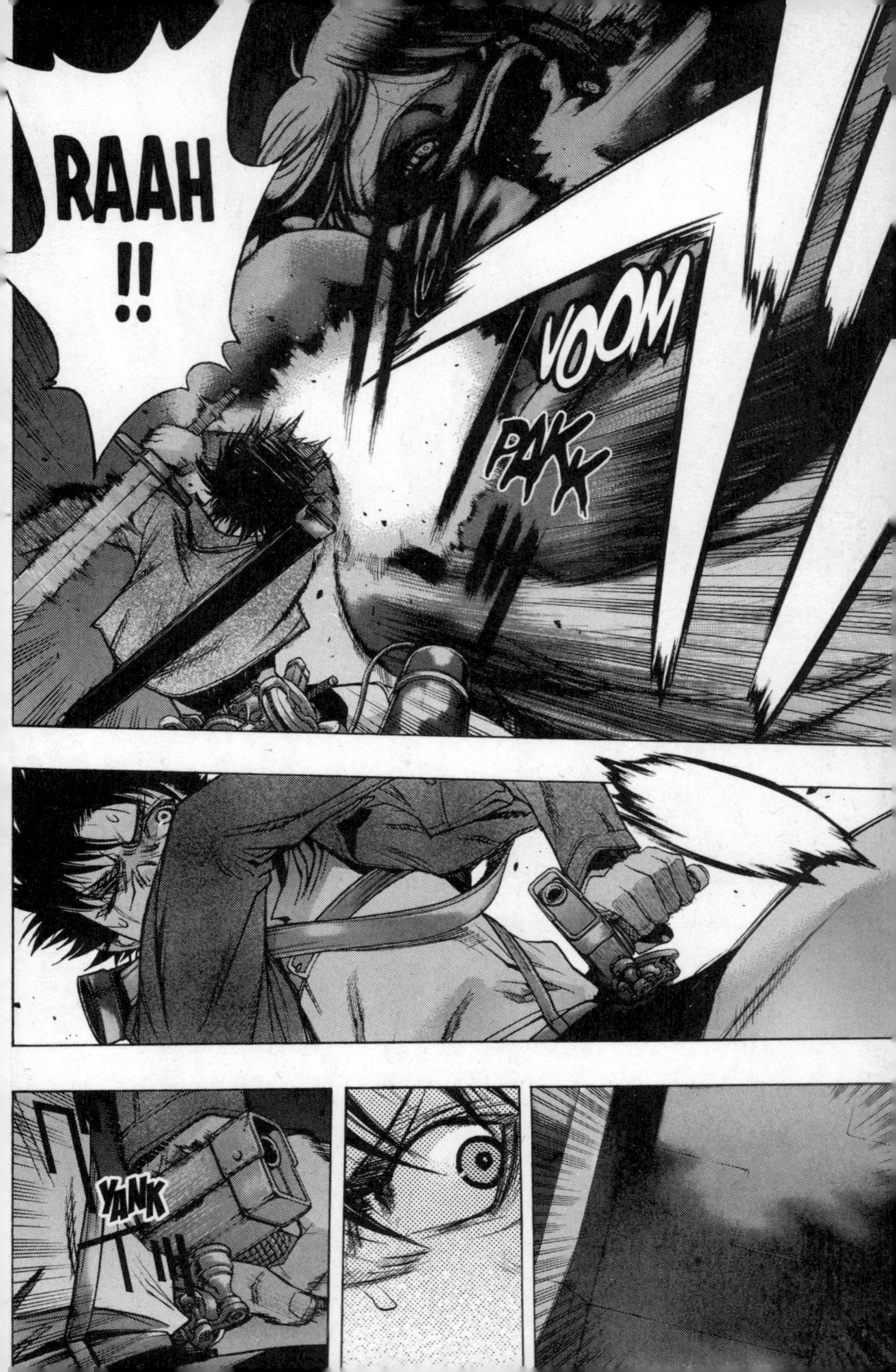
VOOM
PAK
RAAH !!
YANK

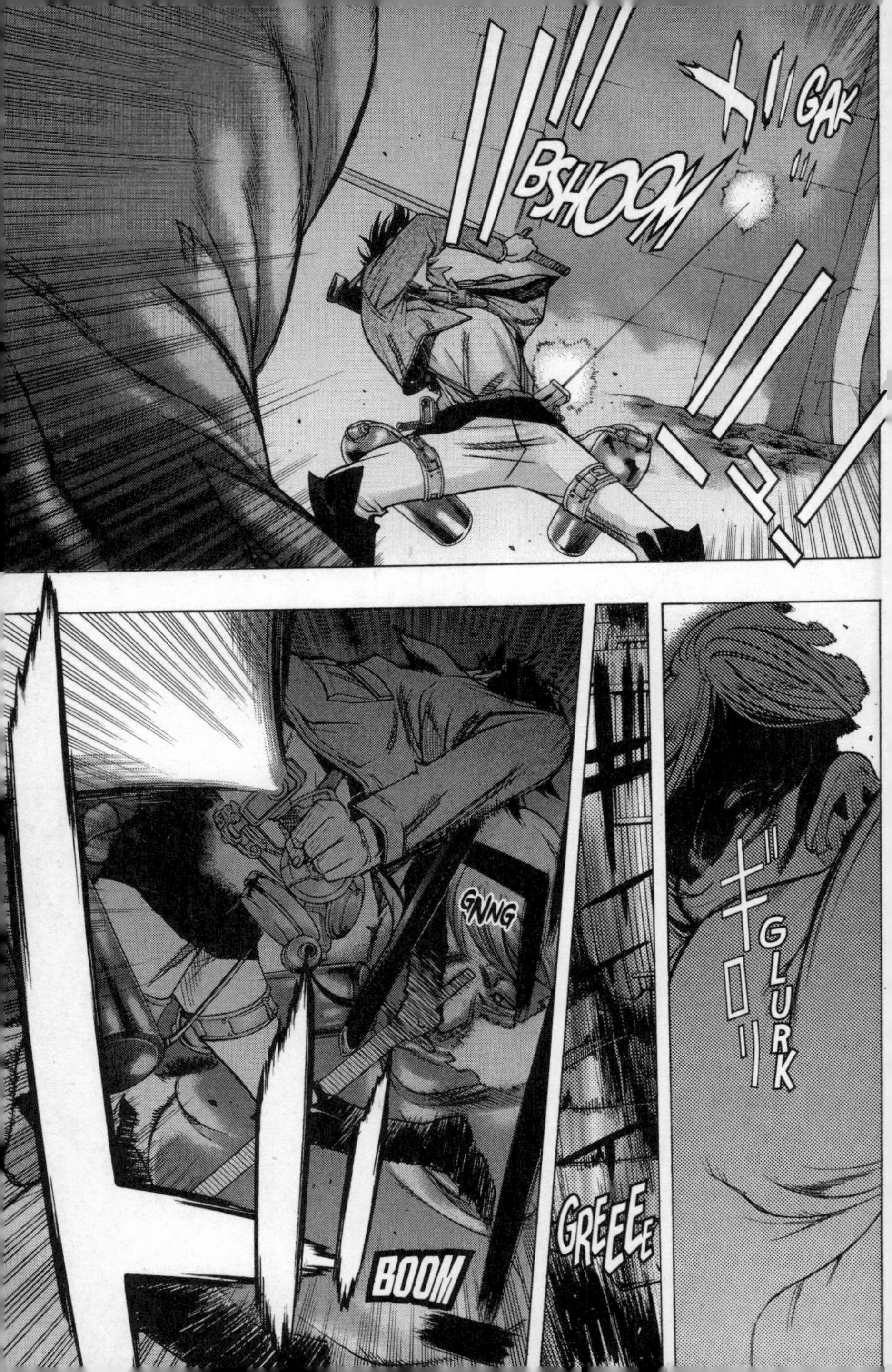
GAK
BSHOOM
GLURK
GREEEE
GNNG
BOOM

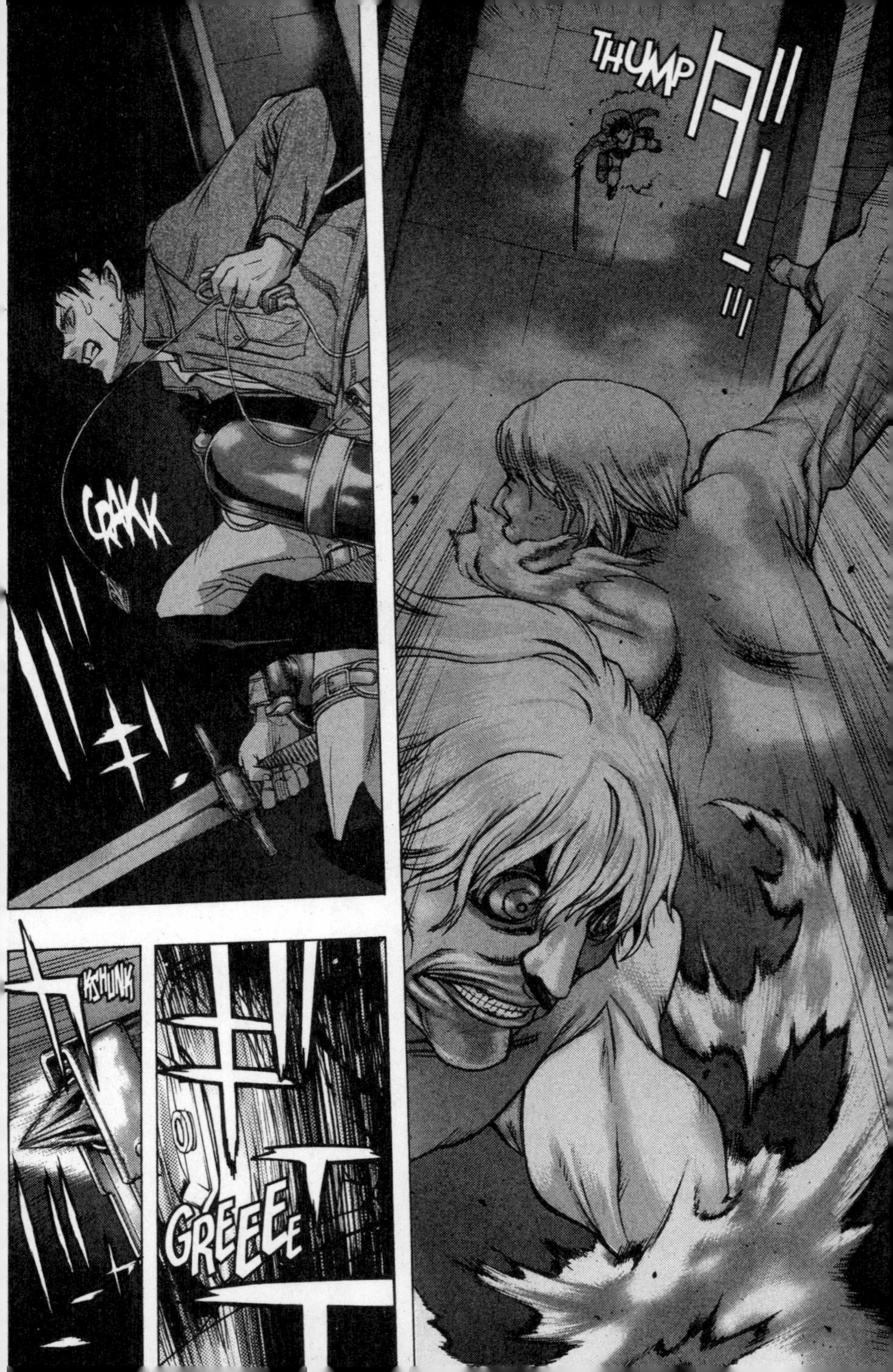
THUMP
CRAKK
GREEEE
KSHUNK

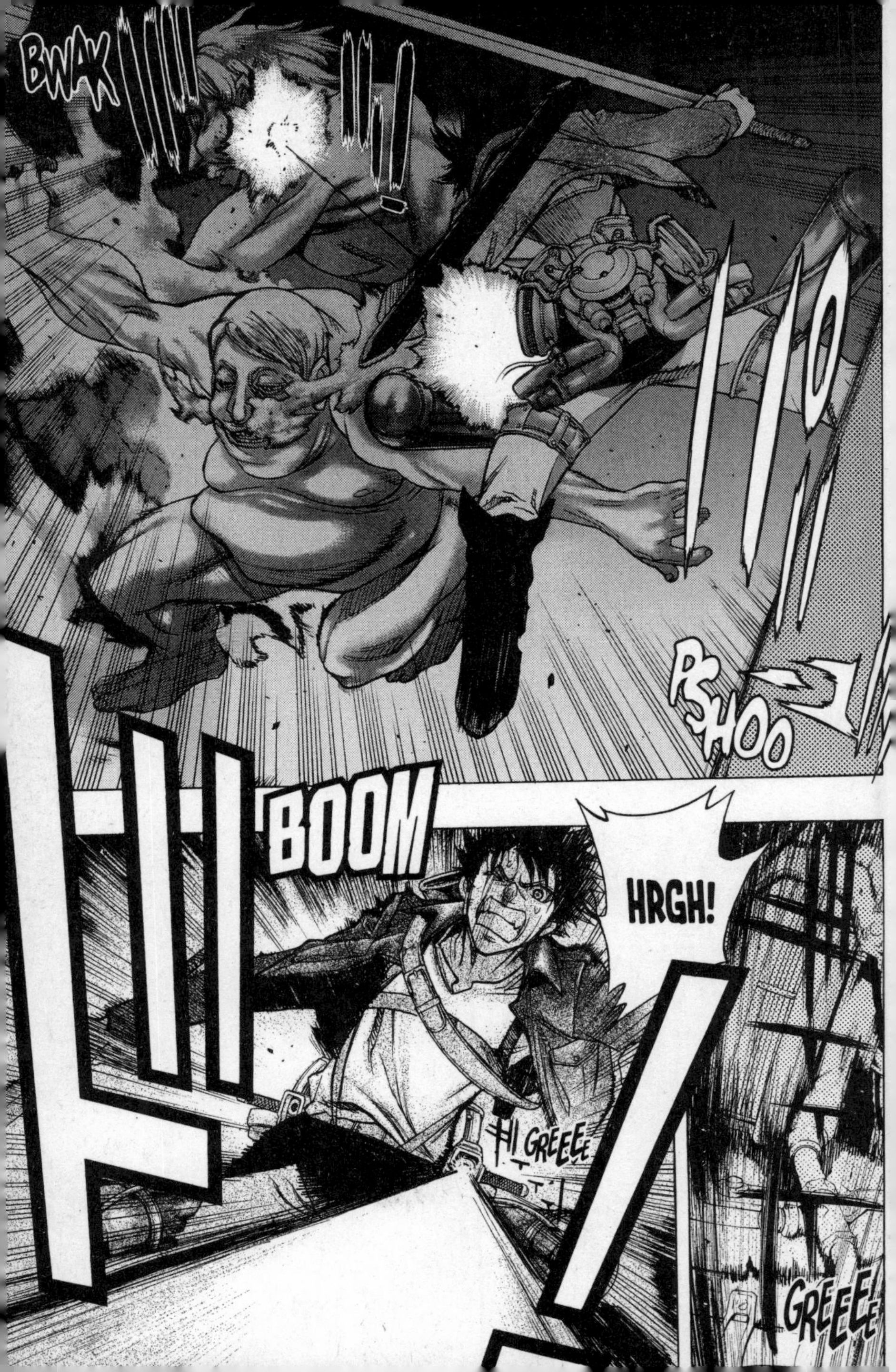
PSHOO
BWAK
HRGH!
BOOM
GREEEE
GREEEE

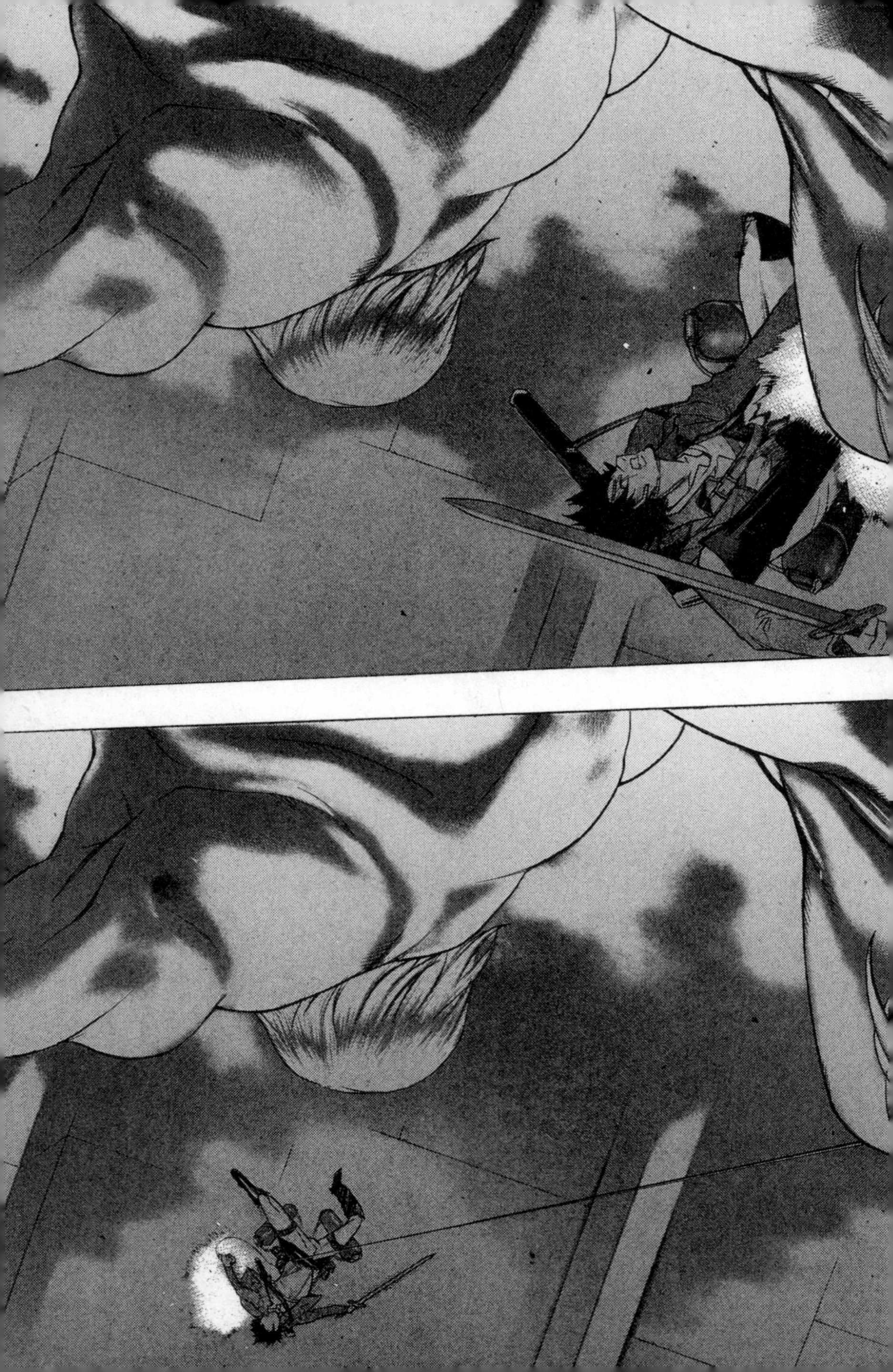

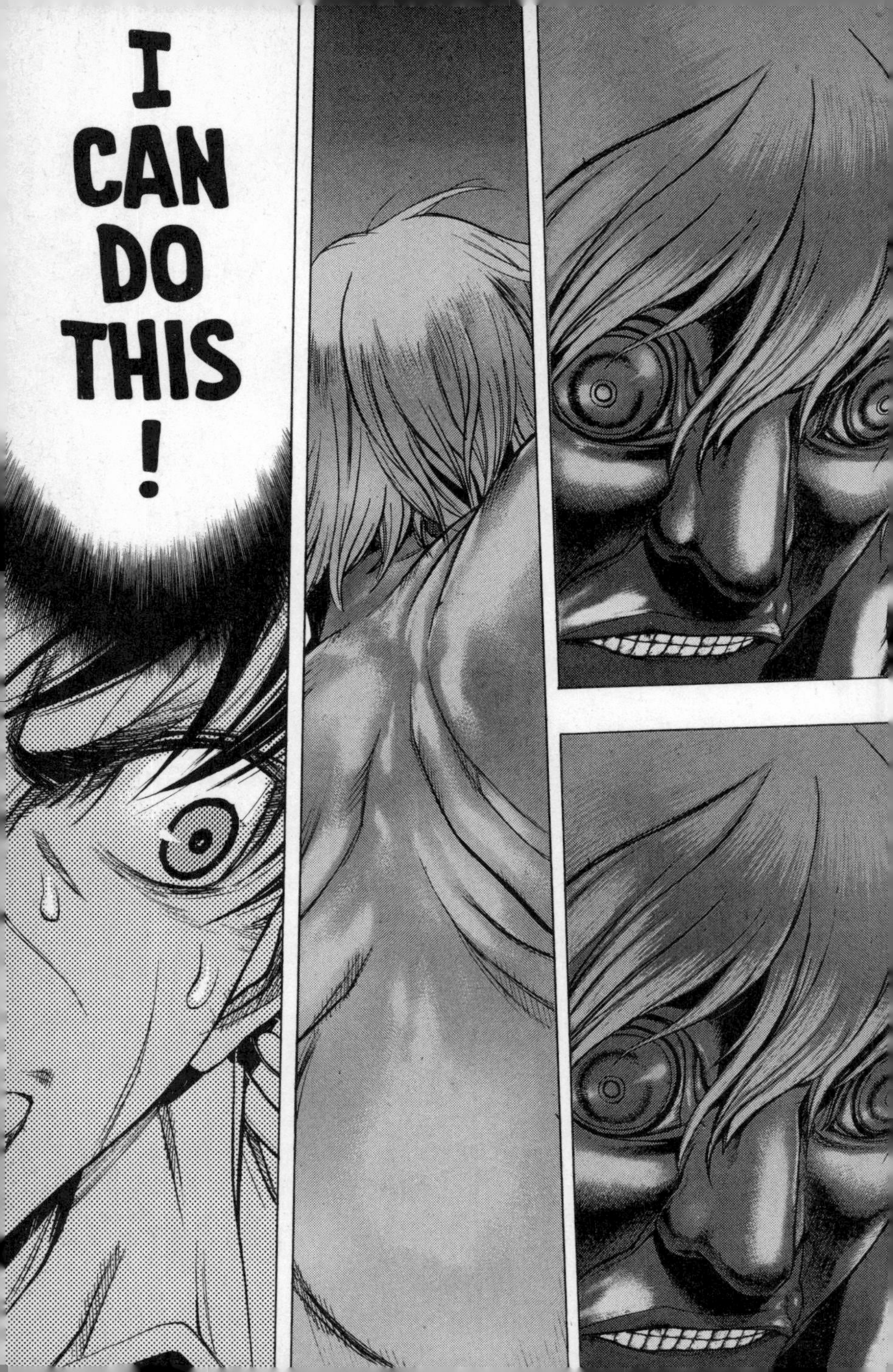
I CAN DO THIS!

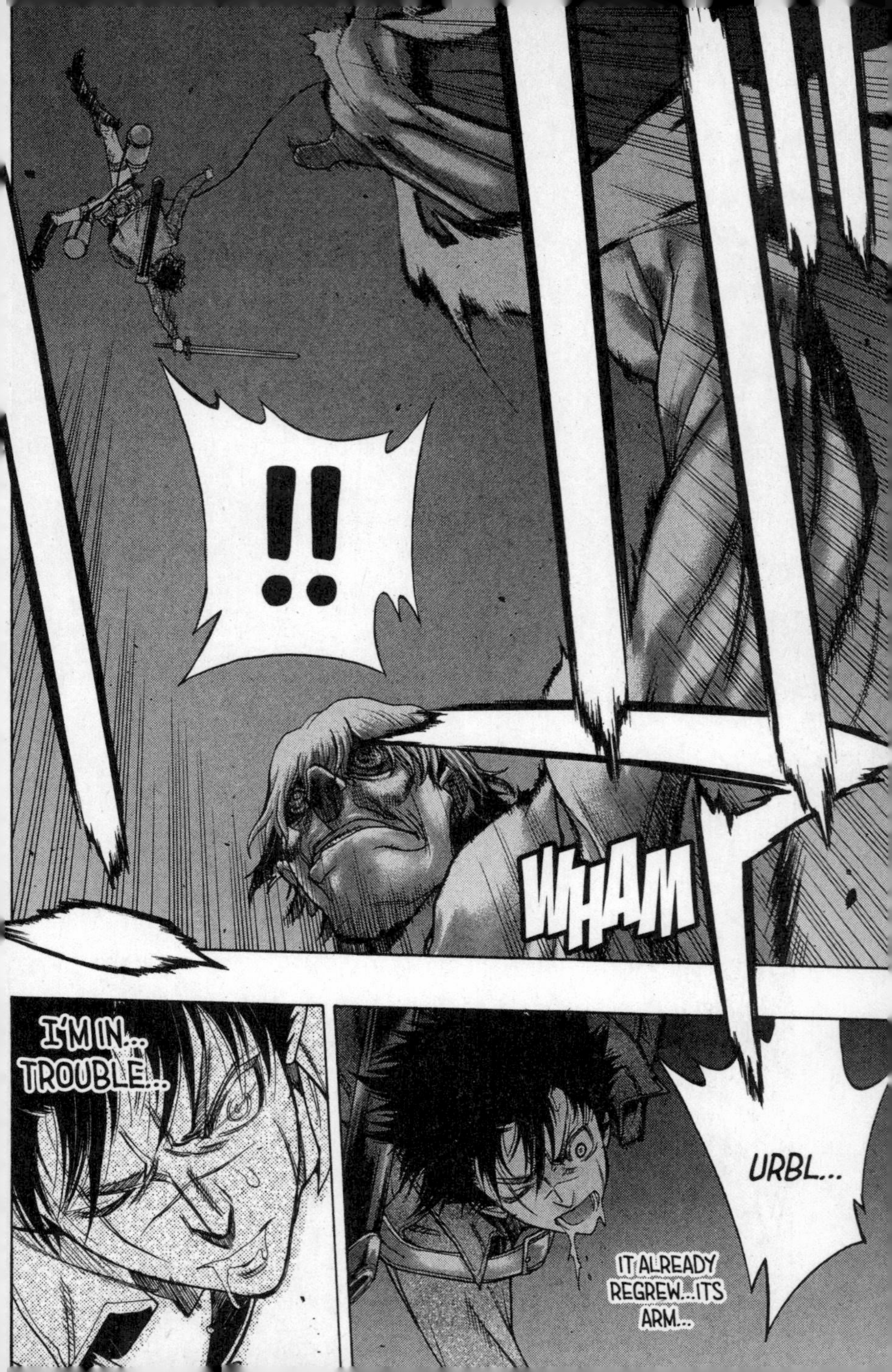
!!
WHAM
URBL...
IT ALREADY REGREW...ITS ARM...
I'M IN... TROUBLE...

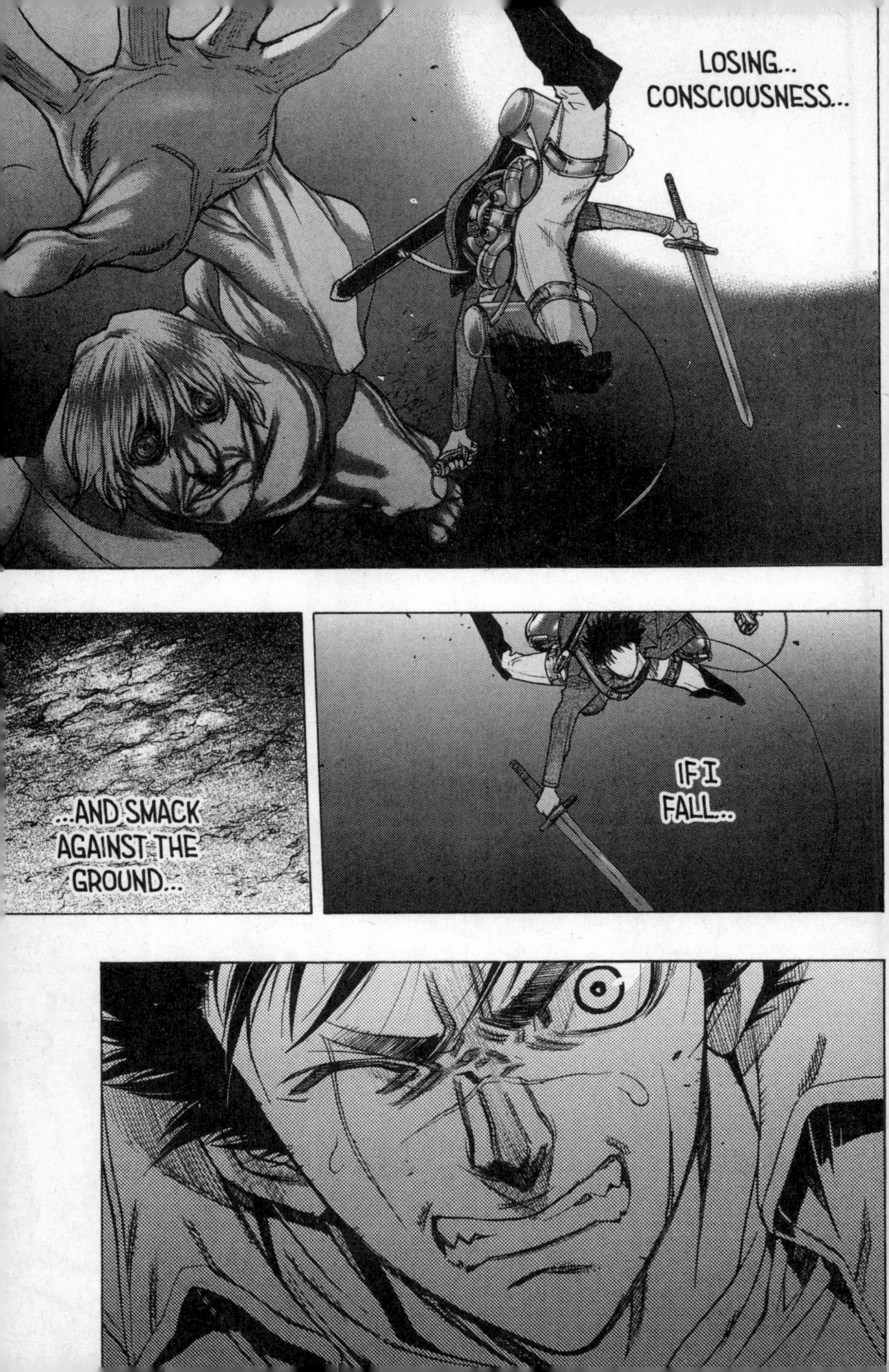
LOSING... CONSCIOUSNESS...
IF I FALL...
...AND SMACK AGAINST THE GROUND...

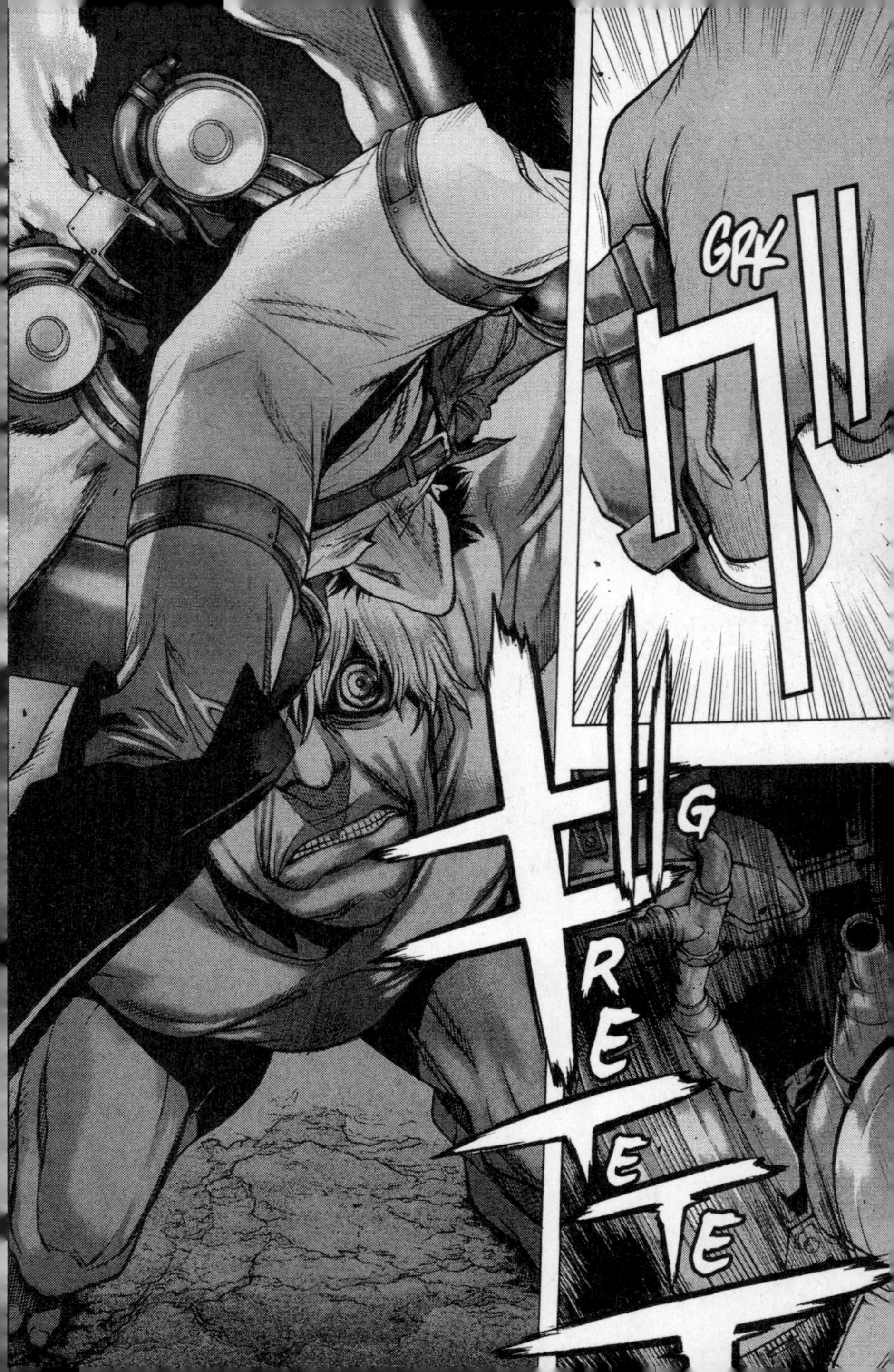
GRK
GREEEE

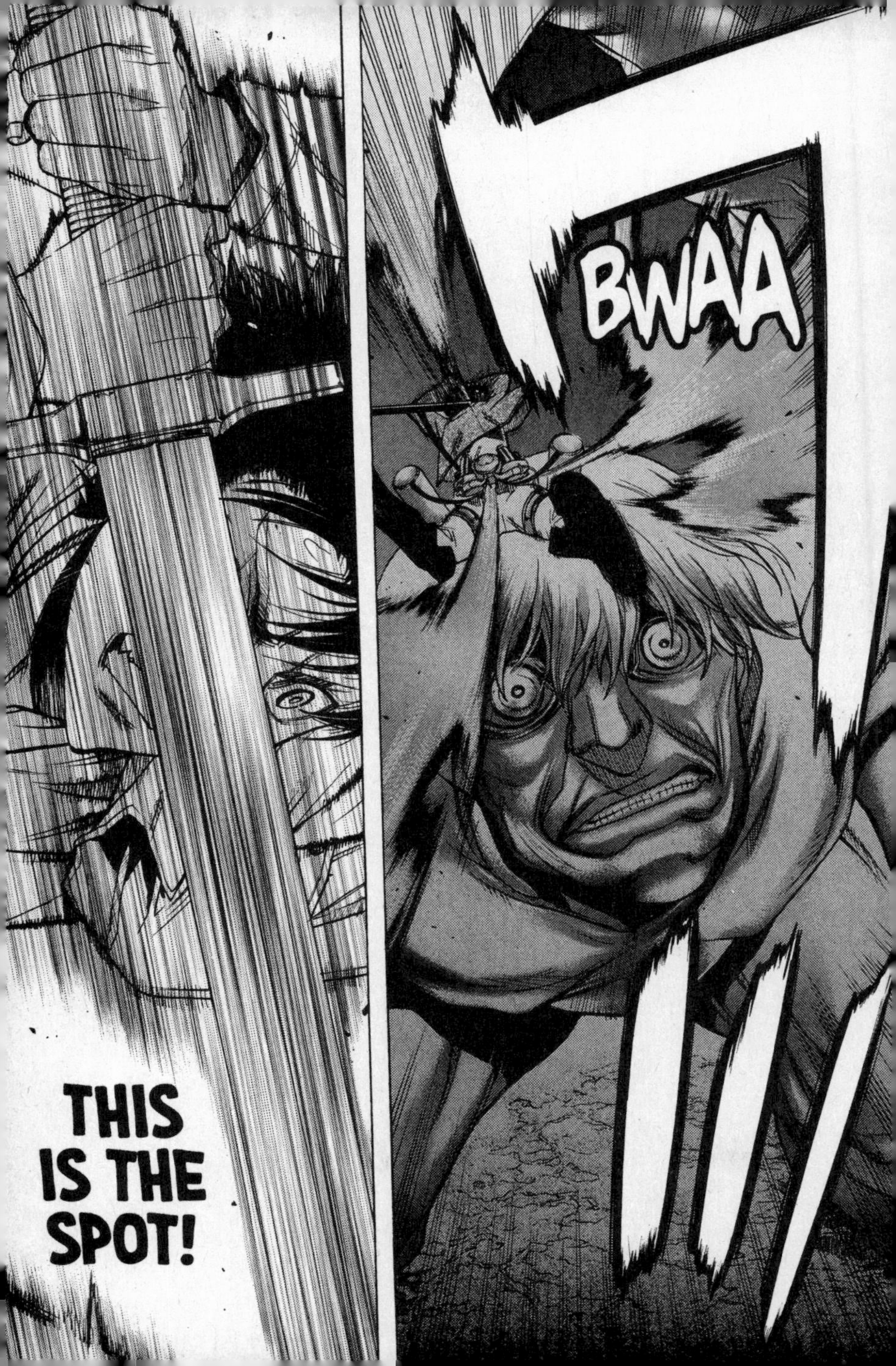
BWAA
THIS IS THE SPOT!

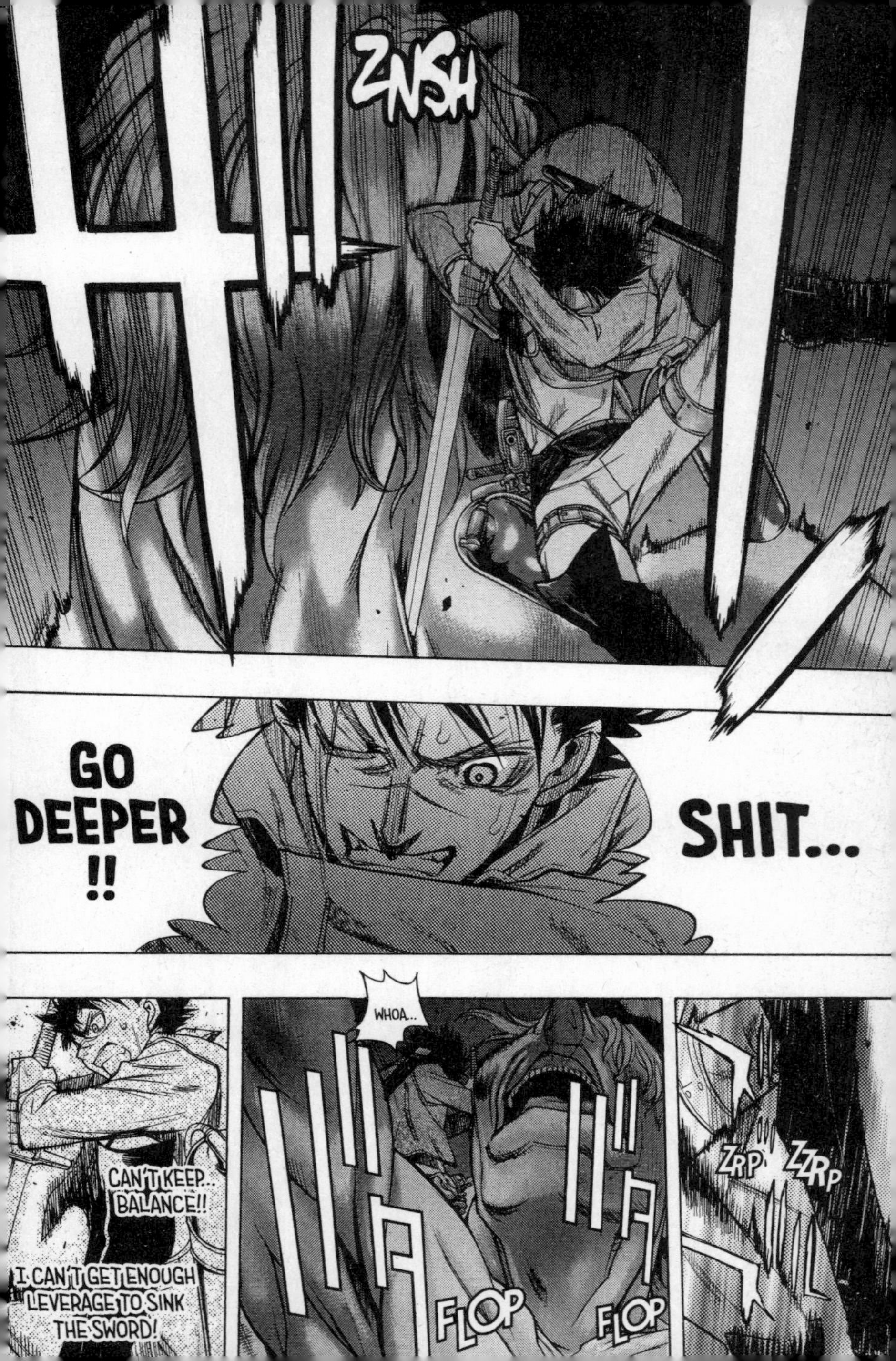
ZNSH
SHIT...
GO DEEPER!!
ZRP
ZZRP
WHOA...
FLOP
FLOP
CAN'T KEEP... BALANCE!!
I CAN'T GET ENOUGH LEVERAGE TO SINK THE SWORD!

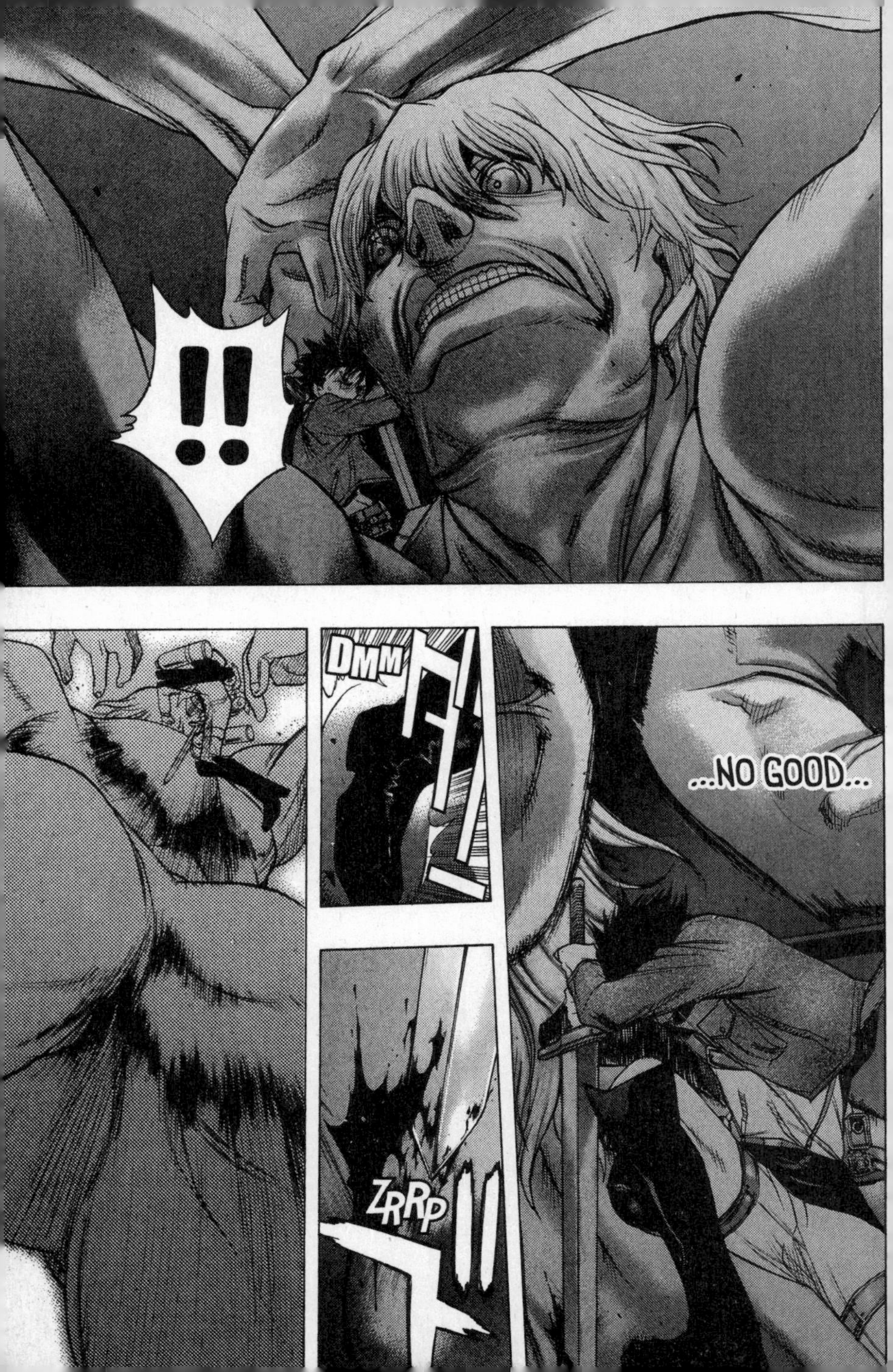
!!
...NO GOOD...
DMM
ZRRP

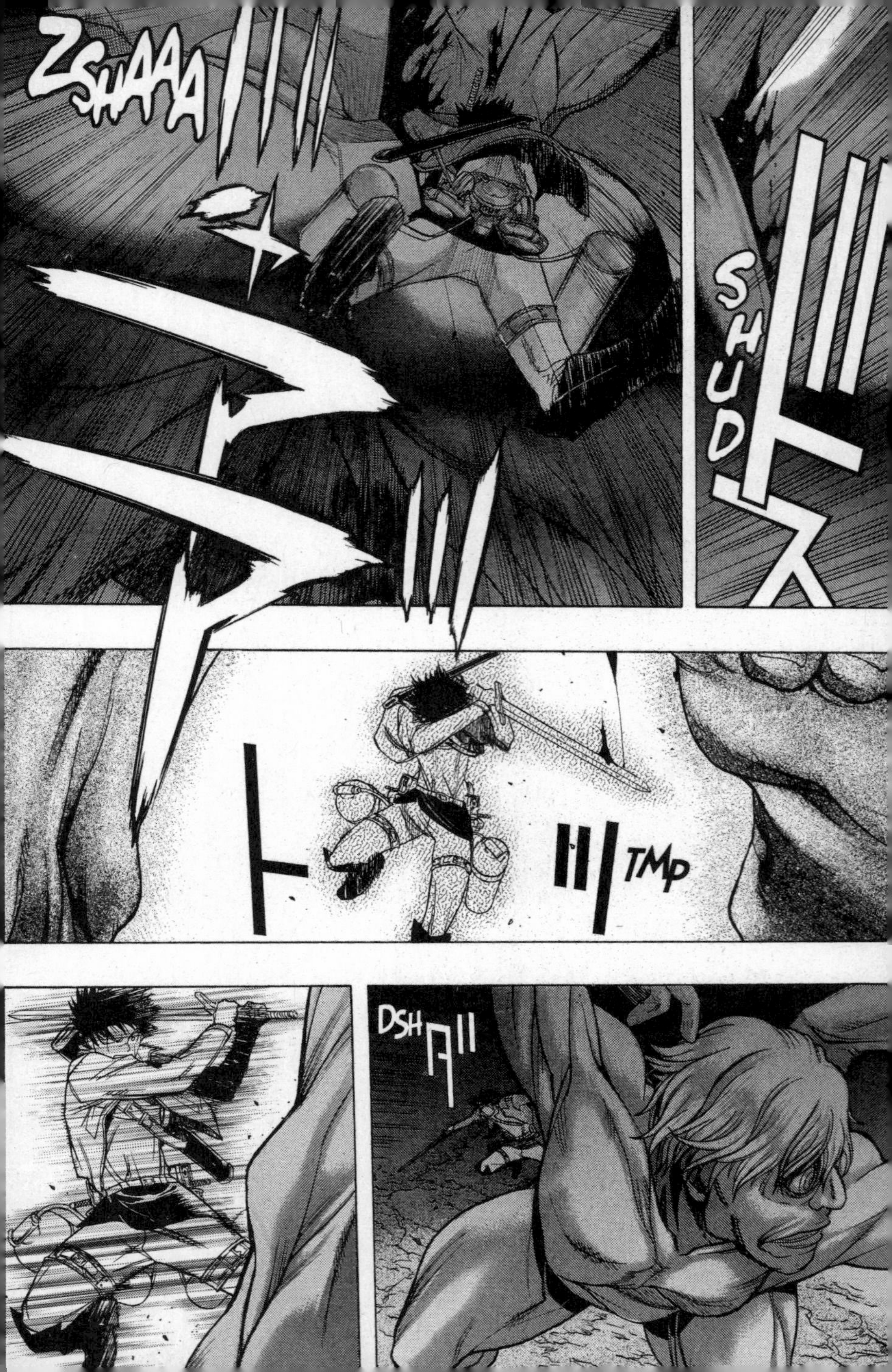
SHUD
ZSHAAA
TMP
DSH

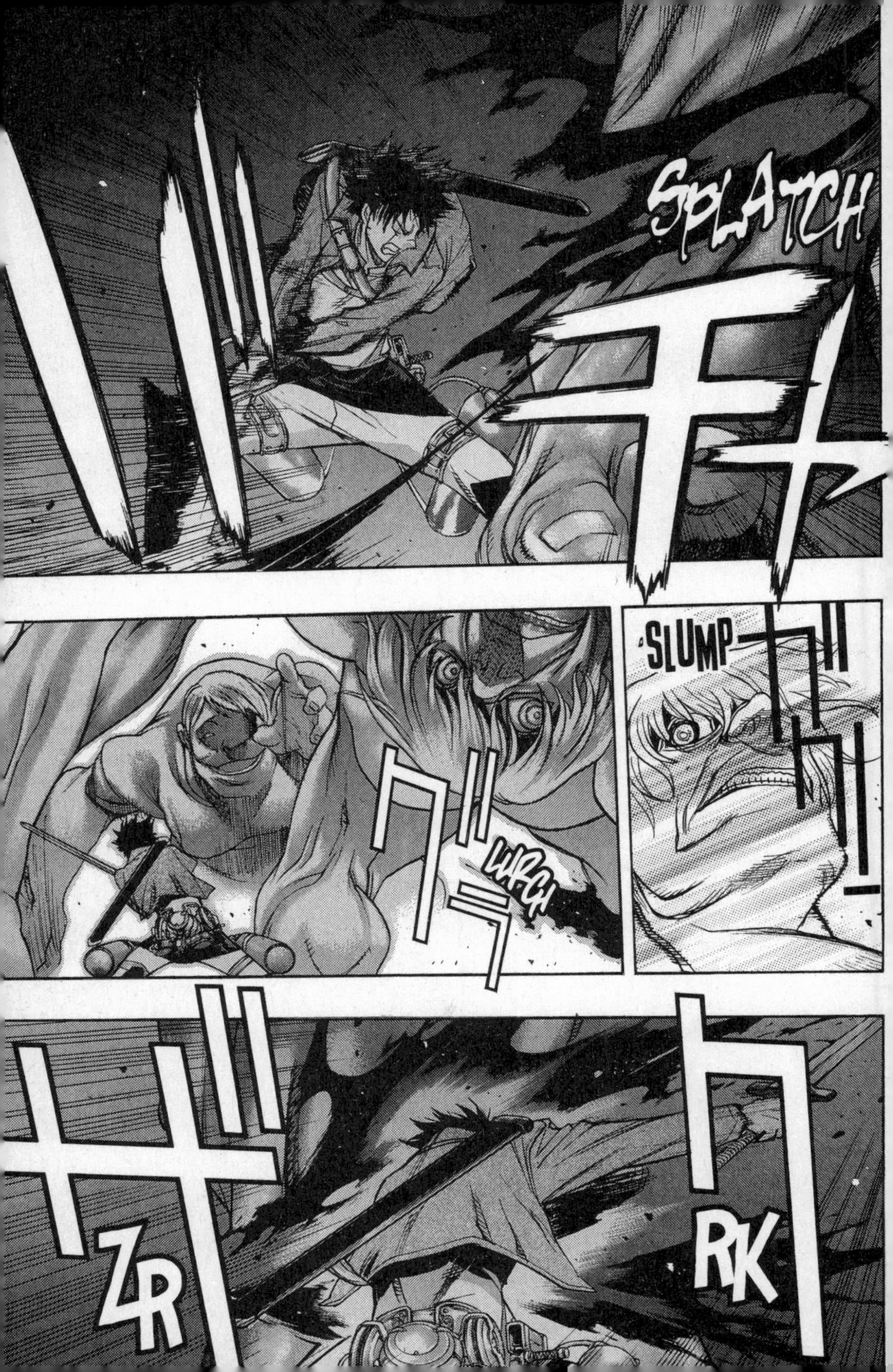
SPLATCH
SLUMP
LURCH
RK
ZR

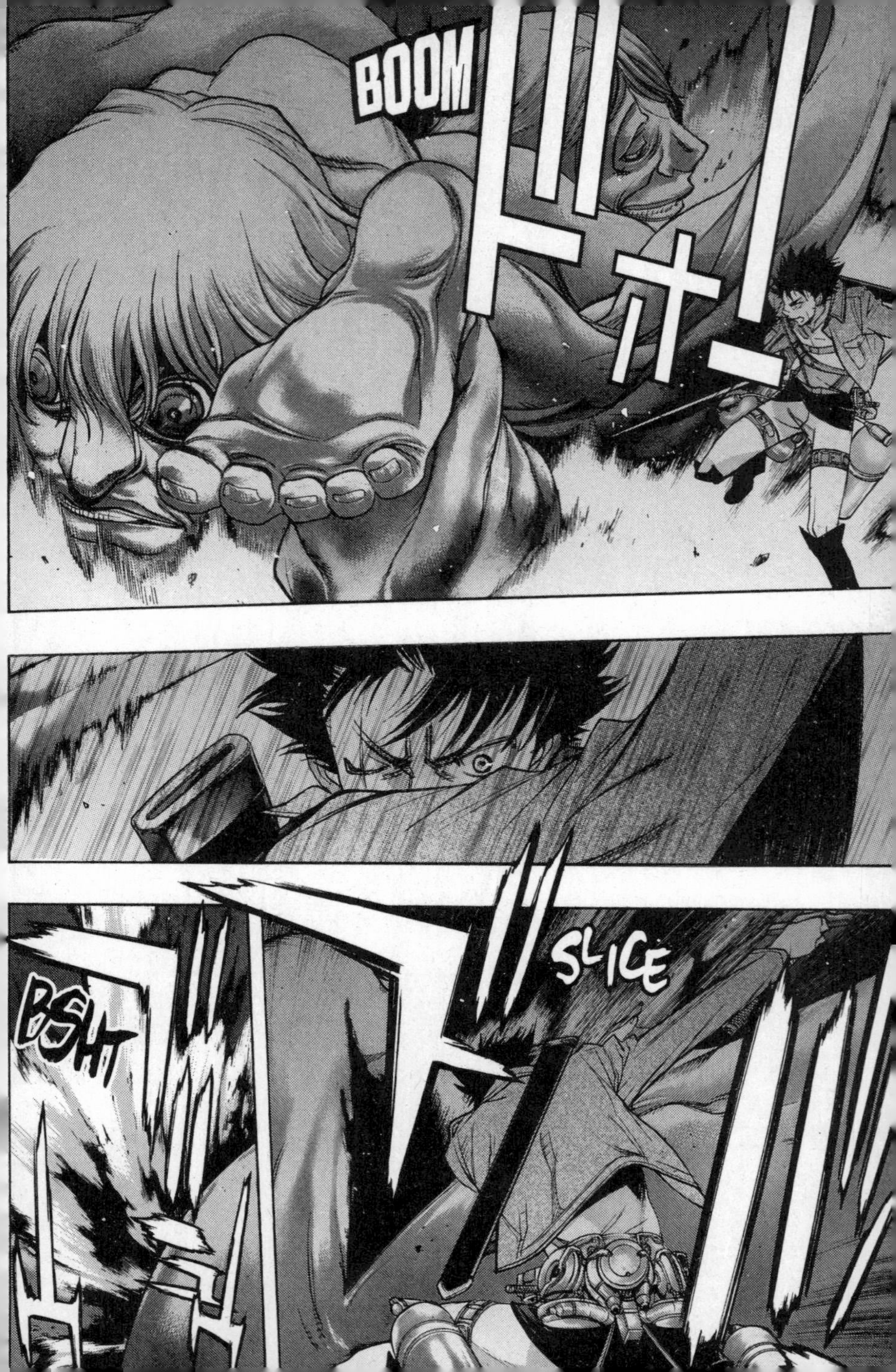
BOOM
SLICE
BSHT

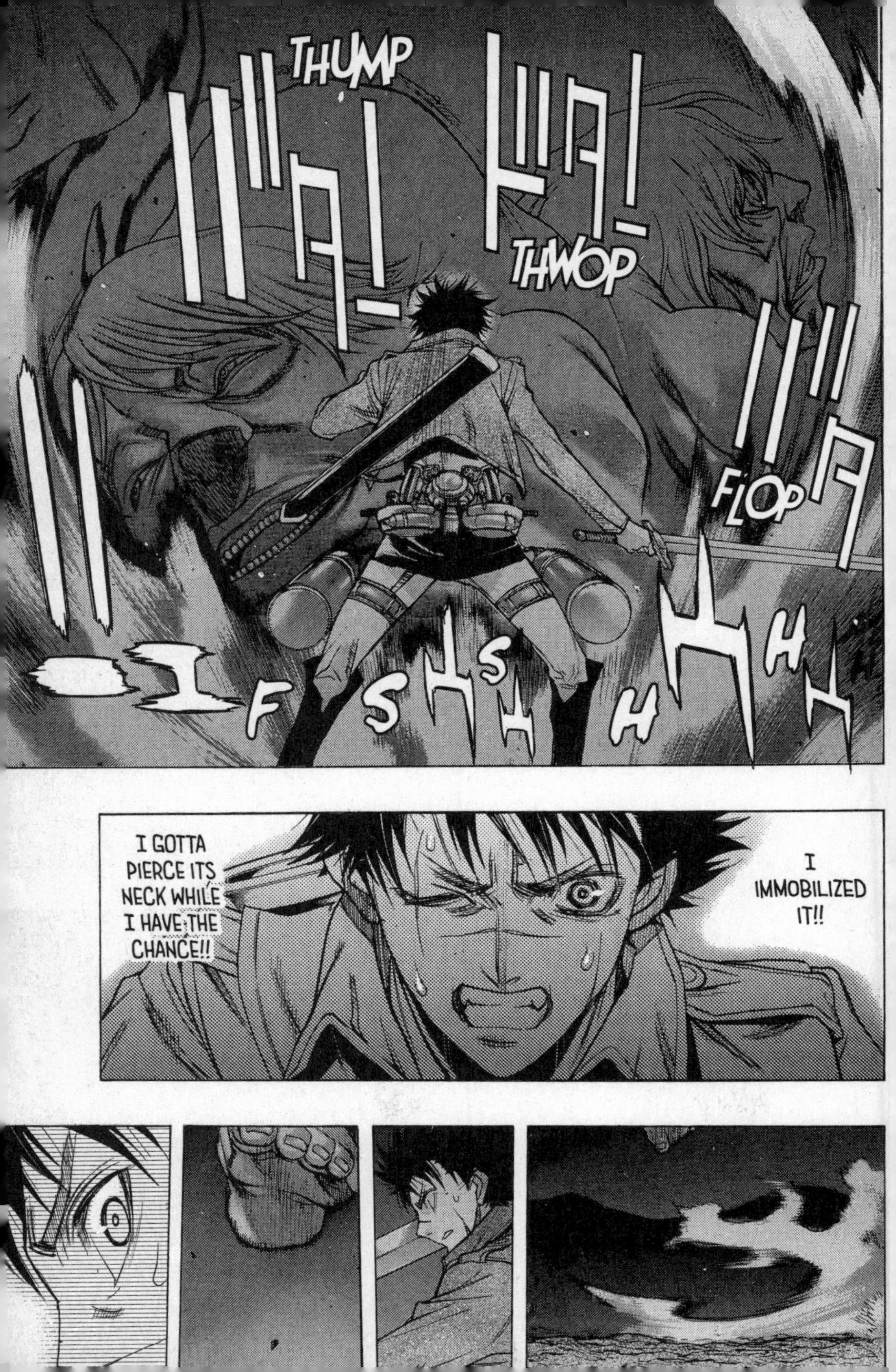
FLOP
THWOP
THUMP
I IMMOBILIZED IT!!
I GOTTA PIERCE ITS NECK WHILE I HAVE THE CHANCE!!

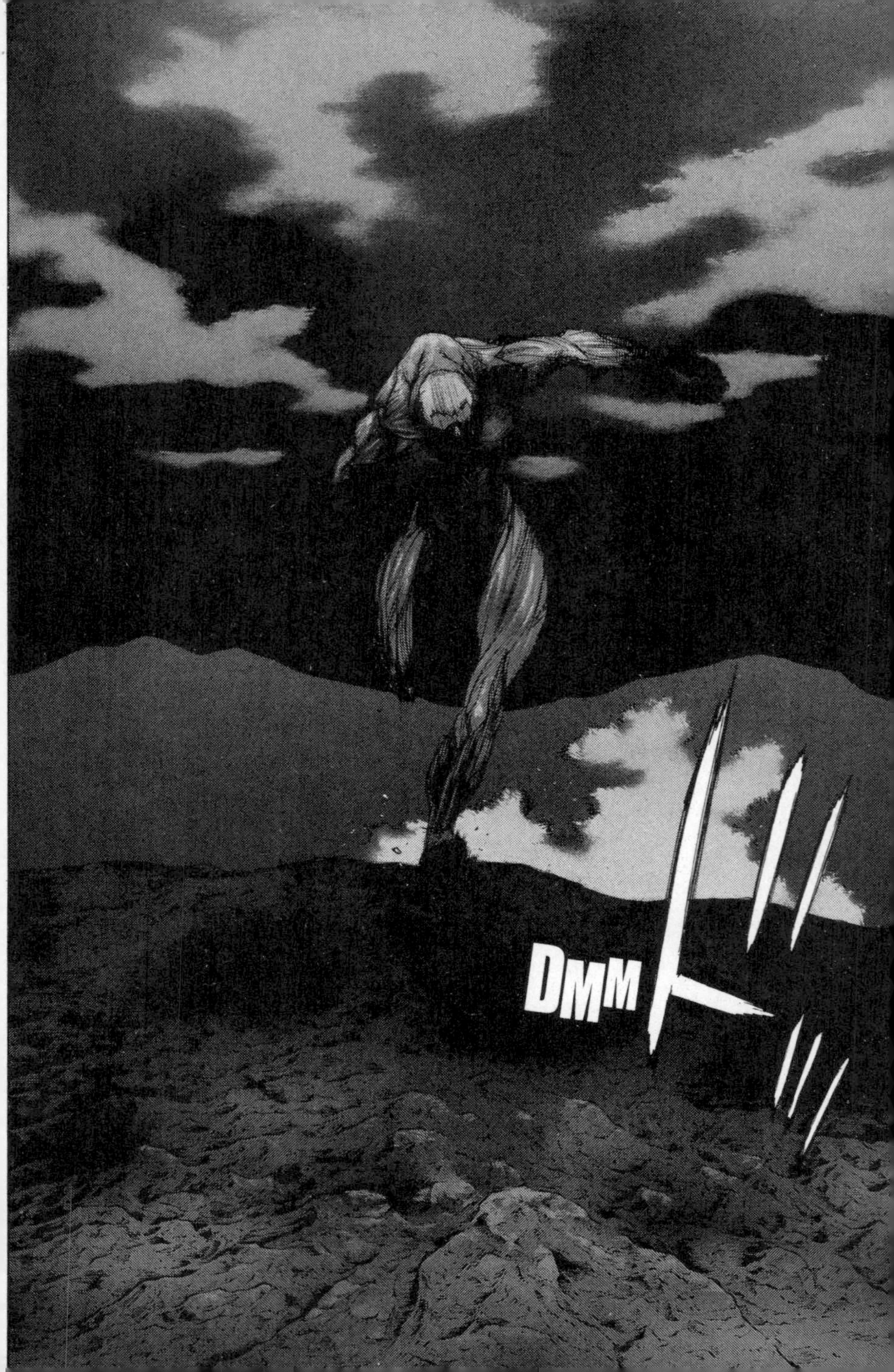
DMM

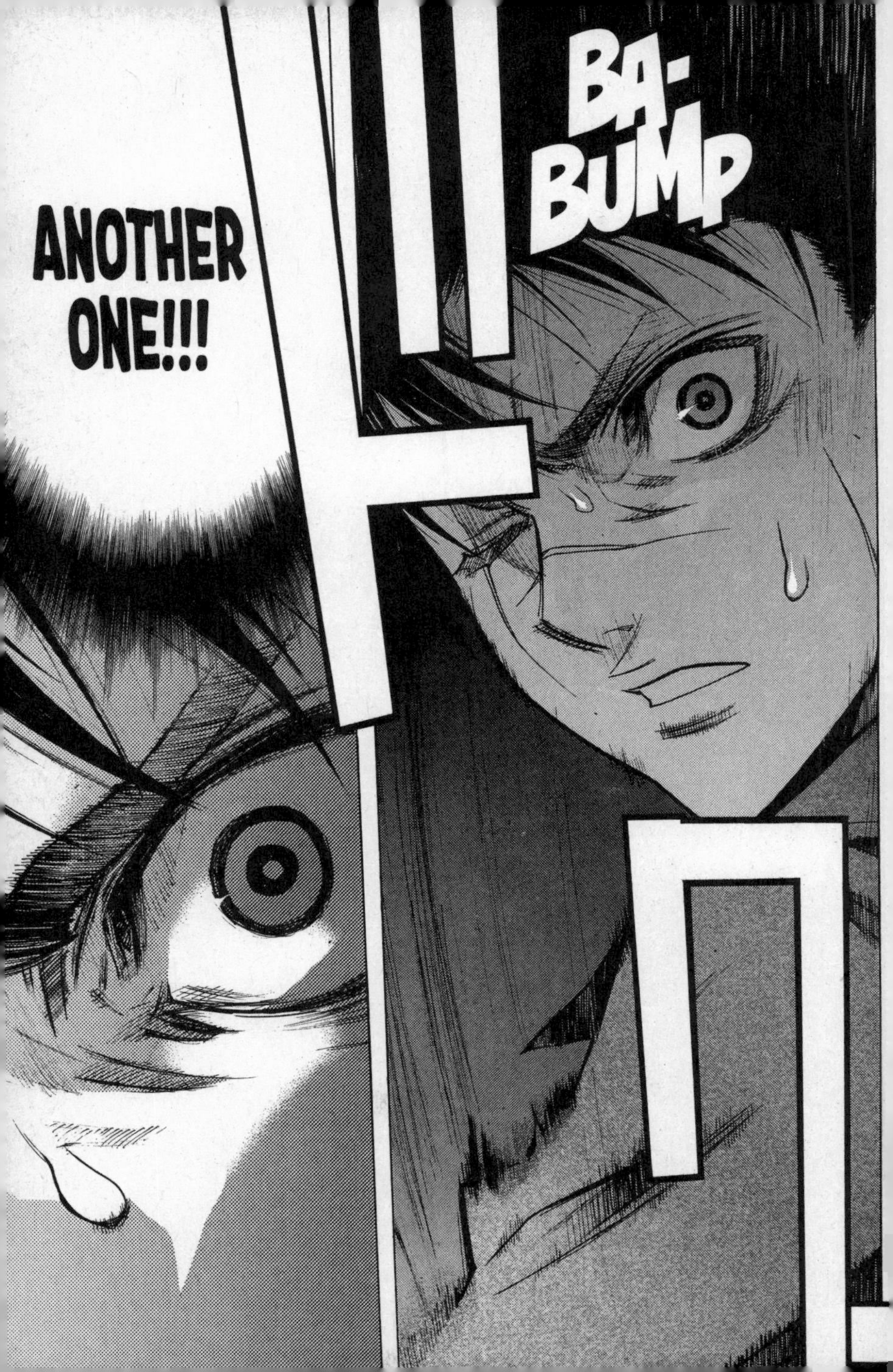
BA-BUMP
ANOTHER ONE!!!

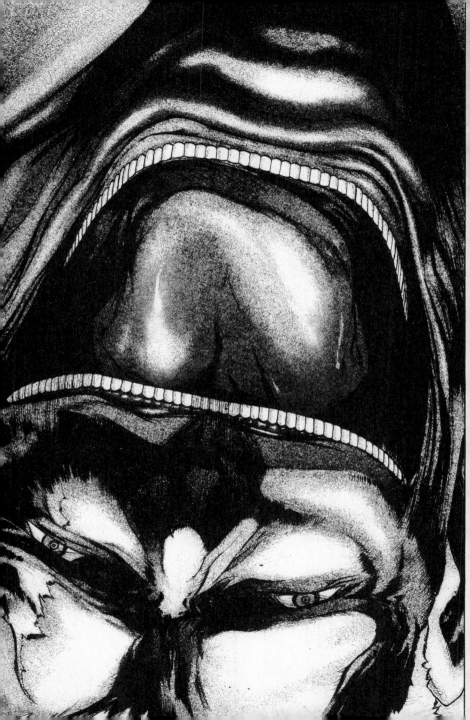

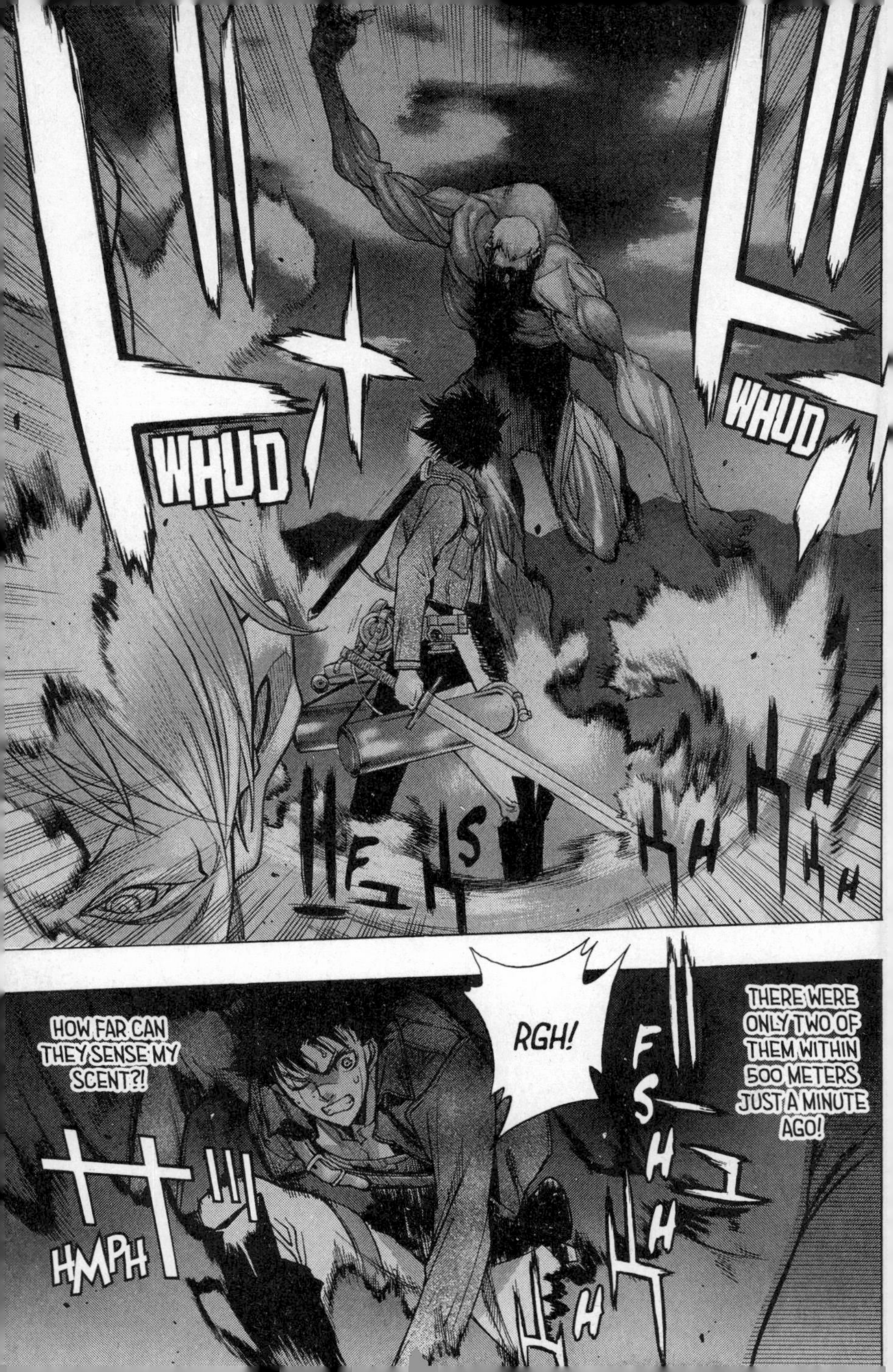
WHUD
WHUD
HFSSH
HHHHH
THERE WERE ONLY TWO OF THEM WITHIN 500 METERS JUST A MINUTE AGO!
FSHHH
RGH!
HOW FAR CAN THEY SENSE MY SCENT?!
HMPH

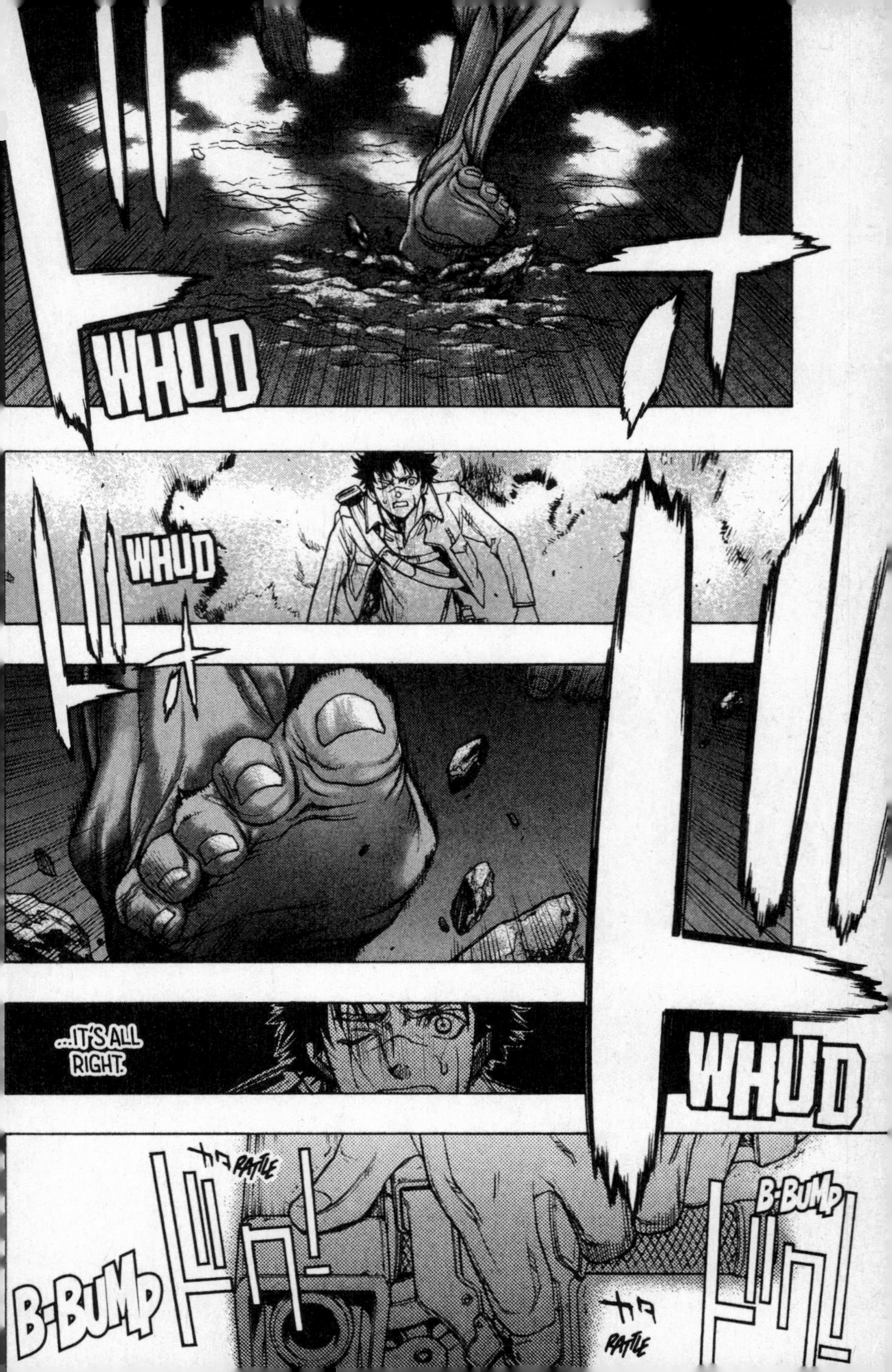
WHUD
WHUD
...IT'S ALL RIGHT.
WHUD
B-BUMP
RATTLE
RATTLE
B-BUMP

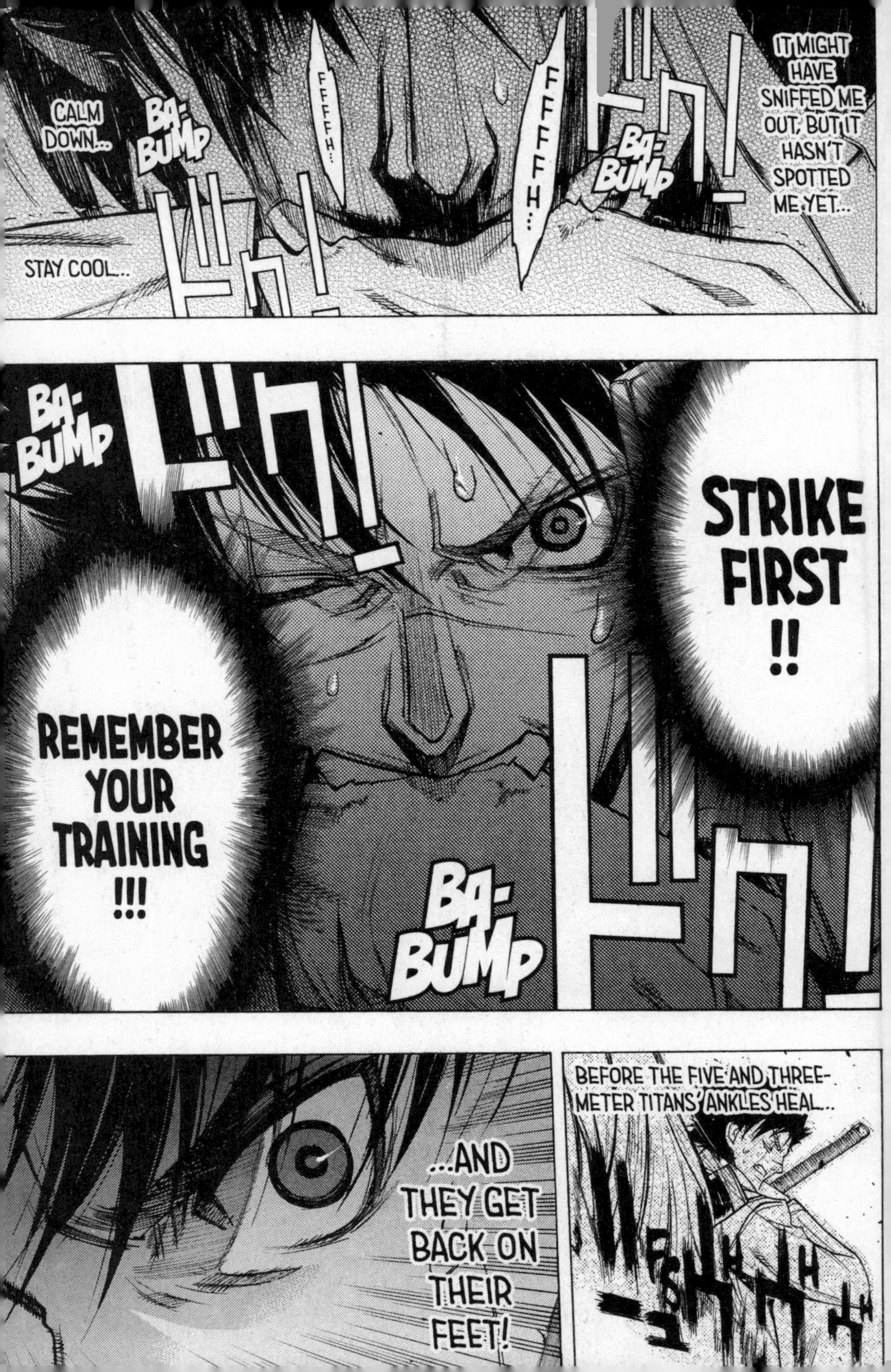
IT MIGHT HAVE SNIFFED ME OUT, BUT IT HASN'T SPOTTED ME YET...
BA-BUMP
FFFFH...
FFFFH...
BA-BUMP
CALM DOWN...
STAY COOL...
STRIKE FIRST !!
BA-BUMP
BA-BUMP
REMEMBER YOUR TRAINING !!!
BEFORE THE FIVE AND THREE-METER TITANS' ANKLES HEAL...
...AND THEY GET BACK ON THEIR FEET!

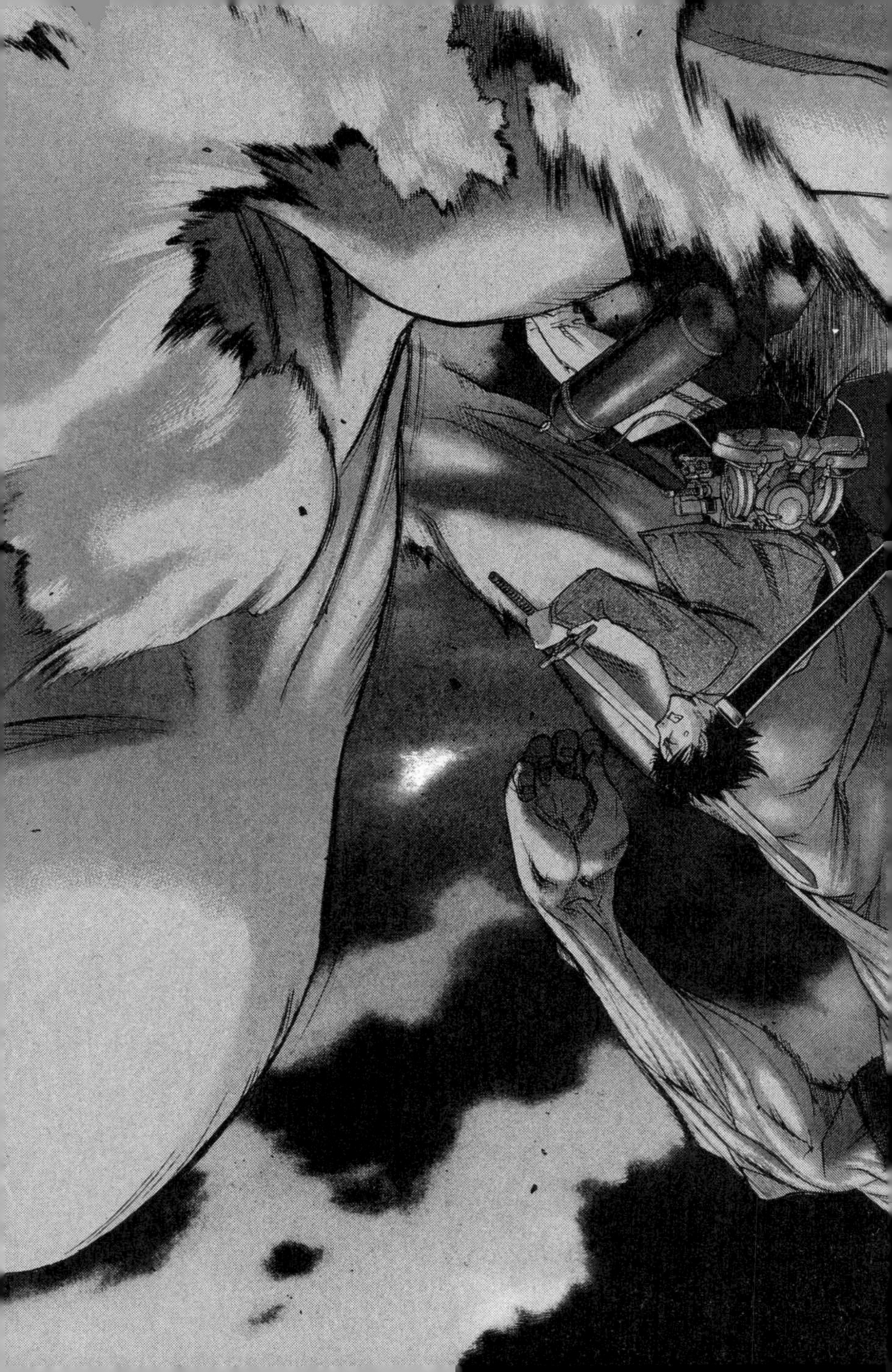

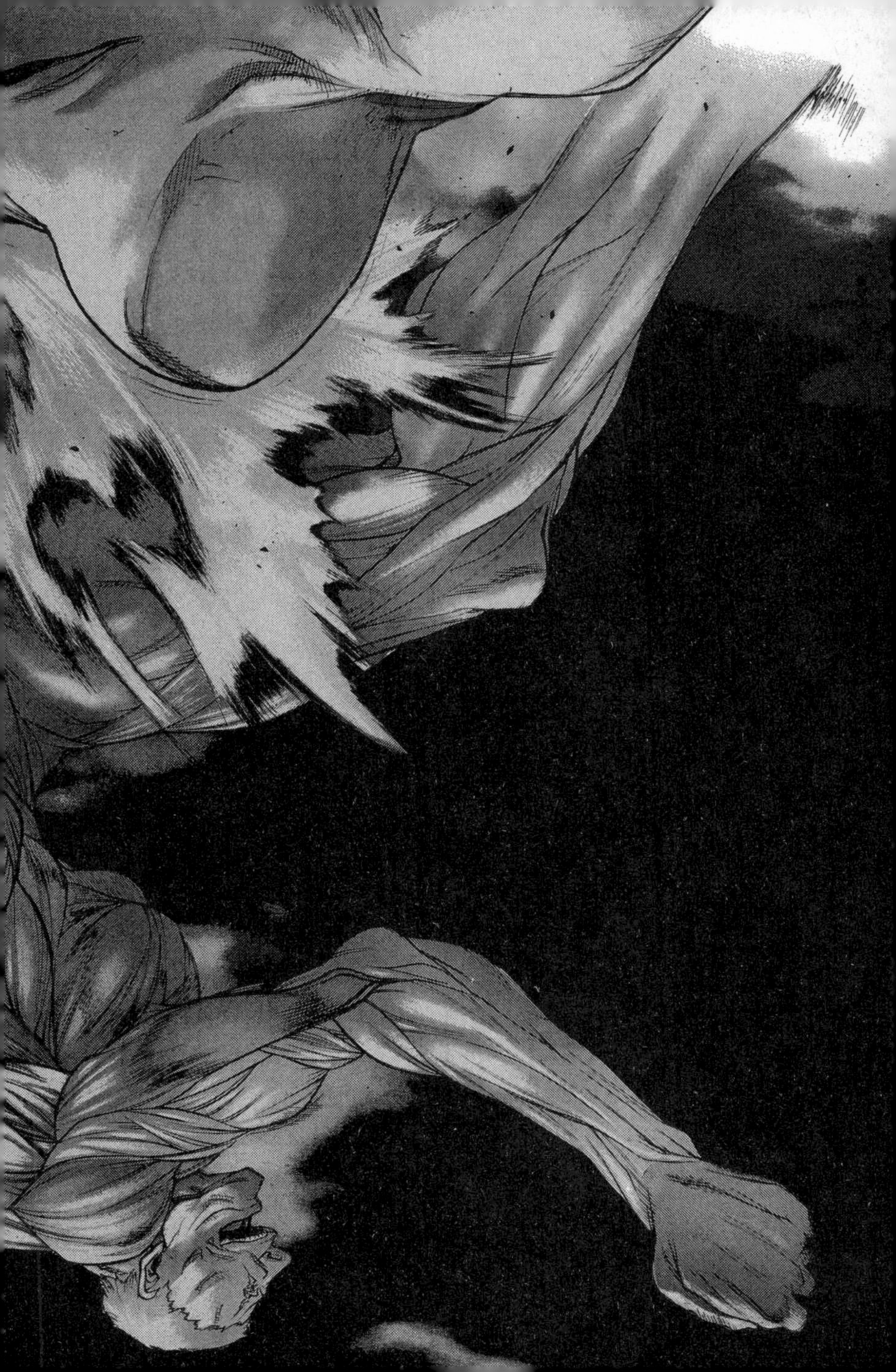

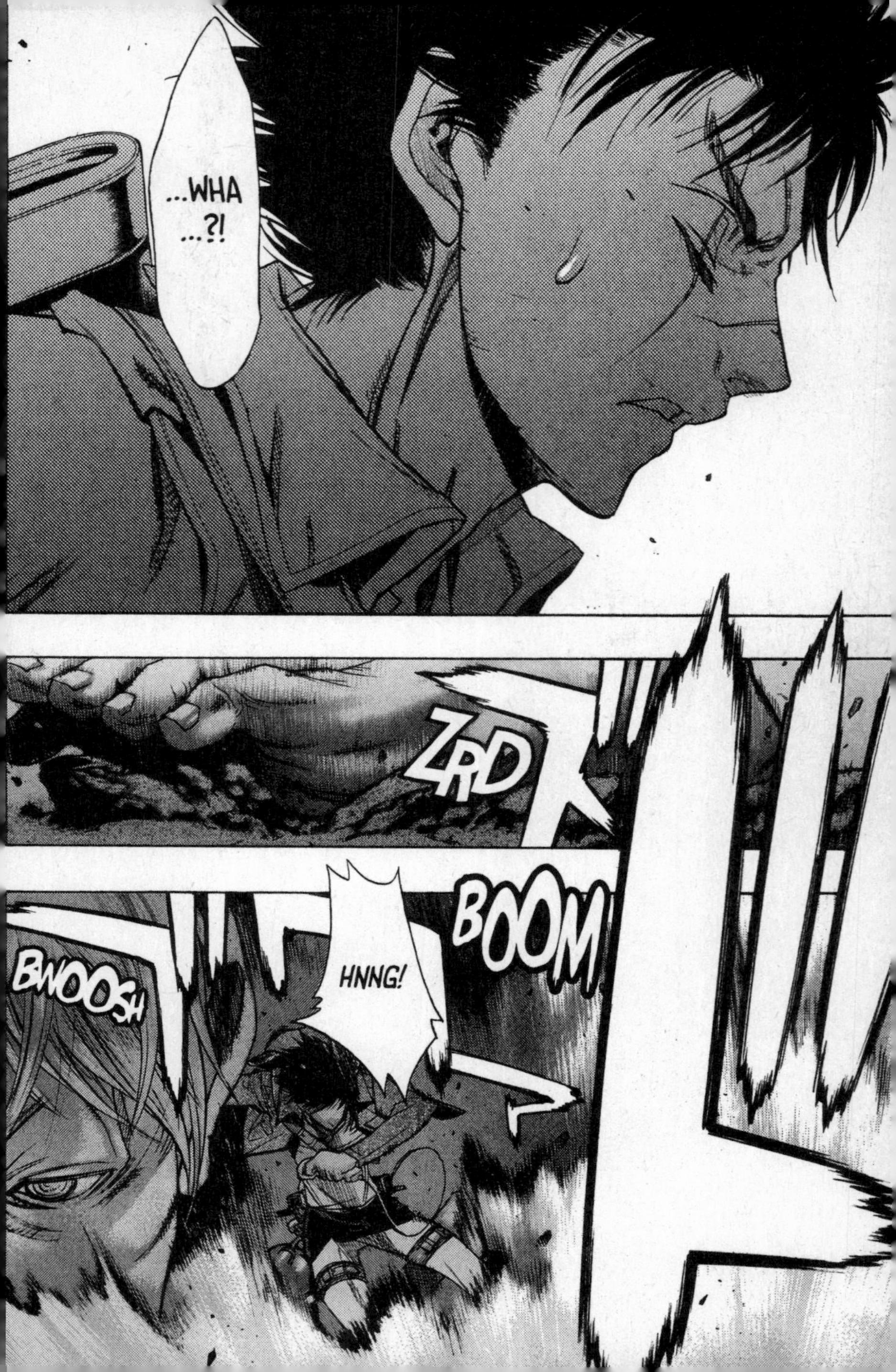
...WHA ...?!
ZRD
BOOM
HNNG!
BWOOSH

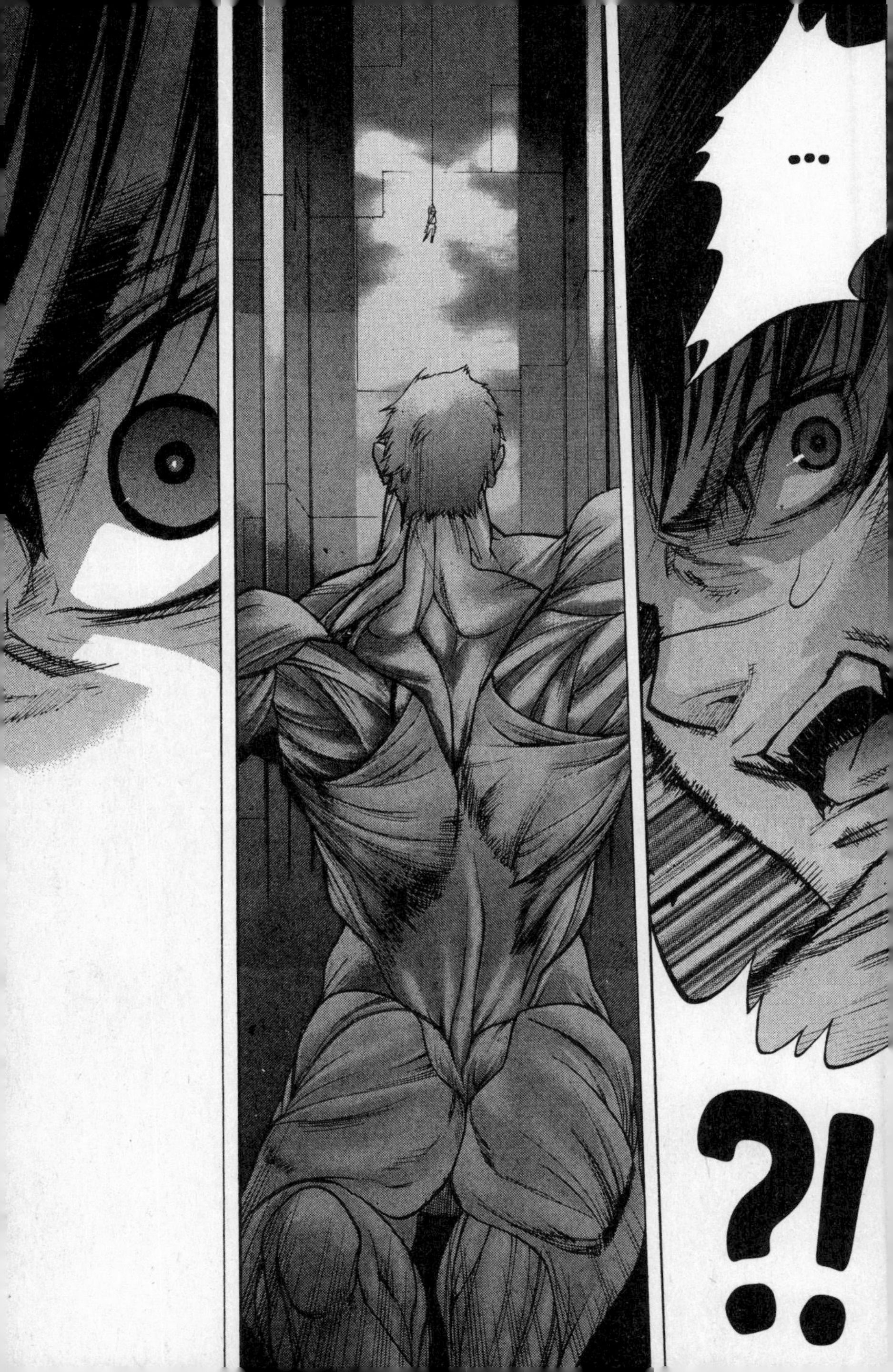
...
?!

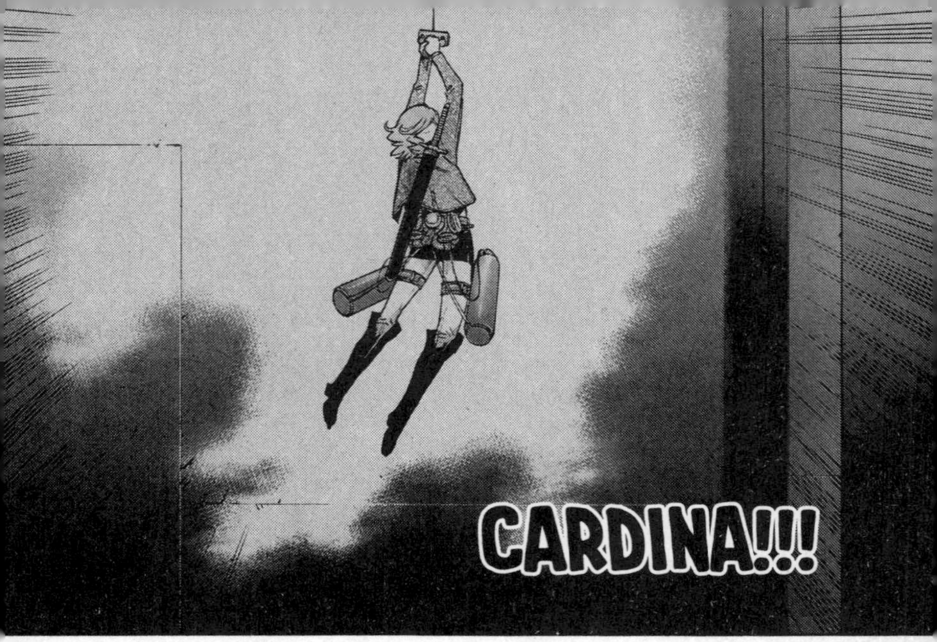
CARDINA!!!
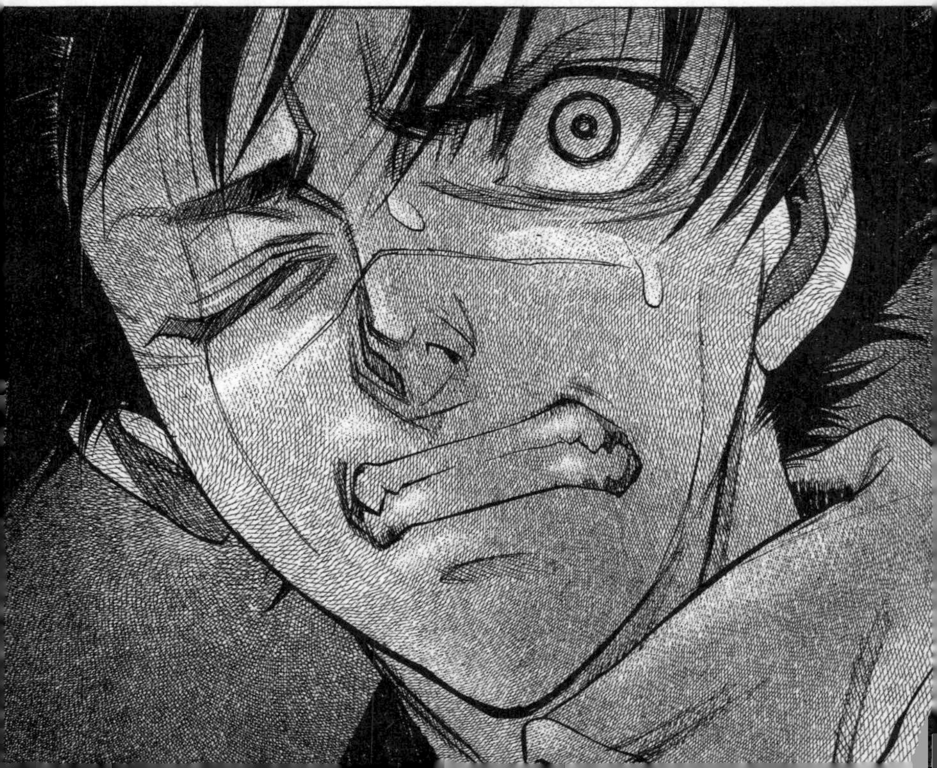

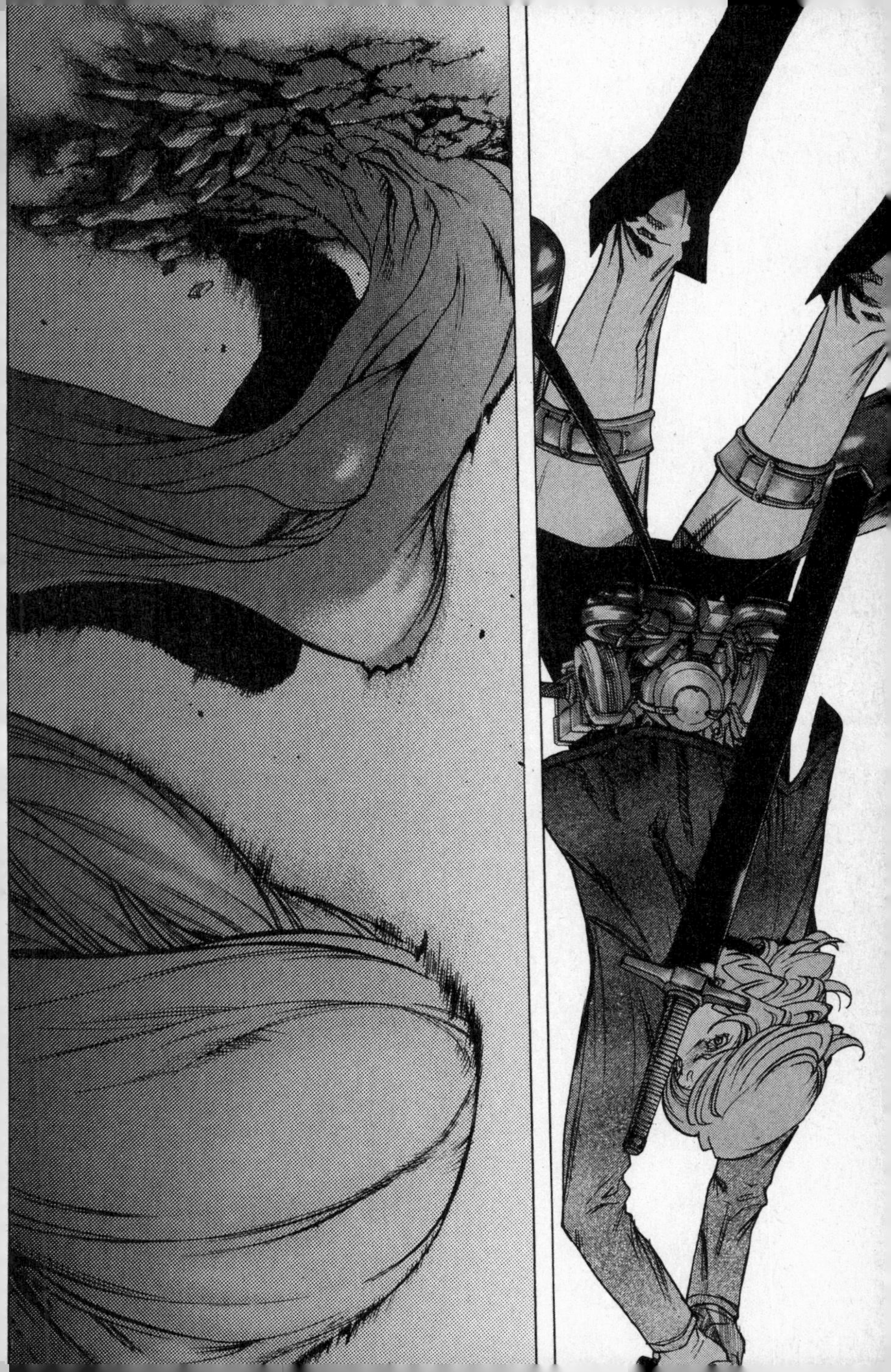

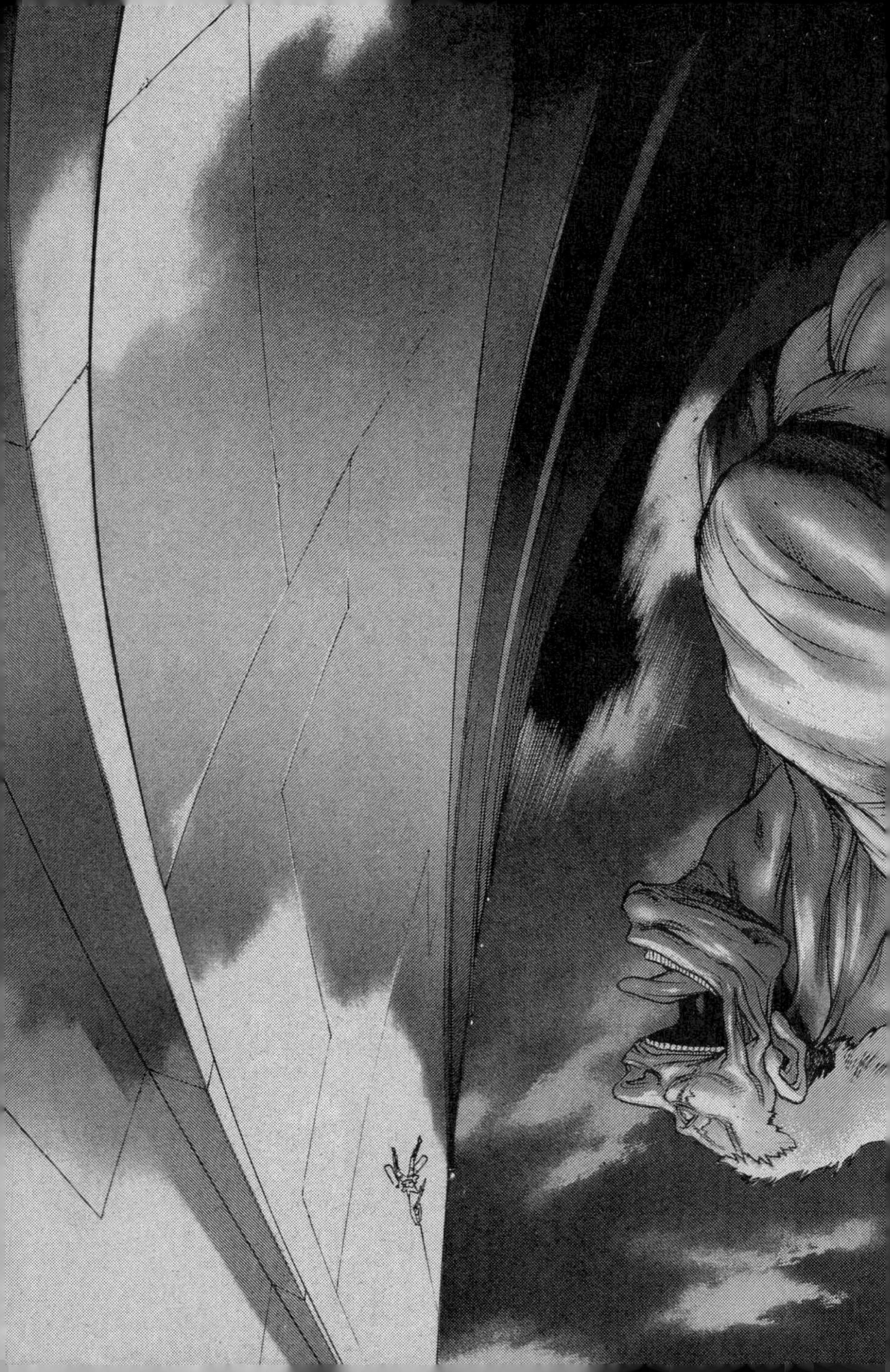

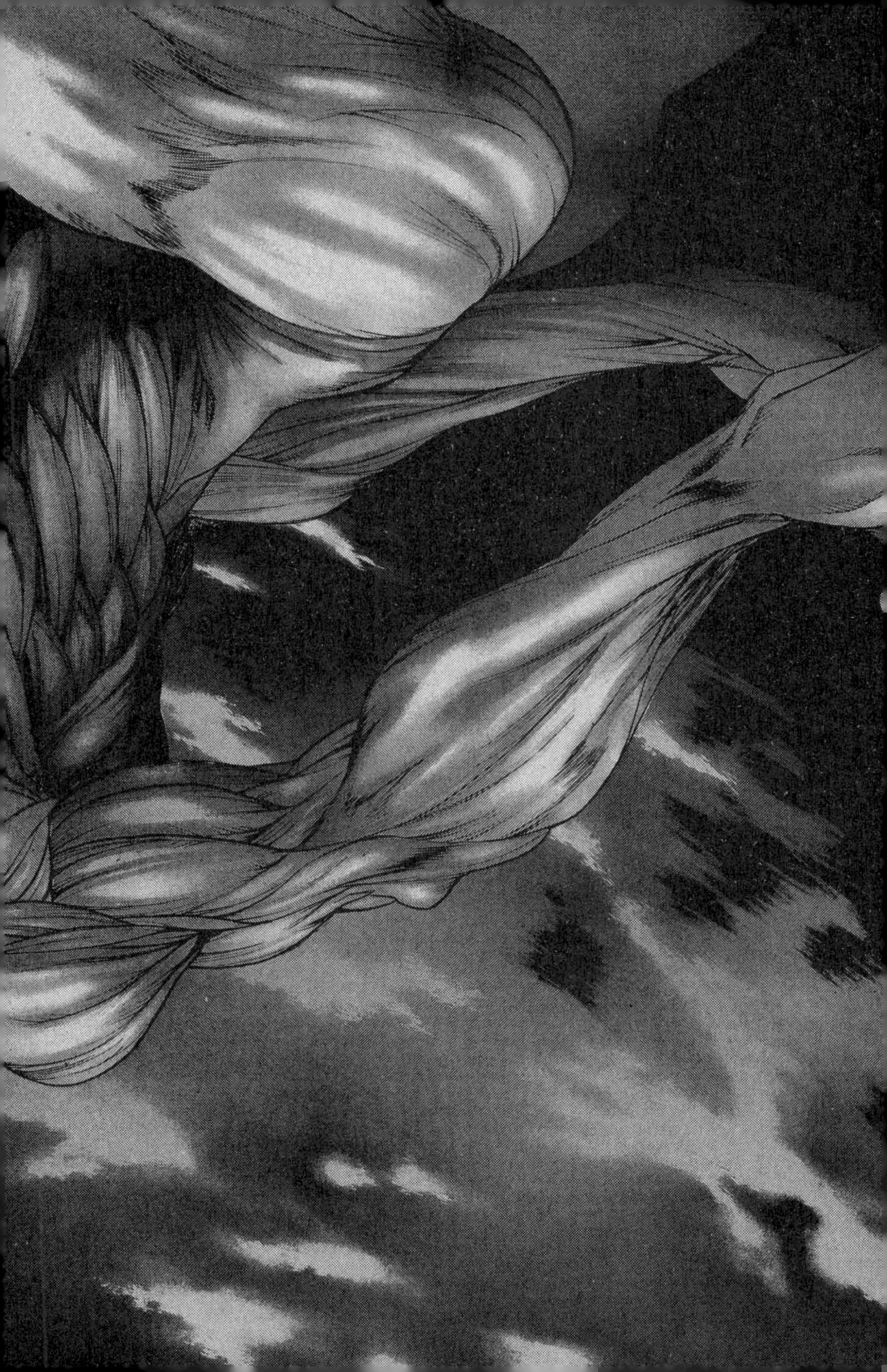

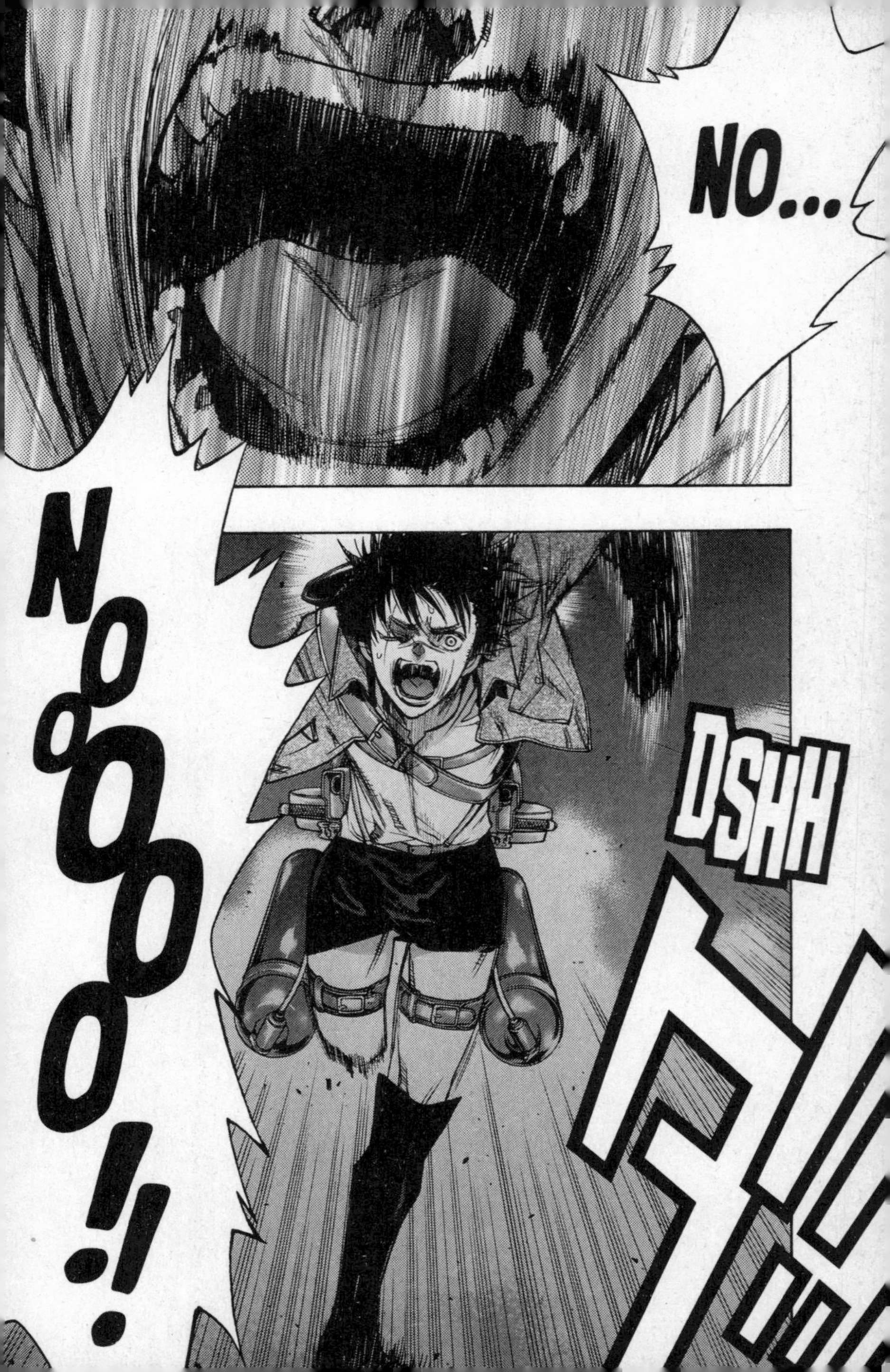
NO...
NOOOOOO!!
DSHH

Chapter 23: Rondo of Darkness · End

ATTACK ON TITAN
BEFORE THE FALL

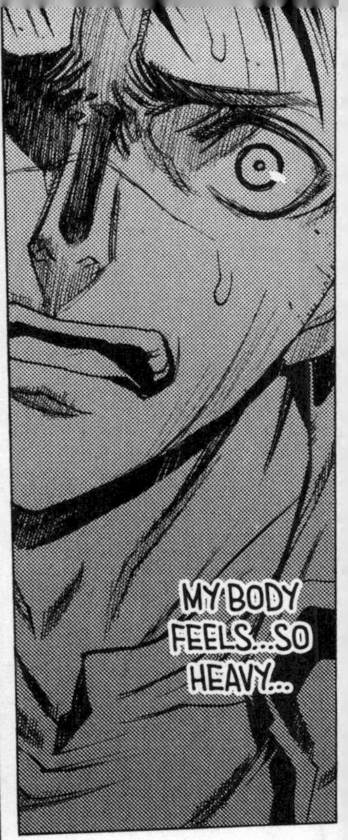
MY BODY FEELS...SO HEAVY...
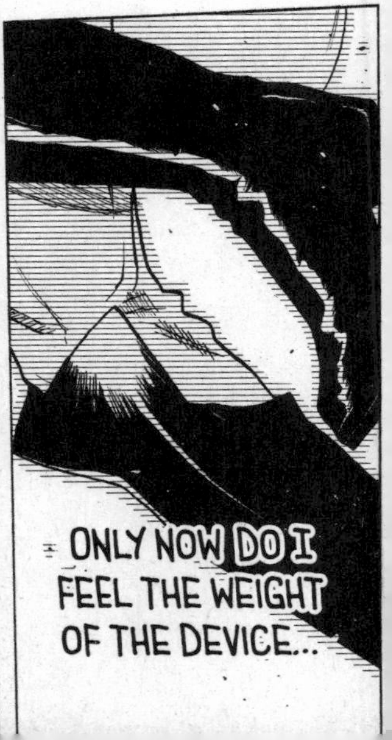
ONLY NOW DO I FEEL THE WEIGHT OF THE DEVICE...
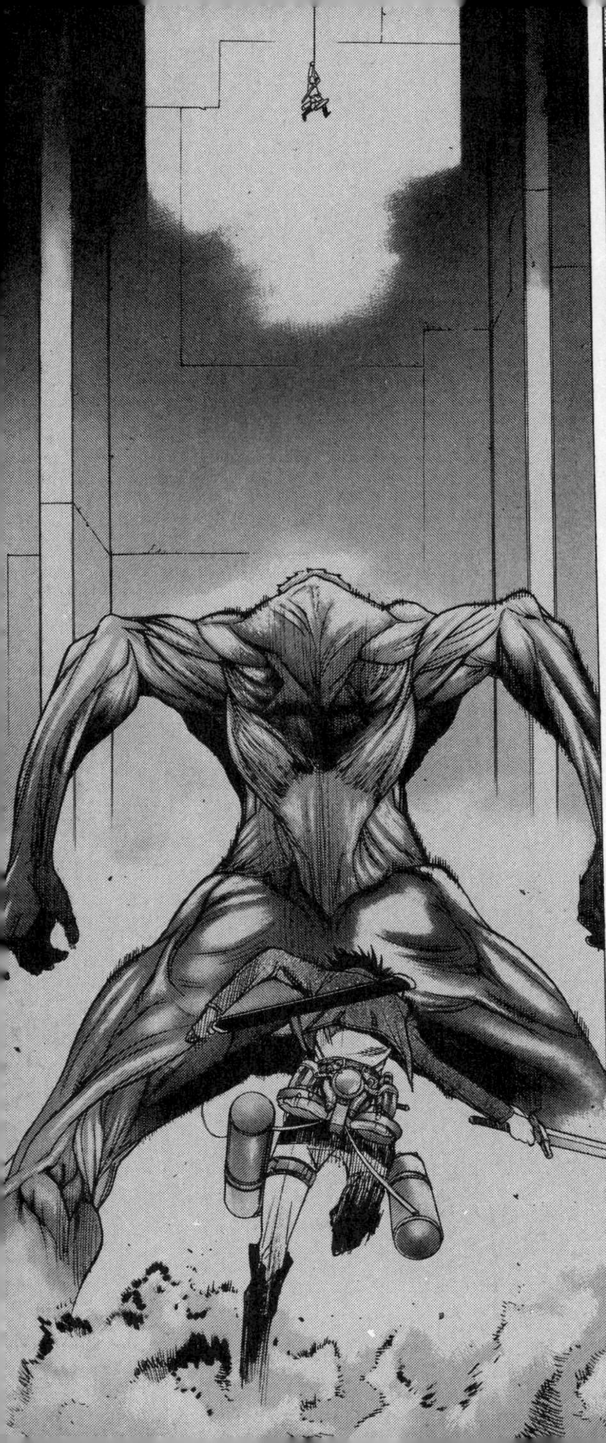

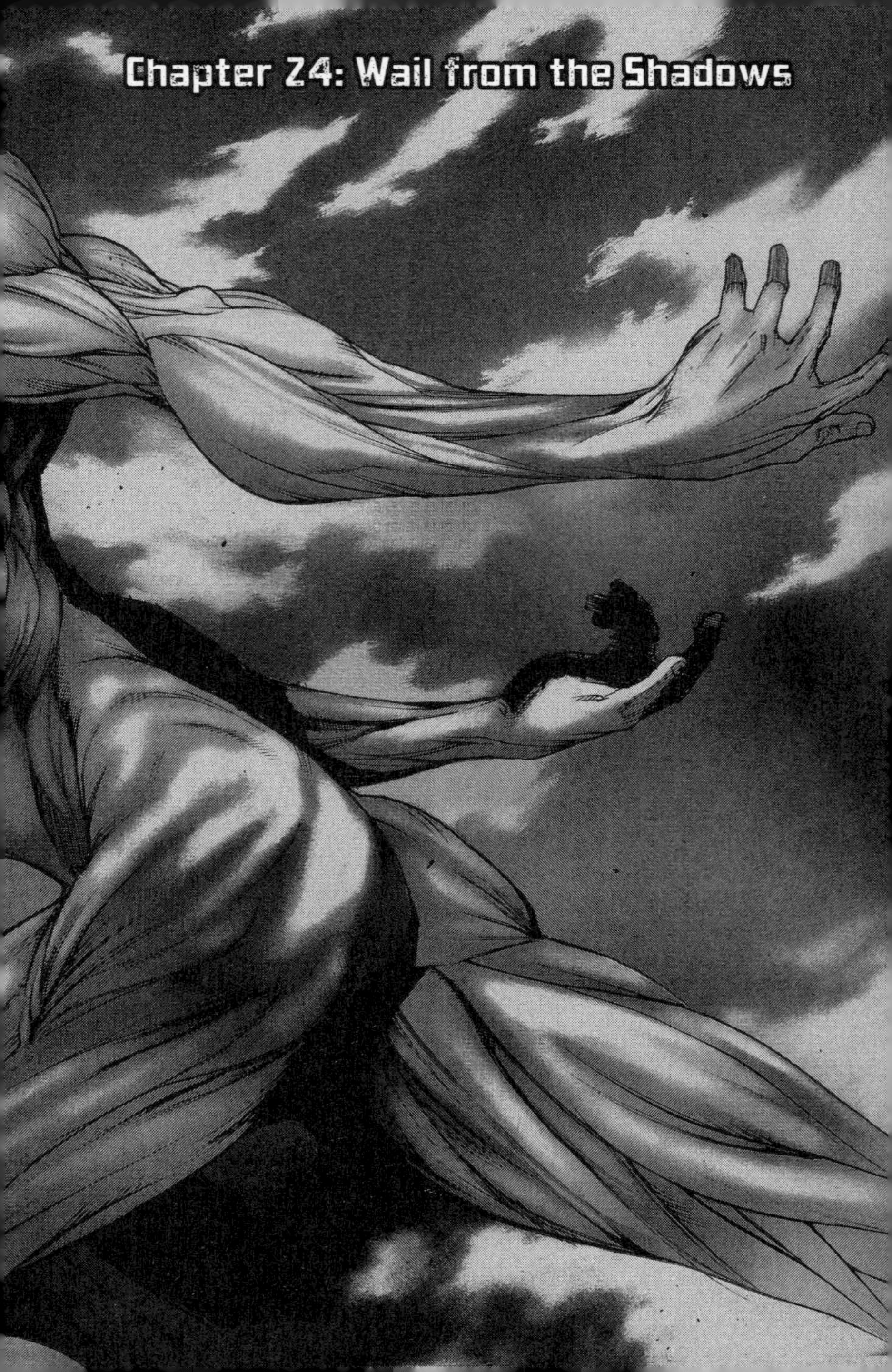
Chapter 24: Wail from the Shadows

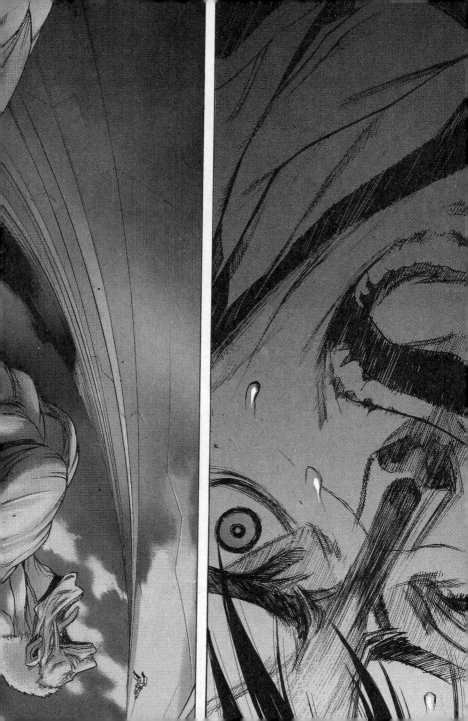

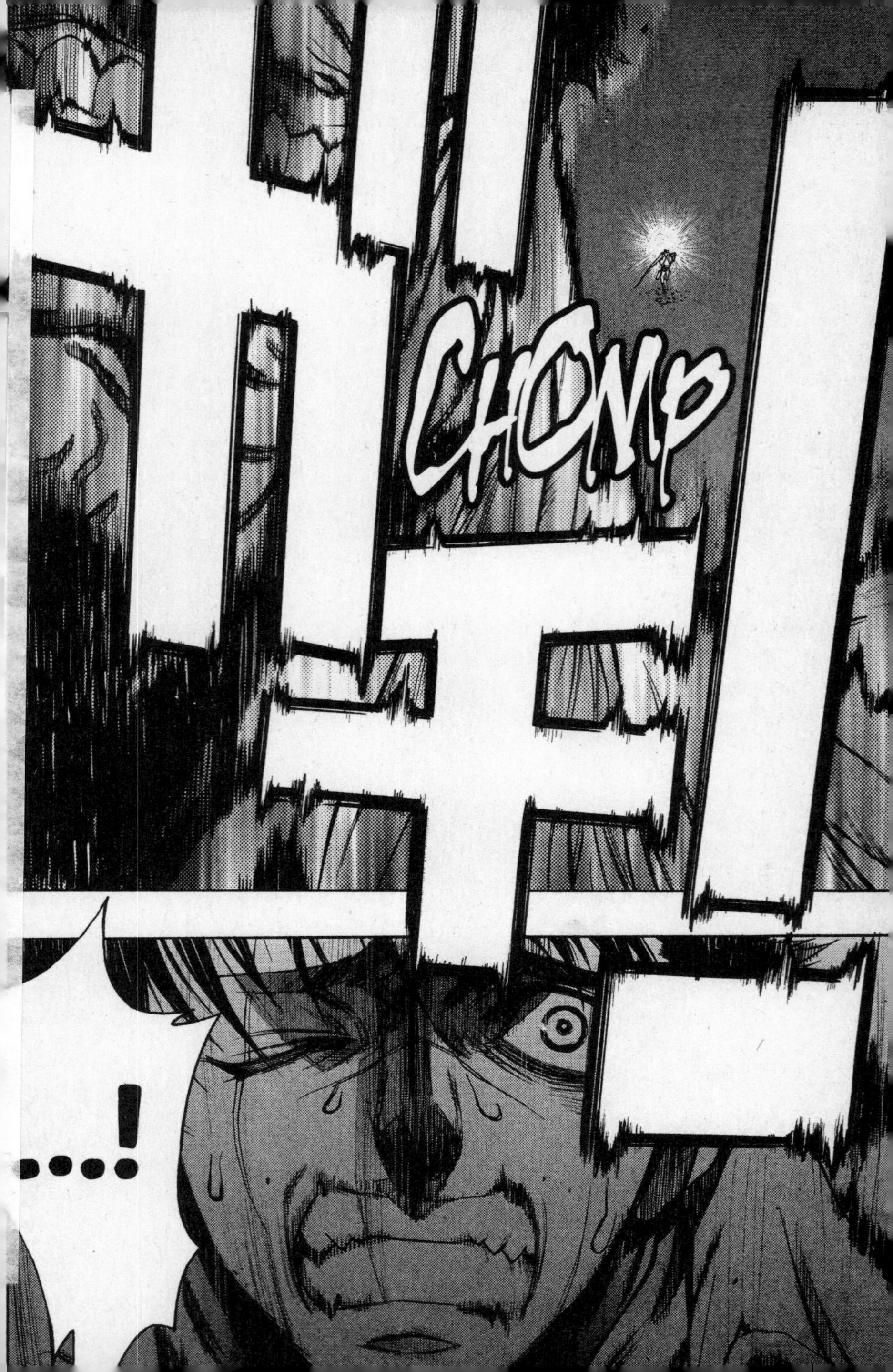
CHOMP
...!

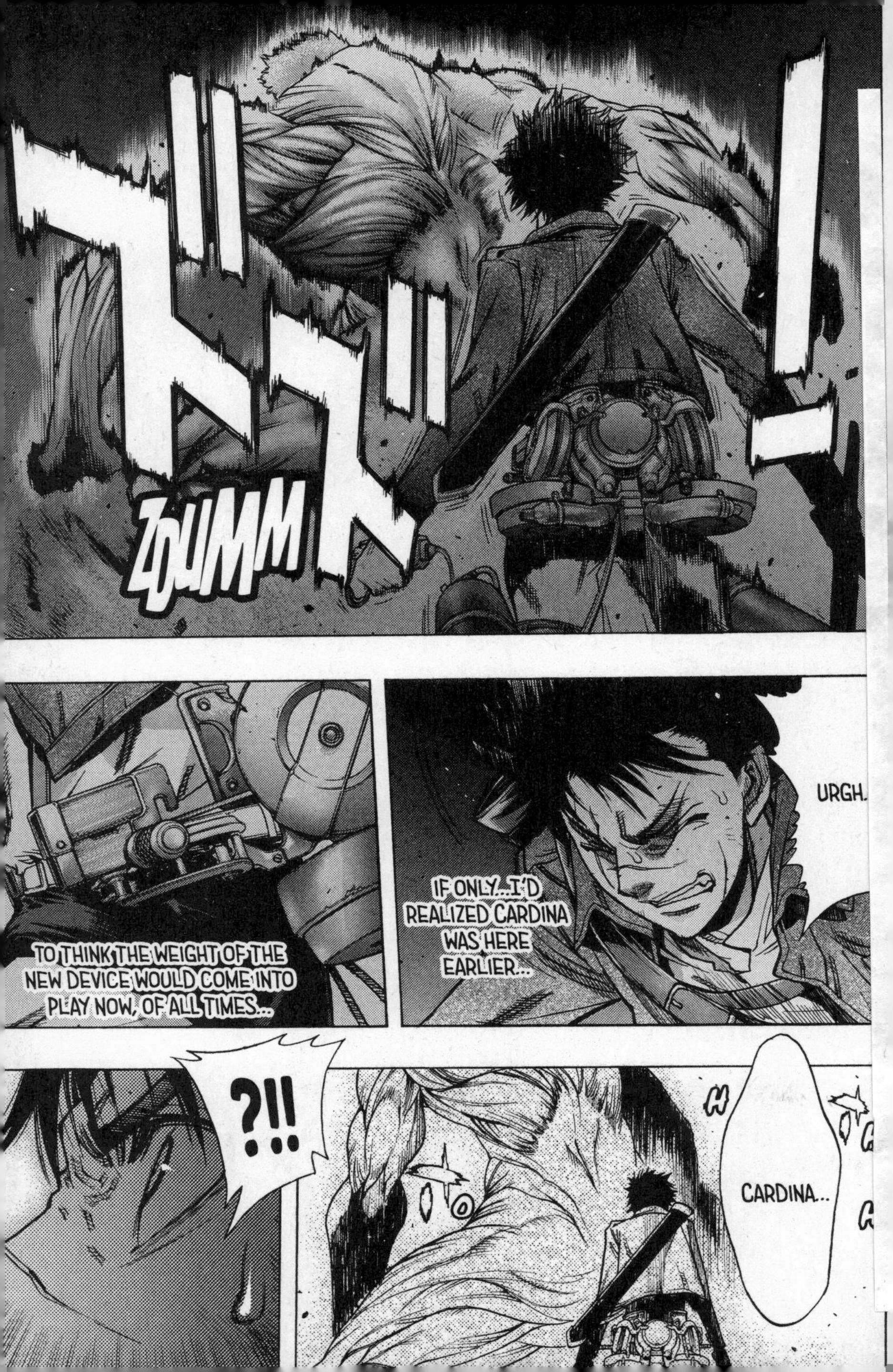
ZOUMM
URGH.
IF ONLY...I'D REALIZED CARDINA WAS HERE EARLIER...
TO THINK THE WEIGHT OF THE NEW DEVICE WOULD COME INTO PLAY NOW, OF ALL TIMES...
CARDINA...
?!!

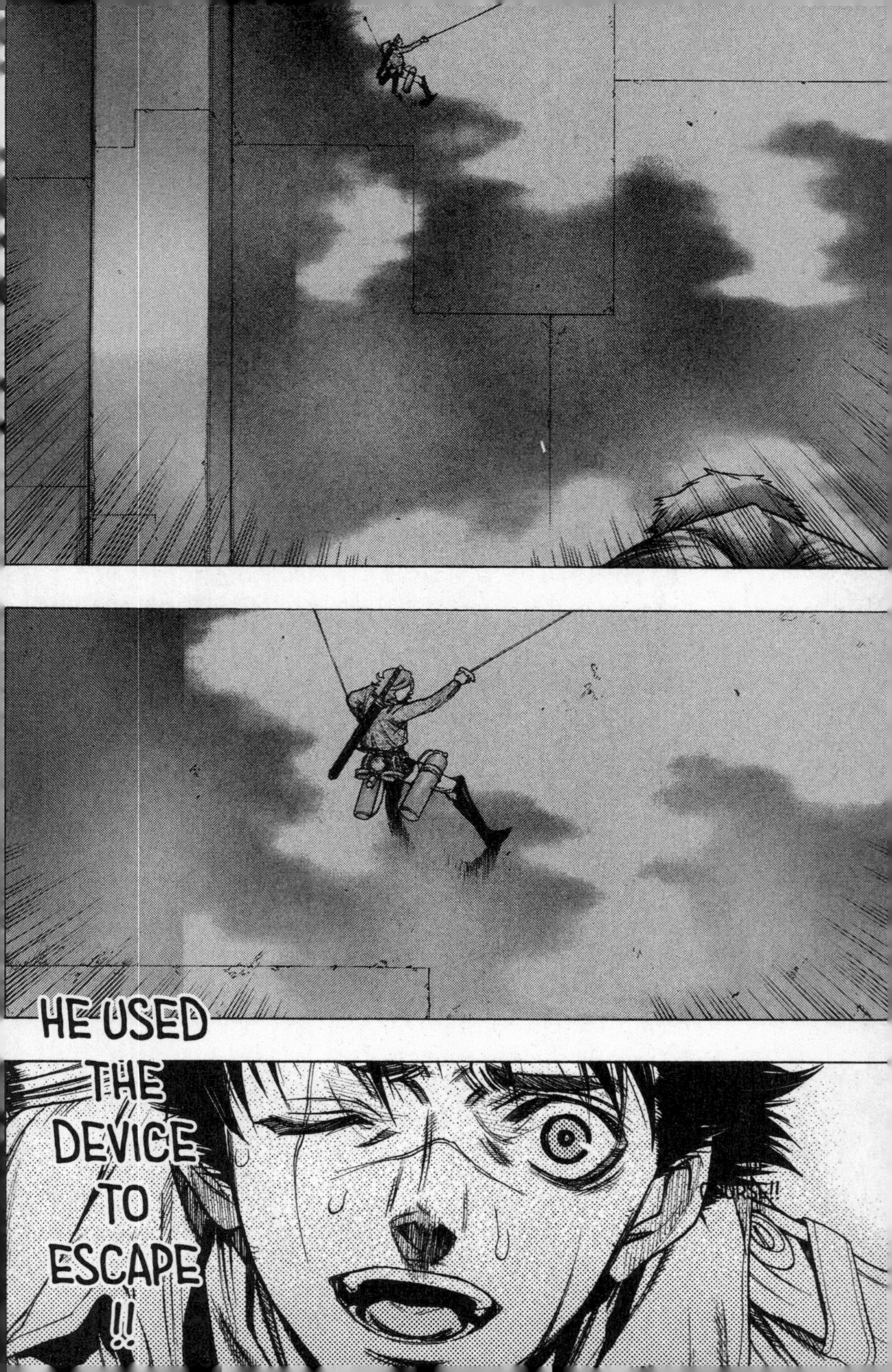
HE USED THE DEVICE TO ESCAPE!!

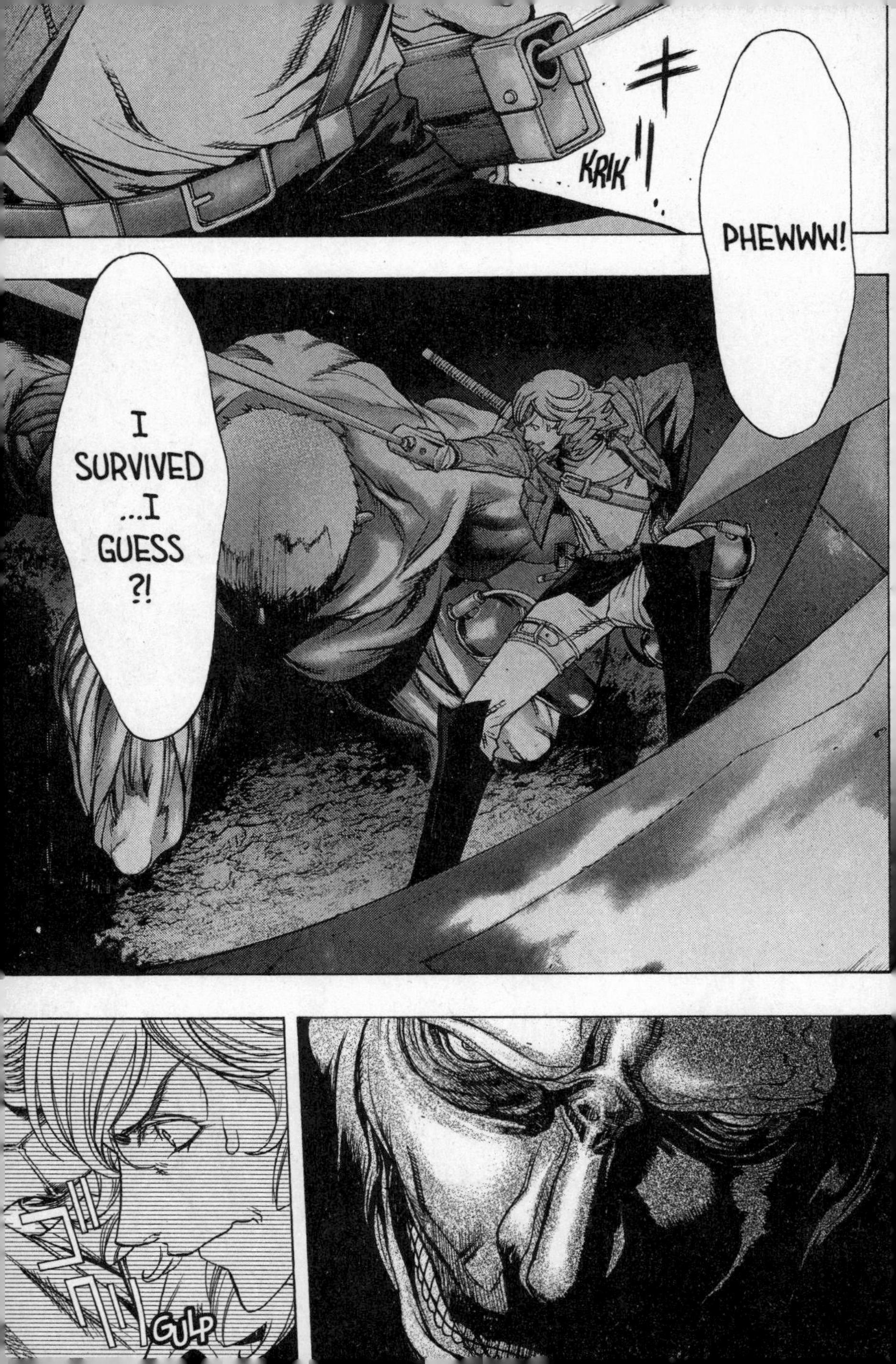
KRIK
PHEWWW!
I SURVIVED ...I GUESS ?!
GULP

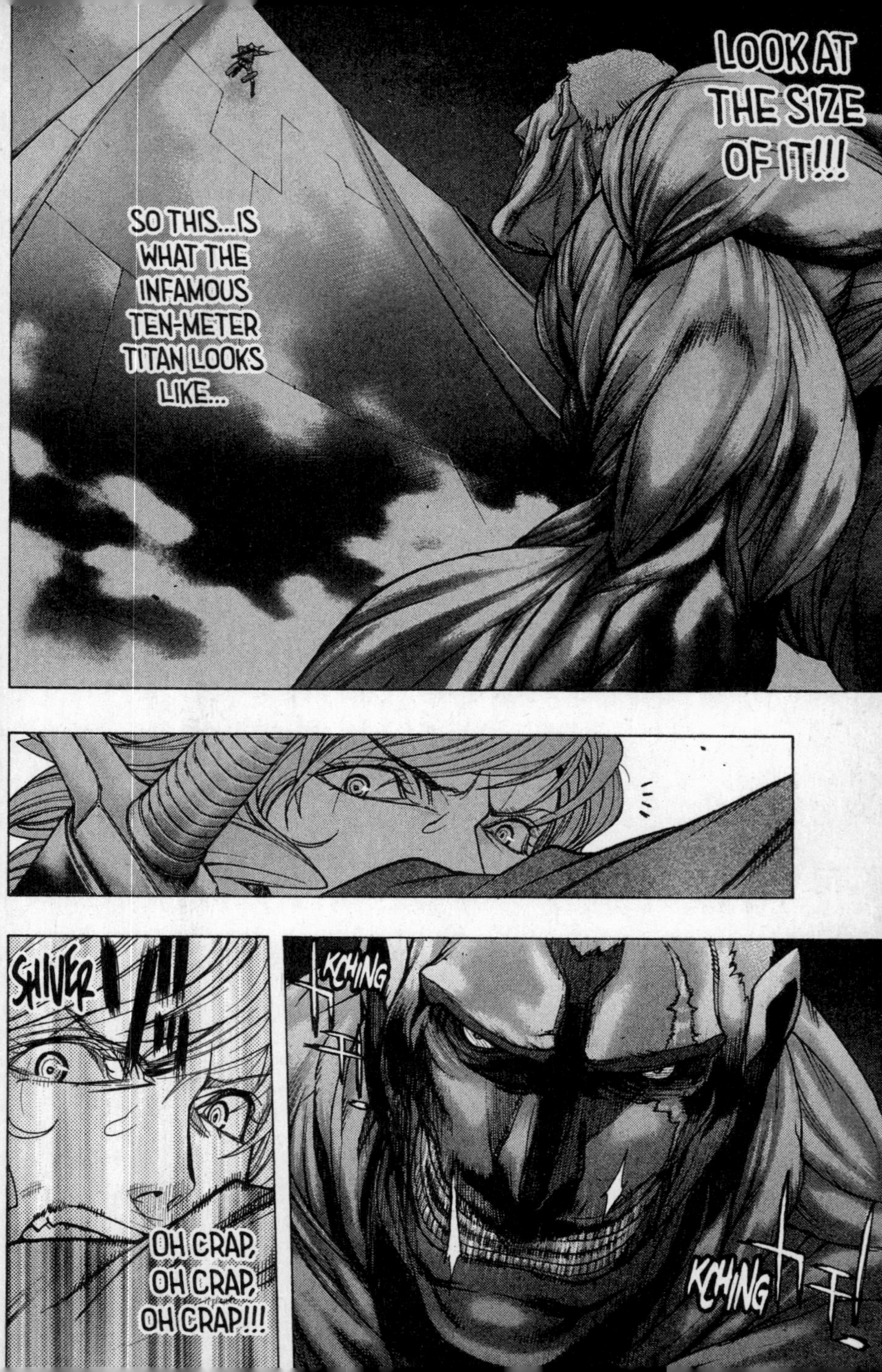
LOOK AT THE SIZE OF IT!!!
SO THIS...IS WHAT THE INFAMOUS TEN-METER TITAN LOOKS LIKE...
KCHING
KCHING
SHIVER
OH CRAP, OH CRAP, OH CRAP!!!

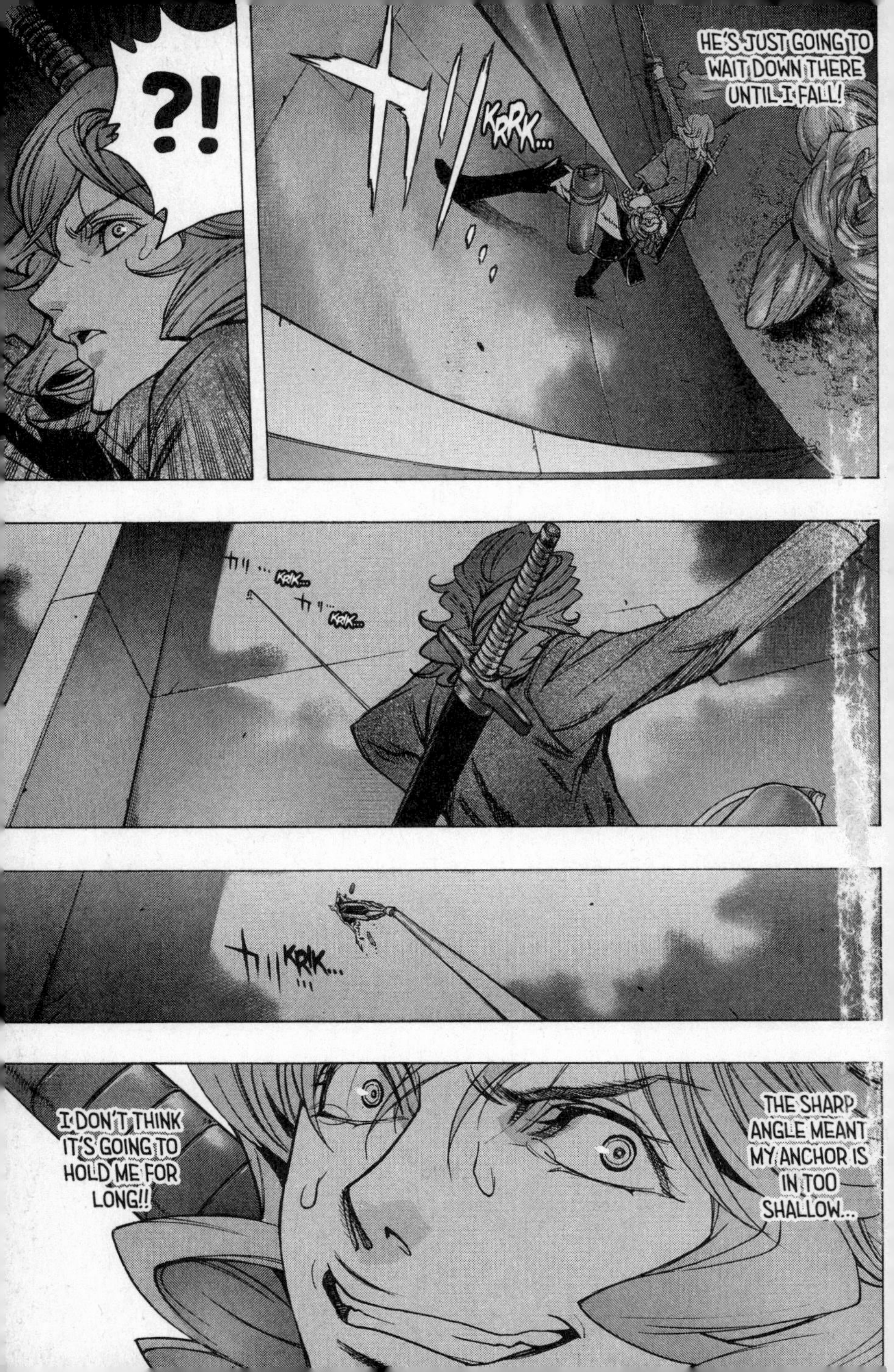
HE'S JUST GOING TO WAIT DOWN THERE UNTIL I FALL!
KRRK...
?!
KRIK...
KRIK...
KRIK...
THE SHARP ANGLE MEANT MY ANCHOR IS IN TOO SHALLOW...
I DON'T THINK IT'S GOING TO HOLD ME FOR LONG!!

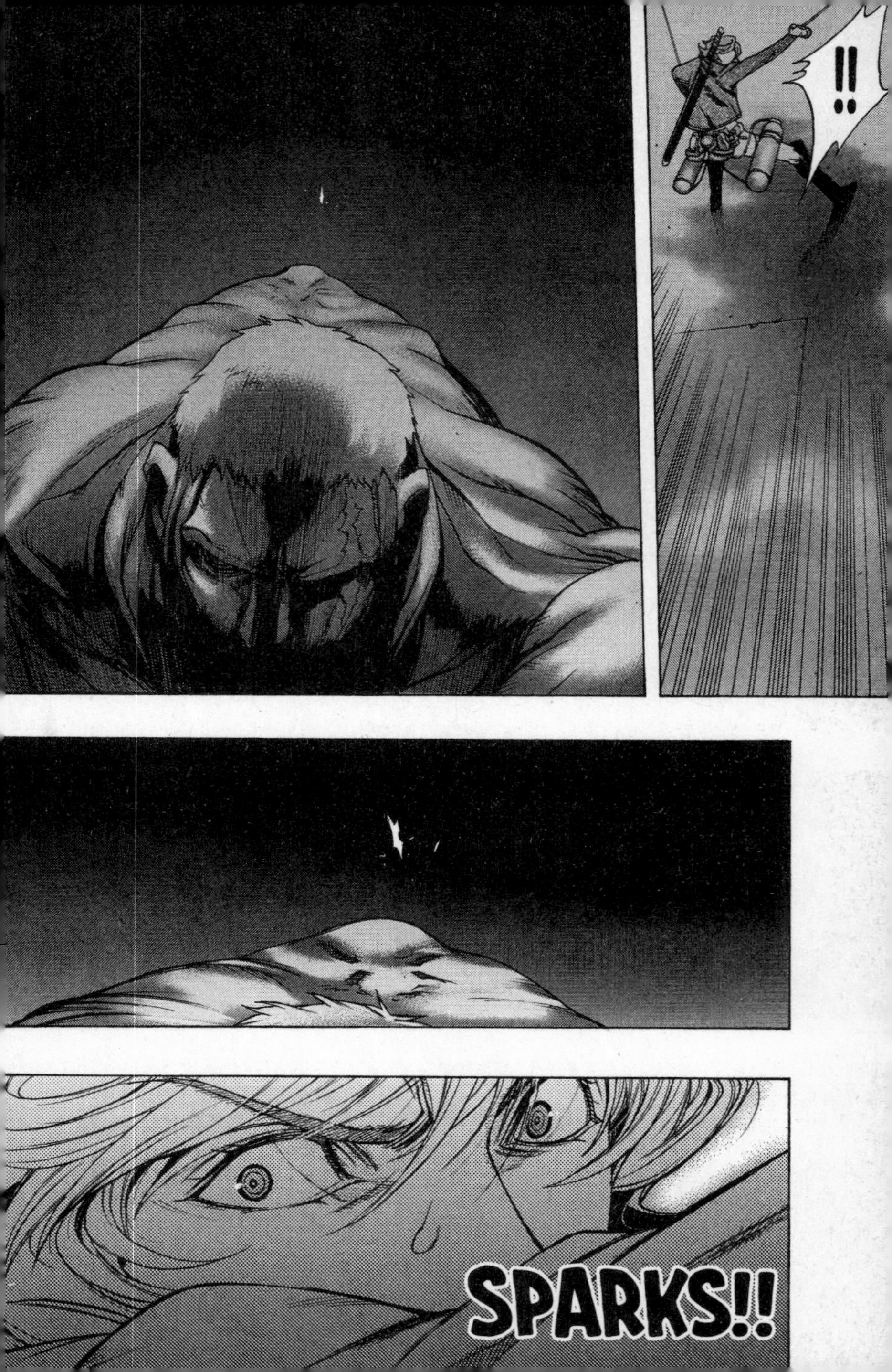
!!
SPARKS!!

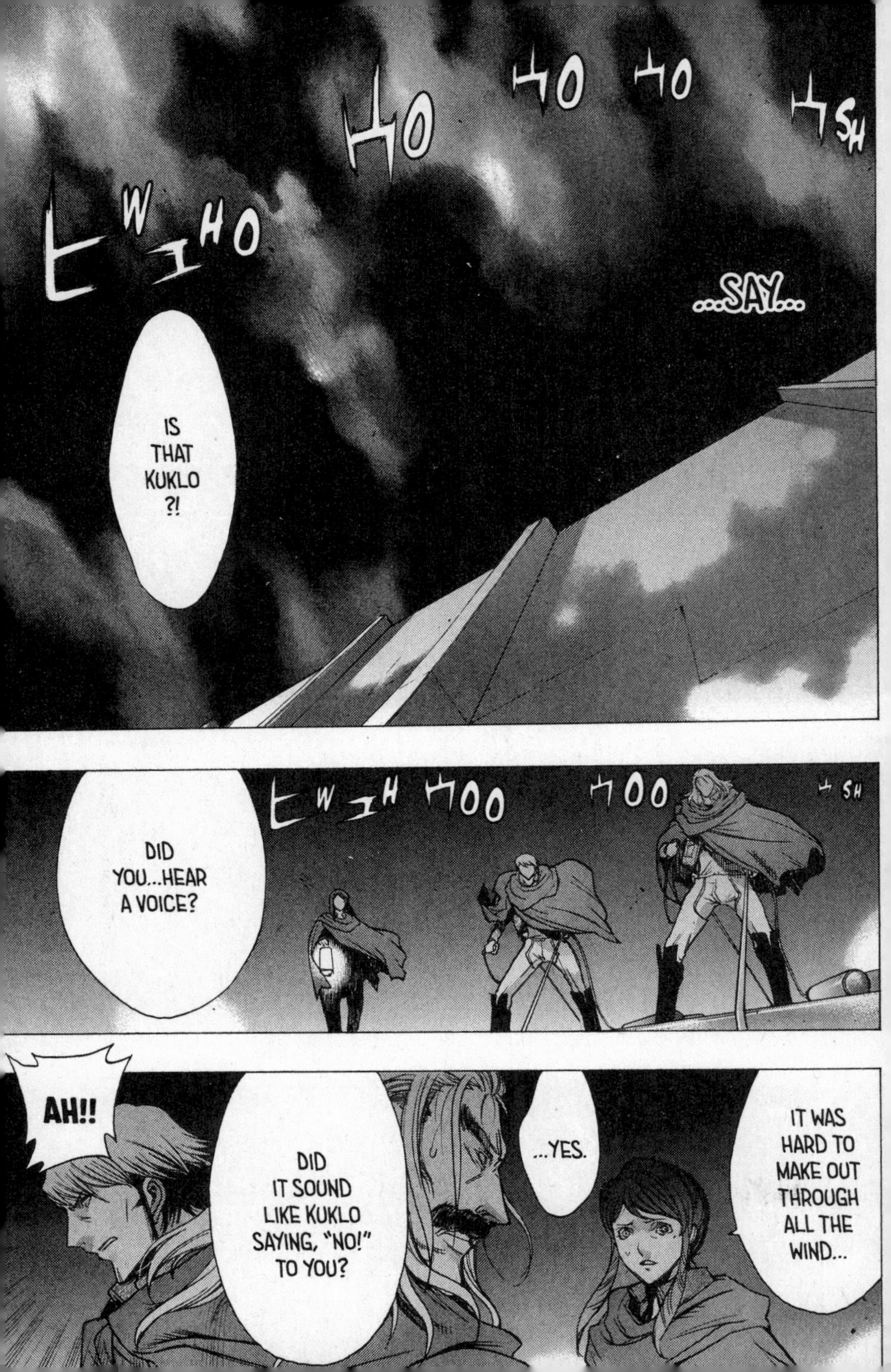
FWHOOOSH
...SAY...
IS THAT KUKLO ?!
FWHOOOSH
DID YOU...HEAR A VOICE?
IT WAS HARD TO MAKE OUT THROUGH ALL THE WIND...
...YES.
DID IT SOUND LIKE KUKLO SAYING, "NO!" TO YOU?
AH!!

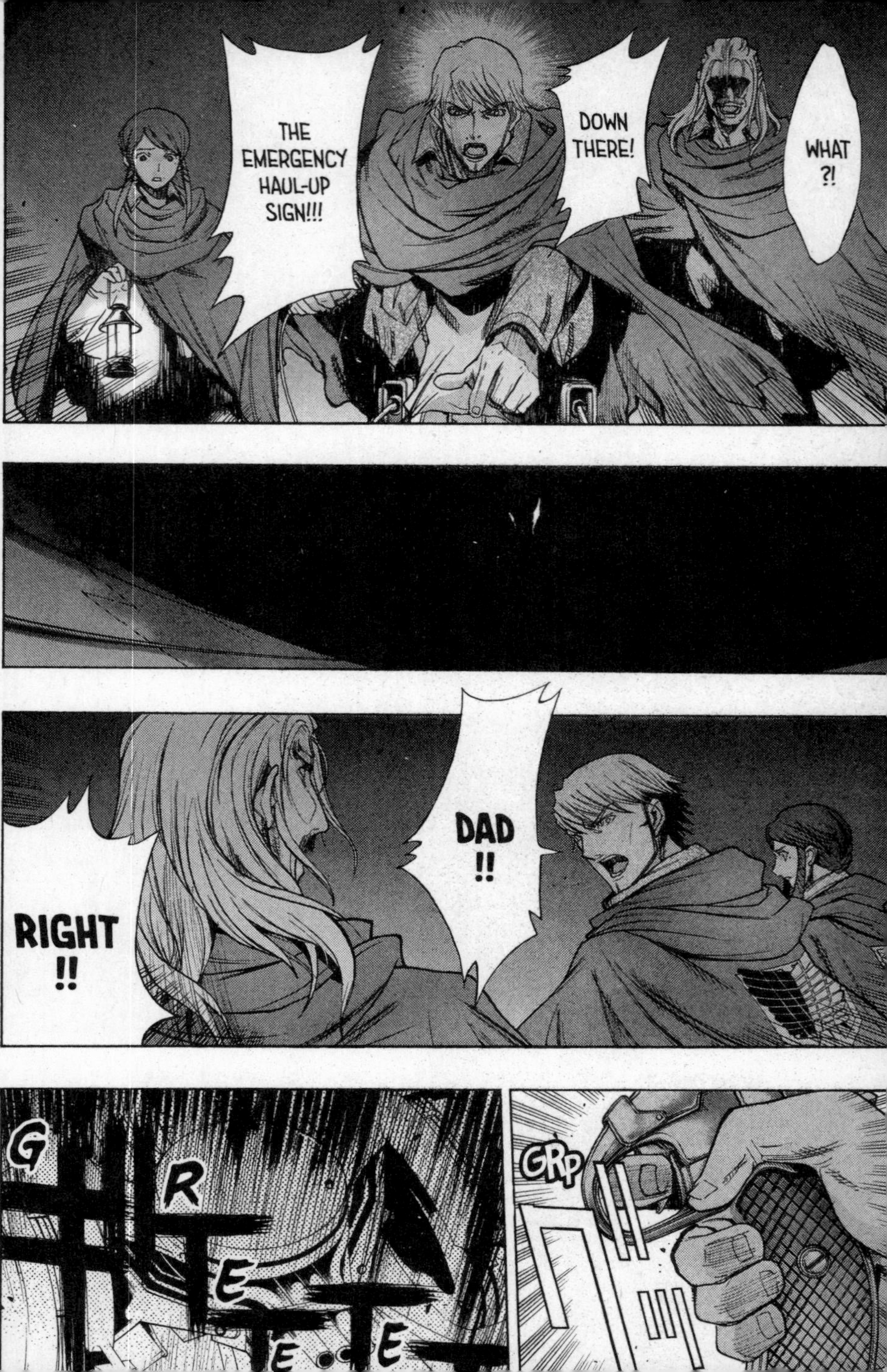
WHAT ?!
DOWN THERE!
THE EMERGENCY HAUL-UP SIGN!!!
DAD !!
RIGHT !!
GRP
G R E E E E

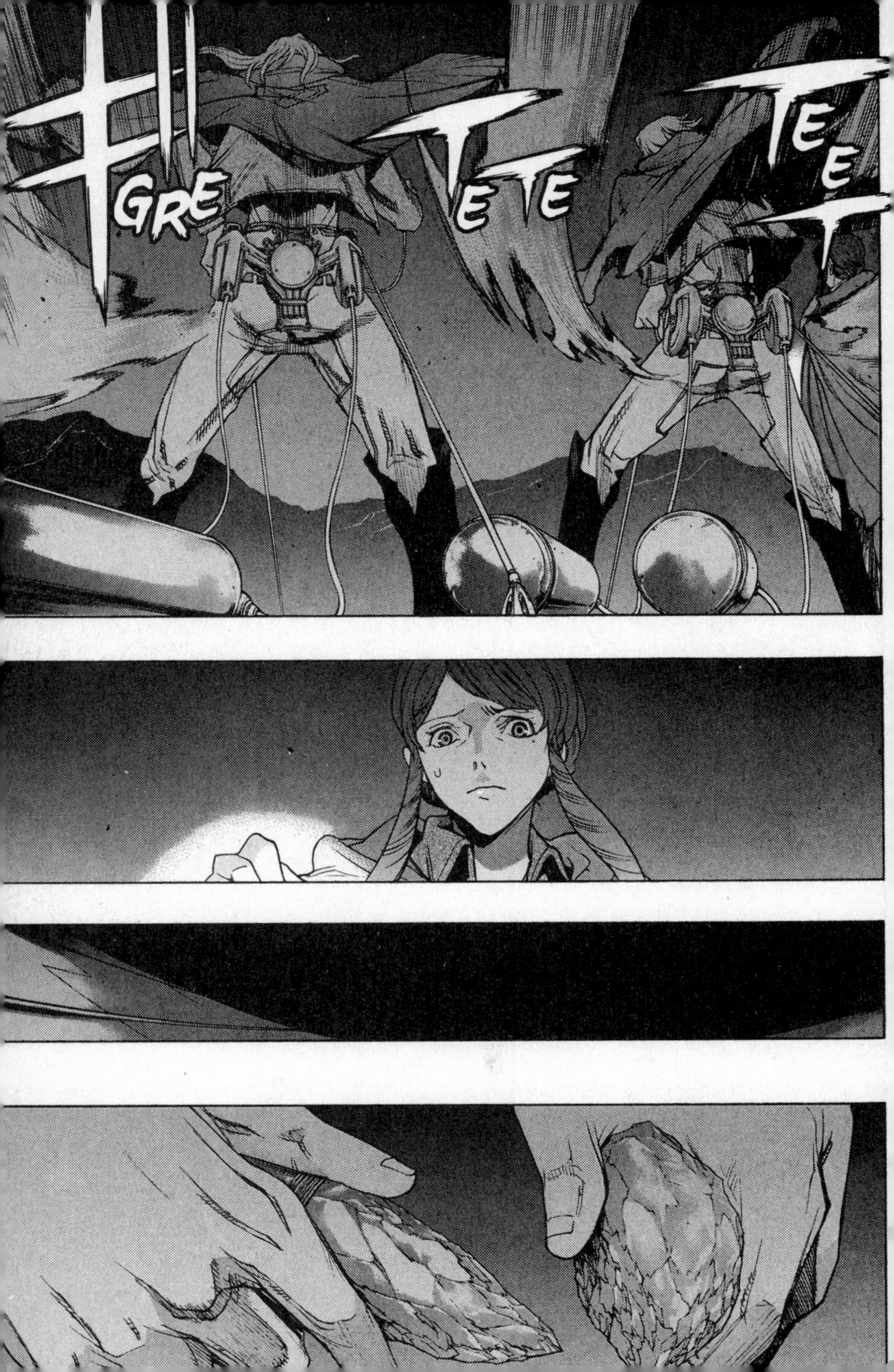
GREEEEEE

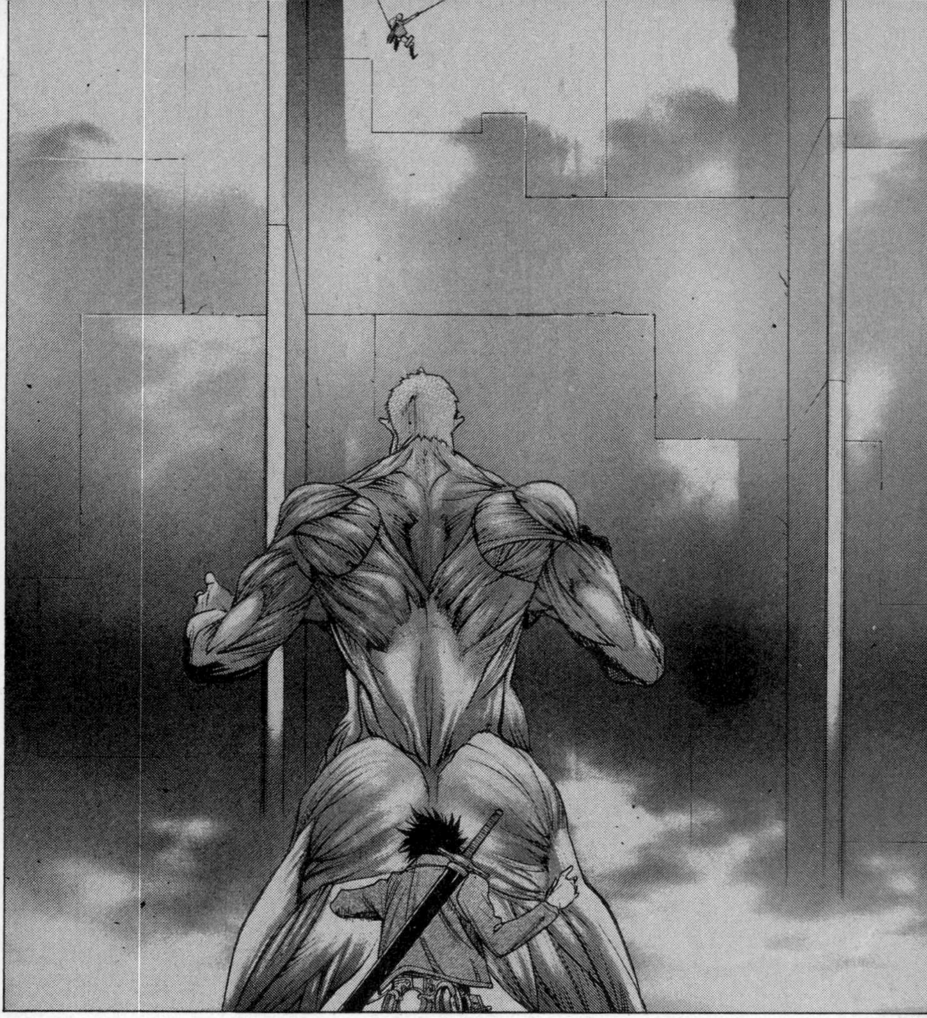

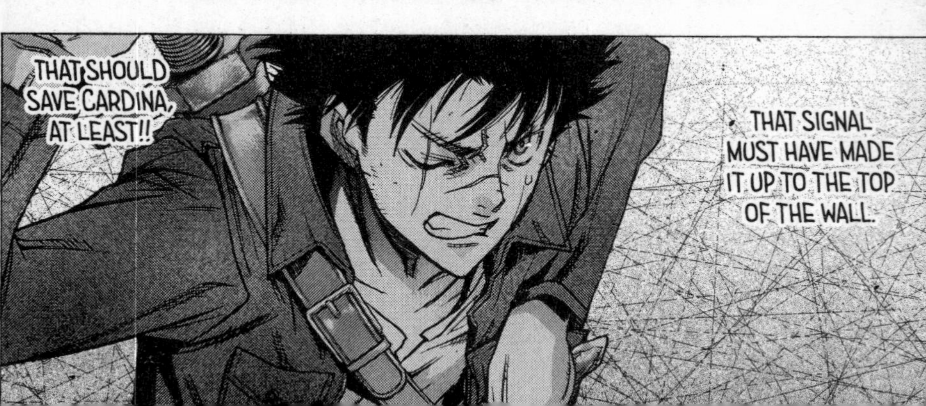
THAT SIGNAL MUST HAVE MADE IT UP TO THE TOP OF THE WALL.
THAT SHOULD SAVE CARDINA, AT LEAST!!

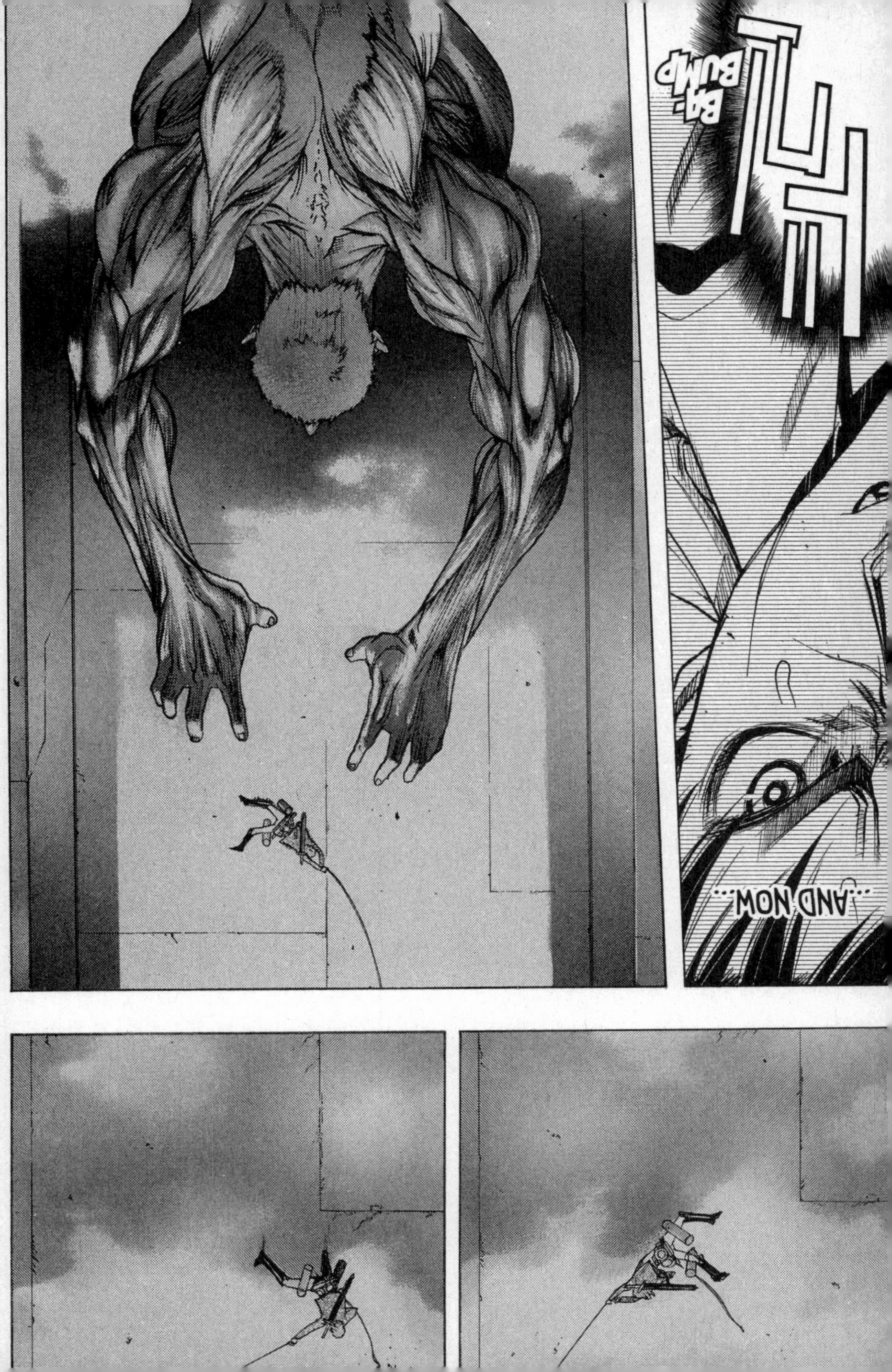
...AND NOW...
BA-BUMP

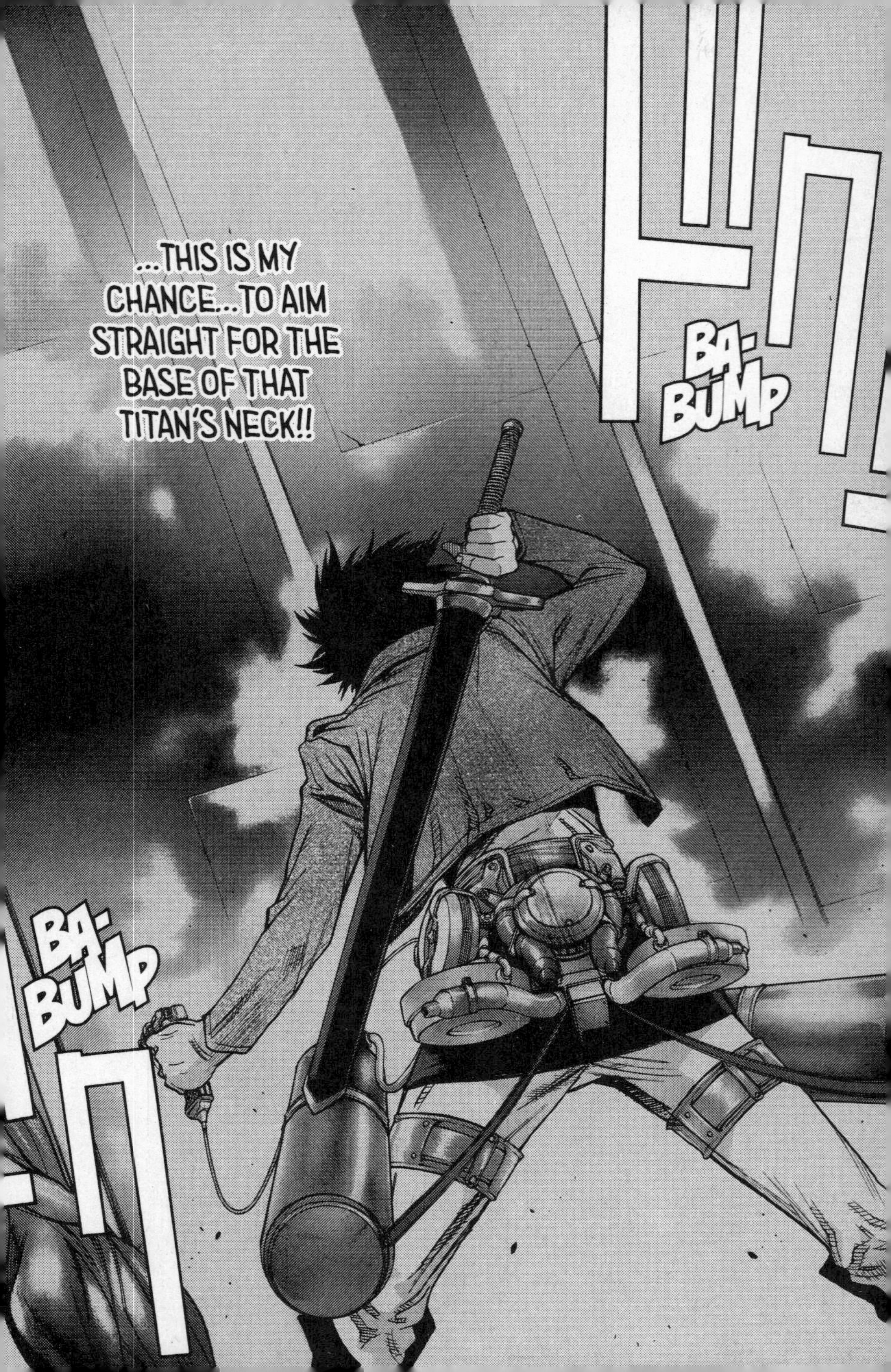
BA-BUMP
...THIS IS MY CHANCE...TO AIM STRAIGHT FOR THE BASE OF THAT TITAN'S NECK!!
BA-BUMP

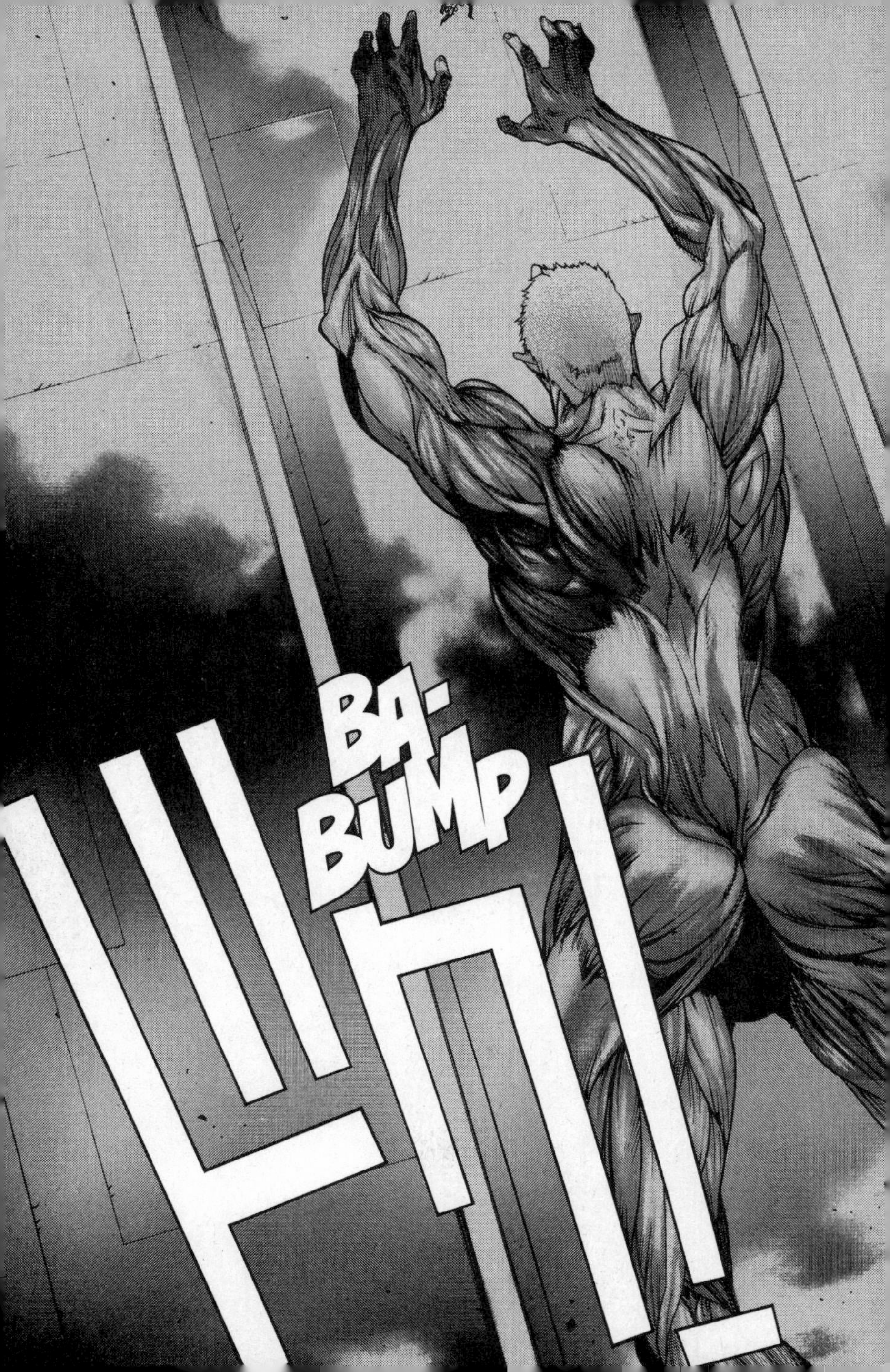
BA-
BUMP

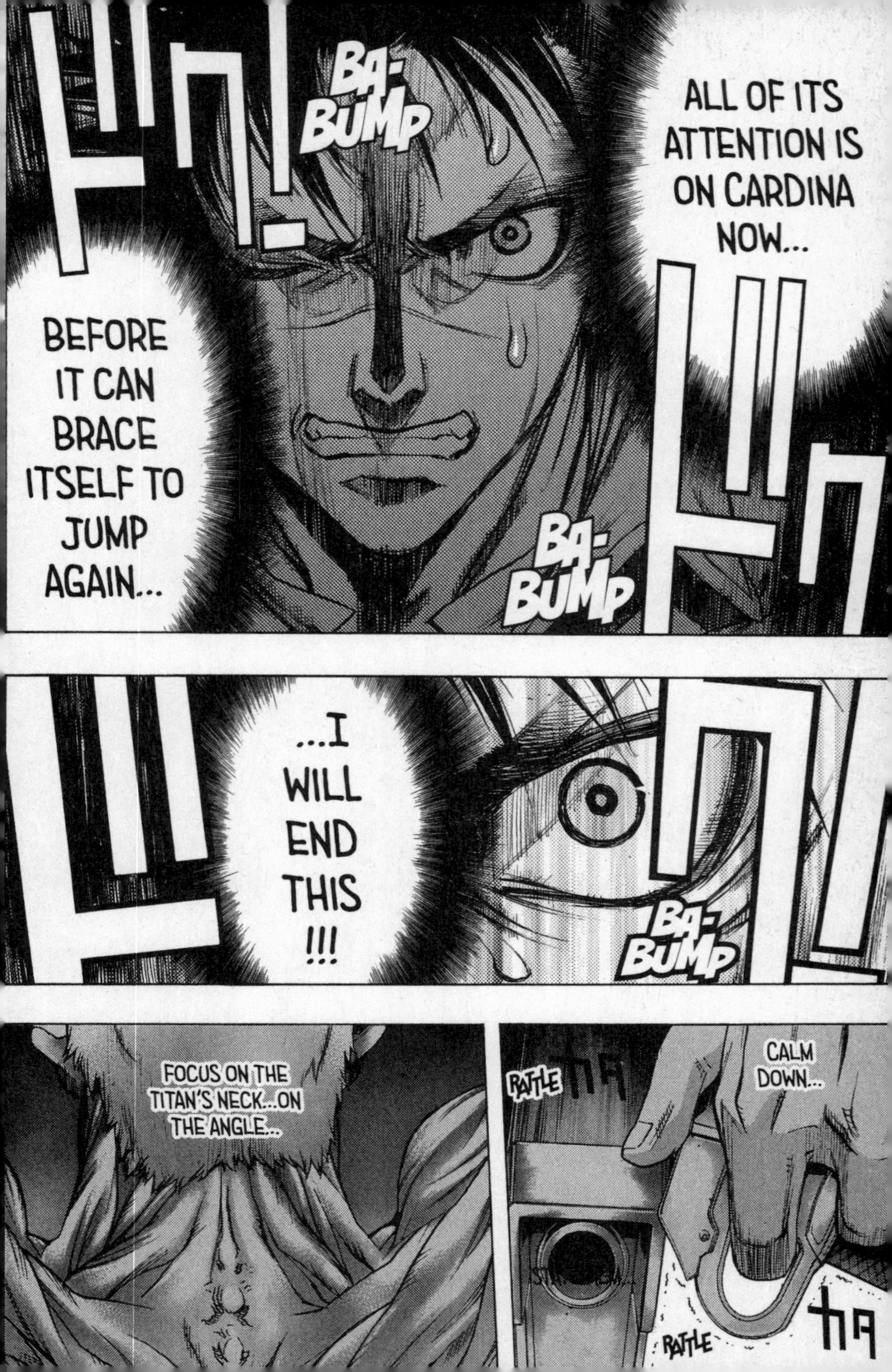
ALL OF ITS ATTENTION IS ON CARDINA NOW...
BA-BUMP
BEFORE IT CAN BRACE ITSELF TO JUMP AGAIN...
BA-BUMP
BA-BUMP
...I WILL END THIS !!!
CALM DOWN...
RATTLE
RATTLE
FOCUS ON THE TITAN'S NECK...ON THE ANGLE...

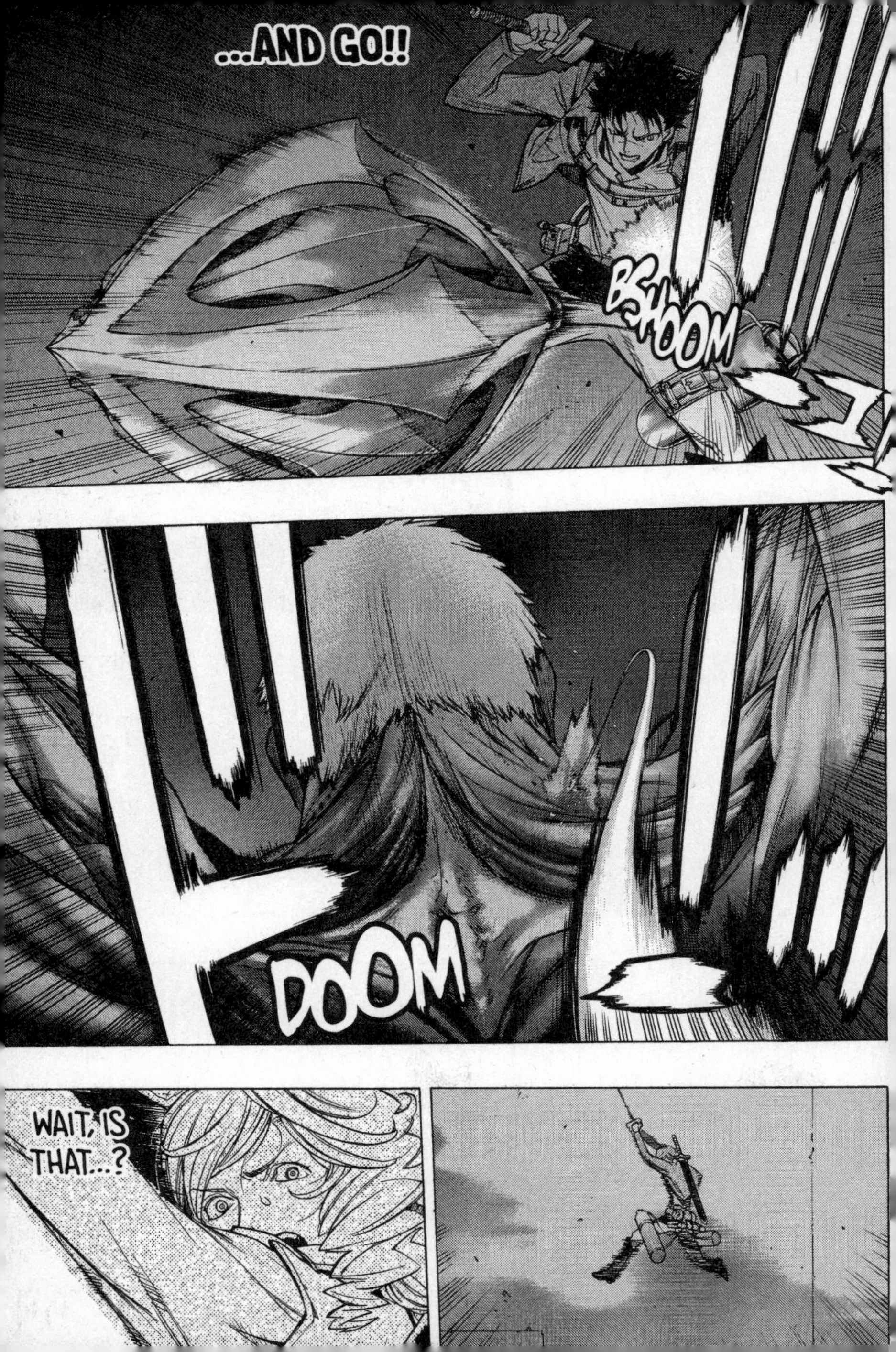
...AND GO!!
BSHOOM
DOOM
WAIT, IS THAT...?

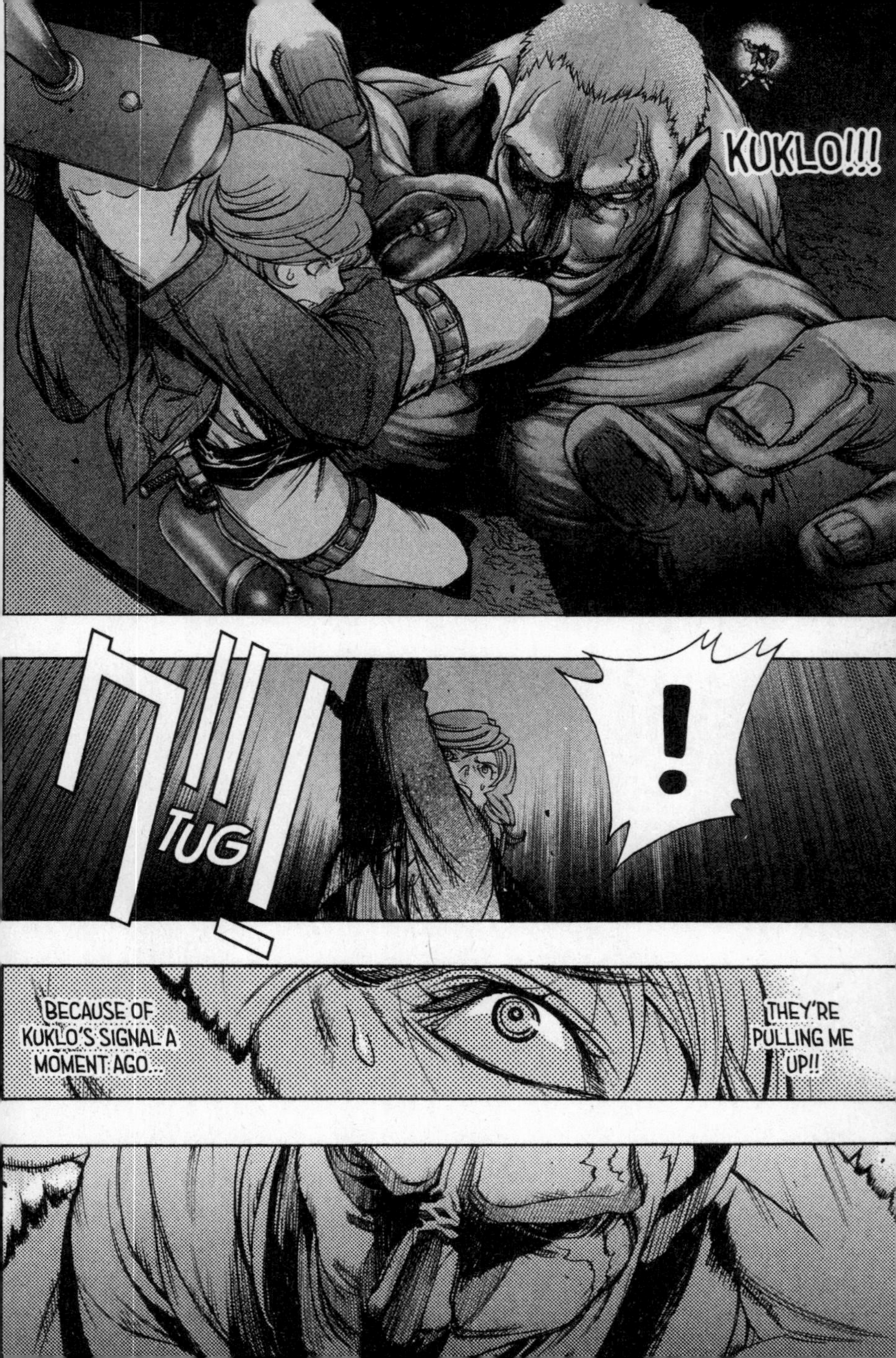
KUKLO!!!
!
TUG
THEY'RE PULLING ME UP!!
BECAUSE OF KUKLO'S SIGNAL A MOMENT AGO...

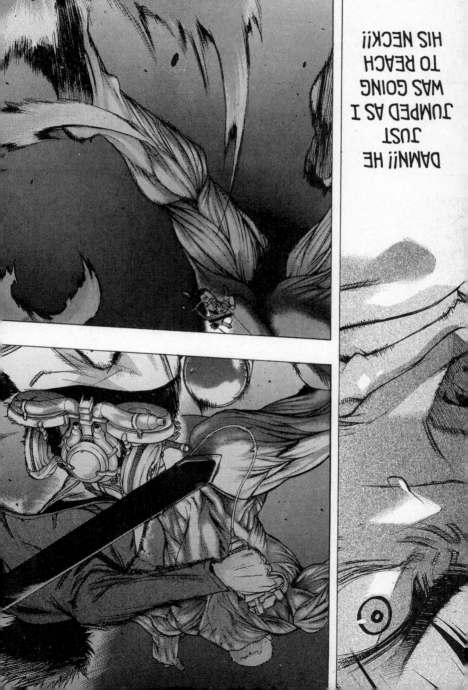

DAMN!! HE JUST JUMPED AS I WAS GOING TO REACH HIS NECK!!

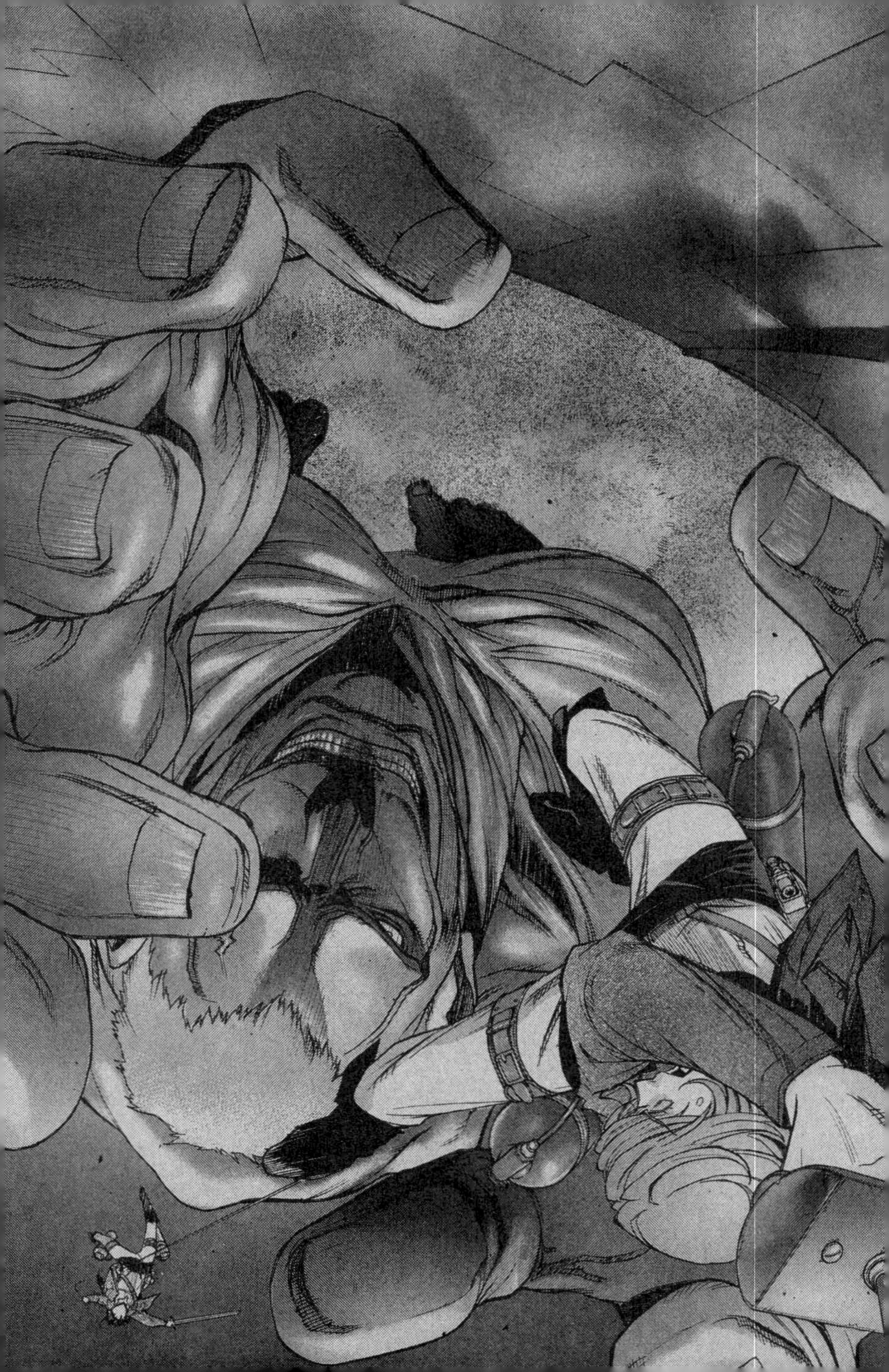

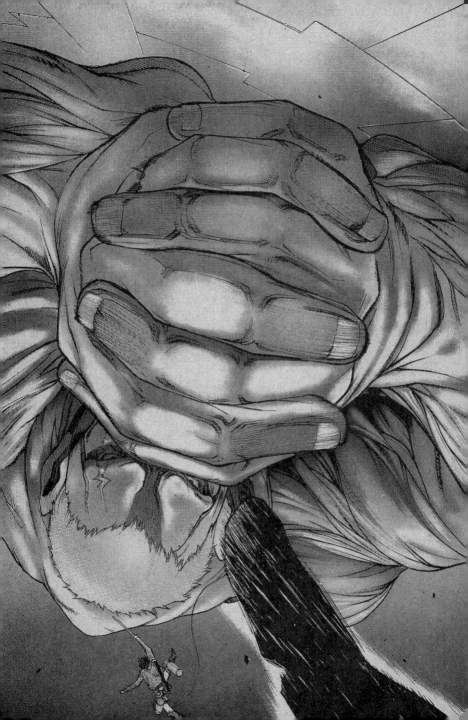

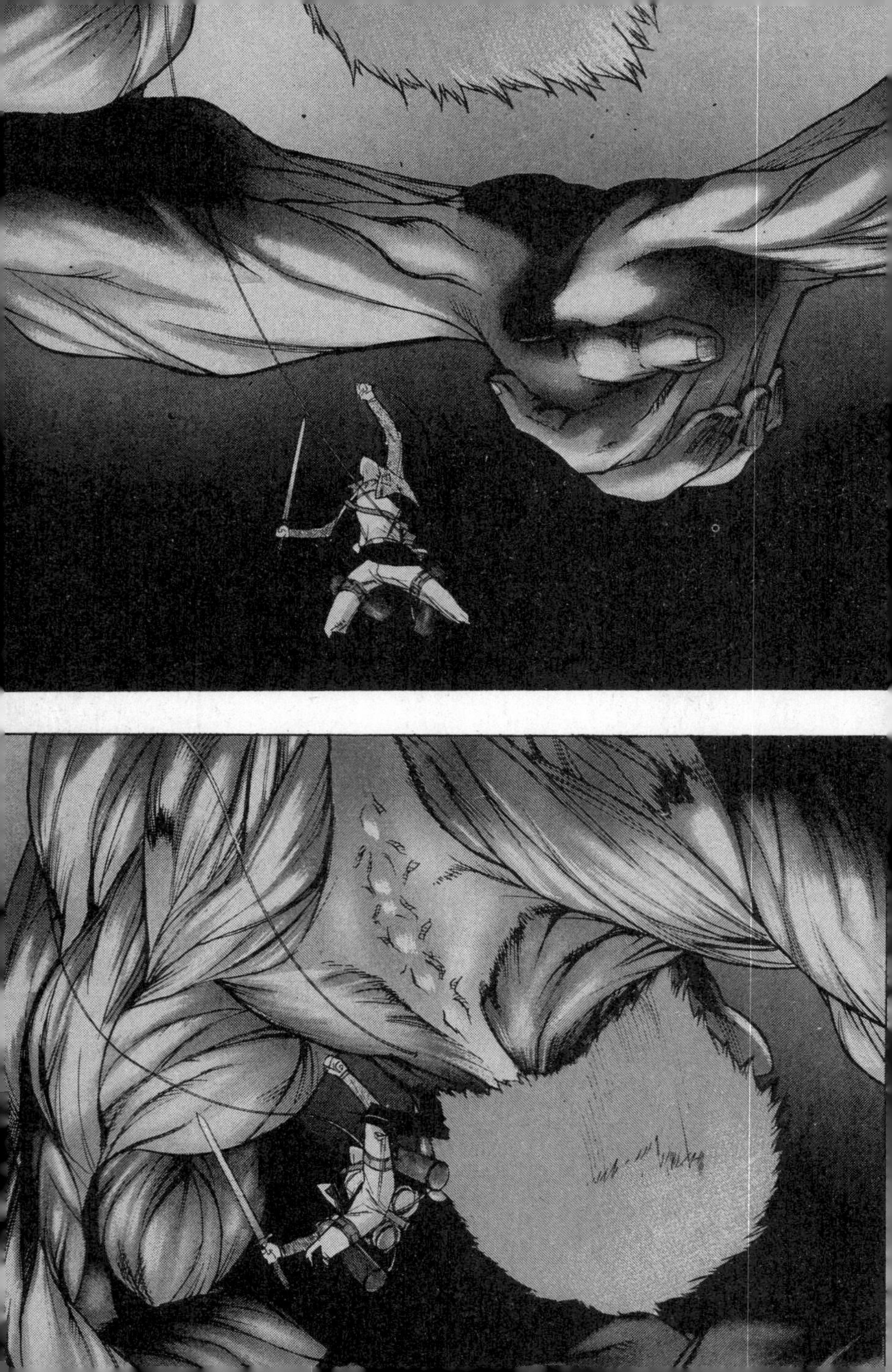

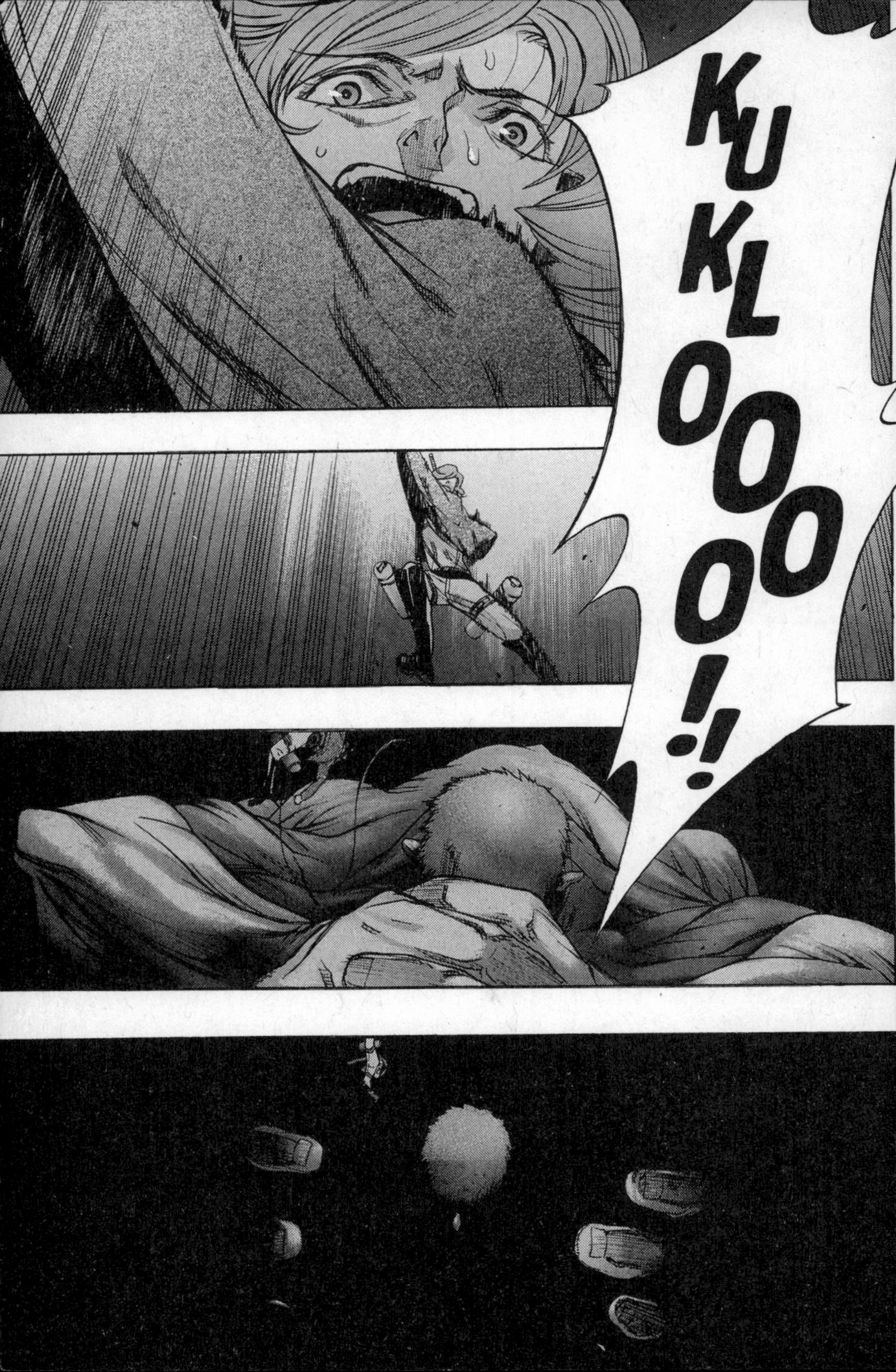
KUKLOOOOO!!

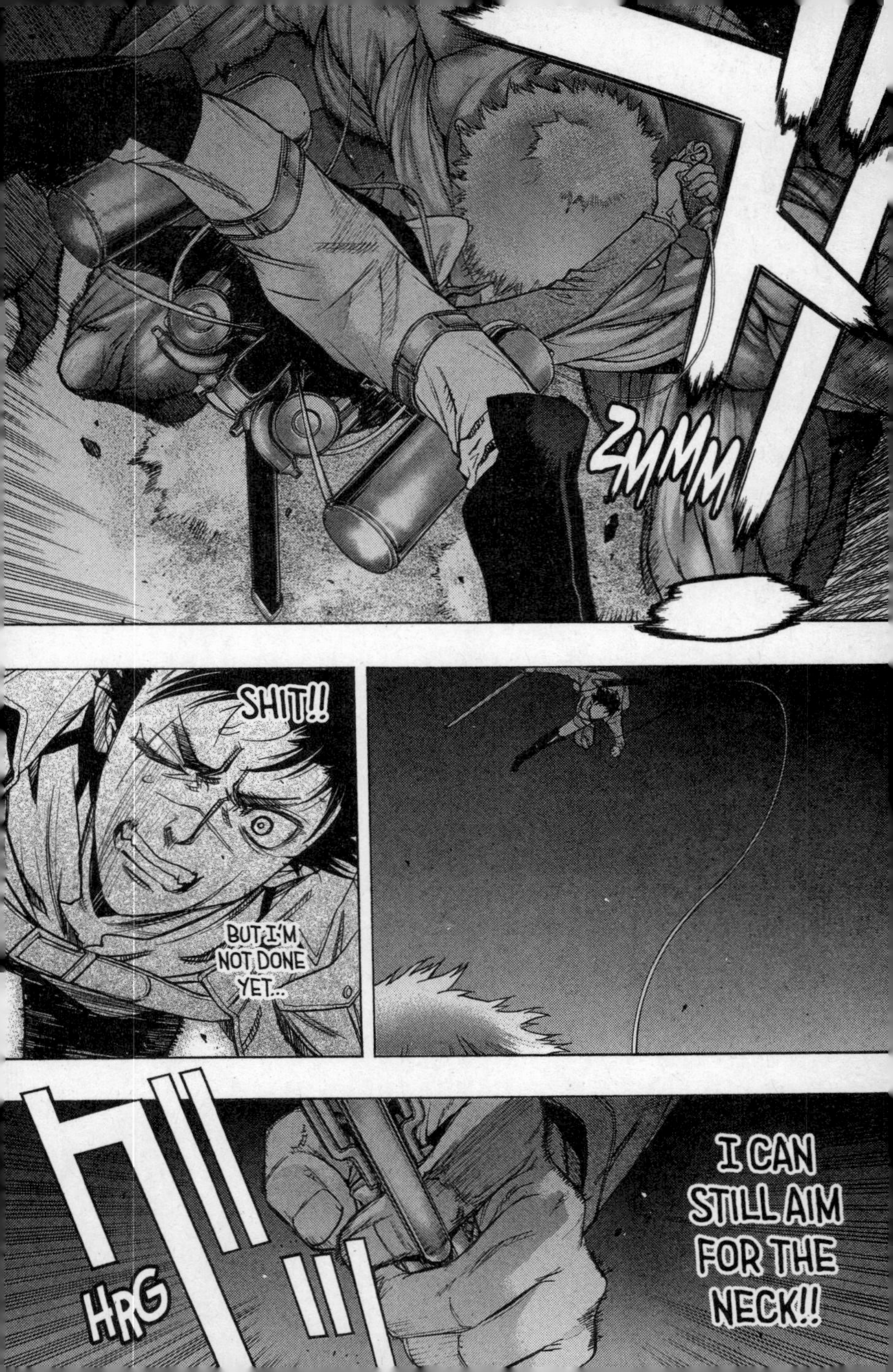
ZMMM
SHIT!!
BUT I'M NOT DONE YET...
I CAN STILL AIM FOR THE NECK!!
HRG

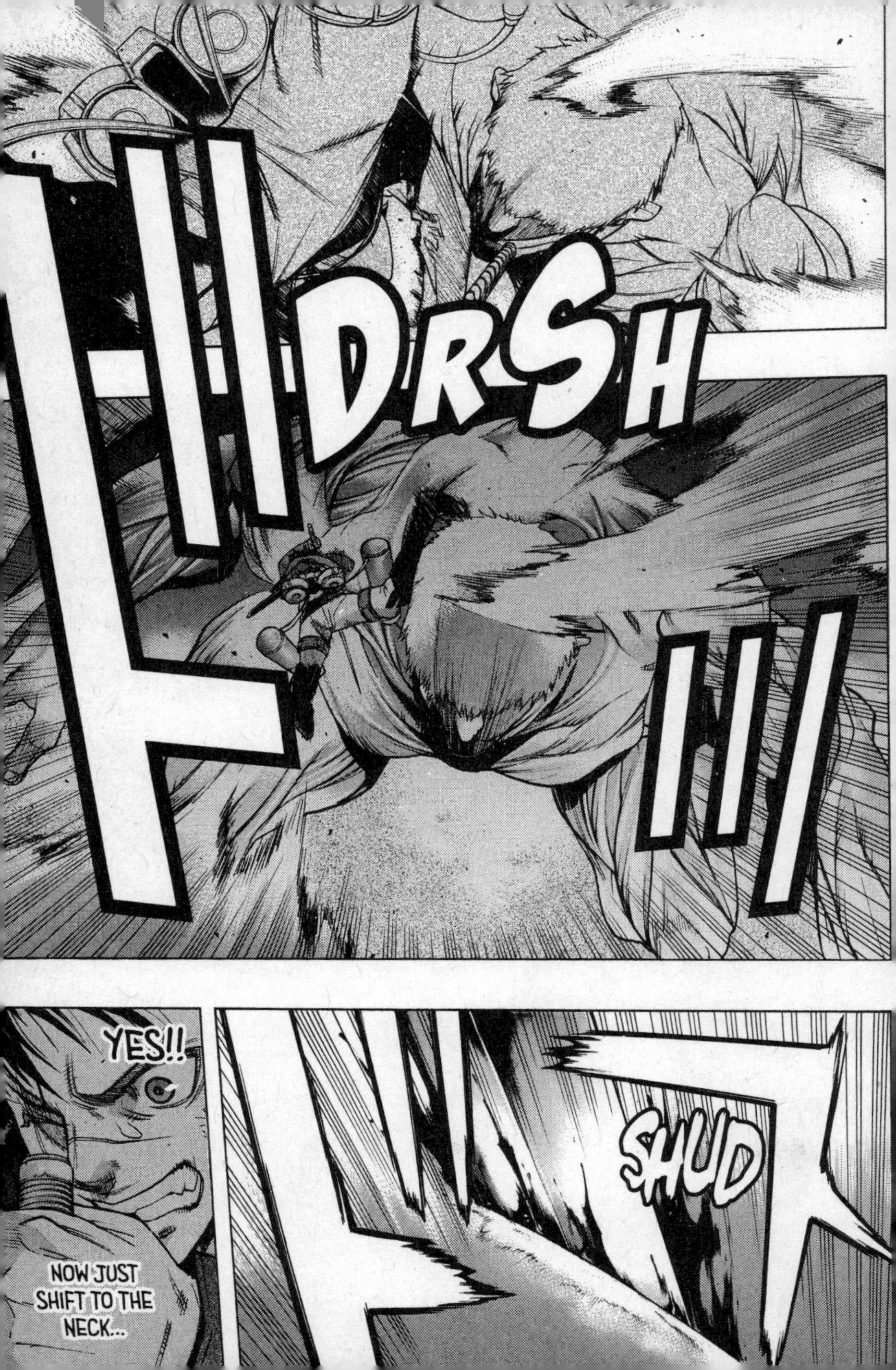
DRSH
SHUD
YES!!
NOW JUST SHIFT TO THE NECK...

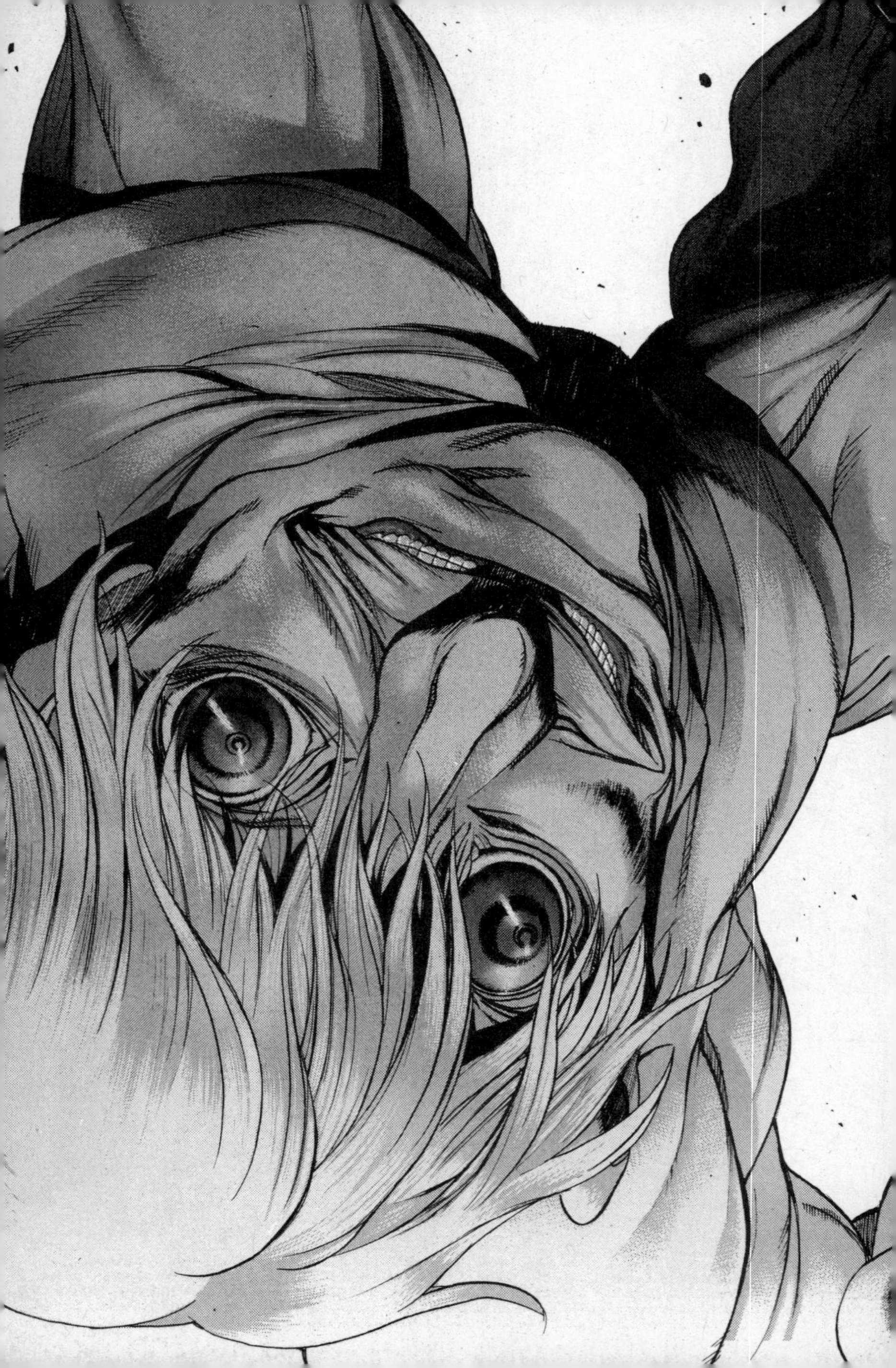

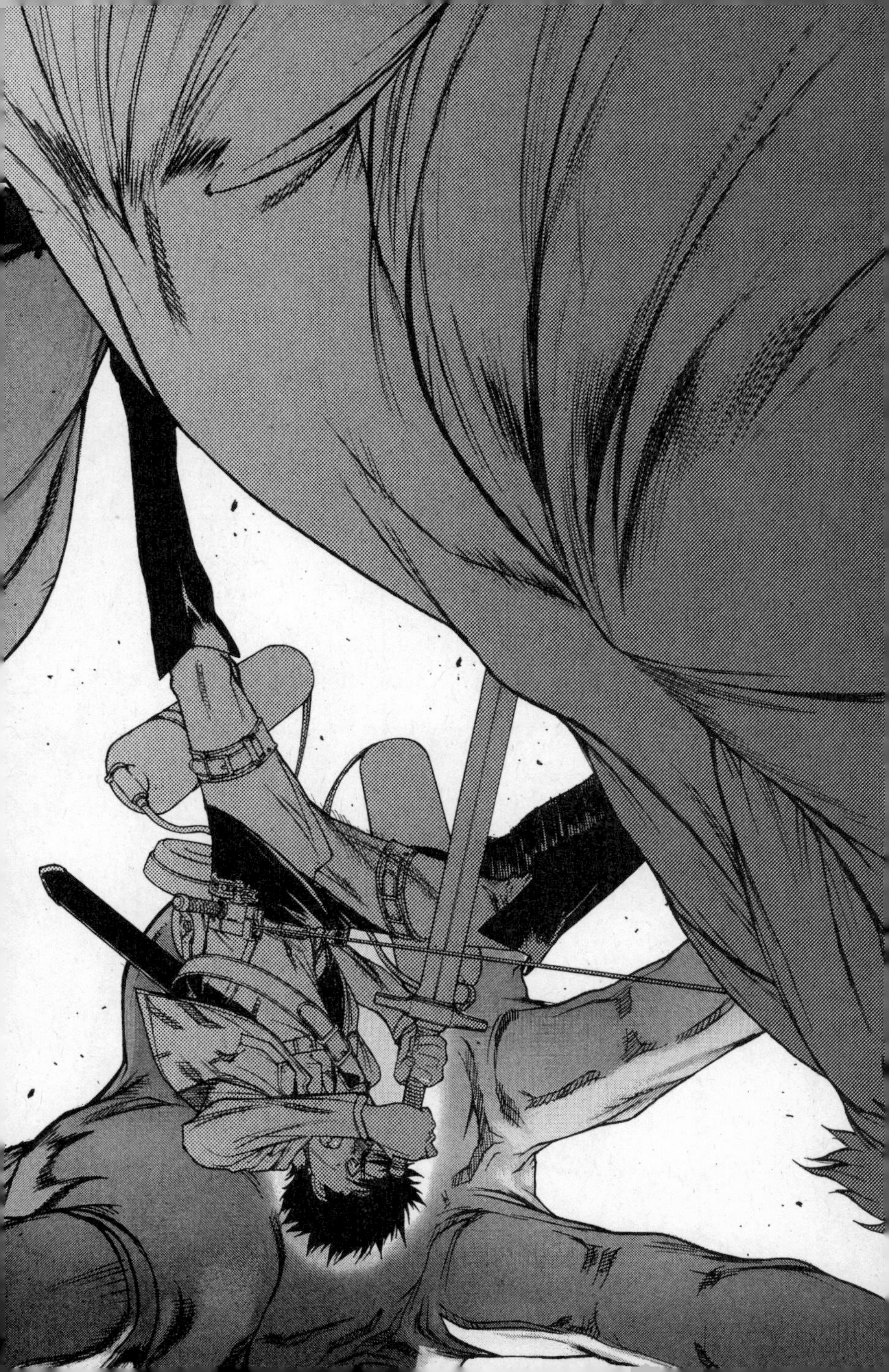

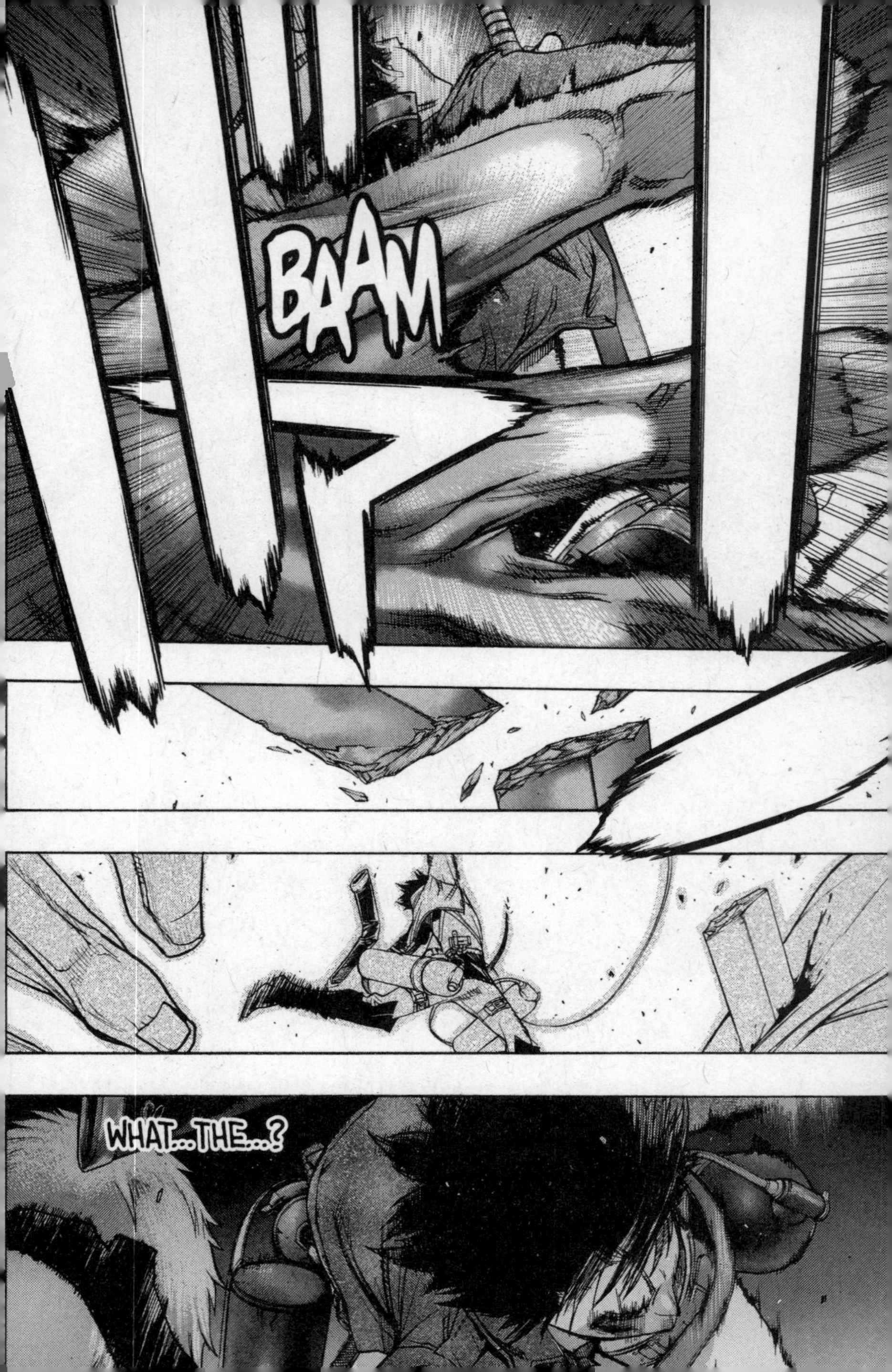
BAAM
WHAT...THE...?

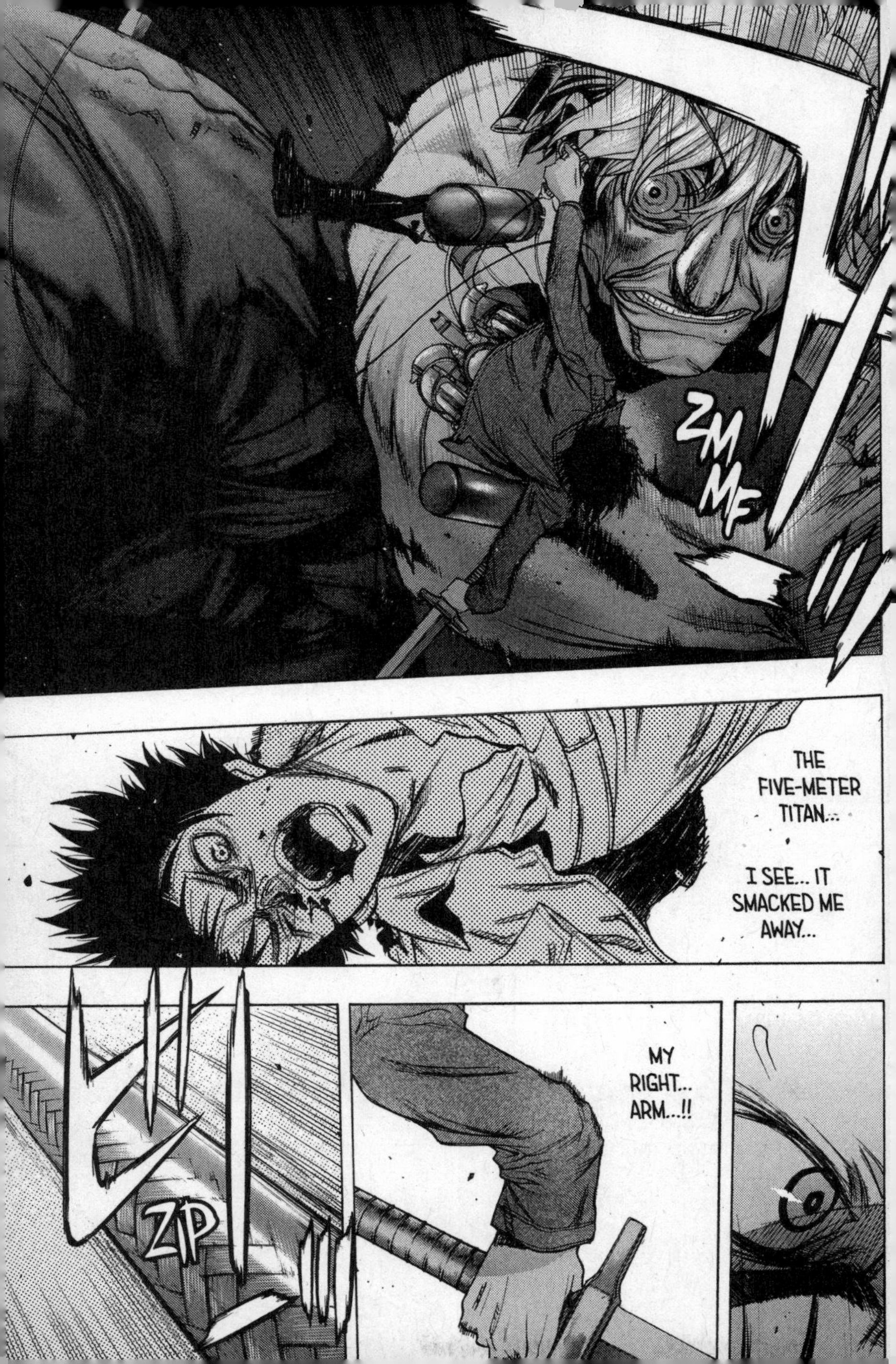
ZMMF
THE FIVE-METER TITAN...
I SEE... IT SMACKED ME AWAY...
MY RIGHT... ARM...!!
ZIP

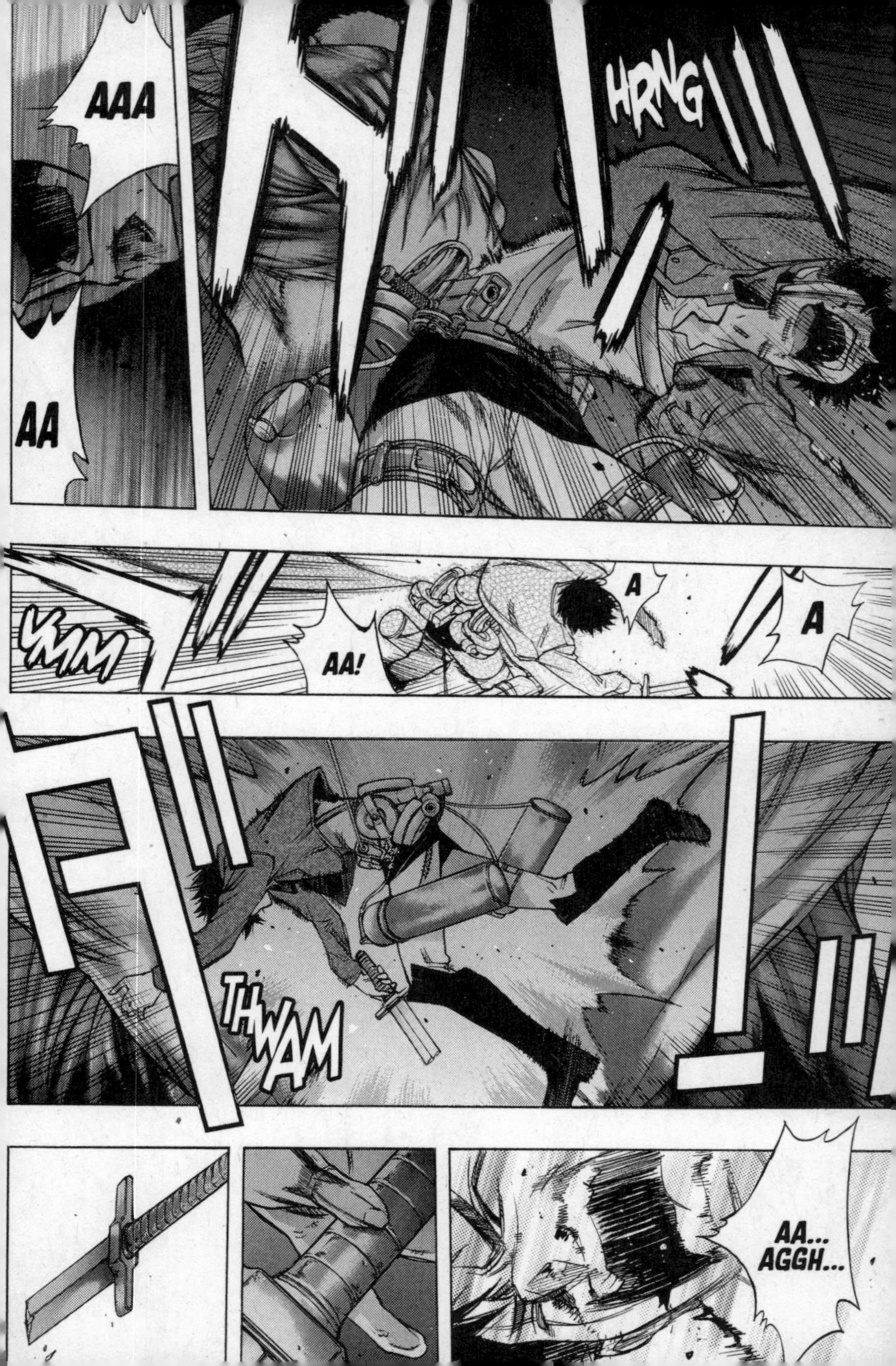
HRNG
AAA
AA
A
A
AA!
VMM
THWAM
AA... AGGH...

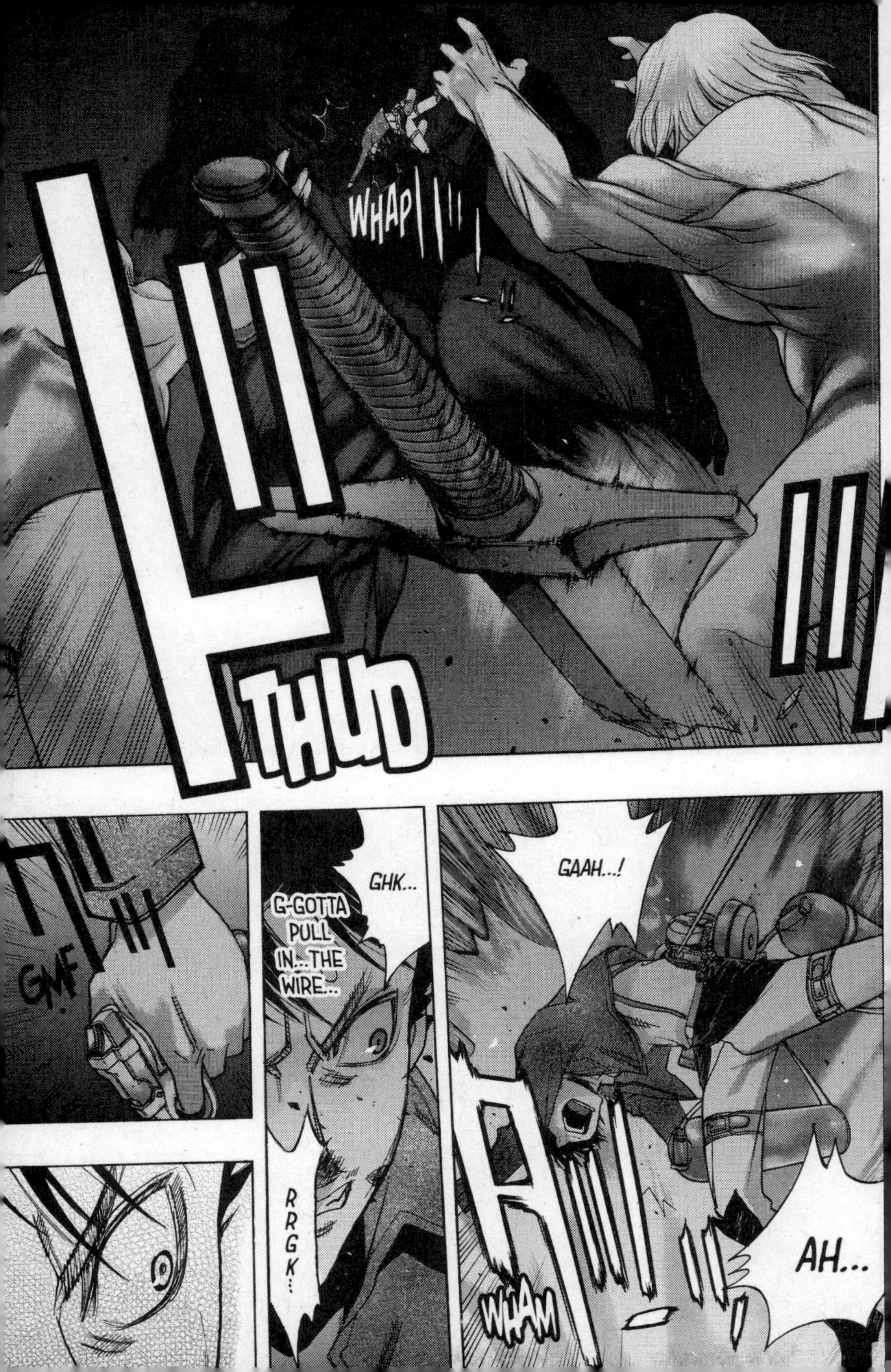
WHAP
THUD
GAAH...!
AH...
WHAM
GHK...
G-GOTTA PULL IN...THE WIRE...
RRGK...
GMF

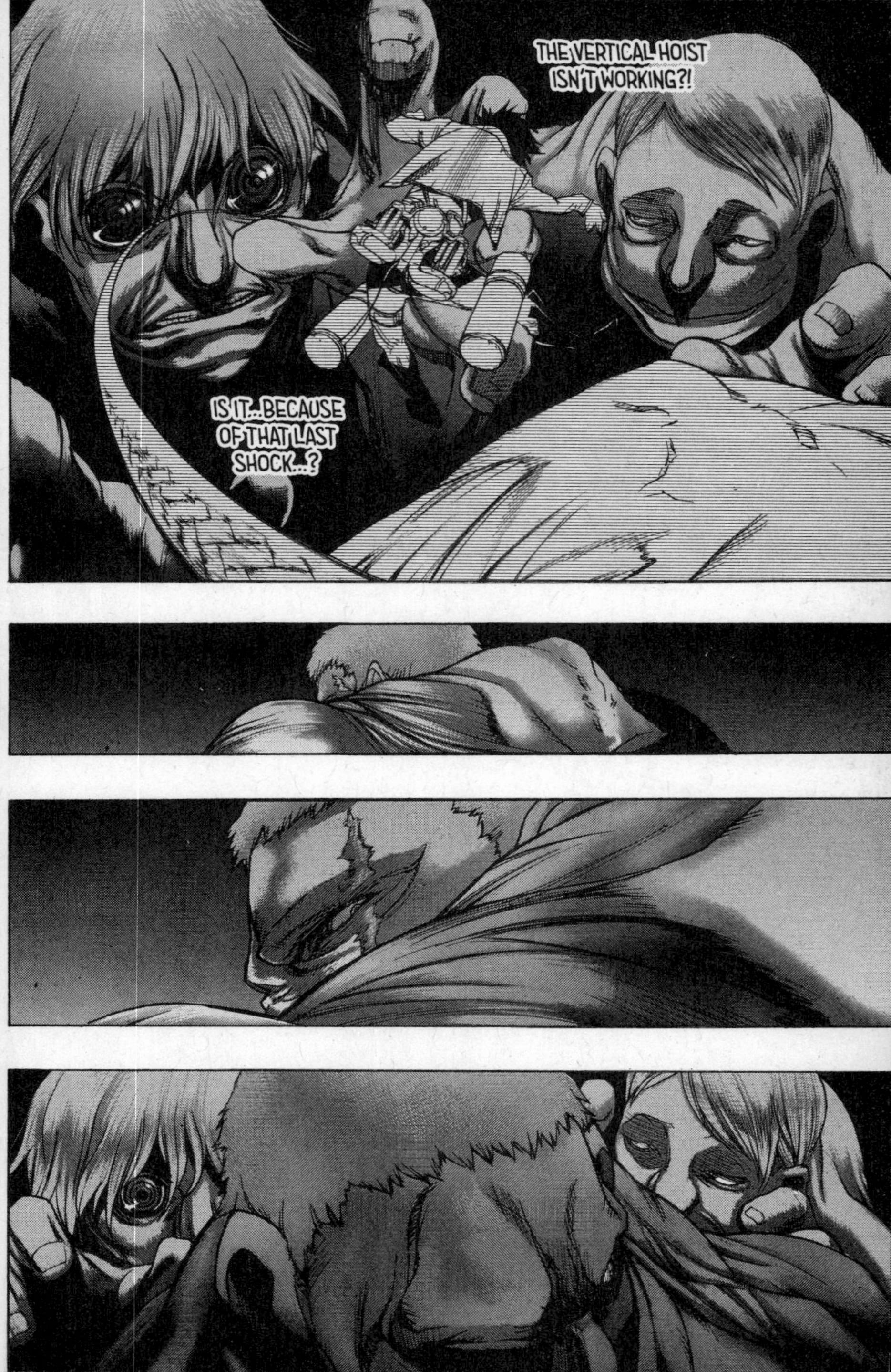
THE VERTICAL HOIST ISN'T WORKING?!
IS IT...BECAUSE OF THAT LAST SHOCK...?

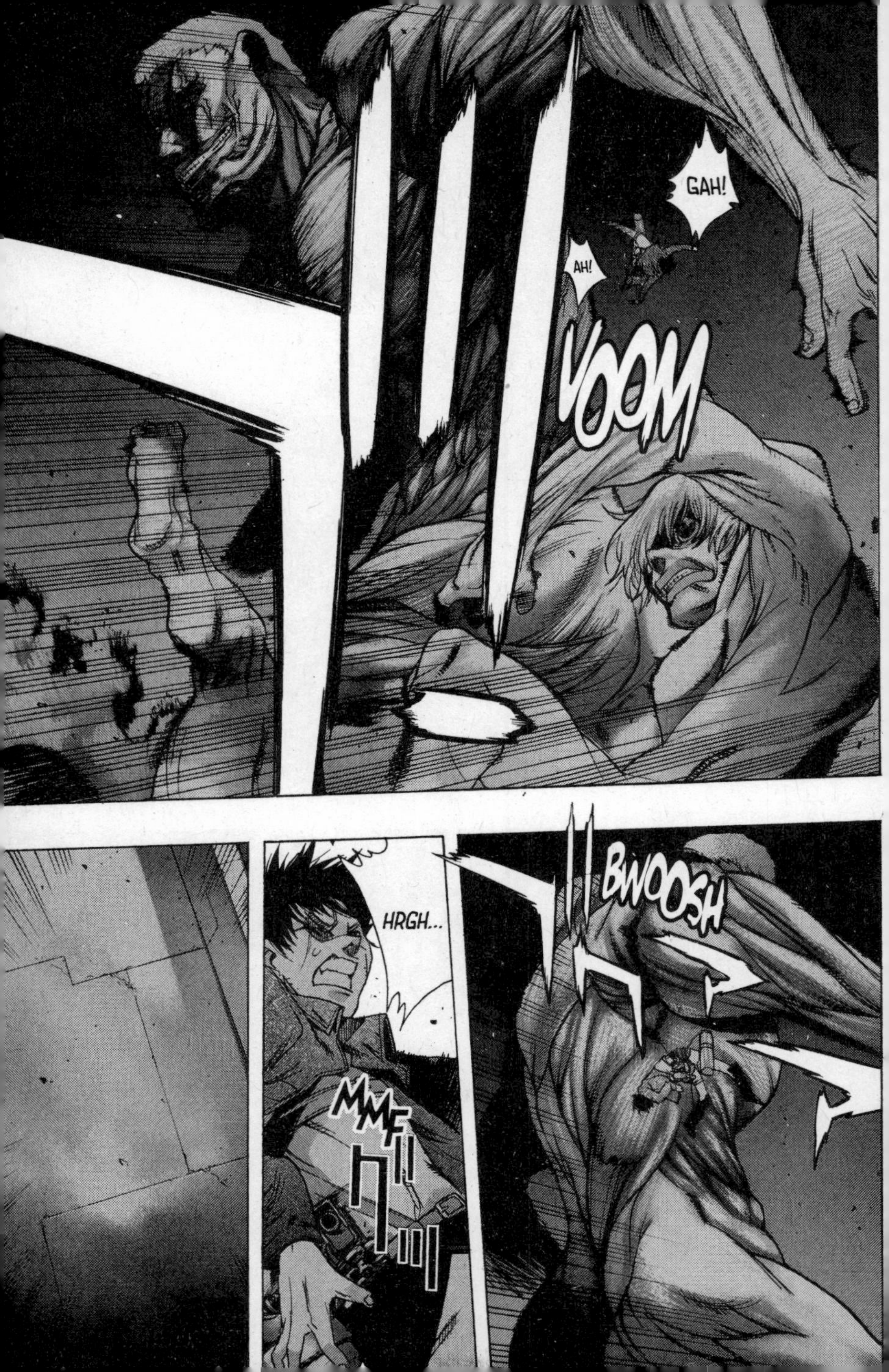
GAH!
AH!
VOOM
BWOOSH
HRGH...
MMF!!

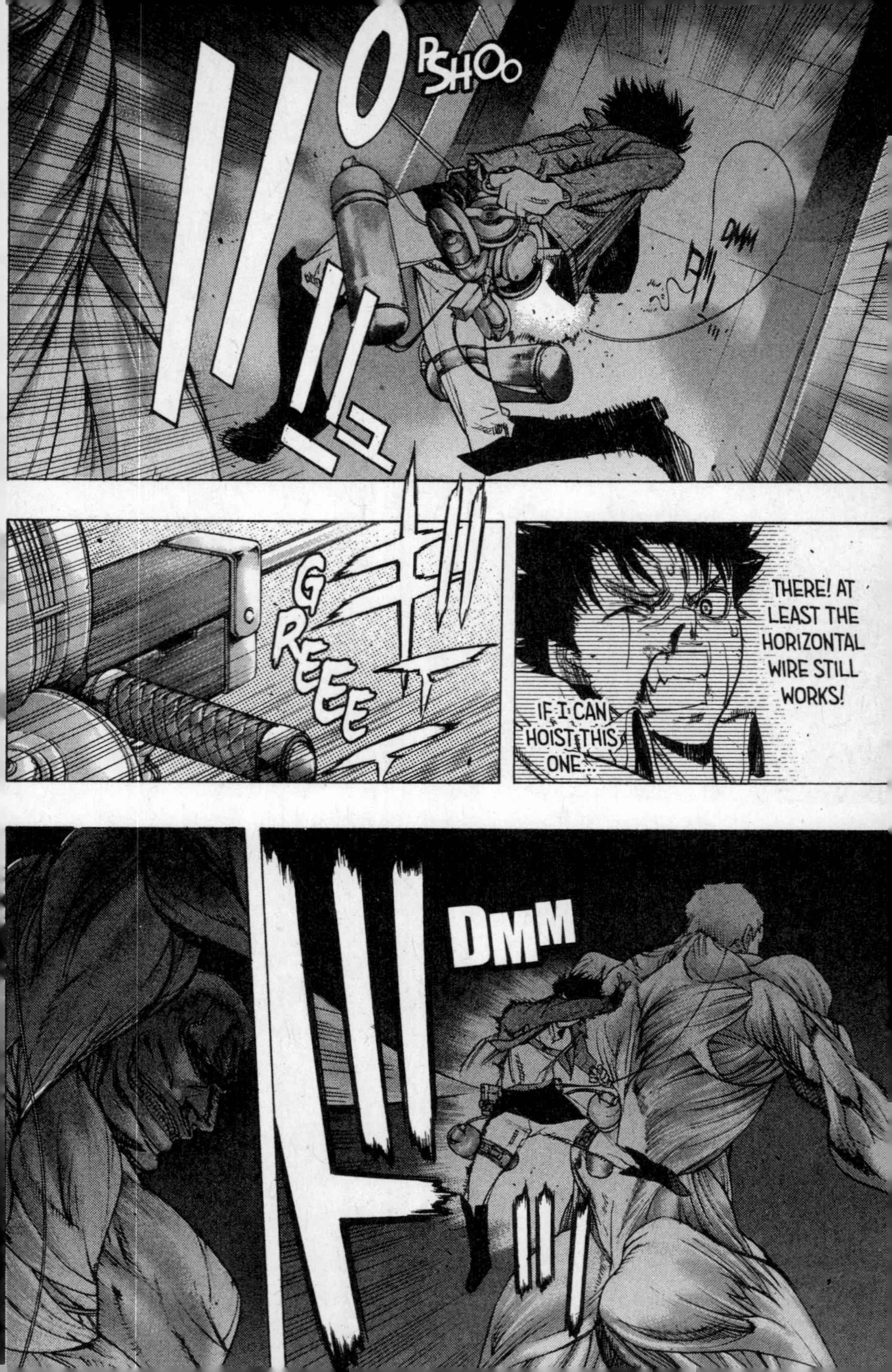
PSHOO
DMM
THERE! AT LEAST THE HORIZONTAL WIRE STILL WORKS!
IF I CAN HOIST THIS ONE...
GREEEE
DMM

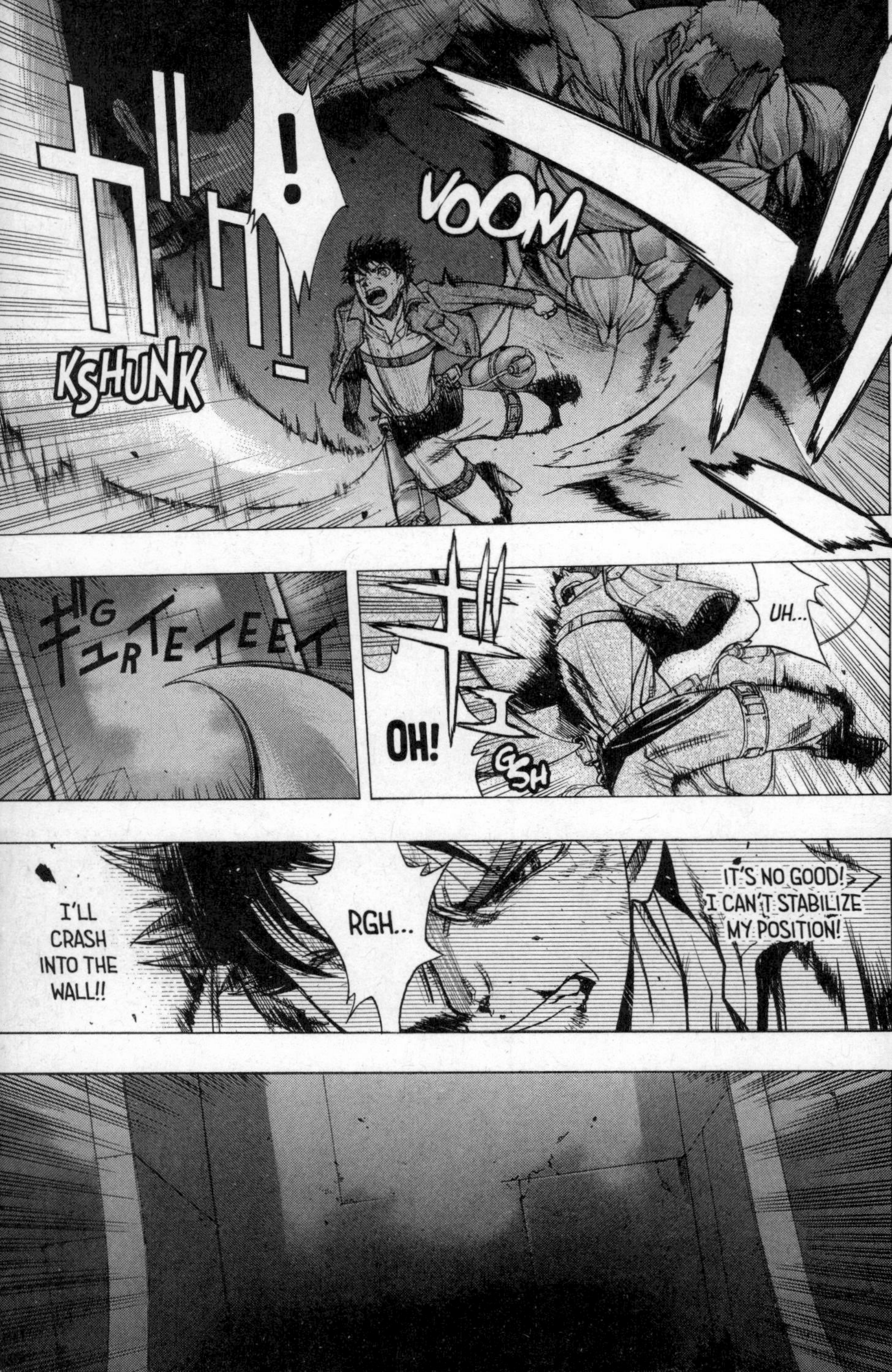
VOOM
KSHUNK
UH...
OH!
GSH
IT'S NO GOOD! I CAN'T STABILIZE MY POSITION!
RGH...
I'LL CRASH INTO THE WALL!!

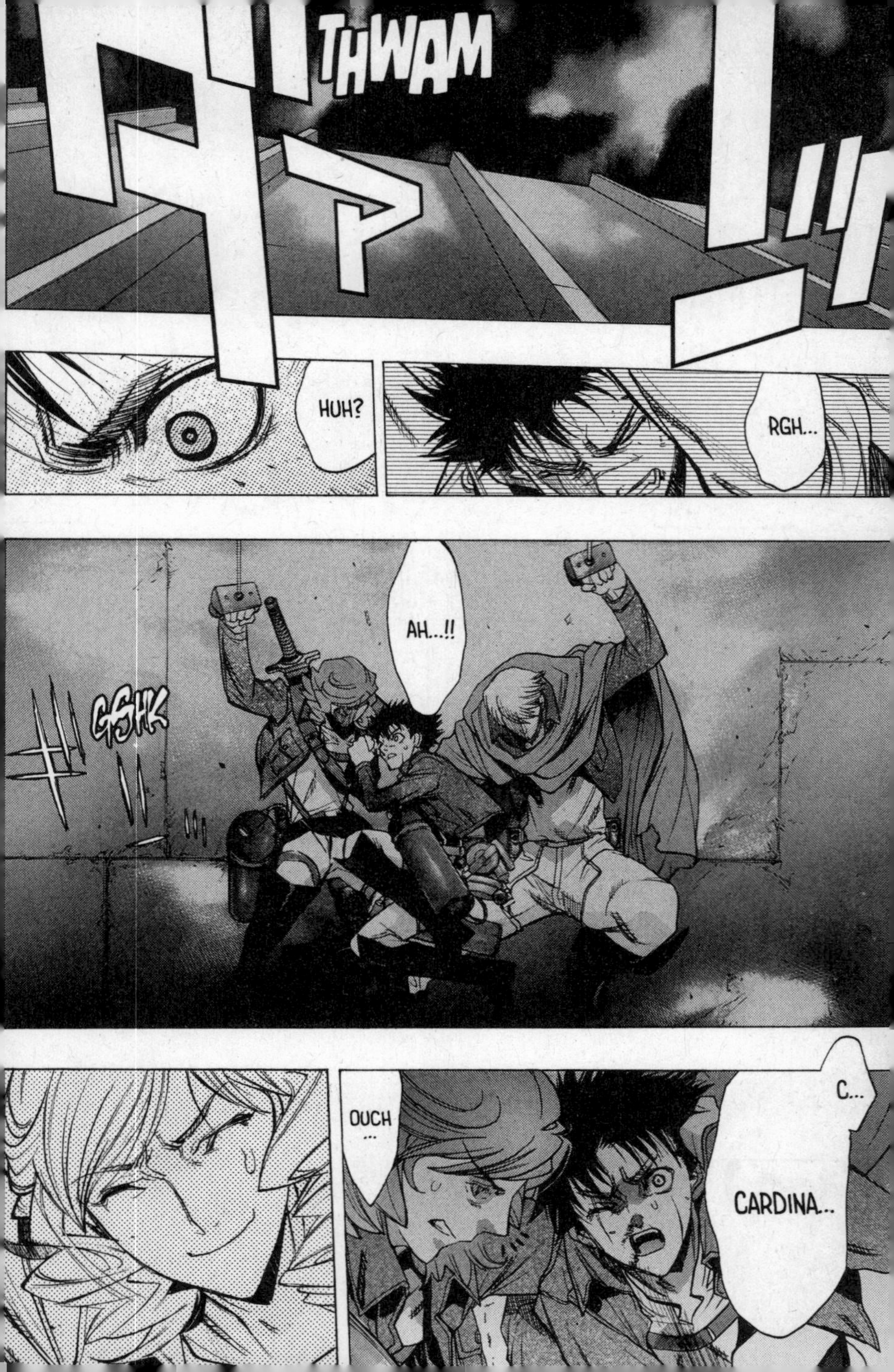
THWAM
RGH...
HUH?
AH...!!
GSHK
C...
CARDINA...
OUCH
...

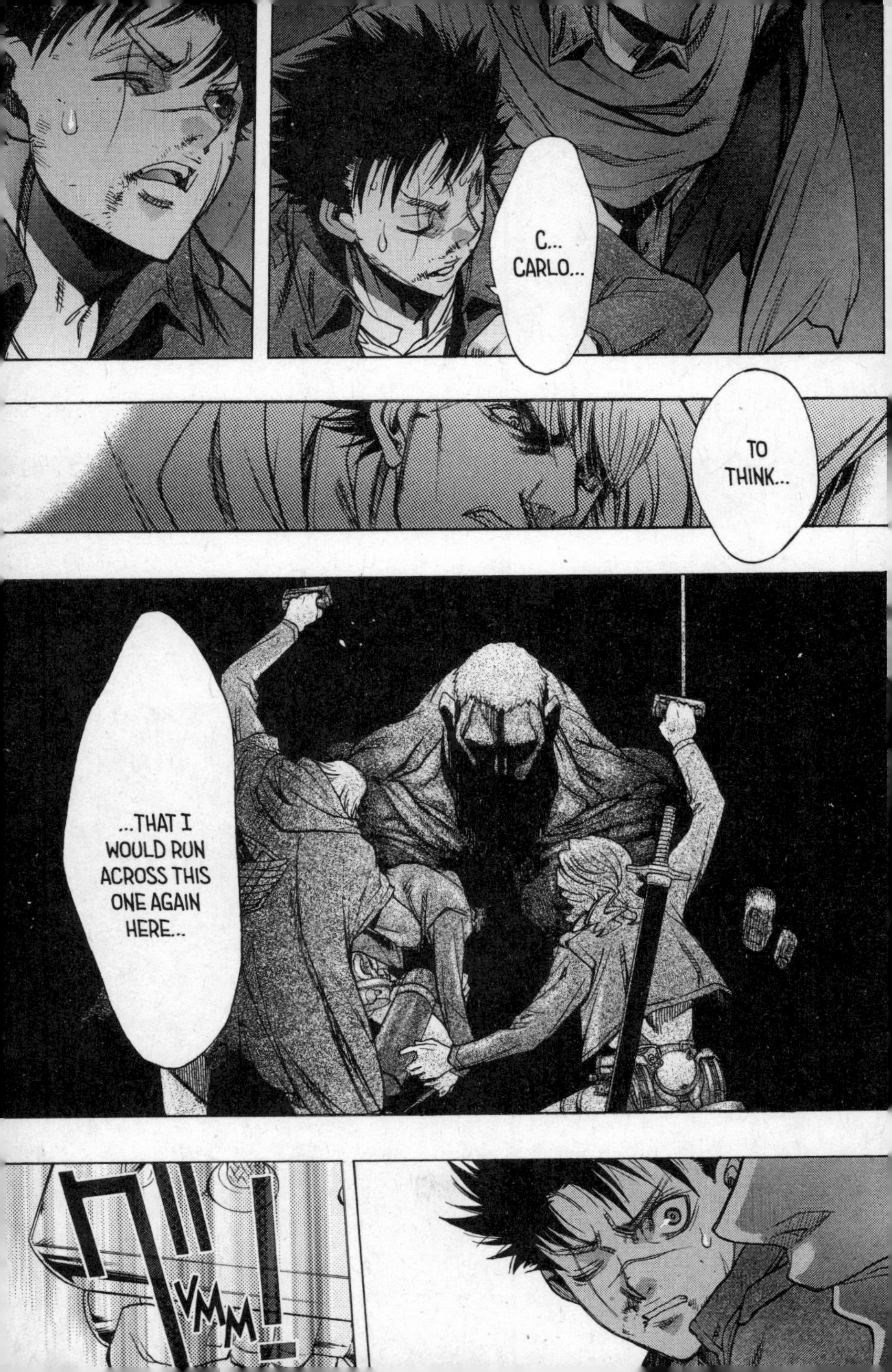

C... CARLO...
TO THINK...
...THAT I WOULD RUN ACROSS THIS ONE AGAIN HERE...
VMM!

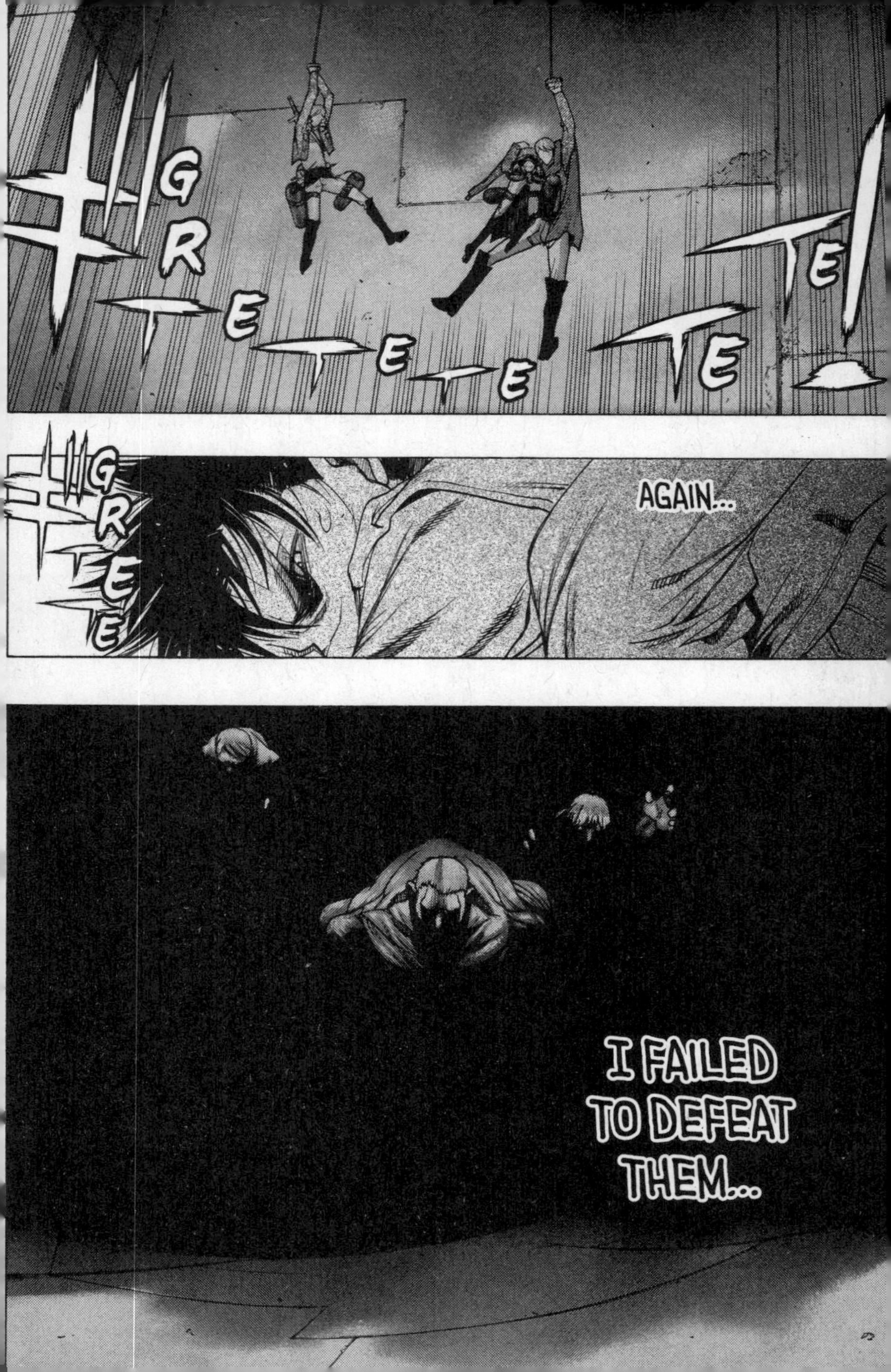
AGAIN...
I FAILED TO DEFEAT THEM...

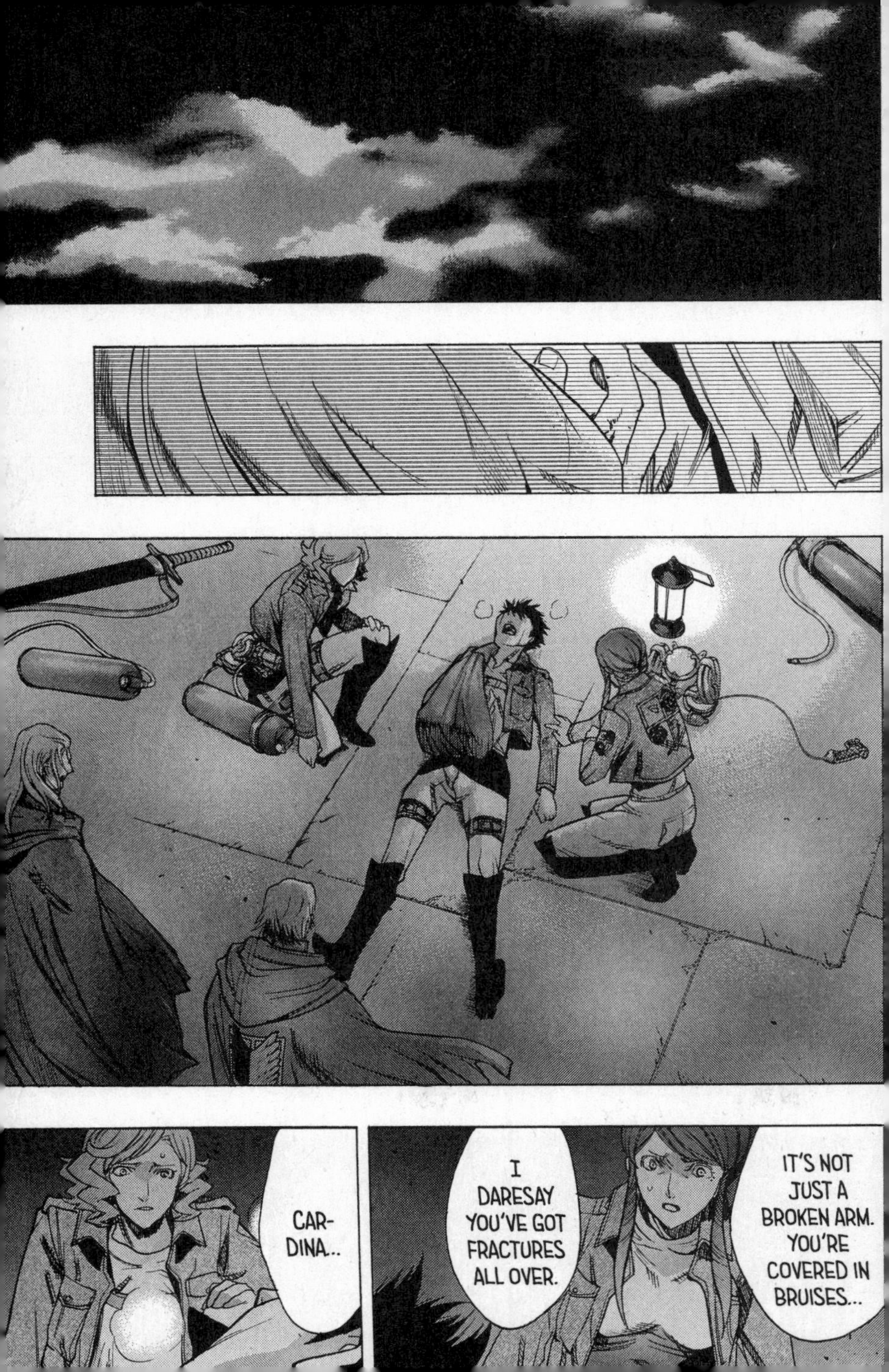
IT'S NOT JUST A BROKEN ARM. YOU'RE COVERED IN BRUISES...
I DARESAY YOU'VE GOT FRACTURES ALL OVER.
CAR-DINA...

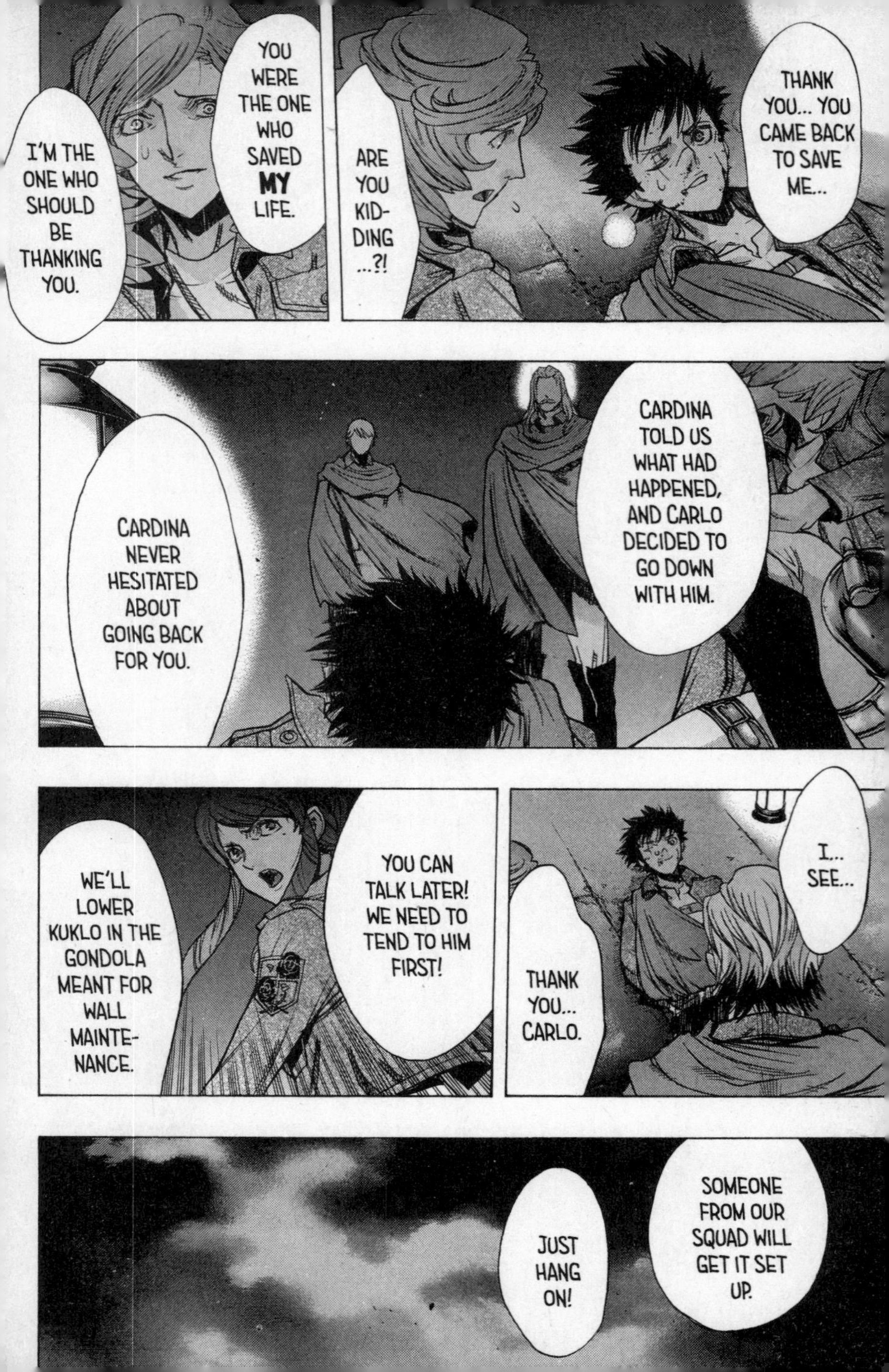
THANK YOU... YOU CAME BACK TO SAVE ME...
ARE YOU KID-DING ...?!
YOU WERE THE ONE WHO SAVED **MY** LIFE.
I'M THE ONE WHO SHOULD BE THANKING YOU.
CARDINA TOLD US WHAT HAD HAPPENED, AND CARLO DECIDED TO GO DOWN WITH HIM.
CARDINA NEVER HESITATED ABOUT GOING BACK FOR YOU.
I... SEE...
THANK YOU... CARLO.
YOU CAN TALK LATER! WE NEED TO TEND TO HIM FIRST!
WE'LL LOWER KUKLO IN THE GONDOLA MEANT FOR WALL MAINTE-NANCE.
SOMEONE FROM OUR SQUAD WILL GET IT SET UP.
JUST HANG ON!

THAT BASTARD ...
...THAT TEN-METER BASTARD WAS HERE THE WHOLE TIME...
...YEAH...

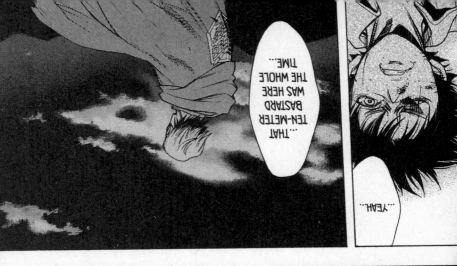

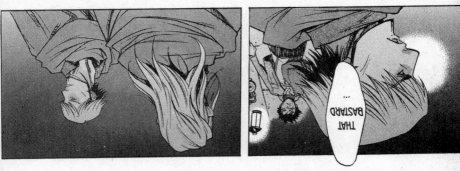

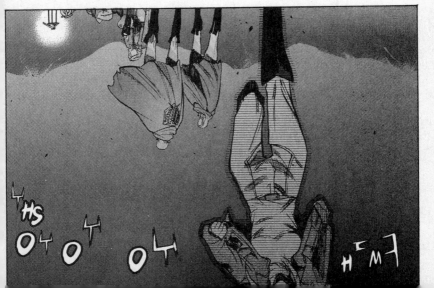

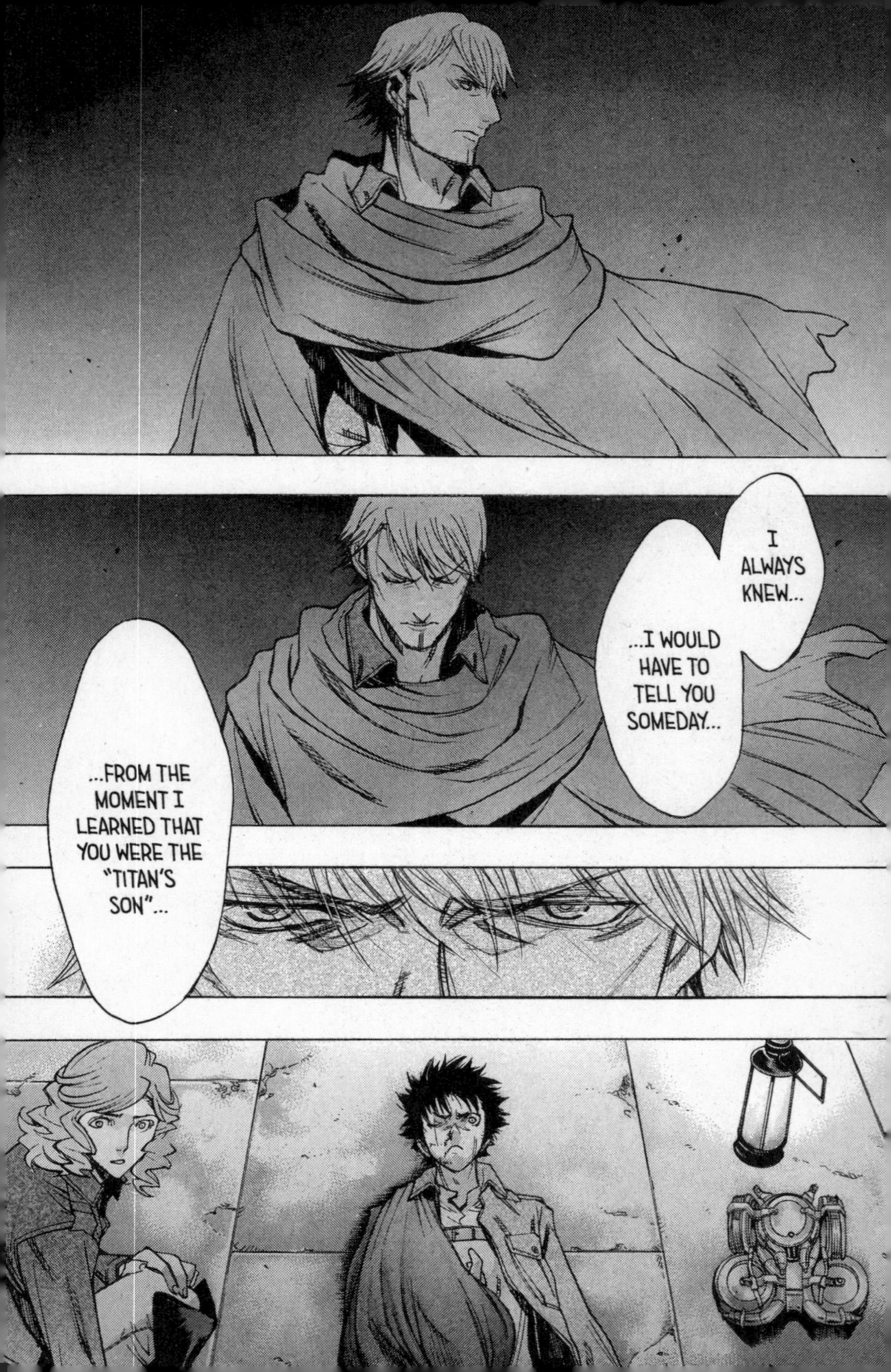
I ALWAYS KNEW...
...I WOULD HAVE TO TELL YOU SOMEDAY...
...FROM THE MOMENT I LEARNED THAT YOU WERE THE "TITAN'S SON"...

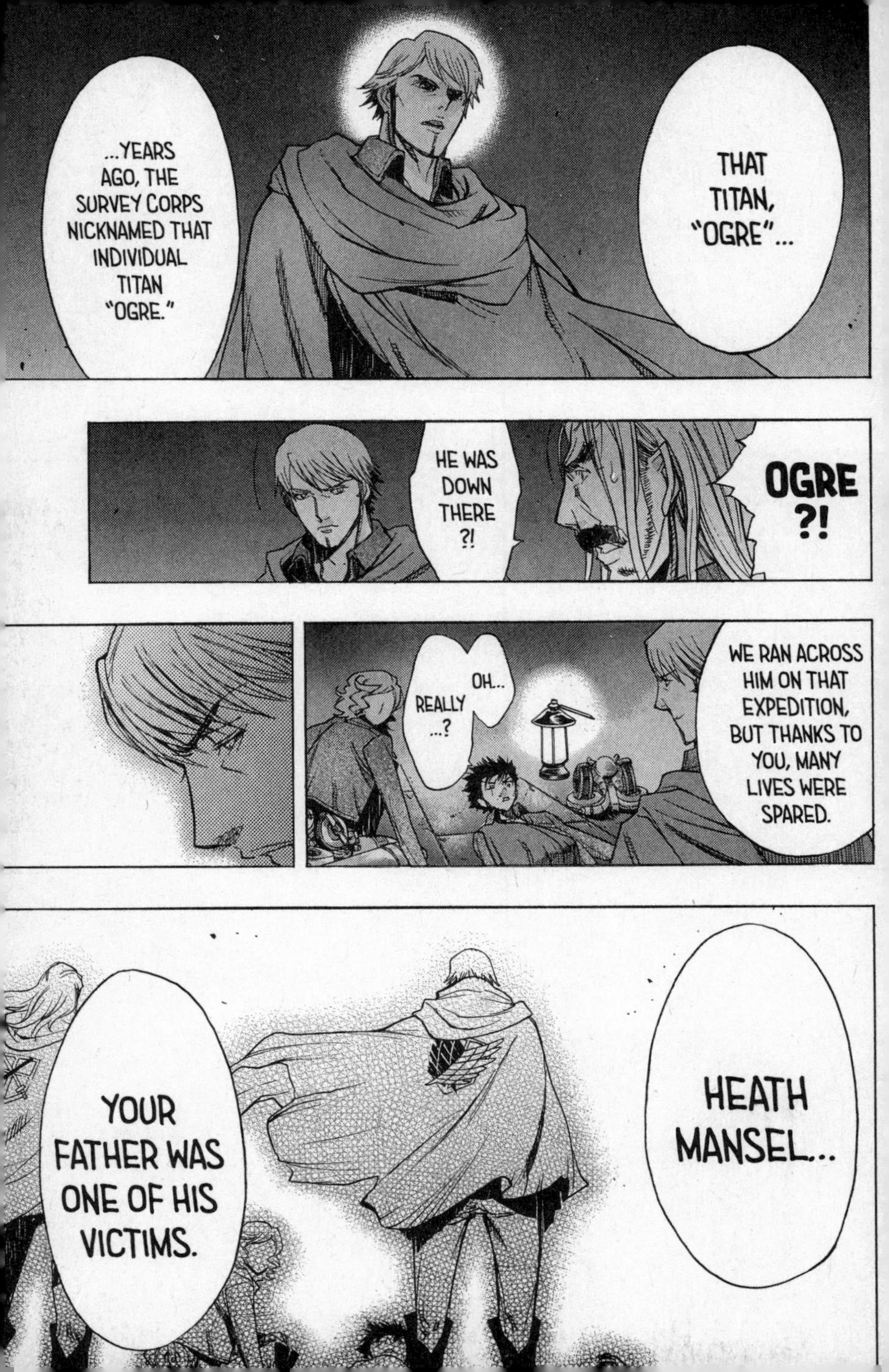
THAT TITAN, "OGRE"...
...YEARS AGO, THE SURVEY CORPS NICKNAMED THAT INDIVIDUAL TITAN "OGRE."
OGRE ?!
HE WAS DOWN THERE ?!
WE RAN ACROSS HIM ON THAT EXPEDITION, BUT THANKS TO YOU, MANY LIVES WERE SPARED.
OH... REALLY ...?
HEATH MANSEL...
YOUR FATHER WAS ONE OF HIS VICTIMS.

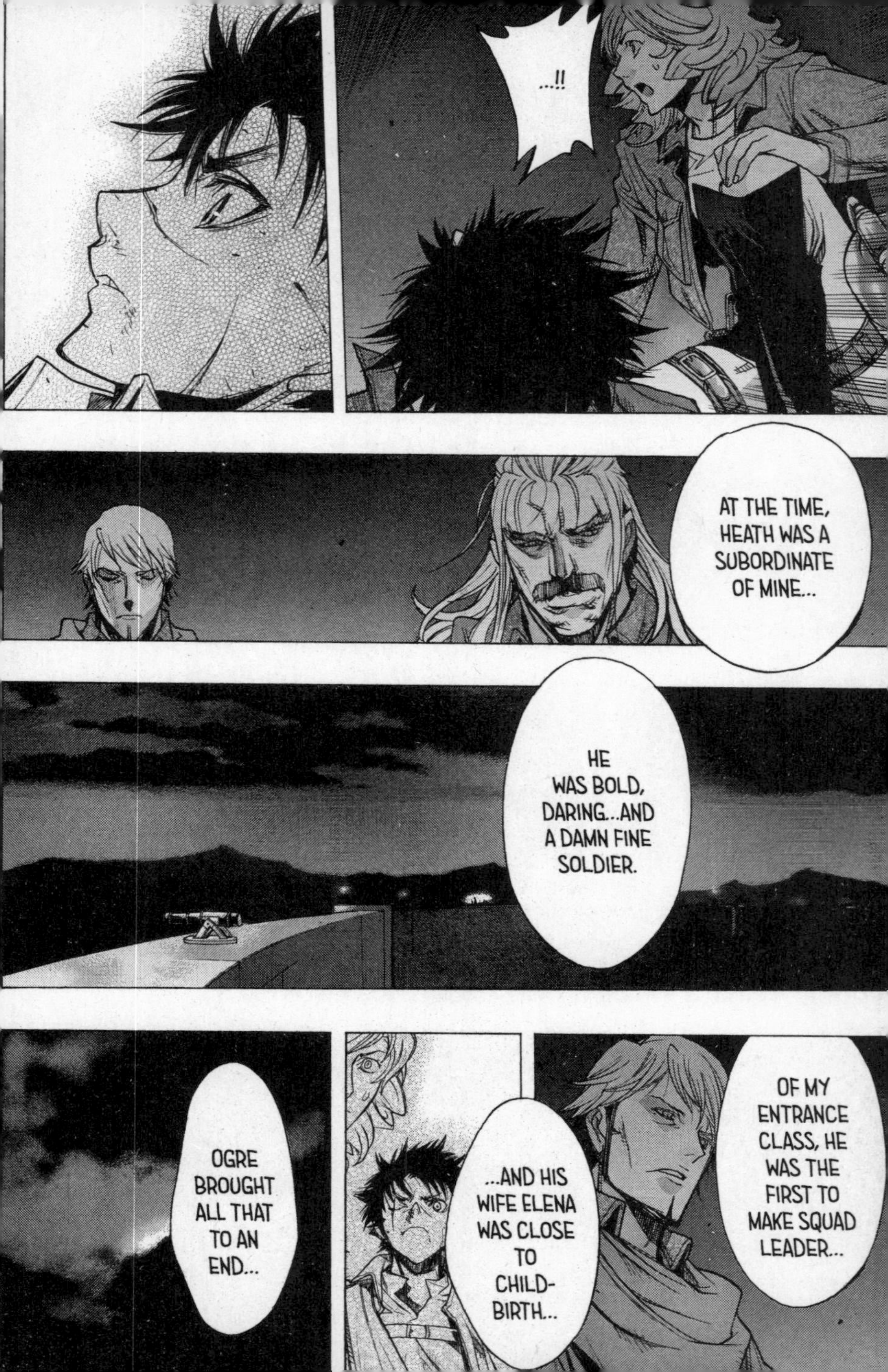
...!!
AT THE TIME, HEATH WAS A SUBORDINATE OF MINE...
HE WAS BOLD, DARING...AND A DAMN FINE SOLDIER.
OF MY ENTRANCE CLASS, HE WAS THE FIRST TO MAKE SQUAD LEADER...
...AND HIS WIFE ELENA WAS CLOSE TO CHILD-BIRTH...
OGRE BROUGHT ALL THAT TO AN END...

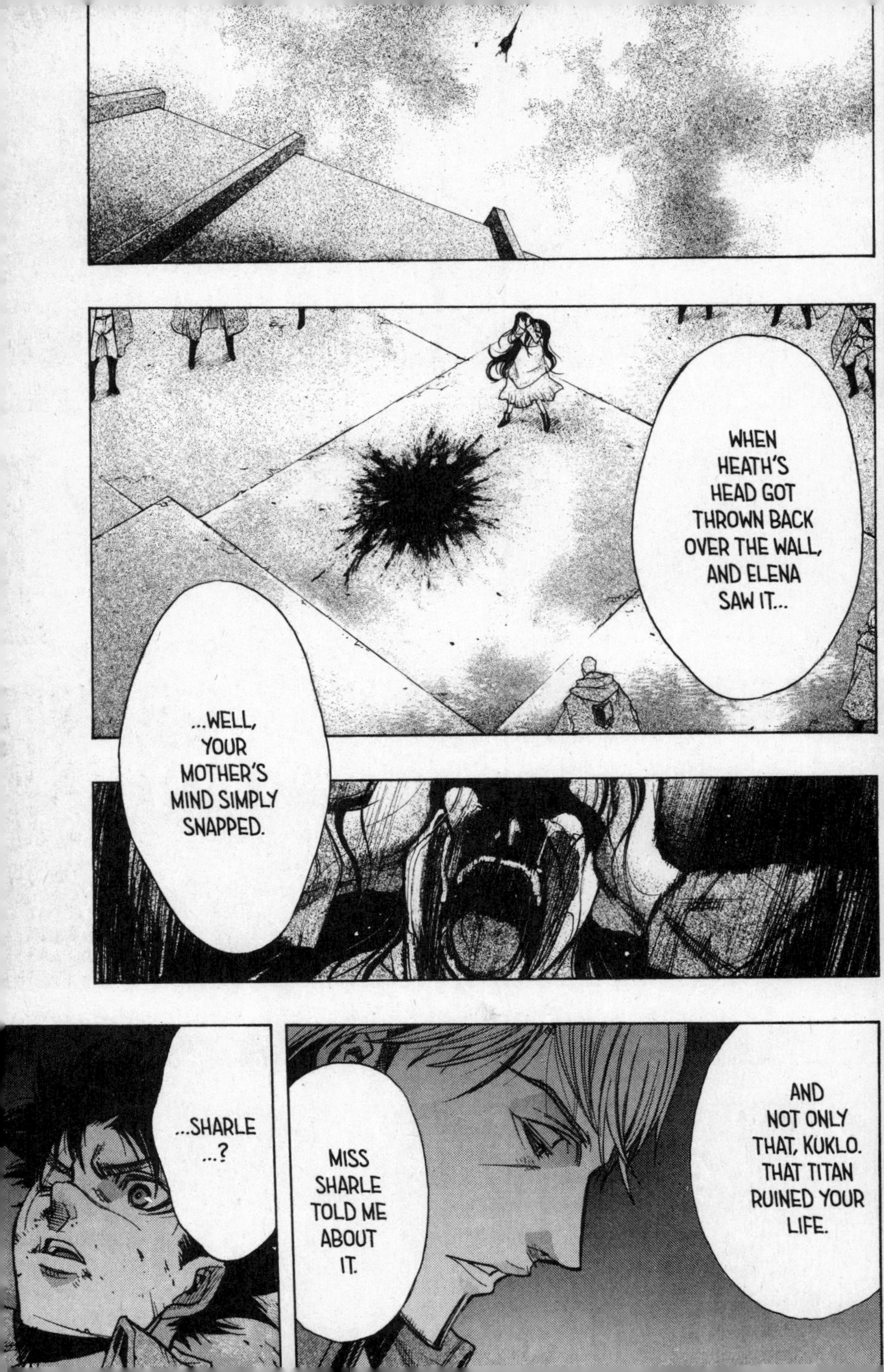
WHEN HEATH'S HEAD GOT THROWN BACK OVER THE WALL, AND ELENA SAW IT...
...WELL, YOUR MOTHER'S MIND SIMPLY SNAPPED.
AND NOT ONLY THAT, KUKLO. THAT TITAN RUINED YOUR LIFE.
MISS SHARLE TOLD ME ABOUT IT.
...SHARLE ...?

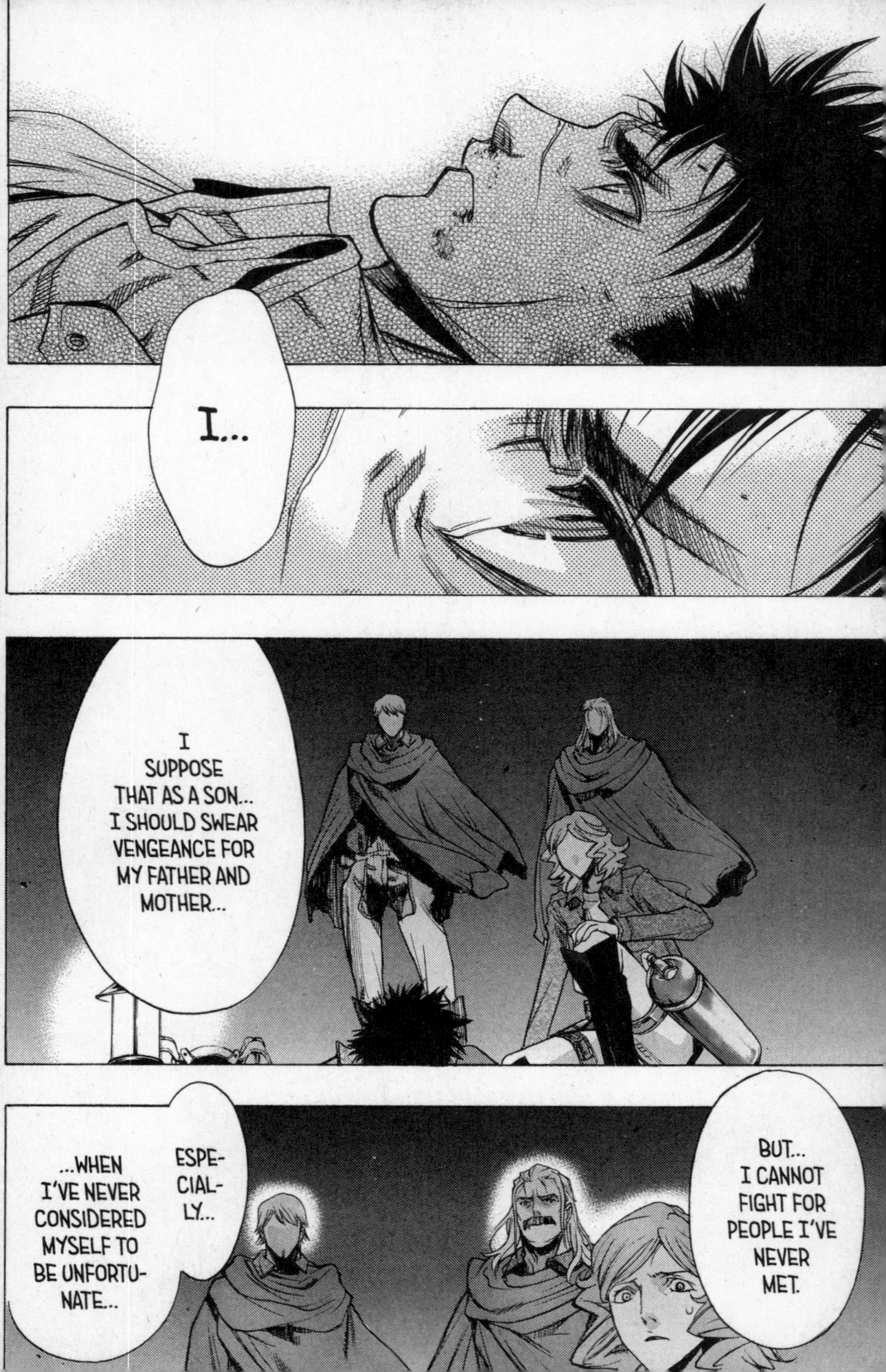
I...
I SUPPOSE THAT AS A SON... I SHOULD SWEAR VENGEANCE FOR MY FATHER AND MOTHER...
BUT... I CANNOT FIGHT FOR PEOPLE I'VE NEVER MET.
ESPE-CIAL-LY...
...WHEN I'VE NEVER CONSIDERED MYSELF TO BE UNFORTU-NATE...

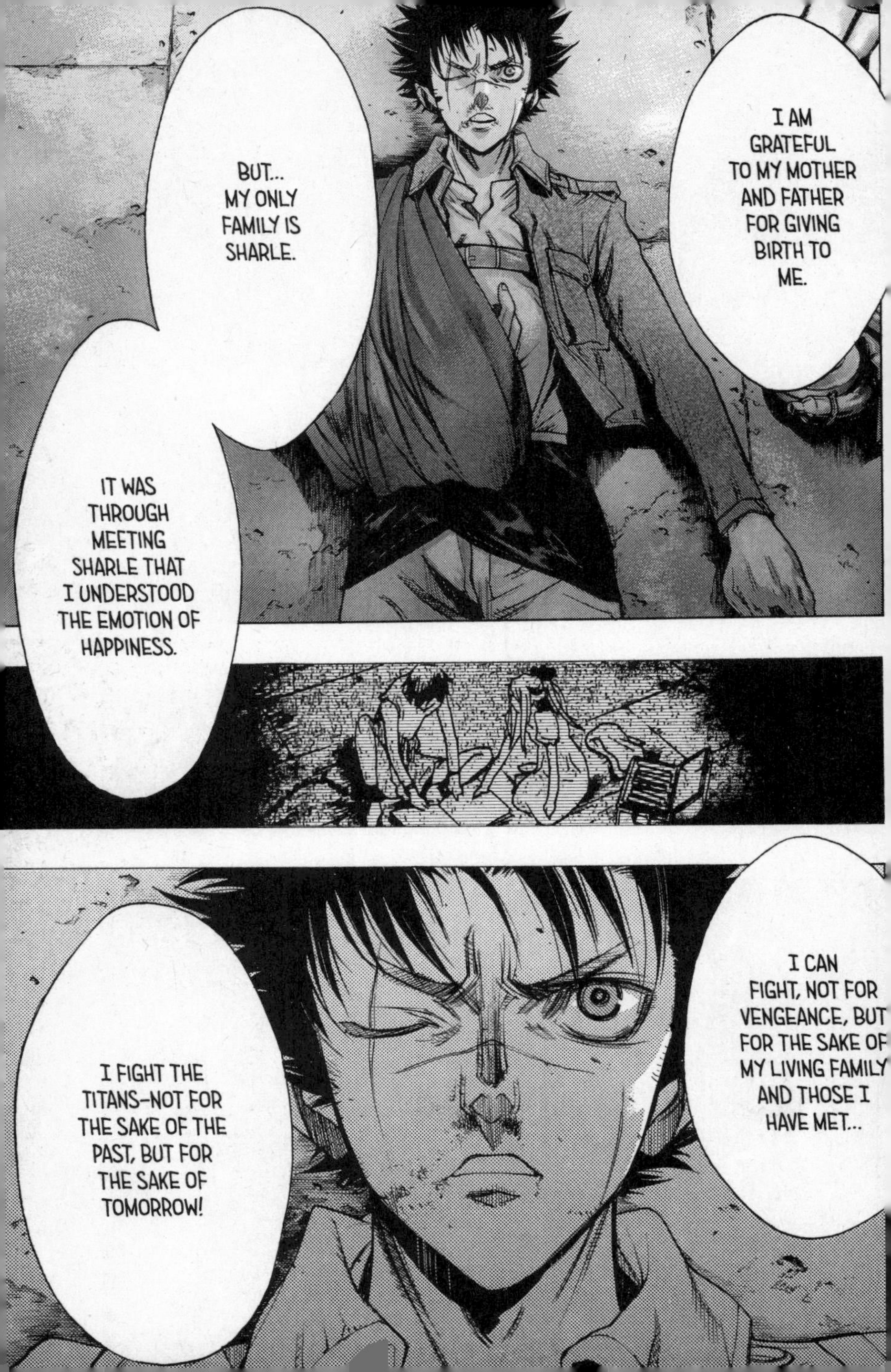
I AM GRATEFUL TO MY MOTHER AND FATHER FOR GIVING BIRTH TO ME.
BUT... MY ONLY FAMILY IS SHARLE.
IT WAS THROUGH MEETING SHARLE THAT I UNDERSTOOD THE EMOTION OF HAPPINESS.
I CAN FIGHT, NOT FOR VENGEANCE, BUT FOR THE SAKE OF MY LIVING FAMILY AND THOSE I HAVE MET...
I FIGHT THE TITANS–NOT FOR THE SAKE OF THE PAST, BUT FOR THE SAKE OF TOMORROW!

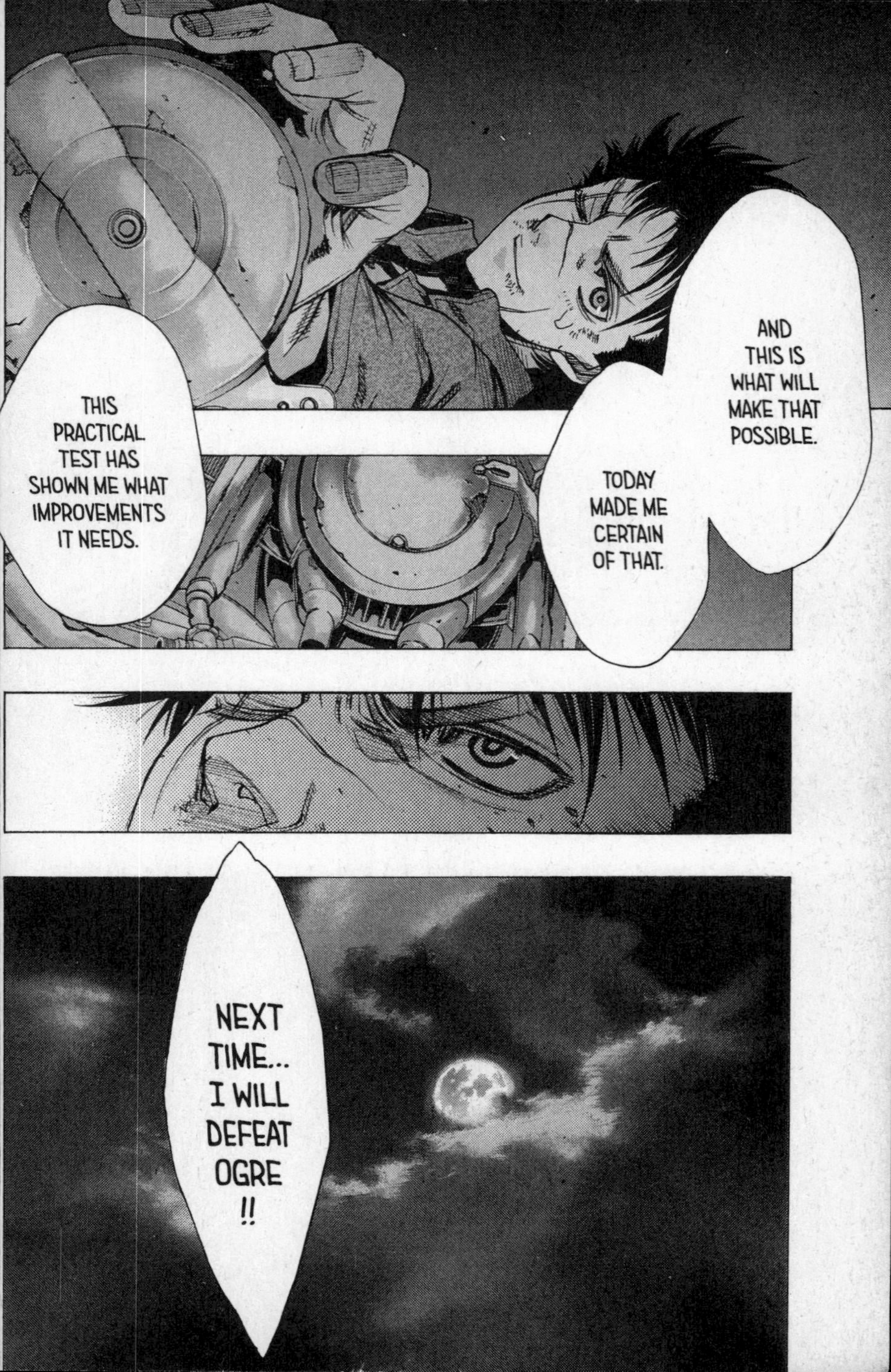
AND THIS IS WHAT WILL MAKE THAT POSSIBLE.
TODAY MADE ME CERTAIN OF THAT.
THIS PRACTICAL TEST HAS SHOWN ME WHAT IMPROVEMENTS IT NEEDS.
NEXT TIME... I WILL DEFEAT OGRE !!

ATTACK on TITAN
BEFORE THE FALL

TO BE CONTINUED

SWEAR UPON WALL MARIA

A story about the relationship between three childhood friends—Sorum Humé, who perished against Mammon in the flashback of Volume 6; his fiancée Maria Carlstead, a member of the Garrison Corps; and the genius craftsman Angel Aaltonen, future developer of the Device.

Originally published: Bessatsu Shonen Magazine, September 2015 issue

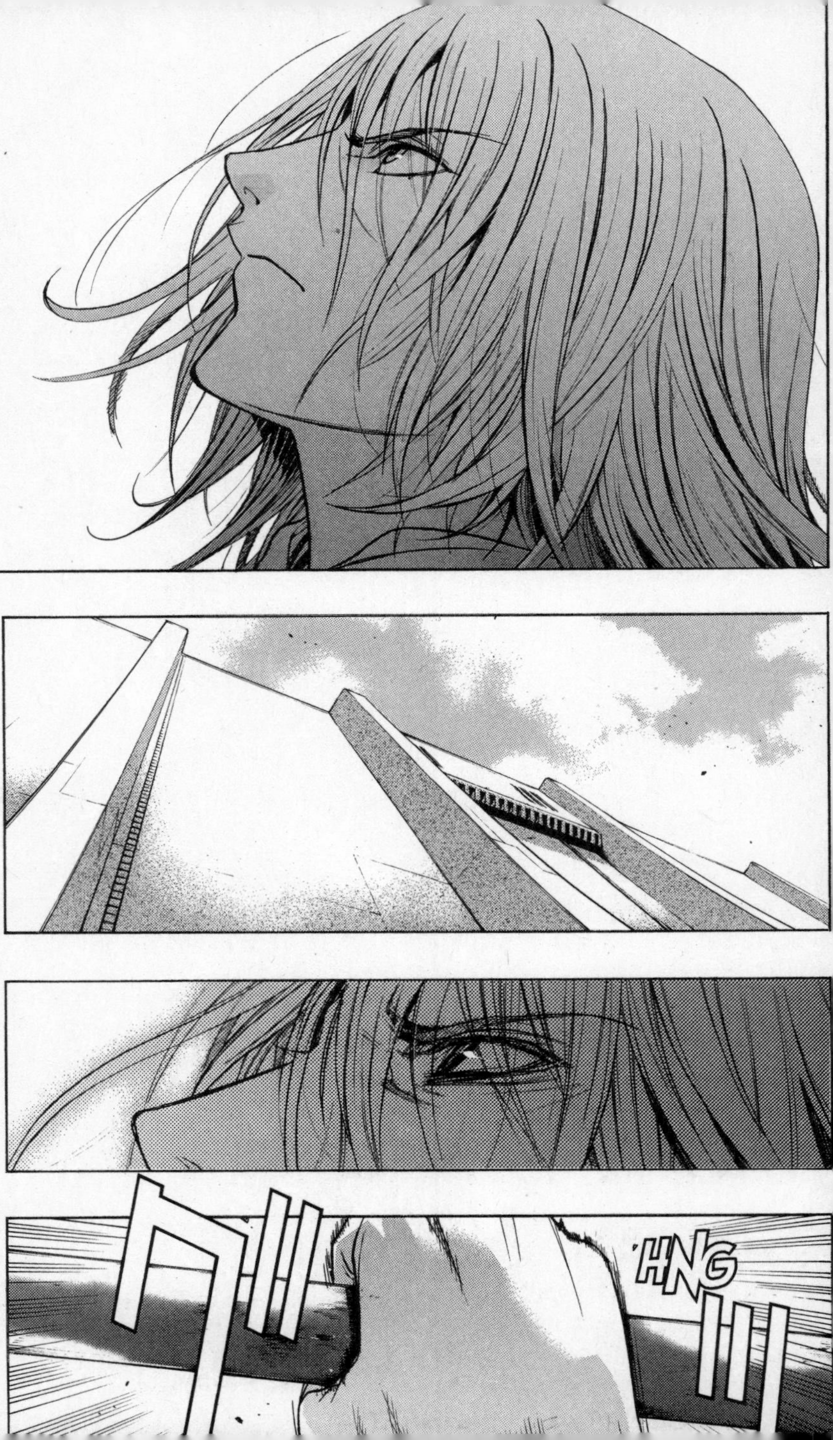
HNG

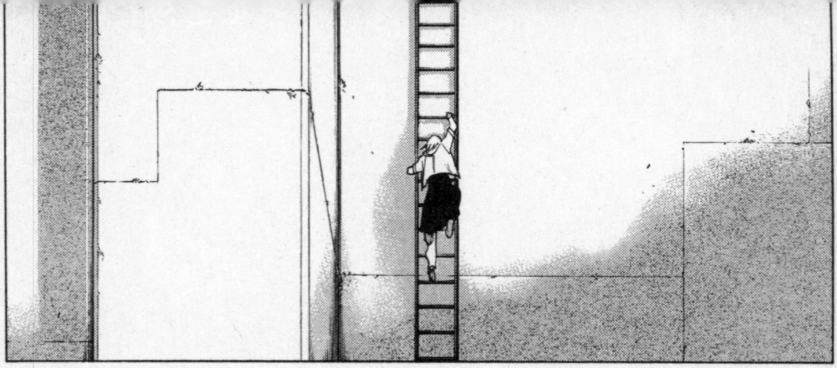
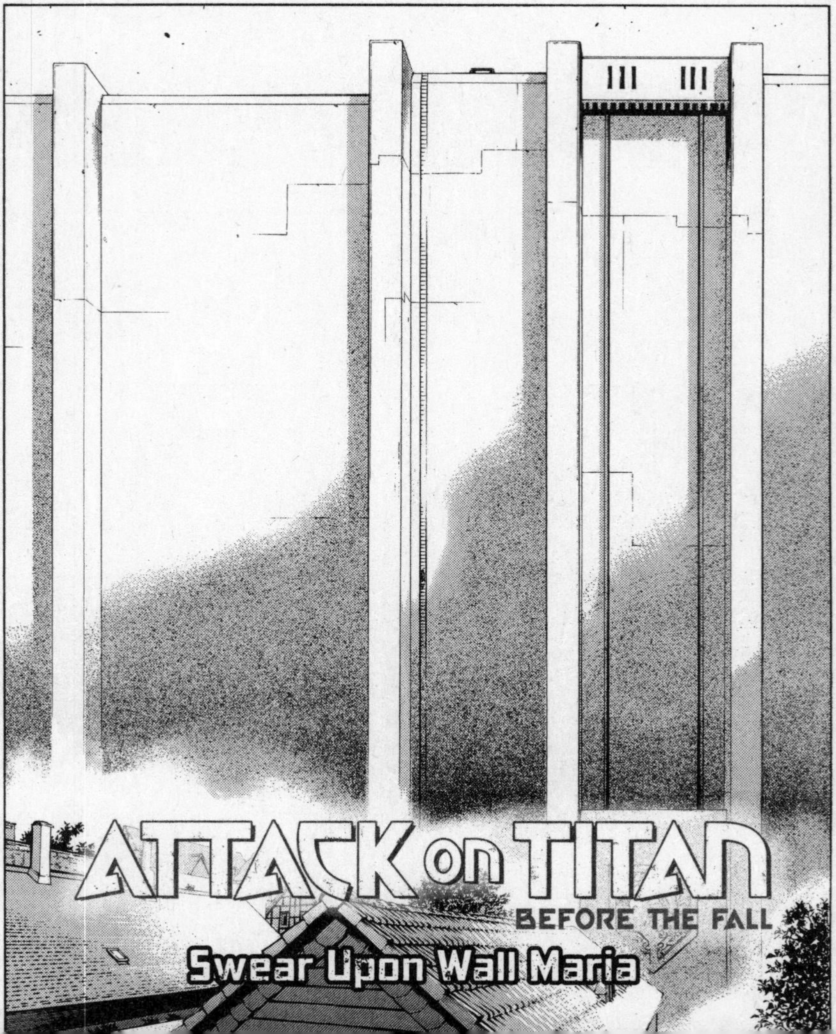
ATTACK on TITAN
BEFORE THE FALL
Swear Upon Wall Maria

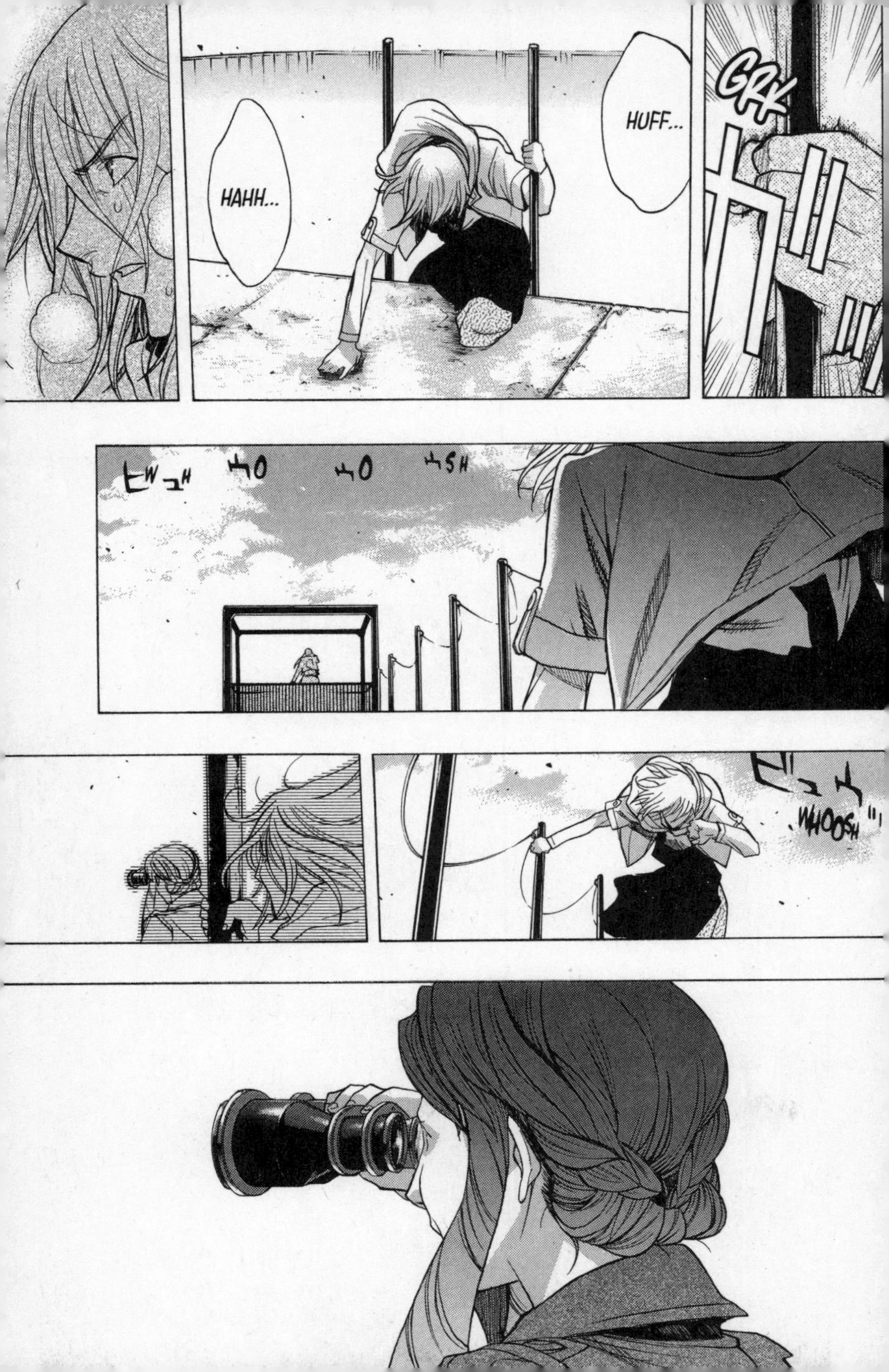
GRK
HUFF...
HAHH...
WHOOSH!!

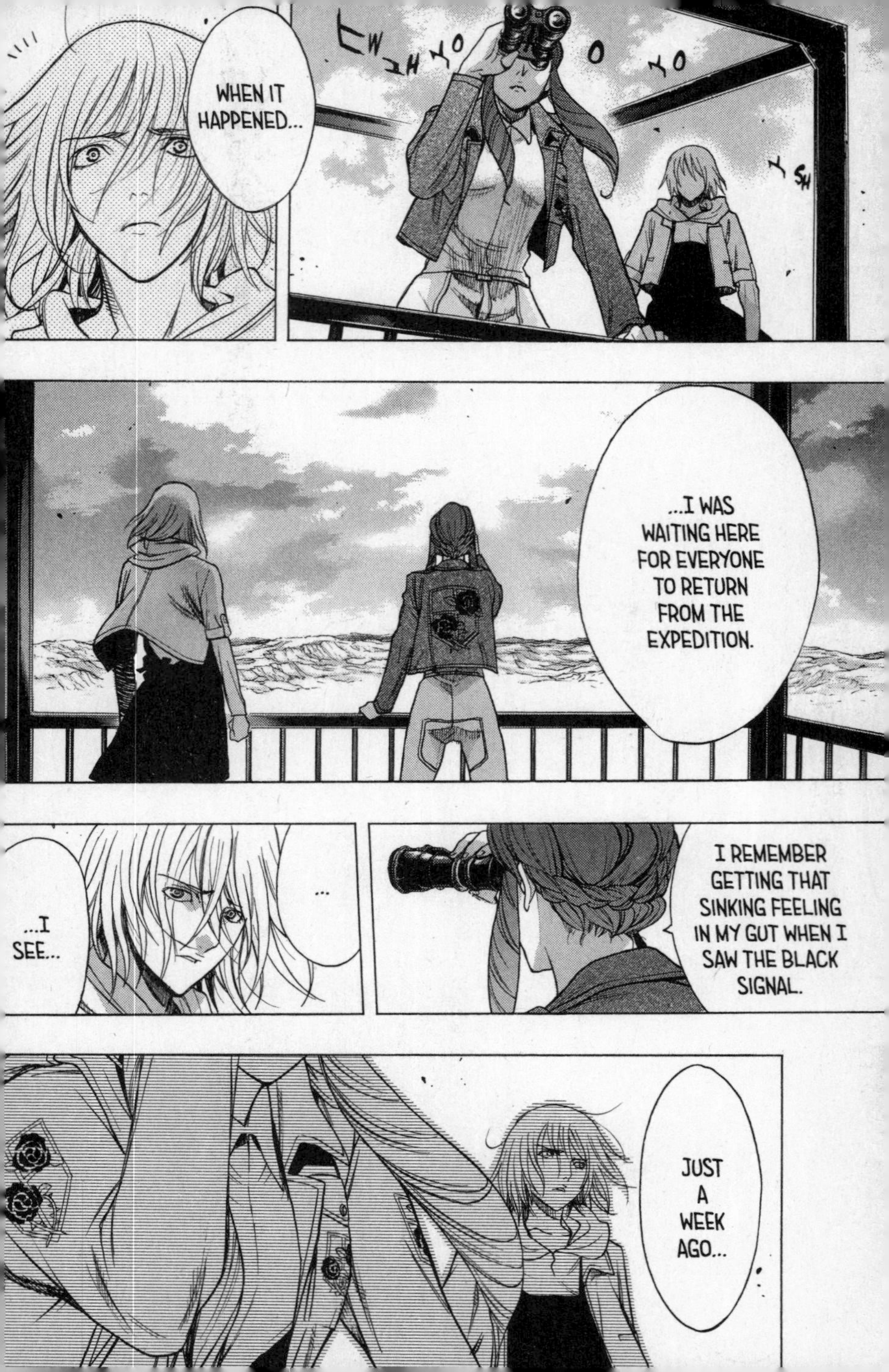
WHEN IT HAPPENED...
...I WAS WAITING HERE FOR EVERYONE TO RETURN FROM THE EXPEDITION.
I REMEMBER GETTING THAT SINKING FEELING IN MY GUT WHEN I SAW THE BLACK SIGNAL.
...
...I SEE...
JUST A WEEK AGO...

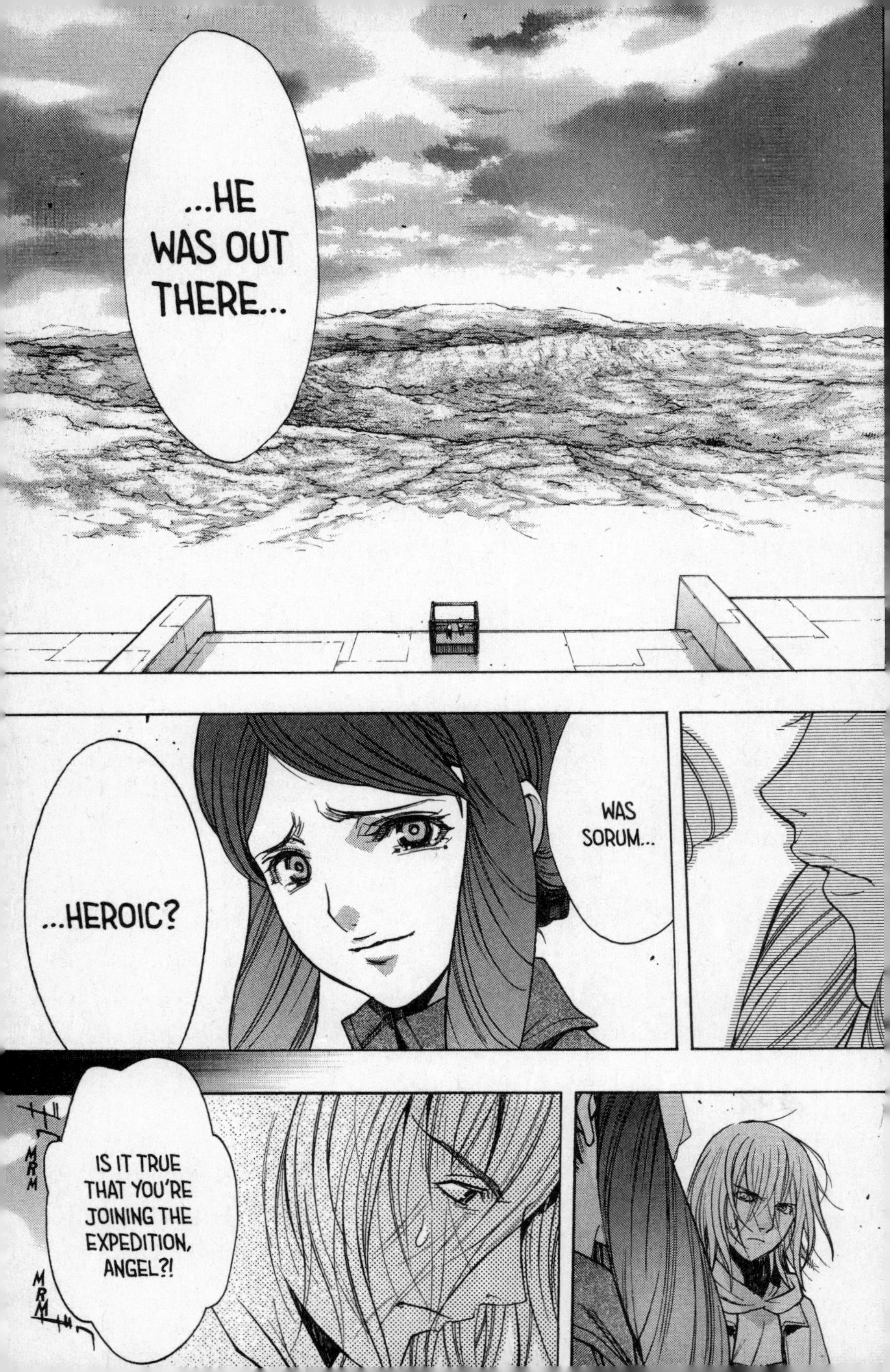
...HE WAS OUT THERE...
WAS SORUM...
...HEROIC?
IS IT TRUE THAT YOU'RE JOINING THE EXPEDITION, ANGEL?!
MRM
MRM

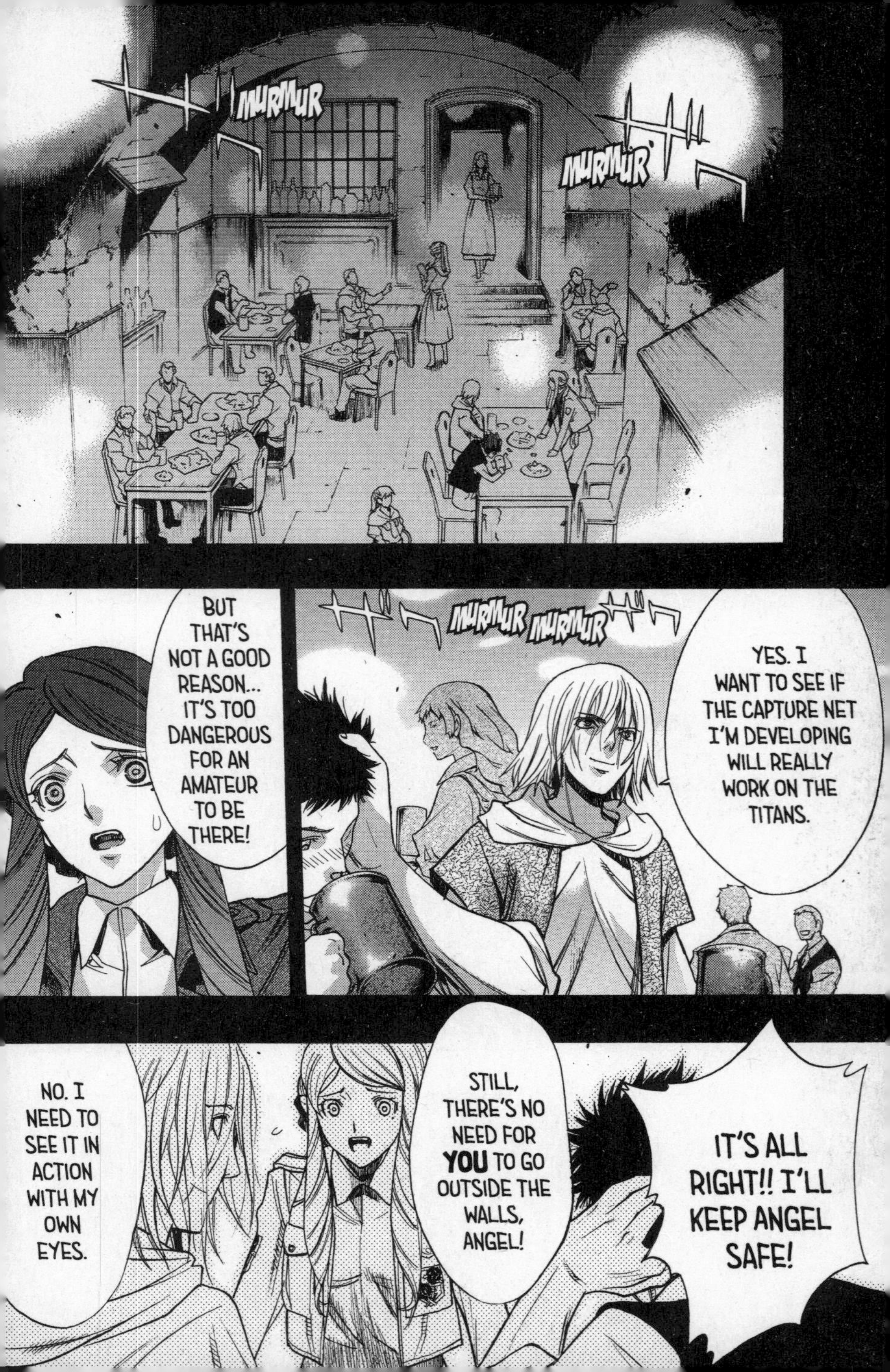
MURMUR
MURMUR
MURMUR MURMUR
YES. I WANT TO SEE IF THE CAPTURE NET I'M DEVELOPING WILL REALLY WORK ON THE TITANS.
BUT THAT'S NOT A GOOD REASON... IT'S TOO DANGEROUS FOR AN AMATEUR TO BE THERE!
IT'S ALL RIGHT!! I'LL KEEP ANGEL SAFE!
STILL, THERE'S NO NEED FOR YOU TO GO OUTSIDE THE WALLS, ANGEL!
NO. I NEED TO SEE IT IN ACTION WITH MY OWN EYES.

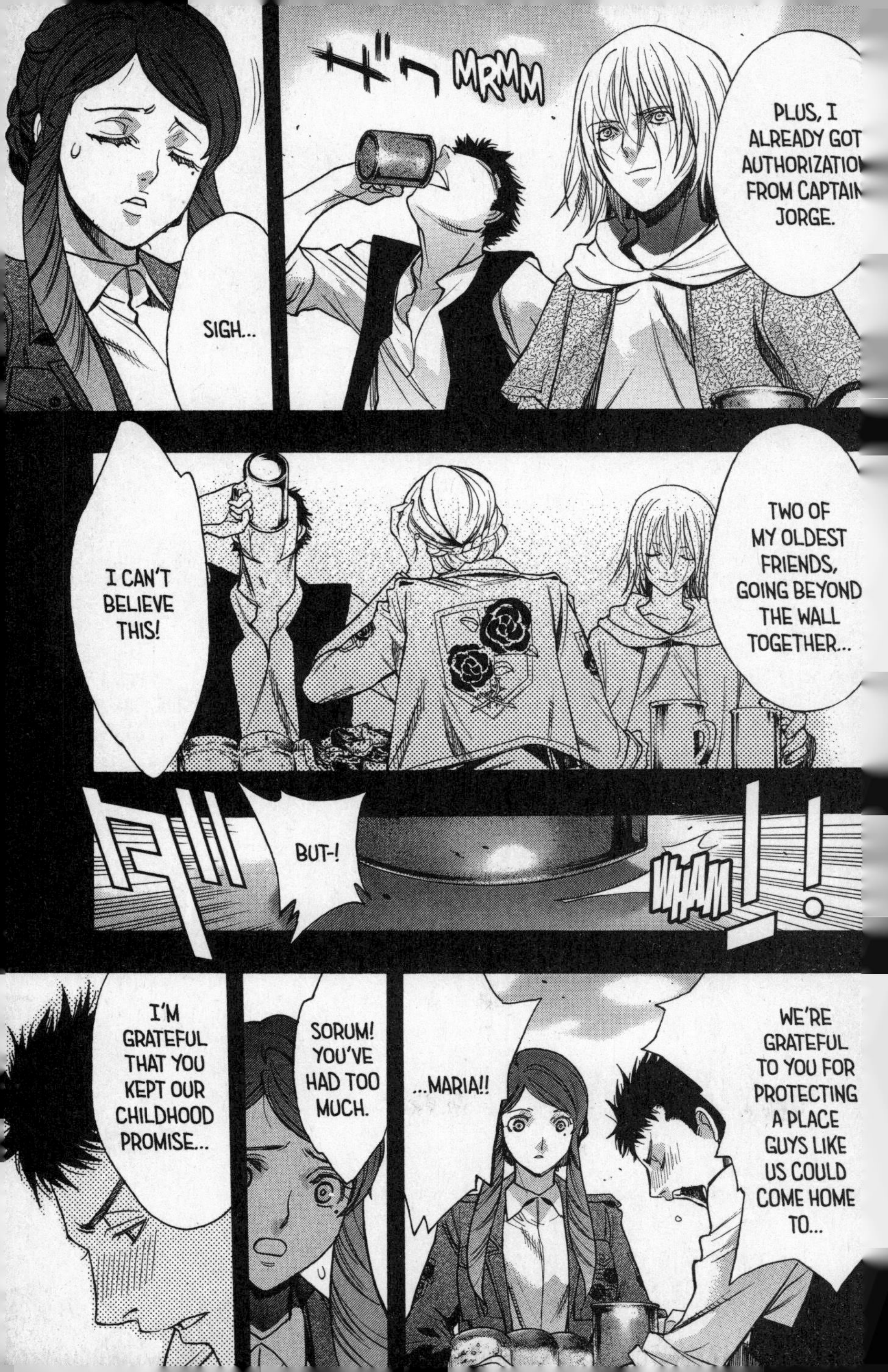
PLUS, I ALREADY GOT AUTHORIZATION FROM CAPTAIN JORGE.
MRMM
SIGH...
TWO OF MY OLDEST FRIENDS, GOING BEYOND THE WALL TOGETHER...
I CAN'T BELIEVE THIS!
WHAM!
BUT-!
WE'RE GRATEFUL TO YOU FOR PROTECTING A PLACE GUYS LIKE US COULD COME HOME TO...
...MARIA!!
SORUM! YOU'VE HAD TOO MUCH.
I'M GRATEFUL THAT YOU KEPT OUR CHILDHOOD PROMISE...

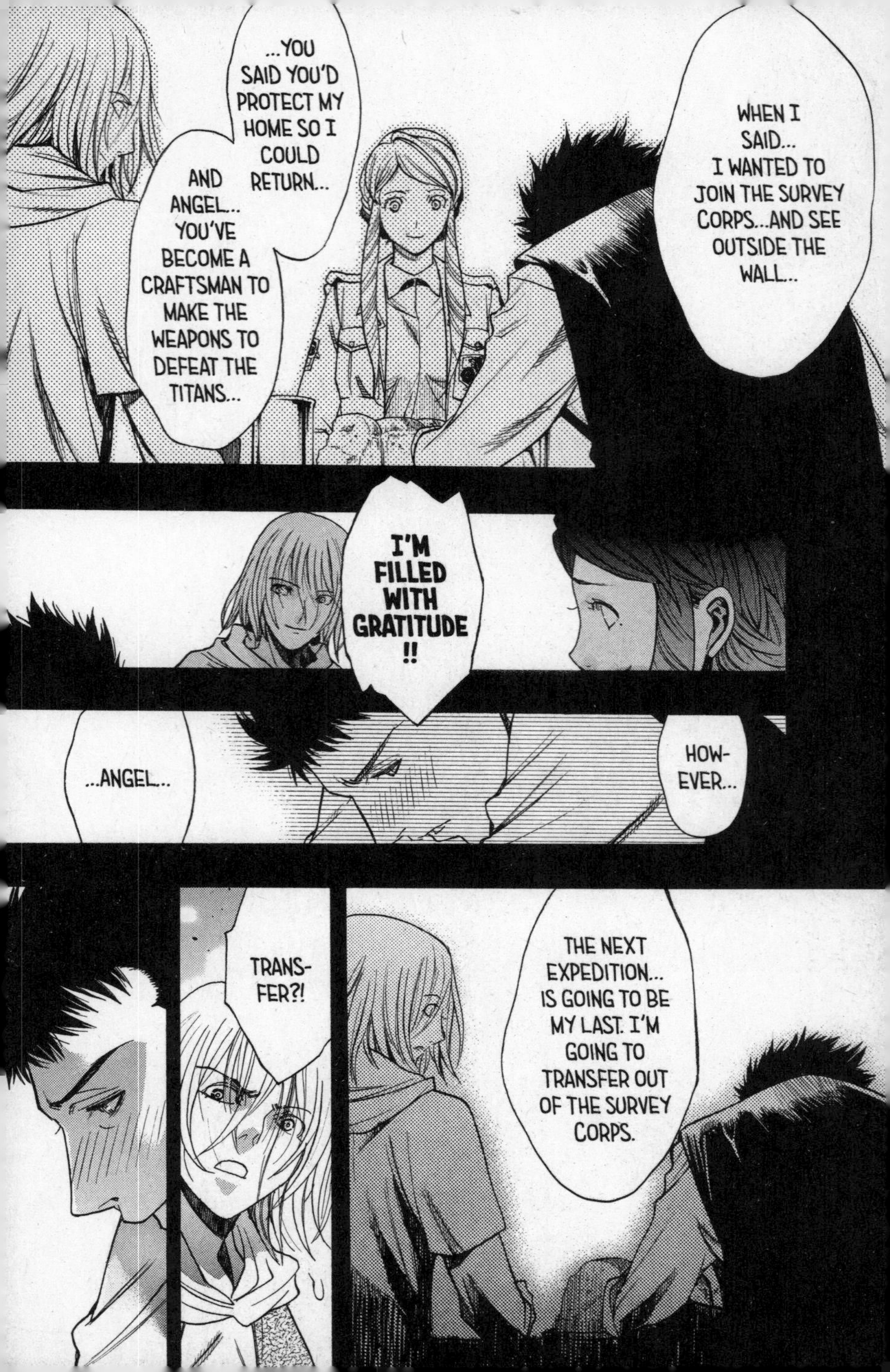
WHEN I SAID... I WANTED TO JOIN THE SURVEY CORPS...AND SEE OUTSIDE THE WALL...
...YOU SAID YOU'D PROTECT MY HOME SO I COULD RETURN...
AND ANGEL... YOU'VE BECOME A CRAFTSMAN TO MAKE THE WEAPONS TO DEFEAT THE TITANS...
I'M FILLED WITH GRATITUDE !!
HOW-EVER...
...ANGEL...
THE NEXT EXPEDITION... IS GOING TO BE MY LAST. I'M GOING TO TRANSFER OUT OF THE SURVEY CORPS.
TRANS-FER?!

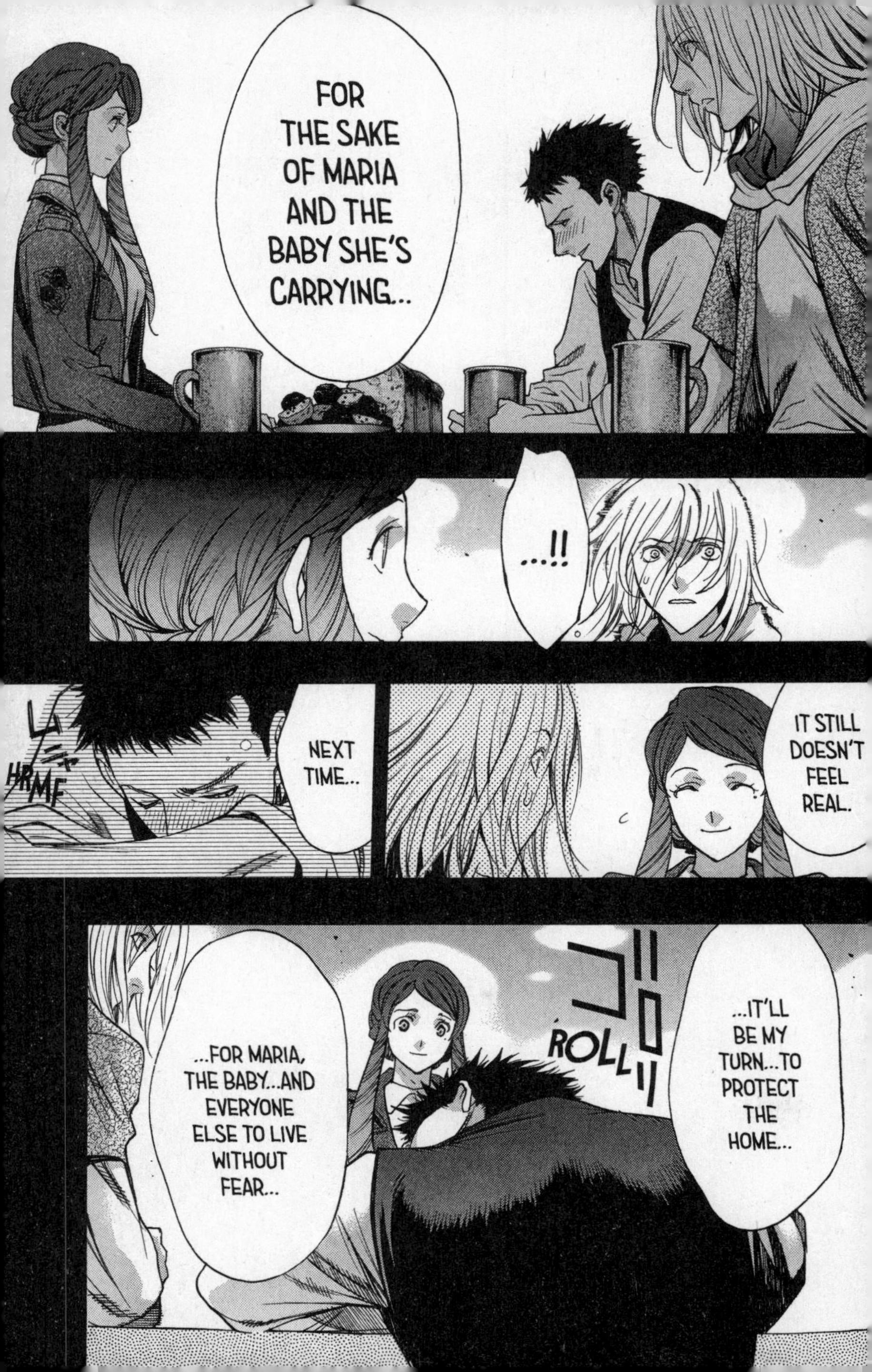
FOR THE SAKE OF MARIA AND THE BABY SHE'S CARRYING...
...!!
IT STILL DOESN'T FEEL REAL.
NEXT TIME...
HRMF
...IT'LL BE MY TURN...TO PROTECT THE HOME...
ROLL
...FOR MARIA, THE BABY...AND EVERYONE ELSE TO LIVE WITHOUT FEAR...

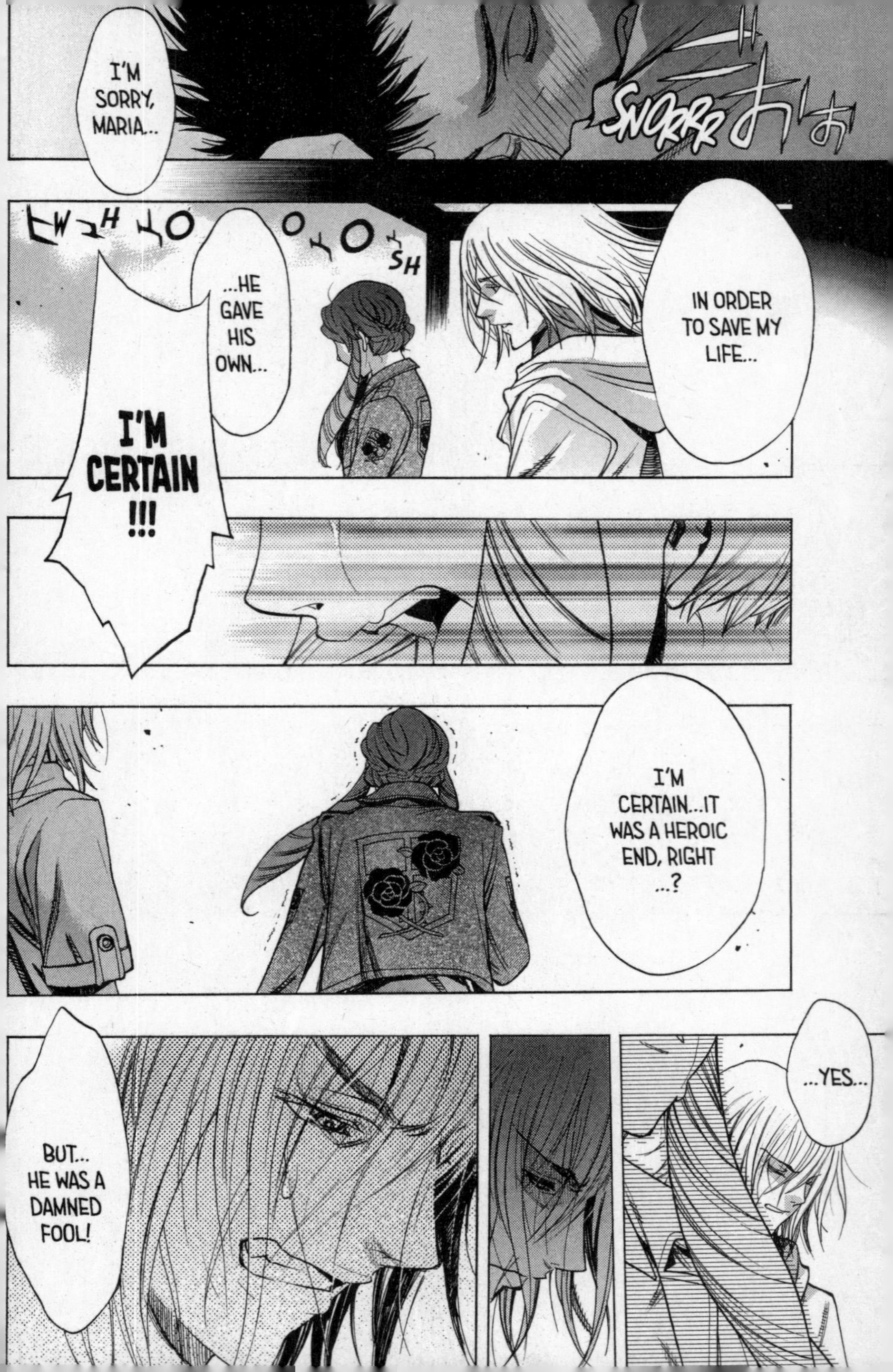
SNORRR おお
I'M SORRY, MARIA...
IN ORDER TO SAVE MY LIFE...
...HE GAVE HIS OWN...
I'M CERTAIN!!!
I'M CERTAIN...IT WAS A HEROIC END, RIGHT...?
...YES...
BUT... HE WAS A DAMNED FOOL!

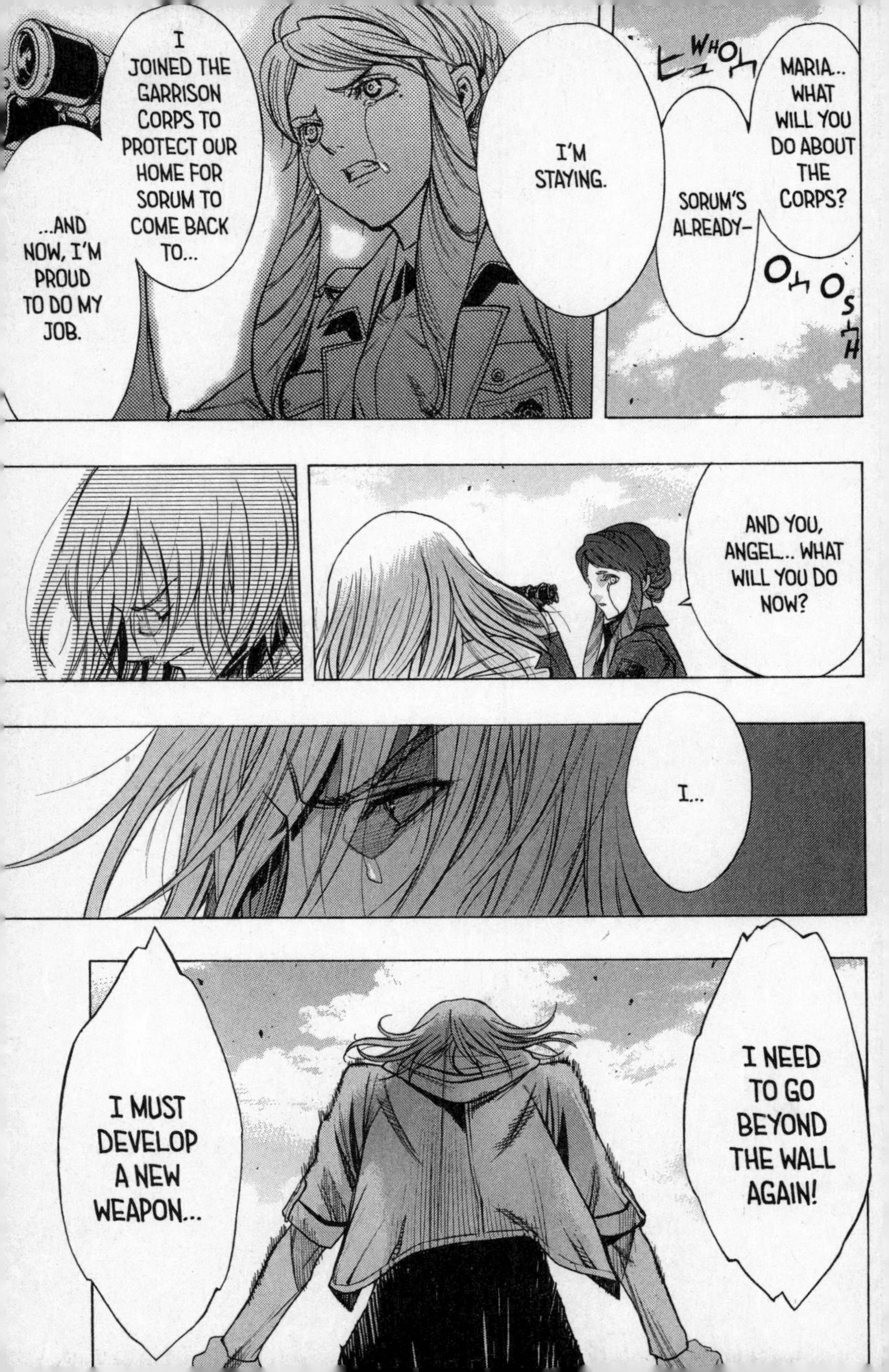
WHOOSH
MARIA... WHAT WILL YOU DO ABOUT THE CORPS?
SORUM'S ALREADY-
I'M STAYING.
I JOINED THE GARRISON CORPS TO PROTECT OUR HOME FOR SORUM TO COME BACK TO...
...AND NOW, I'M PROUD TO DO MY JOB.
AND YOU, ANGEL... WHAT WILL YOU DO NOW?
I...
I NEED TO GO BEYOND THE WALL AGAIN!
I MUST DEVELOP A NEW WEAPON...

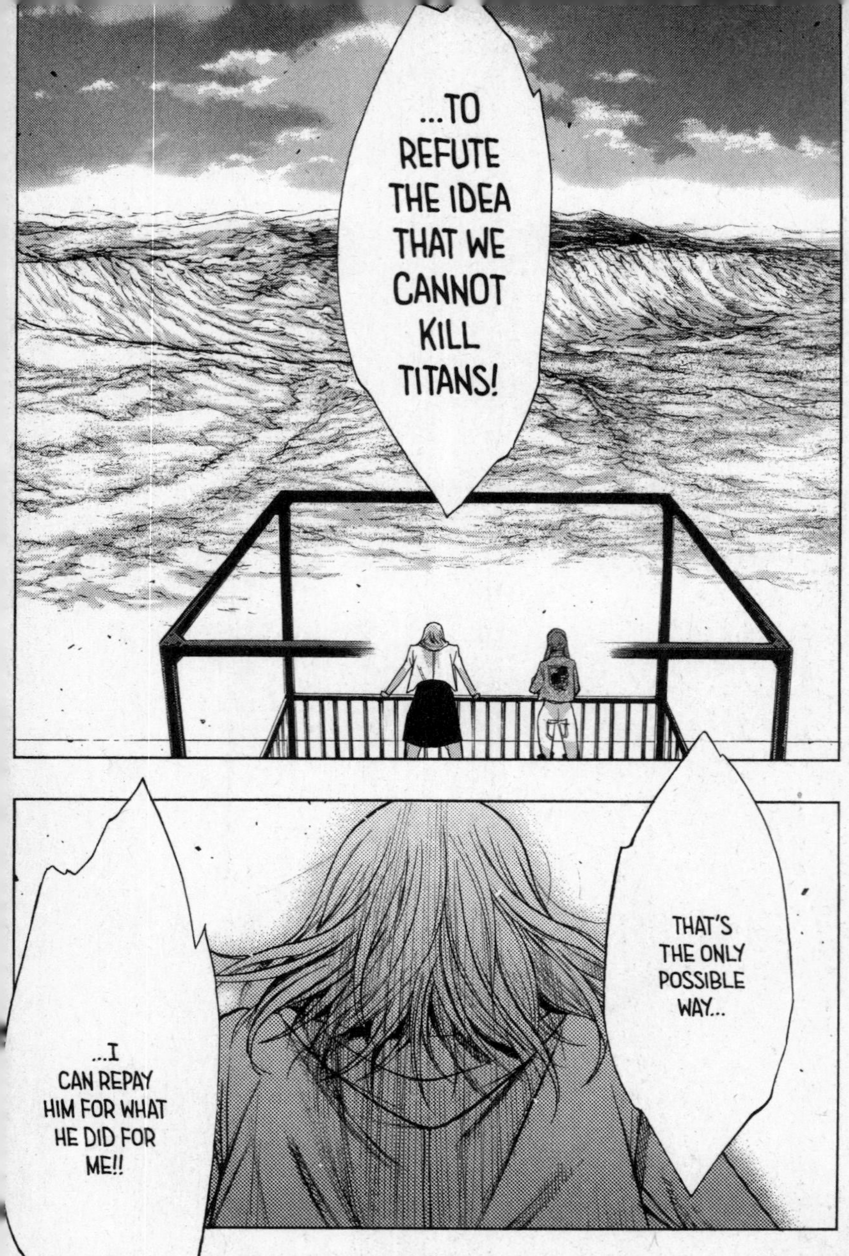
...TO REFUTE THE IDEA THAT WE CANNOT KILL TITANS!
THAT'S THE ONLY POSSIBLE WAY...
...I CAN REPAY HIM FOR WHAT HE DID FOR ME!!

Swear Upon Wall Maria · End

SAVE THE DATE!
Celebrating 15 Years
FREE COMIC BOOK DAY
1st SATURDAY IN MAY!
May 7, 2016
www.freecomicbookday.com
FREE COMICS FOR EVERYONE!
Details @ www.freecomicbookday.com
/freecomicbook
@freecomicbook
@freecomicbookday

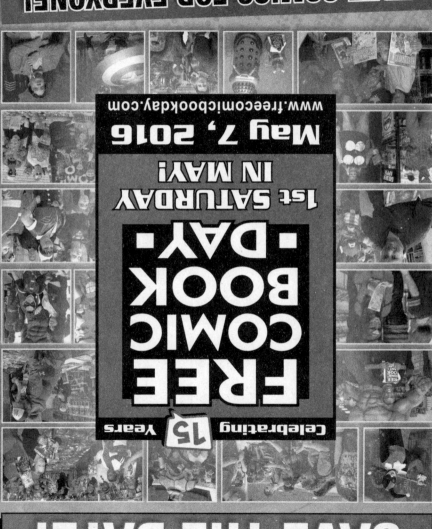

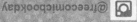

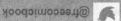

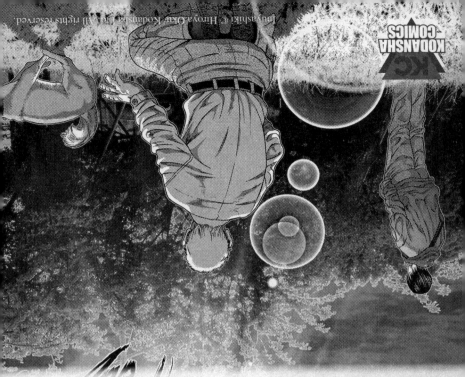

BASED ON THE POPULAR
VIDEO GAME FRANCHISE BY
ATLUS!

AFTER DEMONS BREAK
THROUGH INTO THE HUMAN
WORLD, TOKYO MUST BE
QUARANTINED, WITHOUT
POWER AND STUCK IN A
SUPERNATURAL WARZONE,
17-YEAR-OLD KAZUYA HAS
ONLY ONE HOPE: HE MUST
USE THE "COMP," A DEVICE
CREATED BY HIS COUSIN
NAOYA CAPABLE OF SUM-
MONING AND SUBDUING
DEMONS, TO DEFEAT THE
INVADERS AND TAKE BACK
THE CITY.

DEVIL SURVIVOR

KODANSHA
COMICS
KC

A Kodansha Comics Trade Paperback Original
Attack on Titan: Before the Fall volume 7 copyright © 2015 Hajime Isayama/ Ryo Suzukaze/Satoshi Shiki
English translation copyright © 2016 Hajime Isayama/Ryo Suzukaze/Satoshi Shiki

Published in the United States by Kodansha Comics, an imprint of Kodansha USA Publishing, LLC, New York.

Publication rights for this English edition arranged through Kodansha Ltd, Tokyo.

First published in Japan in 2015 by Kodansha Ltd., Tokyo as *Shingeki no kyojin Before the fall*, volume 7.

ISBN 978-1-63236-225-4

Character designs by Thores Shibamoto
Original cover design by Takashi Shimoyama (Red Rooster)

Printed in the United States of America.

www.kodanshacomics.com

9 8 7 6 5 4 3 2 1
Translation: Stephen Paul
Lettering: Steve Wands
Editing: Haruko Hashimoto
Kodansha Comics edition cover design by Phil Balsman

STOP!

You are going the *wrong way!*

Manga is a *completely* different type of reading experience.

To start at the *BEGINNING,* go to the *END!*

That's right! Authentic manga is read the traditional Japanese way—from right to left, exactly the opposite of how American books are read. It's easy to follow: just go to the other end of the book, and read each page—and each panel—from the right side to the left side, starting at the top right. Now you're experiencing manga as it was meant to be.